FRONTIERS OF JUSTICE

Volume 2: Coddling or Common Sense?

Edited by Claudia Whitman, Julie Zimmerman & Tekla Miller

Biddle Publishing Company
PO Box 1305 #103, Brunswick, Maine 04011

Publisher's Cataloging In Publication Data

1. Frontiers of Justice, Volume 2: Coddling or Common Sense?
2. Miller, Tekla, Ed.
3. Whitman, Claudia, Ed.
4. Zimmerman, Julie, Ed.
5. Corrections
6. Crime Prevention
7. Criminal Justice
8. Prisons & Prisoners
9. Rehabilitation
10. United States, Criminal Justice
11. United States, Corrections

Library of Congress Catalog Card No. 98-70397
ISBN 1-879418-28-2

Published in the United States of America by
Biddle Publishing Company
PO Box 1305 #103
Brunswick, ME 04011
207-833-5016

Cover design by Billy G. Hughes Jr., Death Row, Huntsville Texas
Title by Michael Tenneson, Limon Correctional Facility, Colorado

"The frontier is the outer edge of the wave — the meeting point between savagery and civilization...the line of most rapid and effective Americanization."

Frederick Jackson Turner, 1894
The Significance of the Frontier in American History

FOREWORD

Crime and punishment affect every American. If you or a member of your family has not been the victim of a crime, then you know someone who has been mugged, robbed, raped, or even murdered. If you or a member of your family has never been arrested, you know someone who has faced a judge, paid a fine, sat in a county jail or even "done time" in prison. Crime also touches our lives in more subtle ways: maybe you have voted to increase taxes to build more prisons, or lobbied to decrease taxes by cutting programs for criminals. Maybe you participate in a worshiping group which teaches forgiveness, and struggle with the application of that concept to modern society. Or maybe you volunteer with a community youth group, and feel helpless to stop the abuse or neglect that can turn today's young victim into tomorrow's abuser.

The media and politicians on the election trail encourage our confusion and fear about crime and whip them into anger and votes and newspaper sales. And this "tough on crime" philosophy is changing our society in a way that is much more costly than the dollars we spend to build more prisons. We are becoming a country that values vengeance over reclamation, punishment over prevention. We build "super-maxes" which have been shown to increase, even create mental illness. We lock young men in a cell with nothing to do, provide them with no tools or training to change their behavior, and expect them to be law-abiding citizens when they are released. We treat our prisoners with disrespect, even brutality, and are surprised that they become more violent and angry in prison. We even kill to show our horror of killing, in the most pre-meditated, ritualistic way imaginable.

There are people, however, who are more concerned with results than with the appearance of coddling criminals, and this book is a sampling of the many wonderful programs they have put into place in communities and in prisons all over this nation. The authors of Frontiers of Justice, Volume 2: Coddling or Common Sense? range from a volunteer in Big Brothers to the President of the American Correctional Association, from a Death Row inmate to a crime victim. The programs they are advocating range from Girl Scout Troops to Lifer Groups. The populations being targeted include battered women, drunk drivers, self-mutilators and sex offenders. The skills they are learning include training puppies, learning braille, building motor homes, managing anger and teaching their children to read. And the beneficiaries of these programs? All of us—victim, offender and community —and therein lies the key.

If we continue to see the world in terms of good guys and bad guys, we will continue to feel justified in categorizing certain groups of people as "other"—not really human, not entitled to opportunites for growth and atonement, even if this benefits society as a whole. The alternative to revenge-based criminal justice is not merely less costly and more effective in preventing crime and lowering recidivism. It also preserves the human dignity of the victim, the offender, their families and the body politic—legislators, law enforcers, corrections workers, taxpayers, voters, worshippers, volunteers. We the people.

Tekla Miller
Claudia Whitman
Julie Zimmerman

TABLE OF CONTENTS

LIST OF ILLUSTRATIONS

LIST OF POEMS

SONG OF LOVE

The music plays, yet no one hears.
Listen, I say!

People turn as if to pity,
"poor thang, he's gone mad."

Can't you hear it?
The melody sweet as cotton candy.

Cool like "Grover"...
A horn that wails out a message,
yet no one hears.

Am I mad to hear the birds sing?
First of all
who are they to question —

Listen, I say!
to the music that plays
in my heart.

Willie Christopher Tucker
Bostick State Prison, Georgia

"Song of Love" is excerpted from Trapped Under Ice: A Death Row Anthology (Biddle Publishing Company.

PROLOGUE

The quotes which begin each section of this book are taken directly from letters written by prisoners to me, their penpal. Most of the prisoners I have come to know first made contact through inquiries about publishing. In 1995 my company published Trapped Under Ice: A Death Row Anthology, a collection of poems by death row inmates and other prisoners. I have continued a correspondence with many of those poets and have come to consider many of them friends.

I believe these excerpted letters show, far better than I could explain, that convicted criminals are people, not criminal acts, not monsters, not dispensable. Over time, what is shared between an incarcerated and a free penpal is what is given and received between any two friends: trust, humor, despair, hope, and the knowledge that someone cares. I have been overwhelmed by the generosity and concern I have received from the same men and women whom society dismisses as selfish, worthless, even deserving of death.

On October 22, 1997, I lost one of these friends to execution. Haven't we all struggled to cope with the death of a loved one? Imagine adding to your loss the knowledge that many in America are celebrating his death. Revenge is a state of mind and a political policy that tears at the heart, as well as the fabric of community. Having now lost a loved one to murder and another to execution, I know vengeance does not even the score. It does not feel like justice. It only hurts.

It has been the support and love from my incarcerated penpals that have helped the most in my healing.

October 21, 1997

Dear Julie,

It's just about 12:00 here, though it's still more than an hour before it's midnight in Missouri. I don't know what's happening out there, but I fear the "what" isn't what we've been wishing it would be. I don't expect I'll be spending as much time with this card as I'd like; not because I'm less than thrilled with your company. Because I've a lot of prayer ahead of me tonight.

All that I know of AJ is what I've read and what you've told me, but what I feel in my heart, so fully that no "fact" could be felt with such certainty, is that AJ would want to be remembered in fondness and not with too much sadness, and certainly not with rage. You will grieve his passing, I know, and this is both natural and right—and I wish I had some words to ease the pain. But no one ever does.

But we should take care not to grieve too long. We must live and go about the business of living, taking with us the gifts, the memories, and the legacy AJ has shared with us. By nurturing these, his "better angels," inside us, we honor him. He is at peace now, but he lives on in the lives he's touched. I wish you peace, Julie.

Yours always,

Scott

My wish is that all Americans could learn more of the wisdom and compassion expressed in this letter—by one convicted, incarcerated felon about another. The "better angels" live in all of us, and we are all enriched when we can recognize and nurture them. When we deny them, we diminish ourselves.

Julie Zimmerman

RAMSEY CLARK
"America's War on Crime"

Three decades ago in 1968, for the first year in its history, there was no execution in the United States. The government of South Africa was the leading practitioner of capital punishment, executing over 100 men each year, usually all of them black. The idealism which powered the civil rights, feminist, anti-poverty and peace movements possessed the vision and will to end capital punishment. For nine years there was no execution in the US. We did not want to be like apartheid South Africa.

Millions of Americans demanded laws and programs designed to end poverty and discrimination. More than two millenniums earlier the Athenians identified the roles poverty and inequality play in causing violations of societal norms. Plato proclaimed "poverty is the mother of crime." Aristotle identified the desire for equality as "the chief and universal cause of the revolutionary impulse."

Governments and activists addressed the primary causes of anti-social conduct in society: physical and mental illnesses; substances abuses; family break-up from insufficient personal funds for housing, food, health care, and clothing; failing public schools and high drop-out rates; lack of jobs; racism, segregation and discrimination.

The roles of police, prosecutors, criminal courts and prisons were under careful scrutiny. Police science courses were established through federal funding in colleges and universities in every state. Only a few states had ever provided formal educational programs for police. The ideal was to create a police organization that is skilled, trained, informed with respect to its priorities—crime prevention; family crisis intervention; community service and building trust; diversions of arrested persons to youth programs, special education, drug and alcoholic treatment programs; and a commitment to prevent police violence.

Prosecutors and courts were urged to focus on major crimes of violence, economic crimes by businesses and the rich, with diversion programs for youthful offenders and treatment for substance abusers. Courts were urged to improve procedures, assure fair trials to poor persons accused of crime, use alternatives to incarceration for youngsters, first offenders, persons with family support systems and others wherever feasible. Only short prison sentences were thought to be appropriate and only where incarceration was necessary for public safety.

There was a commitment to reduce prison populations, to place a moratorium on prison construction, to provide small community custodial facilities near homes, schools and jobs for persons able to benefit from them. Corrections systems were to assure health care, treatment for substance abuse, remedial education, job training and placement, family support and special programs for the retarded and handicapped and others.

There was a strong commitment to cause every element of government to deal fairly and constructively with people accused of crime. There was faith that when social conditions assure that infants will be born healthy to stable and loving families in a society that seeks freedom, equality and economic, social and political justice, the incidence of inter-personal violence and property crimes will be very low. Where such acts occur despite best efforts, the priority was to prevent their recurrence by quick, effective action designed to help the offender live a healthy, productive life thereafter. There was a firm determination that the government should always act in a principled way and treat even the most violent and deranged offender decently. That was the kind of society millions of Americans wanted.

It was believed society could protect itself without endangering freedom. Millions of Americans desired to end racism, violence, poverty, war, injustice and suffering. And they worked at it, knowing that though these tragic events might always be with us, enormous differences could be made by passionate commitment, well-planned efforts and perseverance.

Thirty years later we find 3200 persons on death rows across the nation, with executions occurring at a rate of more than one a week. The prison population, an important measure of society's failure, which was excessive in 1968, has increased more than five fold. Isolated and neglected in 1968, prison systems have become America's great growth industry, often run by private interests for personal profit. They manufacture crime and tear at the social fabric of the nation. There is nothing to compare with the US prison population, and America's use of the death penalty among rich countries, or democracies, anywhere in the world. We are far and away both the Lord High Executioner and the greatest gulag archipelago.

South Africa has abolished the death penalty while the US is virtually the only European or First World country to employ it. The US prison population, on a per capita basis, is roughly ten times the average prison population in all such countries.

Conditions of imprisonment have been made deliberately harsh and punitive. The policy is to cause suffering and deprivation. Programs to detoxify, educate, train and return prisoners to the community as quickly as possible as stable individuals have been sharply criticized and curtailed. America has chosen to wage war on its own young people.

The most revealing and damning insight into the real purpose and effect of our prison policies can be seen from the size of the population and its racial content. Today in California, 40% of the African American male population between the ages of 18 and 27 is in prison, or on post-conviction parole, or supervised release. Where in history, or in the world today, have 40% of so large a part of an entire segment of the population been imprisoned? Consider Rwanda, only a few years away from a genocide in which it is claimed one million out of a population of seven million died. In most parts of the country today, it is wracked with insurrection and armed guerrilla warfare. The victorious Tutsi people, representing less than 15% of the nation, claim to hold 108,000 male Hutus in prison. While the ages range from pre teens to septuagenarians, the majority are probably between 18 and 27. The male Hutu population between 18 and 27 is about 10 times the number in that age group who are in prison. California has imprisoned four times (40% compared to 10%) the percentage of the military service age group that war-torn Rwanda has.

The governments of the United States have rejected our most cherished values in their "war" on crime. Individual freedom, equal justice, fair trial and human dignity have all fallen victim to fear and hatred. The media glorifies the power of violence, while ignoring its pity. It daily inflames emotions through sensationalized treatment of violent crime.

Politicians appeal to the worst instincts in society—fear, hatred, racism, greed. They fail to address realistically the meaning of crime in a society and the means of its prevention. Shouts of "coddling" criminals ring out from these political protectors of the people; they rail against programs which have the potential of providing a safe return from prison to society, sentences that are less than draconian, or failures to seek the death penalty. No society has ever coddled people it calls criminals, or the poor from whom most charged with crime come. Use of the word is an appeal to those who want to punish, inflict pain and demonize. Only a demagogue would claim coddling occurs. What occurs is suffering that more often than not makes a meaner person who has learned from society's powerful to seek to have his way by force and cunning. And how many political figures pursuing election as governor, representative, senator or President dare today to oppose the death penalty?

In this tragic social environment, with the negation of our noblest principles by government and the mass media, this volume, its predecessor, and the organizations and individuals who speak here are a sign of hope and a manifestation of faith. They demonstrate a perseverance in the belief that with vision, courage and compassion society can provide a helping hand to each of its members to find peace and fulfillment for themselves, and can treat every person humanely. Only in this way can we finally overcome.

Ramsey Clark served as Assistant Attorney General, then Attorney General, of the United States under Presidents John Kennedy and Lyndon Johnson. He is a teacher and writer, the author of numerous articles and books, including Crime in America, and is actively engaged in the practice of law in the fields of international law, constitutional law, criminal justice, death penalty, civil rights, and the First Amendment. Mr. Clark has spent his entire career advocating for human rights and equal justice in this country and internationally.

I came in here being 'America's Most Wanted,' and I'll be leaving here America's least wanted.

Christian Snyder, "America's Most Wanted"

CRIMINAL JUSTICE IN AMERICA TODAY

Massachusetts

November 1, 1995

"The picture you sent me of the seals is posted on my wall, and I often sit and wonder what freedom really is? It has been some time since I've seen my family. I no longer receive visits from my loved ones as the experience of sitting in a room full of Correctional Officers trying to talk about personal family issues has been dehumanizing for family members, so much of my time is spent looking out my window at the tops of trees, trying to remember what the bottoms look like. As the walls start to close in around me it truly brightens my day to have such a beautiful photograph of these seals to get lost in.

"About a week ago I was informed that the parole board has considered holding a hearing in my case, and there is a possibility that I could be released in the summer of 1998. I pray nightly to my higher power for the courage and will to endure the next two and a half years, and at the same time I fear being released to an ever changing community, that has enacted new laws that would keep a violent offender in prison for the rest of his life. Going into a community with the stigma of being a violent offender, and knowing some people would love to see me in prison for life, is one of the hardest choices I'll have to make."

RAMSAY FIFIELD
"Where The Wild Things Are"

The Youth Center recently bought a chair. The staff have now been trained in its use. I don't know how much it cost; I do know that its only function is to restrain children so that they cannot go to the bathroom, feed themselves, or scratch where it itches. This week the Youth Center is ordering a face mask so that the children also cannot spit at the Training School Counselors who strap them into the chair.

I am a volunteer in an institution which our legislature recently projected to house 110 residents, ages 12-20. Tonight we have 246, of whom 44 boys are crowded into our cottage. As it happens, there are no murderers in the cottage tonight, but we have a generous helping of untreated sex offenders, armed robbers, drug dealers and addicts, as well as a dozen boys whose most serious crime was burglary. Some are here only because they violated technical conditions of probation such as failure to report to probation officers, leaving a prescribed placement, or smoking a joint.

There are two Training School Counselors in charge of the boys until 10:00 p.m., then there will be only one Training School Counselor in charge until morning. The boys will sleep on dilapidated cots in a huge room on the third floor of the cottage where the lights are never extinguished. Maine winter winds come through the window frames. The paint is peeling from the walls and ceiling. Our heating system has no thermostat; it is either off or on. Today it is off.

One of the staff on duty in our cottage has been working for 15 hours straight. A resident has refused to go to school. "Then get your fucking ass on that bench and sit there until I tell you that you can move." Rage floods the boy's face. He sits down.

Our legislature has apparently authorized the payment of virtually unlimited time and a half overtime for Training School Counselors. One third of our cottages are staffed entirely out of the overtime budget. Under this system, a staff member can make much more money and a legislator can point to the economies of the regular budget, ignoring the line for overtime. Once upon a time we had a working farm and splendid vocational programs, all of which have fallen prey to the budget ax. Mathematics was never my strongest subject in school, so maybe I don't understand the economy of this system. Does the system understand about the boy on the bench?

His hair is dyed black in an effort to avoid recognition by the police. His sneakers are torn. His file brands him as an institutional troublemaker; there hasn't been a single day in his two months here that he wasn't confined for at least part of each day in the punishment cells. The file also notes that he has lived on the streets since he was 12; next Thursday he will be 17. His name is Marc.

Our new Superintendent appeared to be a well intentioned person when he came to the Youth Center. He decreed that residents were to be treated with respect and that sitting on isolation was not an acceptable punishment. He has not been in our cottage in months.

I am here more than 40 hours each week thanks to a grant raised from private sources that enables me to bring in other paid volunteers. We have instituted cooking, music, art, automotive mechanics, wilderness survival, poetry, scuba diving, bike repair and a wide range of public service programs in this cottage. We are not professionally qualified to fill the gap of a true corrections curriculum, so we focus on skills-based work. We try to demonstrate anger management, conflict resolution, and other needed correctional pieces through our actions. The cottage down the road rewards good behavior by allowing the residents to count out the squares of toilet paper for use of the other residents. Volunteers have no place there.

The state recently funded a graduate student to teach a patched together curriculum of conflict resolution to a total of 56 residents this year. Hundreds of damaged, angry, criminal children like Marc will come through our gates to be rehabilitated during that time. They will find no institution-wide corrections program of any sort. We offer the federally mandated number of calories, the state mandated number of hours in a school classroom, a chance at foundation-funded drug treatment groups, and whatever program a staff member, his shift supervisor, an isolated social worker, and a volunteer come up with. The program our volunteers have come up with is not popular with many staff outside of this cottage.

Volunteers are outsiders. Perhaps we will speak of what happens Inside. I have been cursed, yelled at and threatened. I have also learned to value and to cherish from the depths of my heart those staff members who try against all odds to make a difference. Places like this seem to attract extreme personality types. So many seem to be here to enjoy domination, power and control. Some days I wonder why I am here.

As a volunteer, however, I am outside of the powerful dichotomy that exists between many of the staff and most residents. Each side clearly perceives the other as Them and knows that Their Side is always either one up or one down in the endless balancing of the equation of power. I have asked to see the young man sitting on the bench. For the moment he is one down in the power equation. He will not speak to me.

I tell him that I don't work here and he doesn't have to deal with me unless he wants to. The end of one sneaker is pried open and he worries his toes with the back of his hand. A disjointed story pours out: he had been put in a class which he felt was reading "third grade stuff." His refusal to do that work led an overworked teacher to give him something easier; his fragile pride was crushed and he responded in the only way he knew—rage and defiance. The institution responded with a heightened assertion of authority, the only way many of its line staff know. What has been accomplished? This scenario is repeated thousands of times each day at the Youth

Center. Is it not possible to teach Marc something besides rage and defiance, and even perhaps to give the staff some tools beyond "Sit down and shut up"?

The problem is the result of an odd marriage between the old woman who lived in the shoe and the emperor who had no clothes. No institution can expect to function in overcrowded and understaffed conditions, especially when the mission of the institution is to deal with the most damaged and dangerous parts of society. This place is not safe. We have so many children and we do not know what to do. We have no leadership; we have no consistent philosophy. The emperor of juvenile corrections theory is buck naked in the real world of overgrown and understaffed correctional facilities. If the emperor has half a brain he is beginning to shiver with fear. The residents are not fooled by what we are doing and their anger is ripening into rage.

My comments may seem out of place in a book which I imagine will be full of good ideas and proposals for enlightened policy. I've heard good ideas and even believe that I have some myself, but right now Marc and I—and 44 other boys and staff—have to get through this Thursday afternoon in October here in Cottage Three.

Marc and I negotiate an agreement. He writes a letter—a very articulate letter—of apology to his teacher. We agree with some difficulty that the only thing stupider than being asked to do easy work is not doing that work well. For every day that he is not locked up, we will put a star on a 3 x 5 card which has his name on it. He will ask to be transferred to another class. He tells me with real pride that he is the best thief in Portland. He only got caught because he got drunk. There is a pause; he looks down. "And," he says, "winter was coming." The first star he chooses is green.

I have no magic. Anyone with time and the willingness to listen could have helped Marc out of the corner into which he had painted himself. An institutional structure which crowds damaged children into crumbling buildings with inadequate staff does not have the time and willingness to listen. Volunteers alone cannot fix this problem. What happens if it isn't fixed?

Our Superintendent says that he supports the presence of volunteers in the institution. We are a dedicated bunch of people, willing to bring our life experiences, our skills, and our time to the residents of the Youth Center. One boy or girl at a time, we patiently work to bring them back from the awful places they have gone. Our successes are anecdotal and not subject to the quantification that systems require; our failures are many and painful to recall. The Superintendent says that he supports the presence of volunteers as humanizers in the institution. Are we reduced to relying on the good will of isolated staff and volunteers?

For a considerable time, the cottage in which I work was run by the so-called Inner Circle—a group of half a dozen residents who had been here for an extended period of time and were allowed by the staff to "take care of business." Residents in that group were given power to run the lives of their fellow residents. Power is a concept which the residents understand well, if in a limited way. You got it or you don't got it. If you got it, you can do anything you want to with it.

Until staff began to provide to the residents alternative means of exercising power, the adults in the cottage were truly powerless. Although they had the apparent authority ("Sit down and shut up"), real power was a clenched fist in the boot room. Or a boy sitting defiantly on a bench refusing to go to school. It may seem paradoxical that only by sharing real power with the residents could staff regain control, but that is exactly how it worked.

It has been a week now. Marc's row of stars staggers across the file card. He has told me how to get pizza delivered to the dumpster in back of the local pizza place and how to steal clothes from upscale stores in the Mall. We have approached the subject of his plans when he leaves here and veered away quickly. Marc has no plans and no dreams beyond getting out and getting high.

We talk about the banner on my wall which reads "Get A Life;" the idea both offends and intrigues him. "I have a life and it works okay, you know. It's just—like, winter is a problem." He has nothing to say about his family; he hasn't seen or spoken to them for more than a year. He agrees to a game I play—a very serious game—in which the resident makes a list of five things he has never done and wants to do. We then figure out how to accomplish the goals. His first item is to eat a chicken sandwich at a named restaurant in the Mall, ["I'm banned from there for life, so that won't be easy."]; another is to find a place to stay "on the outs." When I ask if he means a place to live, the distinction escapes him.

The Youth Center routinely discharges children to shelters. Even more often we return them to the same broken places from which they came. We have been told for years that we will have wrap around services for our residents, wonderful programs that will provide individualized attention in small residential settings "in the community." I know too well the small number of beds, the smaller number of vacancies, and the even smaller number of program directors willing to take a chance on someone like Marc. I spend hours on the telephone each week, begging intake workers to consider our guys. Last year I went to our state capitol to discuss opening another residential aftercare program for boys like Marc. The woman in charge told me brightly that indeed she had funds, but surely not for whole programs. She could buy bikes or perhaps winter coats. No more whole programs. Not for at least two years. I tell Marc about a transitional living program, saying nothing about its waiting list for the present. Marc decides to call them.

This institution quite deliberately infantilizes its residents, depriving them of any decision making power in their lives. I am bending a rule by letting Marc use the telephone in my office. It is just easier to manage too many kids if they all have to do the same things at the same times, and so a vast network of rules grows up. We offer few if any choices to our residents. They need choices; they need a chance in a safe place to try and fail—and try again. Adults look at the rules and believe that their sum total is authority. Residents either comply or rebel for the duration of their stay with us. Do we seriously believe that when they leave here they will take their meals in silence?

A major thrust of the volunteer programs in our cottage is to provide a voice for the residents. The feeling of powerlessness which they bring to us is not healthy, nor is it institutionally safe. We try in everything to offer choice, power, control—and to ensure one resident at a time that these are exercised responsibly.

Freedom Minds meets monthly to write and work on publication of residents' work. Voices of Men records books for daycare programs and distributes them for free. Both programs have waiting lists. They were founded and are run by the residents. Voices of Men's first president was a murderer; its first business manager was an untreated sex offender. When I tell Marc about this program, I can honestly offer him power beyond his wildest dreams—the power to change the life of a non-reading child for good and forever. He would not need to be told this if anyone had ever read to him.

He looks through the stack of books to be recorded until one catches his eye—Where The Wild Things Are. "That one," he says. "I'll do that one—'cause I been there." On the first try he is self-conscious and his voice shakes. Then the magic of the book takes hold and in a clear and gentle voice he begins. "Hi, I am Marc and I am going to read you a wonderful story. So you get all comfy and we'll begin at the beginning."

Marc is at the beginning of a process of healing. Like many boys before him he has just reached out to grasp with both hands an opportunity to do something good in the world. Other than the doing, he will have no reward. No reduction of time to be served, no extra food in the dinner line. He asks when he can do another book. I tell him that I will call him upstairs to do it as soon as I can. Over his shoulder I see the faces of 43 other boys, each needing individual attention, all part of an over-extended and under-staffed system. Triage is a brutal business.

Marc has seven stars. The transitional living program has agreed to interview him. For the first time in our relationship, his eyes meet mine for a moment. I wish him a happier birthday next year. And he smiles.

Neither Marc nor I subscribe to the old saw that a good day in corrections is a day when nothing happens. Boredom and a lack of constructive activities don't create a warehouse for juvenile offenders; they are the necessary components of a factory for adult criminals. Enforced boredom is not the cure for any social ill that I know of.

Young men do not come to us because they lack imagination or ambition. Putting too many together in a place where the prevailing mode is "Thou Shalt Not" simply challenges their already well developed manipulative ability to beat the system. They will ultimately do it. There are more of them than there are of us, and when I look at the system we have designed to repair them, I think that they are smarter than we are.

Today we are talking about Life—the importance of trust or, as Marc puts it, having someone to watch your back. Gangs interest me, but Marc assures me he has never been in a gang. "Cops think we're a gang, but shit, there are only nine of us. We just take care of each other. Who else is gonna do it?"

Really taking care does not mean stealing from the Mall, but my point is lost in the squealing of tires outside the cottage. Marc jumps to the window to report on the excitement. "Missus, they're taking a kid outa the cottage next door. They got two cars—here comes another one across the lawn!" He sits down to explain his version of what has happened. "There were two kids fighting out there. Three cars! Staff really get off on car speed and fights, you know. It is probably pretty boring for them too, just watching us all the time. Three cars—that's what they'd need to take me outa here." I risk laughter, hoping that we have a relationship strong enough to support it. After a startled moment, Marc shrugs and laughs too.

Marc firmly believes that being punished is better than being bored. When punishment becomes boring, he is quite prepared to increase the stakes. Blocking the toilet in the punishment cells creates a flood and the spectacle of people running about with mops and pails. "And when you're there you can yell as much as you want because they can't send you to punishment cells now, can they?" Being deprived of blankets and towels was just a reasonable price to pay.

Given the opportunity, many of these young people will clean up their own messes. Not all. Some of our children are too damaged to repair in any corrections system that I know anything about. If there is no help for them within a mental health system, we may indeed have to contemplate a life for them in isolation from society. In five years at the Youth Center I have met three such residents. Most embrace with eagerness a program that has a clear path (not too long) to an identifiable success. Then another, and another, success breeding success. We need to teach many of these young men how that feels; they have only experienced success in a criminal context. Failure is school, family, perhaps a job—in short, much of the rest of life.

Our local police chief refers to all residents of the Youth Center as "predators." He inspired the Legislature to erect a $300,000 fence around us, promising to keep the people of this state safe from their own children. Institutional policy holds dangerous residents until they "age out" into the adult system. Thus we avoid newspaper headlines that refer to crimes committed by juveniles released from the Youth Center.

Every single resident within that fence is going to get out, no matter how high they build it or how many guards they post around it. It seems fairly obvious that this should be a central component of our program. Each person whom the residents contact within the fence should be a surrogate parent, modeling behavior that we want to see emulated in the institution as well as after release.

Men are particularly important here. Boys in this institution are desperately seeking role models, and they will find them. If we cannot provide men with a wider range than the purely punitive, punishment is what these boys will learn and what they will in their turn inflict on the society to which we release them. Nor is it

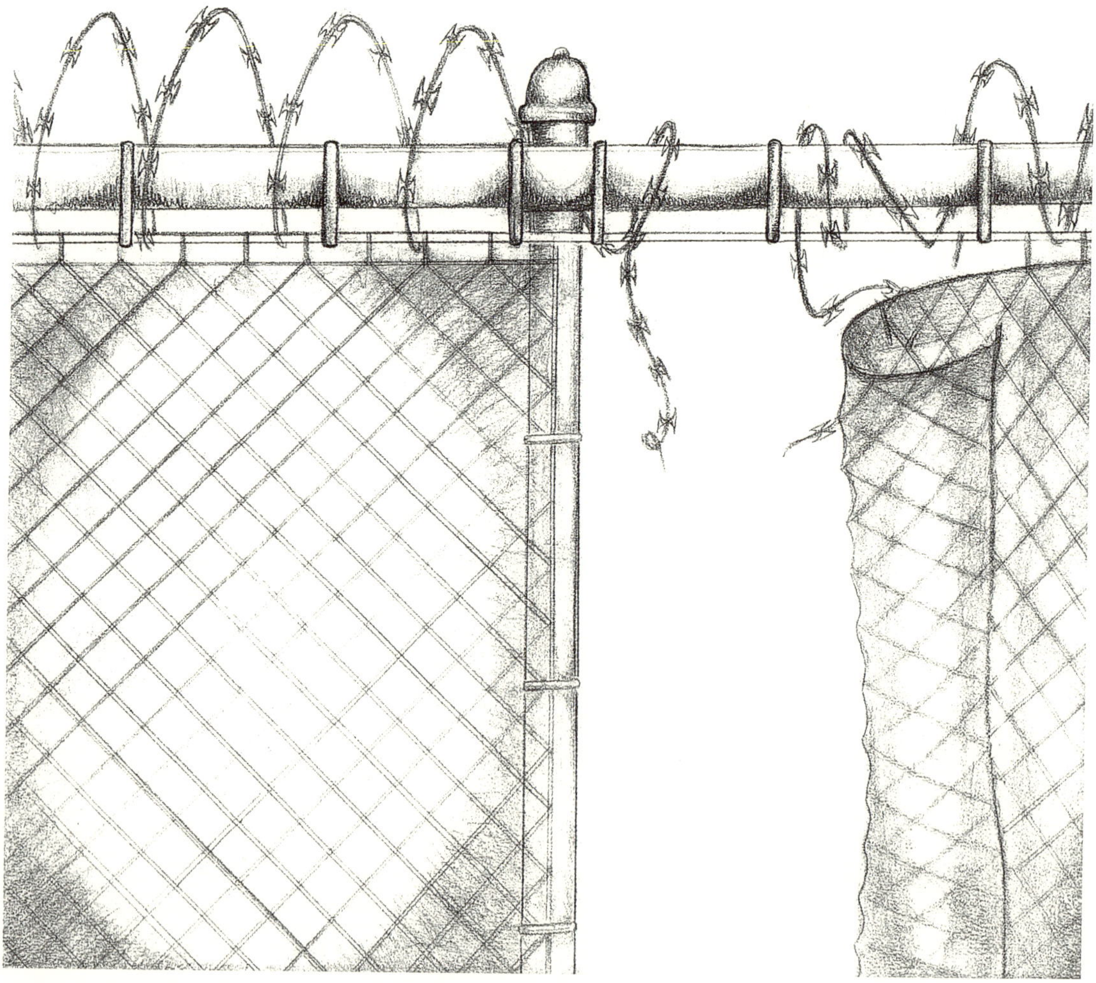

Tony Gagnon, “The Fence”

THE FENCE

I didn't feel so trapped before the fence went up.
I can almost forget it's there,
then I look up and see it.

I hate to look at it -
sad
scared
angry -
being stuck on this side,

but it keeps guys from running -
that only makes it worse for us all.

Is that a hole in the fence?
head for the hole
easy way out
escape -
I want to be out.

I keep hoping I'll wake up and see a hole like that
and be free.

Freedom Minds (a poetry and art club)
Maine Youth Center, Maine

helpful to regard residents as Victims of Society. Well-meaning volunteers, whether men or women, who do not set and maintain a standard of acceptable behavior are part of the problem, not part of the solution. Women behind the fences need to be surrogate mothers who hold their sons accountable for their failures as well celebrating their successes.

Everyone in a corrections facility is familiar with the unstated conflict and power pendulum swing between punishment and rehabilitation—the guards and the "social worker types." In the corrections world there is a place for both; on the street Marc surely would not have chosen to involve himself in Where The Wild Things Are. He needed to stop what he was doing out there before he could start doing something better. In the best of all worlds, the division between the two camps would not be a sexual one. Marc needs to know that a father can do more than punish and a mother can do more than indulge. There is nothing novel in the assertion that a middle course is best, but it is a lesson that institutionally we have not yet learned. If we have not learned it, how can we expect to teach it?

Today Marc is angry. Someone cut in front of him in the lunch line; he shoved the intruder out of the way. Staff saw only Marc's transgression and so gave only Marc a warning write-up. His sense of what is unjust is in high gear. My efforts to broaden the discussion to the justice and injustice of stealing fail utterly. Today Marc sees himself only as victim.

Try as I might I cannot persuade Marc to let go of his anger. We both know that the immediate cause is trivial, unworthy. At least I can see the roots of that anger snaking back through years to God knows what original injury—gathering strength from each real or imagined addition until the accumulation came here to be fixed. Marc sees only that he was dissed in the lunch line. We agree at last that it is not worth getting locked up over. For the first time he chooses a gold star.

Marc and the Youth Center have much in common. Both look at life in terms of success and failure. Marc grew up in a violently abusive family where everything was either absolutely perfect or unspeakably awful. He never learned that mistakes can be fixed much of the time and that life will go on even if they can't be fixed. Everything is either black or white; there is no gray in between. If you didn't do it right the first time, you might as well quit trying. Marc spends a lot of time quitting.

A functional world is mostly gray—lighter, darker, lighter again. It is not only Marc who needs to learn that lesson. We at the Youth Center need to remember and expect that our residents will fail after their first steps toward success. That is why it is so very important that we provide them a place where they safely can fail and fail again until they get it right. Until the hard edges of failure are softened and they learn not to stop trying. Better is good; worse is not so good, but we don't abandon hope or effort when worse happens, as it inevitably will.

As I drove through the gate this morning, I passed a group of staff with hand-lettered picket signs, protesting the overcrowded conditions in the institution. I flashed a thumbs-up and wished that their voices, too, would be heard outside of the fence.

When I asked to see Marc, he was gone. He had slapped the resident from the lunch line and had been defiant when the staff confronted him. It had indeed required a number of staff to remove him from the cottage and he spent the evening strapped in our brand new chair. His locker will be emptied and he will be transferred to a locked cell in the punishment unit. This time he won't be back. Only his voice on tape remains behind, clear and in that moment captured by the magic of hope.

". . . and when he came to the place where the wild things are, they roared their terrible roars and gnashed their terrible teeth, and rolled their terrible eyes, and showed their terrible claws, till Max said BE STILL and tamed them with the magic trick of looking into all their yellow eyes without blinking once and they were frightened and called him the most wild thing of all. . ."

I will miss him.

"Marc" is a composite of two very real boys in punishment cells at the Youth Center as this chapter goes to press. As of February 1998, the Maine Youth Center asked Ramsay Fifield to discontinue Voices of Men, but it is being considered for use in North Carolina, Oregon and Texas.

Ramsay Fifield holds a J.D. degree from the University of California at Berkeley. After 15 years in the private practice of criminal and constitutional law, she was appointed Director of the San Francisco District Attorney's Family Support Bureau. Her mid—life crisis resulted in a teaching credential and several years of traveling the world as a teacher with American film companies on location. She was the founder of FAX, a profitable company run entirely by at-risk teenagers. She has been a full time volunteer at the Maine Youth Center for six years.

DAYDREAMS

Daydreams are exciting - I'm a basketball star!
Daydreams are peaceful - I'm sitting in a field,
there's no noise.
I'm rich, I have money,
I have power,
I have freedom.

If I had freedom I would go home.
If I had money I would buy a car,
a house,
eat lobster, fetticini, McDonalds.
I would travel
to Florida,
to California,
sunshine, beaches...

If I had freedom, I would go home.

NIGHTMARES

Being in the Maine Youth Center is a nightmare!

What scares me?
dying
going to prison someday
UFOs!
really bright lights.
The most scared I ever was
was when I got shot,
was a really bad acid trip.

What makes me angry?
staying here
being separated from family and friends.

The Maine Youth Center is a nightmare.

Freedom Minds (a poetry and art club)
Maine Youth Center, Maine

ROBERT E. LECUREAUX
"Politics of Corrections"

Why did he get out early? Why don't criminals serve their whole sentences? He was paroled after five years on a 20-year sentence. I sentenced him to life and I don't understand why the parole board released him so early.

I've long ago given up on trying to explain or, God forbid, defend the sentencing laws in Michigan or anywhere else in the United States. You can't apply logic to such an emotional issue. It is especially discouraging when you hear judges feign ignorance of the process like the Biblical Pilate washing his hands, or the legislators who voted to establish the sentencing system criticizing it as if the laws were established by the criminals.

Personally, I like the Michigan sentencing model of fixed indeterminate. Under this model, the legislature sets the maximum portion of the sentence while the sentencing judge sets the minimum. That way the legislative branch has a part by setting what is the longest sentence any person sentenced on a specific crime will serve if he/she serves the entire sentence. The legislature can also require a prison term for certain crimes like armed robbery, or a mandatory sentence like life for murder one, or two years flat time for felony with a gun.

Then the judge can set the minimum sentence based on the specifics of the case. Those specifics may be offender variables (i.e., repeat offenders, employment history, family ties, etc.) or offense variables (i.e., number of victims, extent of injuries, viciousness etc.) Then the prison officials in conjunction with the parole board can establish program incentives for positive change and provide re-entry into the community in a rational supportive program that provides for supervision of the offender.

Sounds good, so why all the hoopla? Because when something goes wrong, the key players get amnesia. These key players are the elected officials who always remember that the bottom line is to be reelected.

The offender goes to prison, does well, gets paroled on his/her minimum and while on parole commits a serious crime worthy of a front page article in newspapers and a lead story on the six o'clock news. As reporters start their hand wringing investigation of how could this happen, they discover that the offender was released on parole after seven years on a 20-year sentence.

When asked, the judge gets amnesia and forgets that he really sentenced the offender to five years because that was the minimum, but publically states, "I gave him 20 years and that damn parole board let him out after only seven." The legislators are the next ones to become brain dead and wonder how the judge got around their legislation that set a twenty-year maximum for this crime.

It's no wonder that the general public doesn't understand the sentencing model with these kinds of stand-up politicians.

While I think it is wrong to scrap the fixed indeterminate model and go to mandatory sentencing, I'm beginning to accept the fact that a lot of the rhetoric would be removed if rational sentencing models that made sense to everyone were developed. Right, and I also believe that Elvis is alive and well on a cruise ship in the Bermuda Triangle.

Why can't we develop a rational sentencing model? Ask most people, both general citizens and those in the criminal justice field, and they will talk as though the laws on sentencing terms have come to us from God through Moses on Mt. Sinai. Where do those numbers really come from? One of the simplest examples is the legislative maximum sentence in Michigan for "uttering and publishing" or bad check writing. The maximum sentence by statute is 14 years, while assault with intent to do great bodily harm carries a 10-year maximum; (as a victim I'll take the bad check). Why the discrepancy? A rational sentencing model would state that the sentence is related to public harm. One need only to look at when and why the U & P statute was enacted. It was in the early 1930's and the banks were coming out of the depression and the bank holiday. Checking accounts were becoming available to the common person. The investors needed to be assured of the stability of banks. Bank owners/investors wield a lot of political power, so we get tough on check writers.

Can anybody really explain the disparate sentencing for cocaine possession depending on whether it is in crack form or powder form, except on the political need to get tough on inner-city crack abusers? Under Federal law the penalty for possession of 5 grams of crack cocaine is 6 times tougher than the penalty for possession of 5 grams of powder cocaine. In cases involving major amounts of cocaine it takes one hundred times more powder cocaine than crack to draw the same ten year minimum sentence for drug trafficking.

Watch as legislators respond to the new criminal area of computer hackers or crackers as they are now being called. There will certainly be some tough legislation developed to protect our vast government and business information systems.

I think the saddest example of how politics takes a well intentioned idea and turns it into an aberration is the career criminal legislation. These laws are enacted under a variety of political slogans such as "three strikes and out." It is well documented that a few criminals account for a disproportionate amount of crime. What could be more rational than to provide a severe disincentive for those repeat offenders and remove them from society forever?

The problem is the politics of the process or, as the saying goes, the devil is in the detail. As we approach this effort, we are thinking of the criminal who makes a business out of crime. The professional burglar, the repeat armed robber, the unchanged child molester. So how does politics adulterate the process? The elected official called a prosecutor gets elected by being tough on crime. He or she is not getting enough career criminals caught in the criminal justice net so he/she starts authorizing prosecution on nuisance offenders, i.e. fourth felony of larceny from a building results in a life sentence when the fourth felony could have been treated as shop lifting. A simple possession case becomes 'cause celebre' when the article in the paper notes that the crime is being pursued under a three strikes and you're out law.

It is an old saw that prisoners don't elect anyone, but many politicians are elected because of prisoners. A get tough on crime platform doesn't have to make sense; it just has to appeal to the visceral emotions of the public. Perry Johnson, former Director of Corrections for Michigan and Past President of the American Correctional Association, has written an excellent article on how criminals have become our scapegoats for what is wrong in our lives and society in general. "When we believe that the primary threat to our well-being is the depredations of the convicted and when we distort and exaggerate the extent of that danger, creating a false sense of peril to justify our treatment of these demonized few, we are scape-goating, and our immediate next instinct is to call for banishment of these demons to the fullest extent possible."[1]

Politically it is helpful to talk about crime or criminal behavior as if we have identified a cohesive identifiable group. However, a petty thief is as different from a drug enforcer/murderer as a rock is from an orange. By demonizing this identifiable group of people, we have made them less than human and deserving of whatever the society decides that their punishment should be. They become useful tools for the get elected, anti-crime platform.

When we start from that premise, it is all too easy to support and clamor for a get tough sentencing change that is illogical. Let's double the sentence for any crime if the victim is a senior citizen! Just look at the size of the membership of A.A.R.P. to see what's behind this proposal.

A rational approach to sentencing would be based on public harm, with the intent to remove repeat offenders who score higher on the public harm scale for long periods of time, while those who score lower are diverted from prison to community based programs or are processed through the system more quickly before the system has a negative effect on them. In other words, target our sentencing efforts on the serious offenders, while making room for them by diverting the less serious offenders.

This is called selective incarceration versus the political get tough on crime legislation which results in an increase in general incarceration, i.e., either send more people to prison, or increase everybody's sentence or reduce or eliminate the possibility of parole. General incarceration efforts result in prison building booms and often cause the unintentional consequence of having the overcrowding result in a general reduction of sentences to make room for the influx of prisoners caught in the expanded web.

When the general public (and I include legislatures in this group) is asked, "Is crime going up or down?," most people honestly believe that we are in an unprecedented increasing crime wave. The answer to this question has not changed since former President Richard Nixon discovered what a great political issue "get tough on crime" makes. People do not believe the figures when shown that during the early '80s, crime statistics were stable and that the violent crime rate actually decreased while we were in an unprecedented prison building spree. The average sentence given to state prisoners nationwide went from fifty-five months in 1987 to one hundred-fifty months by 1991,[2] but one Willie Horton makes a greater impact than a book full of statistics. It is interesting that we never hear a discussion about why our country incarcerates more of its citizens than any other nation except Russia. What is wrong with us that we create so many criminals? Are we a morally corrupt society? Perhaps a political discussion of this question would prompt a new look at how we define crime and criminals.

We need to develop a rational sentencing structure, but I'm not sure it is possible in the political arena. It is too easy to describe a worst case scenario as a means of making an irrational sentence seem justified.

After all these years, studies and sophistication, we still don't understand causes of criminal behavior or the effects of punishment. Just how much protection does five years provide over three years? At twenty to fifty thousand dollars a year can we afford those extra two years on a hunch that they make a difference? We need prisons in this country to keep the right prisoners away from society. We also need a rational public harm-based sentencing model to sort out who belongs in these prisons and for how long. Rational equals non-political which equals utopian.

Robert E. LeCureux retired in January, 1997, after 31 years with the Michigan Department of Corrections. The last 12 years were as a warden in the Upper Peninsula of Michigan. Immediately prior to that he was the Director of the Probation Department for Detroit Recorders Court and Wayne County Circuit Court. He and his wife Lynn continue to live in Sault Ste Marie where he teaches part-time at Lake Superior State University and works as an auditor for the Commission on Accreditation.

Footnotes

1 Keynote address to ACA Conference, 1994

2 Bureau of Justice statistics

POLITICAL PRISONER

Caged in the first degree for robbery
My partner armed with a broken B.B. gun
Took forty-five dollars and two pizzas
Didn't harm victim, ate some pizza
Got a twenty-five year sentence.
Was the only African in the courtroom
Was poor and without a job
"A radical from Los Angeles, moved to Iowa
And influenced the blacks to rebel with crime."
That's what they feel.
"You call that a political prisoner?"
Sure, I have much to do with government
Was unemployed, protested with robbery
Tried to liberate my poverty.
It's been the government's mission to put me away
"Was trying to weaken the economy
And overthrow the pocketbooks."
That's what they feel.
I'm not a mayor
But the "city's nightmare."
That's what they say
And try to keep me away
While they get rich in the name of punishment.
Did I need twenty-five years?
Oh, march to liberate my tears.

Vincent Johnson
Iowa State Penitentiary, Iowa

"Political Prisoner" is excerpted from Iowa on the Inside, by Vincent Johnson, Audenreed Press (1997)

LAWSON STRICKLAND
"Prisons As Big Business"

Finally, and perhaps for good, the truth is in the open. In that liberating light which is ever cast about truth, a few brave souls are stepping forward to announce what has long been denied: "Crime pays. I hate saying it, but it really does," concedes Arthur McDonald.[1] Larry Solomon echoes him a little less hesitantly, "What can I say, it's a great, great business.[2]

"Crime Does Not Pay," is a slogan we have often repeated but which is assuredly now in doubt. Crime does indeed pay and handsomely so. It is a force in our society which we love to hate, and and we are going to learn that we possibly cannot live without it. In an ironic turn, thousands of Americans today would have to agree that the presence of crime has benefitted them personally and the country economically. In fact, crime is not only making millionaires of respectable citizens, it has financial analysts betting on its longevity as a recession-proof growth industry.

Of course, neither Arthur McDonald nor Larry Solomon are in any sense criminals. They are merely examples of the growing wave of people and corporations taking advantage of what is being touted by Norwegian criminologist Nils Christie as the "corrections industrial complex."[3] A burgeoning industry which has been in existence for over the last twenty years has only recently (since the mid- to late 1980s) begun to step forward as an economic giant. It includes the construction, maintenance and operation of private prisons; the purchasing of existing state prisons by private firms; the financial underwriting of those endeavors and the selling of goods by corrections market oriented companies specializing in everything from body armor to clog proof waste-disposal systems; personnel management; and the interstate, even international, transport of prisoners. The industry is complete with its own lobbyists, packing political clout from the state level (with hundreds of thousands of dollars donated to state candidates since 1993) up to the national level, the Republican party being the recipient of the majority of donations.

Arthur McDonald was once the owner of the private Houston firm Cornell Cox. Today he is retired, living comfortably in South Dakota, wealthy from the selling of the firm for more than $10 million. Cornell Cox bought California's largest private prison company, Eclectic Communications, Inc., with the backing of Wall Street investment houses Dillon, Reed & Co. and Charterhouse. Eclectic Communications has managed to receive prison contracts worth over $50 million in revenues since 1988.

Larry Solomon, serving as vice-president for the Florida based Joy Food Services Inc., has also reaped profits, the benefit of his access to the ever present and swelling prison population which must be fed.

Crime pays the bills for Fortune 500 CEOs and their finance houses: Goldman Sachs & Co., Prudential Insurance Co. of America, Smith Barney Shearson Inc. and Merrill Lynch & Co. Wall Street giants underwrite prison construction with business-friendly private, tax exempt bonds, such as those usually reserved for the state, at taxpayer cost.

Lehman Brothers in partnership with PaineWebber, working with the nation's largest private prison operator, Corrections Corporation of America, formed C.C.A. Prison Realty Trust in early 1997 for the sole purpose of purchasing existing prisons. The company's Initial Public Offering raised a staggering $388.5 million. PaineWebber describes the sale of prisons to a company such as C.C.A. as "free money," money which a "politician could then use for initiatives that fit his or her agenda, possibly improving the chances for re-election."[4]

Even American Express, always looking for a good return, has gotten into the frenzy of this "boom" industry, having invested $31 million in what is now the private $38 million Great Plains Correctional Facility in Hinton, Oklahoma. This facility houses inmates on contract from as far away as North Carolina.

What should stop private sector companies from entering into a market that is costing the federal and state government $30 billion to operate yearly, with private prison stocks surging on average over 40% yearly. C.C.A., co-founded in Nashville in 1983 by Thomas Beasley (a former chairman of the Tennessee Republican Party) and Dr. R. Crants (its present chairman and CEO), says, "Nothing." Since its original financing by Massey Burch Investment Group of Nashville, it has seen its stock rise from $50 million in 1986 when the company went public to over $3.5 billion in October of 1997.[5]

Wackenhut Corrections Corporation agrees. Based in Miami and the second largest private prison firm in the nation, it houses 23,000 prisoners in facilities spread across this country and those it operates in England. In 1996, the company managed $100 million in revenues with a 26% share of the global market. That same year the company was selected to assume control of a 600 bed facility in Arkansas worth an estimated $7 million in revenues.[6]

Charles Thomas, head of the Private Corrections Project and a criminologist at the University of Florida, believes the private sector can cut construction costs by as much as 25% and operating costs by up to 15%, helping the government to free up needed taxpayer dollars. His Private Corrections Project predicts that by doing so, the availability of private prison beds will grow annually 20% to 25% for the next ten years with capacity topping 276,000 by the end of 2000.[7]

With such figures driving the market, everyone seems to want a foot in the door. Beyond C.C.A. and Wackenhut, which together control over 70% of the global market, 18 other firms are currently in business managing private facilities.

Chances are, if you have your money in the market in either mutual funds or stocks, you are providing for your own future on the interest earned from either housing, managing, caring for or transporting some of the 1.8 million Americans who are incarcerated in the United States.

II

There is an inherent problem with an industry which finds itself economically interested in the perpetuation of a negative aspect of society. Dr. Nils Christie explains, "You get private lobbying for prisons and you get private capital interested in building more prisons, in expanding that system. The industry has no interest in its own abolition."[8]

The more society becomes financially dependent upon crime and its control, the weaker the desire to eradicate it becomes. "Ideally, prisons should be trying to put themselves out of business by doing everything in their power to reduce the recidivism rate," said Jenni Gainsborough, spokeswoman for the National Prison Project of the American Civil Liberties Union. "But the very function of a for-profit prison company is to keep people locked up, as long as possible, because the companies are paid a certain amount per prisoner, per day."[9]

Has economic security become more important than personal security? Are court verdicts and sentences tainted by the corruption often present where money collides with principles? If so, is that not criminal in itself?

Critics of prison privatization and prisoner exploitation are not few in number. Opponents cite the lack of evidence supporting claims that taxpayers' dollars are being saved; the U.S. General Accounting Office released a report in August of 1996 which stated, "Comparisons of operational costs indicate little difference and/or mixed results." The report detailed a comparison of a C.C.A. prison in Tennessee with two other similar state run prisons, revealing that savings of only 1% were realized. The report concluded, "These studies do not offer substantial evidence that savings have occurred."

And yet, while the supposed purpose behind prison privatization has not been definitively proven, there is ample evidence that private prisons end up costing taxpayers more in two areas. The care of hospitalized inmates is turned over to the state and the state must step in and correct problems that private prisons are unable to cope with. In additon, private prisons frequently jeopardize the safety of those prisoners incarcerated within them.

Issues have been raised over the conflict of interest between private prisons' search for profits by the long term housing of inmates and the government's desire to rehabilitate and return prisoners to society. The private sector's drive to streamline and cut corners means efficiency comes before adequate treatment. The result is lack of sufficient governmental oversight; high turn-over rates and inexperience of private prisons' staffs; reports of higher percentages of violent incidences than within state run facilities; and maybe most alarming, the state's inability to protect prisoner rights, such as First Amendment rights, as private prisons are naturally private property.

In August of 1997, after two prisoners escaped from the private C.C.A.-run Houston Processing Center, assaulting a guard and taking his vehicle in the process, the state of Texas was surprised to discover it could prosecute neither of the men for their flight. "They have not committed the offense of escape under Texas law," said District Attorney John Holmes. "The only reason that they're subject to arrest and were arrested was that during their escape, they assaulted a guard and took his motor vehicle. That we can charge them with, and have."[10]

The real shock was that the Houston Processing Center, a facility to hold illegal immigrants awaiting deportation, should not have been housing the two men to begin with; the local authorities had never been made aware of their presence in the state. Neither man was an illegal immigrant; they were two Oregon state prisoners, one serving time for the beating and rape of an 88 year-old woman, and were among 240 other sex offenders shipped to Texas a month earlier by the company.

Had the two prisoners escaped cleanly, then to whose jurisdiction or responsibility it would have fallen for their recapture is in doubt. At that time, C.C.A. itself was not legally obligated to notify the state of the absence of the two men. Texas, which leads the country in the use of private prisons, has since hurriedly passed legislation making such escapes illegal. The incident only underscores opponents' criticisms.

Not only the safety of the public is at issue, but of those imprisoned. Most states do require private prisons to achieve accreditation by the American Correctional Association, but critics argue that ACA standards are inadequate, often not met, and difficult to enforce. Even in states which require state employed monitors to be present in private facilities or visits by independent boards, inmate abuses including substandard diets, the beating of prisoners, inadequate protection from rape and assault, and denial of medical treatment have been well documented.

In 1995, the state of Colorado admitted it could not guarantee the safety of juvenile inmates at the Rebound Corporation-run High Plains Youth Center in Brush, Colorado, after allegations of rape and assault were made by one teenage boy. He had been serially raped for months without intervention by center staff.

The state's director of Youth Corrections admitted, "We were so desperate for beds here in Colorado, we lowered some of our own levels of expectation. The monitors knew if we went in and were too aggressive with it, we had the possibility of losing the contract provider."[11] In this instance, one among many, the state placed its interests before those of the individual in its care. Money took precedence over safety, legality and humanity.

Still, the industry is not defenseless. Dr. Charles Thomas of the Private Corrections Project says, "Private sector companies are increasingly moving to prove their effectiveness, earning better records than public sector systems for seeking and achieving ACA accreditation. This fact may serve to deflate some of the arguments that facilities run by the private sector do not adhere to generally accepted standards and procedures."[12]

The National Rifle Association as well has taken up the cause, in efforts to deflect attention away from itself as pro-gun to the more politically acceptable anti-crime. In 1991, the NRA formed CrimeStrike to lobby for "tough on crime" and prison building initiatives.

In 1993 and 1994, CrimeStrike lobbied up billion-dollar bond initiatives to finance private prisons in Texas and Mississippi respectively. The Texas campaign produced 76,000 beds in that state alone, which have been filled with prisoners from as far away as Hawaii. The butter for the bread is the creation of 12,000 new prison jobs for staff and security.[13]

With a prison population of over 1.8 million in the U.S., which has doubled within the last ten years, there is no doubt a need for more room. It is the simple fact that existing federal and state prisons are bursting, often running at over 125% capacity, filled with the product of the war on drugs. Non violent drug offenders are the largest and fastest growing section of the inmate population. "Three Strikes You're Out" laws such as California's Prop. 184, "Truth In Sentencing" initiatives and "Tough On Crime" mandatory sentencing procedures serve neither society nor the offender. Such "band aid" approaches have not proven their worth beyond creating corporat profits.

While the industry can benefit the economy, it should be held to ethical and moral standards. For that to happen, private prisons and the "crime control industry" must go beyond the status quo. Profits should serve not to enrich individuals, but to combat the social ill of crime and the difficulty of effective rehabilitation.

Financial success in prison privatization provides many benefits: the economic recoveries of cash-strapped rural towns, employment opportunities and investment wealth. But these should take a back seat in importance to providing the country with humane, constitutionally sound facilities whose first priority is to invest the resources necessary to return individuals capable of being re-integrated socially in a fair manner to society. If that standard is not met or even attempted, then the purpose of this venture into privatization is flawed. This does seem to be the case. Lobbyists connected to the industry have been consistently behind tougher and longer sentences while the national crime rate in the last few years has dropped and remained below what it was twenty-five years ago.

The incentive for private prisons is, if they cannot increase the number of individuals entering the system, to influence the length of those individuals' stays. The longer a prisoner remains under their control, the more he or she generates a profit. David Shicher, a professor of criminal justice at California State University-San Bernardino, calls it the "Hilton Scheme": "You want to keep your hotel always full."[14]

"A critical issue is accountability," Marc Mauer of the Washington, DC-based Sentencing Project warns. "You can imagine someone coming up for probation. The tendency of a private prison will be not to release them."[15]

A 1992 study conducted by the New Mexico Corrections Department revealed that women inmates at a C.C.A.-operated prison lost accumulated credit for "good time" at almost 8 times the rate of men at a similar state prison. Prison officials determine when an inmate should have their "good time" debited for disciplinary reasons and guards often are encouraged to write up prisoners. This can lead to not only the loss of an inmate's accumulated "good time," but can also add time to their sentences, up to 30 years in some instances.

Not only do the CEOs and financiers of private prisons have an interest in the bottom line, but often the newly hired guard does as well. Many private prisons offer employees stock ownership as opposed to guaranteed pensions, a money saving plan that compels guards to lengthen inmates' stays at every opportunity, while skimping on such things as food, medical services and rehabilitative activities.

A Prudential Security's report on C.C.A. cautioned, "It takes time to bring up inmate population levels to where they cover costs. Low occupancy is a drag on profits." A similar 1995 report on Wackenhut stated: "The fine tuning of earnings hinges critically on bed count and when new prisons become occupied.[16]

III

The second tier of this industry is inmate labor. Texas Republican Phil Gramm, during a 1995 Senate Judiciary Committee meeting, spelled it out quite clearly. "We ought to build our prisons as mini-industrial parks, where people go to prison, they work, they go to school at night."[17]

The goal is to repeal such laws as the Walsh-Healy Public Contracts Act and Executive Order 11755, both of which place restrictions on the purchase of inmate produced products by the federal government, and the Sumners-Ashurst Act which prohibits the interstate movement of inmate-made goods except for those produced in designated projects.

These laws have either been struck down or weakened by any of the 17 bills concerning inmate labor which were brought before Congress by October 1995. Inmate labor is another "booming" industry netting over 1.8 billion and it is not in danger of being stopped. In 30 out of 50 states today, inmates produce goods in both public and private prisons for the open market. The concept of "factories with fences," championed by former chief Justice Warren Burger in the 1970s, is in full swing. By 1994, more than 70,000 inmates were employed by state and federal correctional industries.[18]

The impetus for private prisons is clear. In a brief to the National Conference of State Legislatures' Criminal Justice Committee, Knut Rostad explained that prison officials believed inmates could pay as much as three times more of their own costs if work programs were increased by 166%.

"Prison officials who manage these prison businesses believe their greatest challenge is creating productive jobs, and that job creation in competitive markets is the business of private enterprise. Most industries' managers have put out the welcome mat for private companies to get involved; they want to talk business," Rostad said.[19]

Inmates now produce circuit boards for Lockhart Technologies Inc. and air-conditioner valves for Chatleff Controls Inc. They make snowshoes for Stowe Canoe and Snowshoe Co., raise pigs in California and sell prison-made "Prison Blues" blue jeans for UniGroup, the title of Oregon Prison Industries. Prisoners have even been used as strike busters by such companies as TWA.[29]

If private prisons can capitalize on inmate labor, then the investment comes full circle. Not only are they paid to house inmates for the state, but they have a captive labor force which requires no benefits, has no lobbying power and cannot strike for higher wages or better working conditions.

Critics are concerned with prison labor undercutting outside wages or removing much needed jobs all together from the private sector. There is also the fear of lax health and safety standards.

Many inmates praise the opportunity to work and earn wages, though. Private sector jobs at prisons pay more than the average "incentive pay" most prisoners in public prisons receive. In some facilities, inmates may also earn more "good time" off their sentences for their work.

Linda Marin of Texas-CURE (Citizens United for the Rehabilitation of Errants) agrees: "If there's a means for them to earn money and get benefits—getting to work on time, having their work valued—that's a good thing."[21] This money can provide for such things as victim compensation, taxes, room and board and child support. All these issues are generally left unaddressed when individuals are sentenced to public prisons without meaningful employment.

What must be decided is if such inmate labor is a means for rehabilitation and for lessening the burden on taxpayers, or if it only amounts to exploitation of a particular class of society. That inmates should be required to work and be charged with victim compensation is a sound ideal. Time in prison should not be idle time, but an obligation to repay one's debt to society.

Yet, if prison administrators only enter into agreements with private companies to make a dollar, which does not benefit the system as a whole by either freeing up or creating more money to fund rehabilitation, then it serves only to harm workers in society in need of employment. The production of wealth by a few, with the exploitation of some, does not justify its existence.

IV

The problem with private prisons and those companies which are strictly oriented towards the prison industry as a whole, at both public and private levels, is that too many have gotten into the business for the wrong reasons.

There is a strong urge to deprive individuals of their liberty for purely economic reasons as the "prison industrial complex," like any other, suffers from the desire to expand. The only possible way for the industry to accomplish such is for it to maintain high confinement rates, while providing the least number of services that cut into profits. This can only lead to the privatizing of the justice system by the influence of the industry's money and lobbying power for longer, tougher and stricter sentences, without chances for parole or probation.

States are consistently lured into the trap by the siren song of savings, most of which never appear. Once there, they find themselves unable to pull away from the commitment. Inmates handed over to private prisons do not have anywhere to go if a prison ends up bankrupt. Once private prisons become imbedded in local economies, politicians are loathe to not renew contracts, even when rates increase by 20% or more and counties find themselves hundreds of thousands of dollars over budget.

As of now, only about 2% of the nation's prisoners are confined within the walls of private prisons. Before that number grows, as experts all agree it will, decisions must be made and exacting standards implemented.

The focus must be shifted away from profits which may be generated by a few individuals and Wall Street finance houses and redirected towards building a system that draws from the best of both public and private sectors. The goal is a system which is cost effective, serves society and produces what prison systems are designed for: a rehabilitated inmate. It is not an unachievable goal; America has done as much with greater problems.

It is already proven that inmate labor and prison privatization can create money and in huge amounts. This money should benefit the taxpayers, and it should, in part, be earmarked expressly for the funding of the justice system, including indigent defender expenses, prison construction, operation and maintenance, and, most importantly, crime prevention measures and prisoner rehabilitation.

Only then will the industry, by cutting costs to taxpayers while partially funding itself and legitimately seeking answers to the elimination of crime, benefit society in a responsible way.

Lawson Strickland was born in Virginia in 1970. He joined the Army at age 17 and served in Operation Desert Storm. On the same day as his honorable discharge from the Army, he was picked up in Louisiana for questioning. Subsequently he was charged with murder for which he still claims his innocence. He is currently on Louisiana's Death Row. Mr. Strickland is a writer of both fiction and non-fiction, frequently writing on capital punishment and the judicial system.

Footnotes:

1 Jan Elvin, "Corrections-Industrial Complex Expands in US," The National Prison Project Journal, Winter 1994/95, p. 4

2 Ibid

3 Ibid, p.1

4 Eric Bates, "Private Prisons," The Nation, January 5, 1998, p. 16

5 Ibid, pg. 12

6 Joseph Epstein, "Wackenhut & CAA; Covicts R Us," Financial World, March 18, 1996

7 Joseph Epstein, "Private Adult Correctional Facility Census, 10th Ed." Private Corrections Project, Center for Studies in Criminology and Law, Univ. FL, March 15, 1997.

8 Jan Elvin, "Corrections-Industrial Complex Expands in US," The National Prison Project Journal, Winter 1994/95, p.3

9 Don Vannatta, Jr., "Private Prison Business Booms, Despite Setbacks," New York Times, August, 1995

10 Eric Bates, "Private Prisons," The Nation, January 5, 1998, p. 12

11 Kristin Bloomer, "America's Newest Growth Industry," In These Times, March 17, 1997, p.16

12 Corrections Alert, "Privatization Census Reveals Continued Expansion," March 6, 1995, p. 1-2

13 Chris Bryson, "The NRA Strikes Back," In These Times, March 17, 1997, p. 18-19

14 Kristin Bloomer, ibid, p. 18

15 Ibid

16 Ken Silverstein, "Jailhouse Stock," In These Times, March 17, 1997, p. 18

17 Gwen Smith Ingley, "Inmate Labor: Yesterday, Today and Tomorrow," Corrections Today, February, 1996, p. 77

18 Ibid

19 Ibid

20 Kristin Bloomer, "A Captive Labor Force," ibid., p. 16

21 Ibid

I understand prison overcrowding has become quite a problem.

Christian Snyder, "Overcrowding"

PATRICIA SPRINGER
"The Influence Of The Media On Our Perception Of Crime"

Americans have become desensitized to crime. Daily headlines that permeate our senses with startling facts about death, photos of human destruction, and cartoons making light of man's inhumanity to man are common companions to our morning coffee. With the addition of news magazine programming on the three major television networks and many cable offerings, crime is as common a part of American life as the elusive American dream.

The power of the media is overwhelming in influencing opinion. When the headline "Inmates Feast On Cake," appeared in the Fort Worth Star Telegram, the public became enraged that prisoners in the Tarrant County Jail were afforded the "privilege" of enjoying cake with their meal. In fact, the story behind the headline, far from depicting an example of privilege, was one of victimization.

Inmates incarcerated in the downtown Fort Worth facility were served cake with their evening meal. By morning dozens of men complained of vomiting and diarrhea. The outbreak was so extensive that authorities were forced to look at the food served, rather than assume a virus had spread throughout every cell block.

Although it was reported that an employee of the food service contracted to provide meals for the Tarrant County Jail was responsible for deliberately putting dish washing soap in the cake batter, the public's focus remained on the dietary offering, rather than inmates' violent physical reactions to the tainted food.

More disturbing is the power of the media in determining pre-trial prejudice toward a defendant. A case in point is that of Diane Zamora, indicted for the murder of a Mansfield, Texas teen rival. Before Zamora's case even went to trial, a book had been published and a movie released, both dubbing the case the "Cadet Murders" after each of the defendants—Zamora was a Navel Academy cadet and her boyfriend, David Graham, of the Air Force Academy.

As often occurs before defendants ever get to trial, critical evidence was leaked to the press. Within the front pages of the Fort Worth Star Telegram and the Dallas Morning News, metroplex readers had an opportunity to read the written statement Zamora gave to police during interrogation. That statement, if true, indicates Zamora's guilt by her own admission. Only as potential jurors are called to serve on the panel to hear the Zamora case will we know the extent of influence the articles had on potential jurors. It is fair to say that a good number of Tarrant County residents will assume Zamora's guilt because they read that statement in the paper.

Prosecutors and defense attorneys are not the only ones who use the media to get their prejudicial messages out to the public. Politicians are perhaps the most expert at utilizing the press. In an age when crime dominates the pages of our newspapers and television news programs, it is beneficial for politicians to project themselves as being "tough on crime." They scream for tougher sentences, tighter appeals procedures, and more prisons. They speak softly when discussing rehabilitation, education, and prison reform.

Thirty-seven Texas inmates died on the executioner's table in 1997—the highest number in the country. In local papers across the state, each executed inmate was profiled for the killings for which he'd been convicted. Then, as a woman headed for the execution chamber, we heard words such as spiritual conversion and forgiveness. One must ask, "Why the media emphasis on one lone woman when thirty-seven men were quietly put to death?"

In 1996, when three of Texas' most high-profile slayings occurred in the North Texas city of Arlington, the city boasted a homicide rate lower than all but one other Texas city. But the public's perception was that violent crime was rampant in the metroplex city. "Residents may have increased fears about crime because the subject has received more coverage in the media," said Arlington Police Chief Kunkle.

Local and national television media tend to exploit tragic, violent crime, bringing it into our living rooms each night. When somebody's child is murdered in Boulder, Colorado, Dallas, Texas, or Union, South Carolina, everybody in America becomes a secondary victim because the media immediately takes us to the scene. We feel the pain, the fear, the anger.

As these front page stories fuel the country's fear of crime and move the people to demand tougher laws and more restrictive parole procedures, we find brief stories of decline in violent crime relegated to the back pages of our newspapers. When stories of stabbings, shootings, and rapes take center stage on the front page, it is unfair that a story titled "U.S. reports decline for second year in violent teen crime" is buried on page five of the Dallas Morning News.

The media has an important job. We just need them to inform, not outrage, the public.

Patricia Springer is a freelance writer in Dallas, Texas. She is the author of two true crime books as well as numerous magazine and newspaper articles.

DENISE QUARLES
"Rehabilitation: An Essential Element of Incarceration"

When one is helping another, both are strong.[1]

Whether our vocation is legal or criminal, we have the same basic human needs—respect from others, personal recognition and a sense of purpose. Contrary to criminals, those of us pursuing legal vocations meet these needs via socially acceptable, constructive avenues. If we are to expect the same from criminals, society must provide them with the appropriate knowledge and skills. There is a segment of society which believes or wants to believe that such efforts are futile. One need only consider the news media's focus on parolees who have committed new crimes, while virtually ignoring those who succeed, to understand why much of society seems to share this belief. However, rehabilitation of criminals is not only feasible, it is essential.

As of January, 1996, $27 billion[2] was spent incarcerating 1,066,011 adult prisoners, which population represents an 8.7% increase of the January, 1995 population.[3] With the increasing cost of incarceration and the large number of prisoners released to the community each year (538,334 in 1995),[4] we cannot afford as a society to ignore the very real rehabilitation needs of prisoners, not if we expect to affect recidivism in a positive manner and to foster constructive, socially acceptable behavior for prisoners upon their release from incarceration. Unfortunately, when the focus of incarceration is solely punishment, as seems to be the current public sentiment, we guarantee a negative fate for criminals and ensure society's self fulfilling prophecy of failure for them. However, the public's desire for punishment can be achieved while at the same time prison officials can implement rehabilitation efforts.

The mere act of imprisonment is punishment. It separates criminals from the community and justifiably results in a loss of basic freedoms available to non-incarcerated law abiding citizens. In order to maintain custody and security, practically every aspect of prisoner's daily lives are controlled by prison officials. This control is exhibited through restrictions on such things as the type of mail they can receive, the amount and type of personal property they can possess, and the amount of time they can spend outside of their cells. While this loss of freedom is essential, so too is the need to provide prisoners with meaningful activities in preparation for the eventual return to the community which the majority of them will face.

The most current data available from the U.S. Bureau of Census for the U.S. Department of Justice (reported by 38 states and the District of Columbia which represented 93% of all prison admissions nationwide)[5] indicate that during 1992 the median age of prisoners admitted to prisons was 29 years. Also, the median level of education completed by these individuals at the time of prison admission was 11th grade, with 46% of those persons having only completed 9th-11th grade. Also, it is estimated that two thirds of inmates had at one time used drugs on a regular basis; approximately 40% had used drugs daily during the month prior to committing their crimes.[6]

It is simply not realistic to expect that by the time adults come to prison after being involved in years of disruptive, criminal and/or self destructive behavior in their youth that a metamorphosis will occur during the service of their sentences. Regardless of the rehabilitation programs which are available and contrary to what many citizens seem to feel, corrections officials cannot force change on offenders—the motivation for change must come from within the prisoner. Prison officials can only offer opportunities for change. The expectation of complete reformation during a prison sentence disregards the responsibility of the individual offender to be motivated to seek constructive change in his/her life and for other segments of society to contribute to the prevention and deterrence of criminal behavior. Prisoners' motivation to change is, in part, based on their belief that rehabilitation program involvement will benefit them.

Evidence from studies has shown that rehabilitation programs can be successful if:

> the programs are offered to high risk offenders
> the specific needs of offenders are identified
> the program matches the offenders' needs and style of learning[7]

In this regard, testing of prisoners upon admission into prison is essential to identify their academic shortcomings and to assess their vocational aptitude to ensure offering prisoners meaningful programs to meet their individual needs, to the extent reasonably possible. In addition there must be an assessment of the type of drugs they may have abused and the degree of that abuse so that appropriate drug education and treatment can be provided. Such therapy is critical to assisting them in realizing the self destructive nature of their drug abusing behavior so that they may become more amenable to involvement in needed academic and vocational pursuits. There are a myriad of programs available in the prison systems in the United States, with offerings varying from one jurisdiction to another. Most jurisdictions offer at least academic and some vocational training as well as substance abuse therapy and a prison industry program.[8] Also, citizen support exhibited through such avenues as volunteerism can be and is used to assist prisoners during their terms of incarceration. Volunteers share their skills by teaching subjects such as art and parenting programs, and they provide spiritual guidance through religious programming. With these programs prisoners can seek to enrich their lives and improve their potential for constructive reintegration into the community upon their release.

One only needs to see the pride and joy of prisoners who substantially improve their reading and writing skills and receive their GEDs to know that academic programming can help prisoners increase their self esteem. One only needs to see the pride and joy of prisoners who learn a new meaningful skill to appreciate the value of vocational programs in allowing them to receive positive personal recognition from others. One only needs to see the pride and joy of prisoners who manufacture clothing, furniture, cleaning supplies and numerous other products to know that prison industries can provide a prisoner a sense of purpose and hope for meaningful employment when released. Even for prisoners who are not initially highly motivated to participate in such programming, their achievement of success in the programs can become, in and of itself, a source of motivation to continue their self improvement efforts.

One of the seemingly greatest incongruities in a prison setting is to witness hardened criminals take pride in caring for plants and vegetables they have grown in a horticulture program, in food they have cooked in a food preparation technology program, in having repaired or constructed something in a building trades program, etc. Learning a new skill, realizing success from a new effort from which they receive personal recognition from staff and other prisoners allows prisoners the opportunity to visualize, usually for the first time in their lives, that they can be involved in efforts which achieve constructive ends instead of criminal and self destructive behavior.

The ultimate test for the success of prisoner rehabilitation programs is not only the attitude and effort of prisoners upon their release from incarceration, but also the willingness of employers to give them a chance to hold meaningful jobs. Without this support of the community we cannot hope to reduce recidivism. Too often communities ignore the returning motivated offender and yet expect his or her behavior to become lawful. Positive reintegration of offenders into the community cannot solely be supported by government agencies. Various segments of society such as the prisoner's family, place of worship and potential employers all must play a role through their support in encouraging offenders to lead a life free of criminal behavior. Society can only be strengthened by this provision of support to offenders and for the rehabilitation programs offered in prisons.

To get the best out of a man, go to what is best in him. Daniel Considine[9]

Denise Quarles is a Regional Prisons Administrator who supervises the wardens and oversees the operations of 16 prisons for the Michigan Department of Corrections. She has over 26 years of experience with that agency for which she has worked in many positions which had previously not been held by females: 1 of 2 females to first supervise a male felon probation caseload, manager of a half-way house for male prisoners, Assistant Deputy Warden of a male maximum security prison and manager of a male prisoner reception center. During her career she has served as the warden of four prisons containing male and female prisoner populations of various security levels. Ms. Quarles also served in the capacity of Deputy Director of the Bureau of Field Services which operated the state's parole and probation services, half-way houses for prisoners and alternative to prison incarceration programs. While holding this position, she was responsible for the development of several new programs which were alternatives to prison incarceration for probationers, parolees and half-way house prisoners such as probation detention centers and technical rule violation centers. She has bachelor and masters degrees in sociology.

Footnotes

1 German proverb, 2715 One-Line Quatations for Speakers, NY, NY, 1996, p. 102

2 The Corrections Yearbook-1996, South Salem, NY, 1996, p. 65

3 The Corrections Yearbook-1996, South Salem, NY, 1996, p. 1

4 The Corrections Yearbook-1996, South Salem, NY, 1996, p. 47

5 Sourcebook of Criminal Justice Statistics 1995, Washington, DC, 1996, p.567, US Department of Justice, Bureau of Statistics

6 Durham III, Alexis M. Crisis and Reform: Current Issues in American Punishment, Boston, MA, 1994, p. 158

7 Durham III, Alexis M. Crisis and Reform: Current Issues in American Punishment, Boston, MA, 1994, p. 156

8 The Corrections Yearbook-1996, South Salem, NY, 1996

9 2715 One-Line Quotations for Speakers, NY, NY, 1996, p. 24

REGINALD A. WILKINSON
"The Emergence of Restorative or Community Justice in the United States"

Picture yourself as the victim of a serious assault. Although you are making progress in the healing process, several recurring questions plague you: "Why did he choose me?" "Am I still in danger?" "What kind of person is the man who assaulted me?" "Is he sorry for what he did to me and to my family?" Victims of crime, who wish to, may now ask those pressing questions of their assailants through a process called victim/offender mediation. Mediation is only one facet of many in a national movement called restorative justice.

In restorative justice, crime is seen as something done against victims and the community, not just a violation against the state or government. The Center for Restorative Justice & Mediation (1996) at the University of Minnesota described crime as "any wrong that weakens relationships between people or harms community living. In restorative justice, the offender becomes accountable to those he or she has harmed. Justice is done for victims, victimized communities, and offenders."

A case can be made that restorative approaches to addressing crime date back thousands of years. The Babylonian Code of Hammurabi (c. 1700 BC) and the Sumerian Code of Ur-Nammi (c. 2060 BC) required restitution for offenses of property and violence. Convicted thieves were ordered to pay double the value of stolen goods as dictated by the Roman Law of the Twelve Tables (c. 449 BC). Germanic tribal laws (c. 496 AD) promulgated by King Clovis, called for restitutional sanctions for both violent and non-violent offenses. The Laws of Ethelbert (c. 600 AD) included detailed restitution schedules. As much as any ancient people, the Hebrew culture promoted the concept of peace.

The Norman invasion of Britain can be described as the end of crime being perceived as injurious to persons and the beginning of the concept of crime as an offense against the state. William the Conqueror developed a legal system for centralizing power and accruing funds. William's son, Henry I, issued laws concerning offenses against the King's peace. Infractions that violated this "peace" were considered to be an offense against the king; the actual victim was denied any significant role in the justice system. William and his descendants developed a justice system that has lasted for centuries.

It is possible that in the next millennium we will reverse the trend of crimes being violations against the King's peace and revert to the philosophy that crimes are injurious to real people. Many people point to our costly criminal justice system, our crowded prisons, high recidivism rates and disregard of victims as signs that our current system is unsupportable and simply does not work. Perhaps our society is ready for a comprehensive justice system which incorporates all aspects of crime, victims and justice into its framework.

As the twentieth century comes to a close, restorative justice is receiving considerable attention and rightly so. Umbreit (1996) examined the growing awareness in restorative justice. "Interest in the United States has grown the most extensively during the past five years. Representing one of the oldest and most visible expressions of restorative justice, the practice of victim-offender mediation, which began in the late 1970's, is now occurring in more than 280 communities throughout the U.S."

Many jurisdictions, including the Ohio Department of Rehabilitation and Correction (DRC), prefer the term "community justice" to "restorative justice" because most people have some concept of what community means as it relates to the justice process, i.e., community corrections, community policing, community prosecution, community courts and the like.

Our justice system ranges from retribution to rehabilitation and back again. In community justice, however, crime is recognized as more than just a violation of the law. Community justice is concerned with repairing harm done to the victim and the community through a process of negotiation, mediation, victim empowerment and reparation. It is inclusive by bringing all those involved or impacted by crime into the decision making process. DRC has acknowledged that the key stakeholders in the community justice process are the victims, the community, justice professionals and offenders.

The victim's involvement and perspective are essential to the process of defining the harm of each crime and identifying how that harm might be repaired. Victims are given a voice in determining what will happen to the offender. It may come as a surprise to many that victims of crime, rather than seeking vengeance, are prone to favoring fair sentences. Victims prefer the idea of punishment paired with reparation, rehabilitation and responsibility.

The community is often engaged as a resource for reconciliation of victims and offenders and as a resource for monitoring and enforcing community standards of behavior. The entire community is given the opportunity to participate. There are many ways citizens can be involved. For example:

1. Volunteers in a parole or probation office may assist by verifying an offender's attendance at work, school or counseling; compiling and submitting statistics; developing employment referrals; providing child care; performing pre-release investigations; developing community resources; participating on advisory committees, and much more.

2. Citizens may choose to mentor an offender by offering support, guidance and someone to listen. Citizens can also be involved by providing jobs so offenders may contribute positively to their neighborhood and be able to make restitution payments to their victims.

3. Local organizations and churches can work together to provide assistance and support to victims and offenders. Neighborhoods can also get involved in prevention programs and internally enforce community standards among community members. Such participation reinforces to community members that crime is everyone's problem and that crime is not acceptable and will not be tolerated.

The justice system is the key to seeing that the wrongs that have been committed are addressed in a fair and equitable manner. Criminal justice professionals facilitate "balance" in the justice system by understanding stakeholder viewpoints and ensuring that all are fairly represented. Criminal justice professionals need to have an open mind about the principles of community justice and lead the way by supporting victims and by being visible and accessible to the community. Justice professionals need to gain greater understanding of victims' issues and a heightened awareness of the victims' perspective. For example, attendance at victim impact panels help professionals understand how victims feel and how they are treated throughout the justice process.

Offenders often rationalize that they didn't hurt anyone or that someone else can easily pay for the damages. Community justice ensures that they bear personal responsibility to correct the damage they have done. Offenders participate in the process by paying restitution, offering an apology, performing community service work or participating in mediation. Offenders may be less likely to commit another offense if they have to face what they have done. By removing the barriers that separate the offender from his or her victim, and by making offenders face the human costs of their actions, crime is personalized for the offender.

All the stakeholders are needed for a truly restorative or community justice response to crime. By giving a voice to all concerned, and by raising awareness about all stakeholders involved, community justice brings balance to the justice system.

There are many restorative and community justice initiatives at work across the country.

- The State of Vermont has restructured its Department of Corrections to include Reparative Probation Boards comprised of community volunteers who meet with eligible offenders to determine appropriate sanctions for the offense.
- The City of Boston teams police officers with juvenile probation officers to monitor violations of probation in the community. They work closely with community members and help to resolve conflict in the neighborhood.
- The Crime Repair Crew in Minnesota is comprised of offenders who respond to the scene of property crimes to repair damage such as graffiti and other types of destruction.
- Community prosecution in Austin, Texas is conducted in decentralized locations in the city, in an attempt to resolve conflict and disagreement in the community without having to utilize the court system.
- Organizations such as the Mothers Against Drunk Driving and Parents of

Murdered Children provide victim impact panels for offenders and other groups to raise awareness about victims' issues.

The Ohio Department of Rehabilitation and Correction has implemented several community justice initiatives.

The DRC created an Office of Victim Services to address the needs of victims both in the prison and parole jurisdictions. The office is staffed by victims or advocates who provide information and support to victims of crime. The staff have trained a victim coordinator in each prison and parole region to assist victims of crime in getting their questions and concerns addressed.

We have opened our parole hearing system to victims, enabling them to have a greater voice in the process. Office of Victim Services staff assist victims in preparing for Parole Hearings and may also accompany the victim to the hearing. Ohio also appointed a victim of crime to the Ohio Parole Board to provide a more complete insight to the process.

We have piloted Victim Sensitive Offender Dialogue, in which victims meet with their offenders to help achieve closure. While this process is not for everyone, and is carefully monitored and painstakingly coordinated, many victims and offenders derive a great benefit from the sessions. Prisoners at one of our largest institutions are also involved in paying restitution for their offenses.

Ohio did not start from scratch. Many existing programs reflect the principles of Restorative Justice. For example, our Bureau of Community Service oversees a program in which inmates volunteer literally millions of hours to community service work. We also field community advisory boards at all our prisons. Our offender services network, which endeavors to provide tools for rehabilitation after release from prison, is growing steadily. We support community corrections (alternatives to prison incarceration) through funding, design, technical assistance and networking through Community Corrections Act Planning Boards.

Our most recent effort is perhaps the most comprehensive. The DRC has formed a diverse Community Justice Cabinet to provide oversight and guidance as we progress toward a more balanced system of justice.

In the years ahead, Ohio corrections professionals will work as a team with all stakeholders to establish linkages and create an umbrella of community justice that is inclusive of all entities affected by crime and punishment.

Reginald A. Wilkinson is director of the Ohio Department of Rehabilitation and Correction. In his 25-year career in corrections, he has served as superintendent of Ohio's first Corrections Training Academy, first warden at the Dayton Correctional Institution, and first regional director. A strong advocate of professionalism, Wilkinson is a member of many professional and civic organizations. In 1996, he was proud to be elected president of the American Correctional Association. He has a B.A. Political Science, The Ohio State University, 1972; M.A. Higher Education Administration, The Ohio State University, 1973; Post M.A. Educational Leadership, The University of Cincinnati.

References:

Center for Restorative Justice & Mediation. "Restorative Justice". St. Paul, MN: University of Minnesota, School of Social Work, in cooperation with: The Minnesota Department of Corrections, Balanced & Restorative Justice Project, and the National Organization for Victim Assistance, 1996.

Ohio Department of Rehabilitation and Correction. "A Community Justice Agency". Columbus OH: State of Ohio, Department of Rehabilitation and Correction, 1997.

Umbreit, Dr. Mark S. "Responding to Important Questions Related To Restorative justice." St. Paul, MN: University of Minnesota, School of Social Work, Center for Restorative Justice and Mediation, 1996.

SHAPING ATTITUDES

Death Row, California

August 23, 1997

"California adopted a 'no frills' ideology when it went on its prison building boom in the 80's-90's and all of the new prisons are built purposely bleak, sterile and block-like, no paint, no grass, nothing but concrete, razor wire and gun towers. The insides are like grey cinder block beast bellies...the grounds around the buildings are bare dirt, sterile of any green growth...really depressing, and oppressive, sites. The older prisons did manage to keep some semblance of human habitat and maintained their landscape, but the new sterile joints outnumber the old, therefore more prisoners are affected by the bleak environment than are by the old."

Connecticut

March 12, 1995

"I feel something happening in this country, I smell fear of the government by common ordinary citizens, like never before. I hear meanness being uttered from the mouths of those we vote into office to have authority over us, and I sense a deep chill in my soul. Our privacy and Constitutional rights have been eroded almost to non-existence, and the average citizen is only now beginning to feel the heavy hand of oppression. I believed in Justice at one time, I certainly learned about her in school, but, Julie, she's missing now in our court system. I hope we can continue to communicate, because prison is an intellectual desert, in which you have to create your own reality. I feel a need to voice the injustice I see...and hope you can help me be a voice for those facing this idle abandonment."

MAIL CALL

Today I got my brother's letter
The dog died
But mama's doing better

Little Billy has a bad cough
The phone's disconnected
And the electricity is off

Rumor is that your wife left town
With Jody Lee
And the pickup truck broke down

Downsizing cost daddy his job
He's very depressed
Poor man can only sob

Oh, and when you're released from prison
Don't come home
I think you know the reason

You're not wanted back this time
We are embarrassed
By both you and your crime

You should consider leaving the USA
Go to Asia
Or somewhere else far away

Have to close now - got stuff to do
Wanted to write
And send best wishes to you

John Yarbrough
Federal Bureau of Prisons, Texas

MICHAEL TENNESON
"From the Cocoon"

My earliest memories came out in 1988 after being sentenced to multiple life sentences. For years I had terrible nightmares of being strangled and beaten as a child. There was so much pain and violence in these dreams that I would wake up in a cold sweat. When I told my mother about my dreams she said I was too young to really remember what had happened, but when I gave her specific details, she realized that I was having clear recollections of my earliest experiences.

Included in my memories is a man's face sneering at me and smothering me with a pillow when I cried. I remember that face pointing guns in my face and saying, "click...click," as he laughed and pulled the trigger. When I'd laugh back, he'd slam my head into the wall or hit me in the face. My father was a very disturbed young man who was thrown in jail frequently for a gamut of drunken offenses, including raping a neighbor's retarded daughter. In each case he was immediately bailed out of jail by his wealthy parents. One night he tried to rape Mom and that was the last straw! She got a restraining order, filed for divorce, and we were on our own.

My father died when I was eight years old. The monster was dead, or so I thought. I didn't realize that the monster was inside of me, growing silently.

When I was four years old I was snatched away from Mom by social services because a woman in our apartment complex got jealous when her husband came down and talked to Mom. The woman called social services and said my mother was involved in criminal activities. Mom was arrested and I was put in a foster home for almost a year.

The foster parents told me that my mother was bad and that I would never see her again unless I did what they said. They gave me drugs that made me sick and dizzy; when I spit them out, the woman sat on me and forced me to swallow them. When I cried, they locked me in a closet and kept me in it for long periods. It was dark, I was scared and often forced to urinate and defecate on myself.

Sometimes they would sit me at the table and play a game with me: "Mikey, want to see your mommy tomorrow?" I'd get all excited and say "Yes!" Then they laughed and got ugly looks on their faces and said, "You can't, because your mommy's bad!" I'd begin to cry, then get beaten, then...the closet.

Many months later, Mom was finally proven innocent of the charges against her and was released. The neighbor woman had come forward and told the truth, confessing to her lies and motives. I came from the foster home stuttering terribly, twitching (from being hit in the face so often), and peeing the bed frequently. I was also on a number of drugs to "control those dysfunctional behaviors..." and was required by social services to see a shrink regularly. Mom was furious and wanted to know what the hell had happened to her little boy. I could offer no insight; I was only five years old.

When I began kindergarten that year, I stuttered and twitched so badly that the kids laughed at me. I hated them and lashed out physically, eventually learning to be left alone by attacking them first. I never got good overall grades because of my undeveloped social skills, even though I excelled over most of them academically. My constant violent responses led to my being expelled.

The next year I began school in another district, which was just as bad. I was expelled for being assaultive and assigned a home tutor. Social services was always threatening Mom to "keep your son under control or else..." We were both terrified of the ramifications; she tried to comply by becoming an obsessive perfectionist. Nothing I ever did was good enough, and I couldn't understand why one day she would be so nice, and the next so violent.

Those developmental years were filled with constant school changes and taking psychotropic drugs prescribed by various psychiatrists. I learned that drugs made me good, and not taking drugs made me bad. Those perceptions were reinforced by the erratic behavior of my mother. When she'd have problems, she'd tell me what a rotten son-of-a-bitch I was, then reach for her bottles of nerve medications; a few hours later she would be "normal" again.

I hated having to be around other people because they belittled me. I felt like a freak. As I grew into my early teens, I was an isolated loner, rejected by my peers, shunned by my teachers and noticed by the authorities. By the age of twelve, I was using illegal drugs and alcohol to numb the pain and loneliness.

In my fourteenth year I had a very violent summer and was sent to reform school. There I received none of what I desperately needed which was love, compassion and understanding. I was dealt with clinically, coldly, systematically and shot back to society when my parcel of time had been served. I was more scared, paranoid, resentful and wary of the system, as well as more suspicious of people and of my own human worth; I was not at all rehabilitated—debilitated and denigrated is more accurate. I spent high school on dope, becoming more sneaky, stuffing my feelings more deeply, and even further withdrawn. The monster was stirring inside.

I did crime to pay for my habits. My crimes became more brazen. I became more violent. In 1980 I was arrested after a long night of burglaries—it snowed, and the footprints led to my front door. I was read a long list of charges and told by a public defender to plead guilty or I'd face close to 100 years. I said I didn't commit all those crimes and he said, "Take it, or leave it." I capitulated, accepting my fate.

Self esteem? Self worth? I was an abysmal failure in everything I tried. From my earliest years I was constantly told I was a rotten piece of excrement and would never amount to anything—just like my father. It was indeed prophetic. I couldn't hold a job even when I had adequate skills. I could not even begin a friendship, much less maintain one. My entire world was filtered through negative conditioning and a drug-induced state that I had come to know as simply "normal."

I did very hard time for my six-year sentence. I was terribly disillusioned and desperately wanted to change what I was. The programs they offered sounded good on paper and no doubt the public paid dearly for them, but in fact they were largely ineffective.

I went through them all and learned the facts, figures, and latest theories about drug abuse. I was told I had to learn to feel good about myself without drugs, though none of the programs offered me practical opportunities to do the things that would help me develop those positive feelings about myself. I had a stack of certificates saying that I had completed this and that program du jour and I fully believed that I would take the lessons I had recited for six years in the sensorily-deprived environment of prison and be able to use them in the real world and live a normal life. The problem was that all those paper facts and figures did nothing to erase the nightmares that haunted me. They did nothing to heal the emotional wounds I had suffered all my life. They did nothing to change my twisted perceptions of people, the world, and myself.

The first night home was a wild kaleidoscope of confusion. I went into extreme depression and psychological overload. I went straight to the dope man and bought a bag of dope, and then to a liquor store. I spent the next couple of months quickly spiraling to a point where I finally lost all remnants of sanity and human dignity. I went on a suicidal crime spree and had no intention of going back to prison. In fact I had no intention of living to see the new year—I planned to "hold court in the streets" whenever the authorities caught up to me.

June of 1987 found me in the Denver County Jail charged with five counts of first degree murder. I stared at the TV in the block watching the headline story of this monster who had gone on a murderous rampage. The monster was me. In 1989 at the conclusion of my death penalty trial, I was spared a place on death row by the vote of one dissenting juror. When asked why she did not impose death, she said, "I had a gut feeling."

Today I am consumed with remorse for the crimes I have committed. There are no words capable of expressing the depth of sorrow I feel for taking five innocent lives. I still shudder when I reflect on the mind set that caused so many people so much pain. In 1987 I felt I was paying back every "rotten-son-of-a-bitch" that ever hurt me. I wanted to dehumanize, demean, and violate the society that sat back and ignored me as I cried out all of my young life when the same things were happening to me and Mom. It was blind rage. Does that seem horrible? Sick? Of course it does. At that time I was a very sick individual.

Society screams out in vengeance to "Lock-em-up-for-life! Take away everything that a normal human being relies upon to define and develop his human identity. Don't waste money educating "them," re-training "them," and damnit—Don't coddle "them!" In effect society says, "To hell with prisoners." Predictably, prisoners respond likewise and end up saying, "To hell with you too!" Violence begets violence. Hatred breeds hatred. Ignorance uneducated remains ignorance. Human beings that are brutalized, dehumanized, violated over and over for an extended period of time will generally assimilate those same behaviors.

Ignorant people come to prison, are exposed to constant ignorance, and leave prison unchanged for the better. Violent people come to prison, are exposed to even more senseless violence, and leave prison more violent and less equipped to deal with it. Perverts come to prison, are surrounded by perversion, and they leave worse. People who have been abused most of their lives come here where they receive constant emotional and psychological abuse and leave—just waiting to pay somebody back.

Please understand that I am not excusing, nor justifying my actions. There is no one I blame. But there are reasons why I thought, felt and acted the way I did. Until society understands the cause and effects of psychological disorders and is willing to put its own vengeance, hatred and irrationality aside and look objectively at what is really needed to change the mind sets of the people in prison, this problem will continue to grow rampantly.

You cannot murder murderers to show that murder is wrong and expect murder to cease. You cannot abuse children and then expect them to have the skills necessary to raise their own offspring without abuse. And the Golden Rule points out the obvious again: You cannot exact your vengeance upon prisoners, who are already victims of "society" in one twisted sense or other, without those victims coming back and re-paying you with generations of interest. Our collective motives, mind sets, and sick needs to hurt each other have to change. It is not "us" against "them" because we are all part of one society. The greatest obstacle that has prevented any true rehabilitation in this country has been the stigmatization of people convicted of a crime. We are not animals, but we quickly become animals when we are treated as such.

Where does the cycle stop? The first step would be to rewrite policy from a common-sense standpoint, not a political one where there are vested interests.

Why should society give a damn about a prisoner? Allow me to share a glimpse of who I am today and draw your own conclusions.

While I was sitting in the hole in 1988 for assaulting two correctional officers, the mental health staff and warden came to visit me. I was belligerent, violent and ended up getting the hell beat out of me. Deservingly.

Months later we met again. This time I listened and begged for the chance to do something constructive with my life. The warden suggested I take the Commercial Art course offered there. I said, "I can't draw...!" He said, "Try!" After eighteen months of working 16-20 hours a day, sprawled out on my concrete floor, I graduated. For the first time in my life I finished something I'd started, and I excelled! I cried when I got my certificate, and have tears in my eyes even now as I remember that turning point in my twisted life. My whole attitude toward myself, others and life began changing. It wasn't the art so much as the entire process I learned as I studied: reflection, analysis, concentration, discipline, honesty, interpretation. Also it was something that I wanted to do. I soon surpassed the skills of my peers, the expectations of my teacher, and the limits of the simple materials I was allowed (i.e. colored pencils). I began petitioning the administration for permission to buy painting materials which are water-soluble and non-toxic. I was repeatedly told, "No." I resubmitted my proposals with increasingly focused rebuttals. My tenacity paid off. I was given the chance I had requested so passionately, with the warning that if I so much as sneezed wrong, I would lose it all.

I threw my TV away in 1990 and began studying art intensively, often waking up on the floor with a pencil, brush or book in my hand. I learned that the more I focused on my studies, the more my skills improved, and the better my entire outlook became. Common sense to most? For me it had a profound life-changing effect!

I have been the mural painter at this new medium/close security facility for four years. Again, I asked for the chance to expand my skills, and do something positive with them to benefit others. I was given permission to do as I requested. The warden gave me his trust, and the reminder, "Strike one...and you're out." Since then I have operated as an independent. I have been trusted with the responsibilities of handling every aspect of my work from designing the murals, ordering the materials with purchase orders, inventory and accountability for all the materials, building the frames and hanging the finished work. I have even been granted a "special permit" to possess in my cell the materials that I need to do all the various design work to make abstract ideas become focused compositions, another skill that translates directly to solving problems in everyday life.

The result of being allowed to earn these privileges has been a dramatic change in my attitude, temperament and motivation. The resultant self-esteem has given me the courage and ability to overcome my past. If you were to see my art, or hear my music you would never suspect that it was done by a man who made the headlines ten years ago as a monster. Today the headlines tell of the beauty these hands have learned to create.

The majority of criminals are not incorrigible, like the "experts" would have you believe. Prisoners are not inherently bad. I offer the extreme case of myself for irrefutable proof! If someone as bad as I was can come so far with so little, then what does that say about the experts' opinions?

Though I have expressed numerous complaints about the current state of things here, I must also thank the administration and staff who have given me the latitude to do the things which have been paramount to my growth as a human being. Tenacity and sincerity have helped open many doors of understanding, and a certain level of trust has been developed as a result. I realize that all the opportunities in the world will not change a person who simply does not want to change.

Those who demonstrate exceptional sincerity and determination should be allowed to earn privileges commensurate to their efforts, actions and attitudes. Such wisdom would not only encourage, but allow highly motivated inmates to realize the potential within themselves and maximize it. It would also offer a powerful role-model to lesser motivated inmates and inspire many to reach for these higher goals.

The lack of any such provisions are the crux of my complaints about current prison policies—these are minor changes that could have a major impact on the developmental potential of tens of thousands of prisoners across the nation.

In conclusion I will offer this thought: from it's humblest beginnings, immersed in darkness, the ugly caterpillar struggles within its little world, entangled in the strands that will one day become its wings. American prisons are filled with ugly caterpillars. Who, not knowing of the metamorphosis, would ever suspect such beauty could come from such ugliness?

Michael J. Tenneson was convicted of five murders (in Colorado and Wisconsin) in 1987, and only spared the Death Penalty because one juror said she had "a gut feeling..." Driven by feelings of deep remorse, his life's goal is to give something back to society through his art, music and writing. For four years, he has been a member of the Redirections Therapeutic Community at the Limon Correctional Facility, undergoing extensive drug, alcohol and behavioral modification therapy. Mr. Tenneson is conclusive confirmation that even the worst can change dramatically. He says, "Yes, the prisoner must have the true desire for change, but the system must also allow us to earn the very tools, education and opportunities that are condusive to radical change."

Michael Tenneson, "Through a Child's Eyes"

Michael Tenneson, "Julia Belle Swain at Riverside"

MARCIA BUNNEY
"Finding Self-Respect for Battered Women"

"The subject of past abuse emerges frequently in recovery programs, yet it is basically overlooked in most curricula. Clearly, domestic violence in an inmate's background, whether experienced as a child or during adulthood, results in long lasting damage that needs to be addressed. For many survivors it may be at the root of many socially maladaptive behaviors."[1]

More than two decades ago, books such as Del Martin's Battered Wives began to focus public attention on the issue of domestic violence. The body of related literature amassed in the ensuing years contains little, however, which directly addresses the concerns of incarcerated victims of abuse: battered women in prison.

Controversy has long surrounded the issues of abuse and victimization, particularly as applied to those who break the law, and most especially to women who commit crimes under the duress of abuse, or who kill or assault the men who abuse them. Our criminal justice system is engaged in a continuing struggle to balance compassion for the abused against a visceral fear that acknowledgment of reduced culpability sends the wrong message to offenders.

The correlation between domestic violence and women's criminal conduct is demonstrated in numerous studies. Statistics indicate that as many as 88 percent of women in prison today have been victims of domestic violence and sexual or physical abuse prior to their incarceration, either as children or adults.[2] Violent offenders in particular were determined to have been victims of physical or sexual abuse prior to incarceration. This abuse, according to researchers, "was likely to be at the hands of their husbands or boyfriends."[3] This correlation is particularly important in rendering in-custody assistance to battered women who have killed or assaulted their abusers.

It is exceedingly difficult for the average person to understand the daunting challenges faced by abused women in prison.

Prison administrators and guards, like the public, often err in assuming that "domestic violence" is an exclusively physical phenomenon. Experts in family violence, on the other hand, urge that physical violence is but one factor, albeit the most readily perceived by the average layperson. Battered women frequently report to researchers and therapists that "the psychological harm is much more significant than the physical harm."[4] The psychological effects of battering are numerous, including depression, anxiety, insecurity, and suicidal thoughts.[5] The development and nurturing of self-esteem in these women is thus absolutely vital in motivating them toward, then sustaining them through, recovery.

Typically, a woman who is convicted of killing/assaulting her abuser arrives in prison in an utterly debilitated state, suffering not only the physical and emotional effects of jail confinement—often, of several years' duration in murder cases—but the terrible grief and disorientation resulting from having committed a violent act against the man she loved.

The majority of women convicted of such offenses have no criminal record, no history of violence. In many cases, a woman has been intimidated by attorneys who use the threat of the death penalty to induce her to accept a plea bargain, or forego her right to a trial by jury. Engulfed in remorse, paralyzed by fear, and convinced of her utter worthlessness in the face of the State's apparent willingness to kill her for having fought back against her abuser, she is likely to capitulate and enter a plea of guilty, just to get the process over with.

Having thus condemned herself in every sense, it is extremely difficult for her to focus inward to activate her survival instinct, and make the best of her lot in prison. The reserves of strength and determination that enabled her to survive abuse are the key to her healing and her survival in prison. Yet, while a woman remains immobilized by the combination of her own emotions and memories, amplified by the inescapable fact of her imprisonment as "proof" of her failure as a human being, she is unable to help herself. She is, in her own eyes, unworthy of the effort to save herself, totally at fault for everything that has happened to her—just as her abuser always told her she was. As long as she continues to think and feel this way, it is as though he is still alive, still abusing her, still in control.

This, then, is the starting point for battered women sent to prison as punishment—punishment for striking back to save themselves and their children, for breaking under the pressure of more threats, more beatings, more sexual abuse in the guise of conjugal relations. It is the purpose of the prison's battered women's group to assist these women in their efforts to overcome the effects of combined negative messages, to cope affirmatively as survivors rather than victims, and to foster the growth that will enable them to avoid violence in future relationships.

Among California's five state prison facilities housing female offenders, two currently operate self-help/support groups for battered women: the California Institution for Women (CIW), and the Central California Women's Facility (CCWF). Initiated by the women themselves, then formally implemented through administrative proposals, each group functions under the combined supervision of prison staff and counselor-facilitators from a local battered women's shelter/support agency.

An auxiliary function of the groups is the presentation of informal workshops on domestic violence. Conducted on a voluntary basis by senior group members, these loosely-structured dialogues occur within the framework of other self-help/motivational prison programs, such as Substance Abuse, Parenting, and Pre-Release. Each inmate facilitator is free to draw upon her own experience for anecdotes to stimulate the interest and involvement of the class. Hand-out literature and short videos provide more detailed information and reinforce the speaker's message.

Experts in family violence recognize the unique value of peer input and support in a battered woman's long, painful, and often frightening odyssey through recovery. Abused women themselves say that the most effective assistance they receive comes from groups and shelters utilizing the input and presence of women who have experienced domestic violence.[6] In the prison setting, this inmate-to-inmate approach is acknowledged as a major strength and source of effectiveness for self-help groups,[7] as it encourages a degree of sharing, frankness, and insight not generally achieved by more traditional methods and exercises.

New members of the group receive an extensive orientation regarding basic aspects of domestic violence, including identifying and understanding the emotions related to their histories. Gradually, they explore constructive means of emotional expression appropriate to the peculiarities of the prison environment.

In the process of their recovery, senior group members have developed personal strategies for healing, particularly those of us who came to prison during the years preceding a more general recognition of the scope and dynamics of domestic violence. In these early years, a woman convicted of killing an abusive mate was treated as nothing more than a vicious criminal. She was no different, in the system, than a gang member involved in a drive-by shooting, or a drug dealer who executed a competitor. Although she, too, was a victim, it was as though her victimization was nullified by her criminal conduct and resulting conviction. While many correctional entities, including the parole board, continue to view us this way, some are beginning to acknowledge the critical importance of recognizing and validating the grief and other emotions of women who have attacked, even killed, their abusers.

The prison environment, however, is not conducive to self-assertion; most expressions of personality are viewed as tantamount to criminal offenses, and making decisions is considered a luxury.[8] Women prisoners frequently say that prison staff encourage them to focus on the positive aspects of their situation, to forget about their depression, to stay out of trouble. The prevailing attitude is that remaining silent about their feelings will make them go away. In the community, depression is treated as a natural response to loss; in prison, it is viewed as inappropriate behavior rather than a valid response.[9] Expression of this grief, as well as the anger and depression likely to follow without counseling and support specific to their needs, is likely to be interpreted as a lack of self-control.[10] Left to themselves, they are at risk, and some eventually do lose control. Typically, the response of the system is punitive; the women are designated "management problems," caught up in an endless cycle of disturbances and segregation placement. This, unfortunately, has the effect of exacerbating prisoners' difficulties while adding to the burdens on prison personnel; it is a sad and unnecessary misuse of resources.

Any battered woman in recovery travels along a fine line between awareness of her victimization and the compelling necessity to proceed with her life, a victim no more. This line is even more finely drawn in prison, where the microcosmic culture itself can be a tremendous obstacle to true healing.

For many battered women confined in prison, the physical abuse, emotional manipulation, and terror we suffered at the hands of our abusers is far from over. The inherent brutality and abusiveness prevalent in California's prisons spawn high levels of stress and physical violence, posing a serious threat to the health and safety of all, and creating a cruel irony for battered women. Thus, although we are physically removed from the presence of those who abused us prior to our commitment to prison, conditions within the institution continually re-invoke these experiences, often with devastating results.

If a woman is being beaten or emotionally tormented by another prisoner in her dorm, for example, a typical staff response is, "Deal with it," or an offer to move her to another dorm. Being moved fosters the impression that she, not the abusive other, is the problem—a parallel to situations in which women have been forced to abandon their homes in order to escape abuse. Generally, assaults occur unpredictably and infrequently, the woman "hurt just enough to 'keep her in her place.'"[11] The relatively minor effects of such violence do not mean that its overall effect is insignificant; in fact, "the psychological and social effects of the violence can be very great, even when the physical damage is minuscule."[12]

Employing my own history as an example, the sole disciplinary offense on my prison record—which was clear for the first eleven years of my incarceration—stems from such a situation. Despite my repeated verbal complaints, pleas for help, and written grievances submitted according to procedure, I was forced to remain in that dorm until I was attacked, and was subsequently placed in segregation housing. I was given a disciplinary report because my behavior—complaining about the abuse—had ostensibly caused the attack. In reality, having "made my bed" by coming to prison in the first place, I was expected to "lie in it" by virtue of my silence, and was indirectly punished for my refusal to do so. In the ensuing five years, placement in similar situations has continued. I was last attacked in June 1997, by a roommate known to be violent: she had battered another woman in our dorm less than two months prior to her attack on me, and in that case, the victim, not the abuser, was moved.

My experience of violence and abuse in the confines of this particular prison is not merely a personal phenomenon. Rather, it is representative of other incidents in the same vein. It is symptomatic of a continuing refusal to deal with serious problems at root level, a failure to operate from a preventive, rather than remedial, philosophical base. One member of our group described it thus: "Living in the average dorm at CCWF is like living with seven abusive husbands."

Incarcerated battered women who receive the education and support available through groups learn to cope with the dynamics of interaction with personnel in the prison setting, and minimize detrimental interaction with their sister prisoners. Most importantly for re-integration into society, they acquire knowledge and develop resources, both internal and external, which will enable them to take a pro-active position in dealing with an abusive mate, or recognize—and avoid—a potential batterer. They learn the importance of seeking help before things go too far, as well as safe methods of involving the appropriate agencies. They learn to stop the violence—a goal which benefits the women, their families, and their respective communities. The woman who develops an awareness of the shadow presence of abuse possesses an invaluable tool for directing and accomplishing her recovery, overcoming her self-image as a victim, and rejoining society as a responsible and empowered citizen.

The paramount needs of incarcerated battered women are safety and means of exercising self-assertion in a constructive fashion. It should be obvious that it is difficult at best to achieve true healing while abuse is permitted to continue, even encouraged in some cases. The fostering of dependency and maintenance of a climate in which abuse can continue to occur virtually unabated is not merely cruelly ironic; it reinforces the very role we women are striving to escape.

Self-help/support groups for incarcerated battered women are thus an effective and increasingly important means of promoting valid correctional goals, while affirmatively confronting an uncomfortable truth: the prevalence of domestic violence.

Marcia Bunney is a California prisoner, sentenced to 25 years to life for the shooting death of her abusive lover. Incarcerated for 16 years, she has been active in the formation of two self-help groups for battered women, at the California Institution for Women and the Central California Women's Facility, where she also facilitates domestic violence workshops for prisoners. She has earned her A.A. Degree while in custody, and is exploring means to continue her formal education, emphasizing the areas of journalism and law. Her work has been produced in various media, including workshop literature distributed at the U.N. World Conference on Women (Huairou, China, 1995) and articles/ essays appearing on the Internet. She serves on the Advisory Boards of the National Network for Women in Prison and Catholic Charities' HIV/AIDS in Prison Project, and is an elected member of the National Steering Committee of the National Lawyers Guild Prison Law Project.

Footnotes

1 Owen, Barbara and Bloom, Barbara, "Profiling the Needs of California's Female Prisoners" National Institute of Corrections, US Dept. of Justice, February 1995, p. 42.

2 All Too Familiar: Sexual Abuse of Women in US State Prisons, Human Rights Watch, Women's Rights Project, Human Rights Watch, December 1996, p.19, n. 18.

3 Owen, Barbara & Bloom, Barbara, "Profiling the Needs of California's Female Prisoners" National Institute of Corrections, US Dept. of Justice, February 1995, pp. 8-9.

4 Walker, Lenore, The Battered Woman Syndrome, 1984.

5 Ewing, Charles Patrick, Battered Women Who Kill: Psychological Self-Defense as Legal Justification; Lexington Books/D.C. Heath & Co., Lexington, Mass., 1987.

6 Bowker, Lee H., "A Battered Woman's Problems Are Social, Not Psychological," in Current Controversies on Family Violence, Richard Gelles and Donileen Loseke, editors; Sage Publications, Newbury Park, CA, 1993, p. 157.

7 Owen, Barbara & Bloom, Barbara, "Profiling the Needs of California's Female Prisoners" National Institute of Corrections, US Dept. of Justice, February 1995, p. 42.

8 Jose-Kampfner, Christina, "Coming to Terms with Existential Death: An Analysis of Women's Adaptation to Life in Prison," Social Justice, Vol. 17, No. 2, Summer 1990, p . 117.

9 Ibid., at pp. 118-119.

10 Ibid., at p. 117.

11 Bowker, Lee H., in Currents, Spring 1984, 4(2):37-42, at pp. 38-39.

12 Ibid., at pp. 38-39.

CHARLES M. DENNISON
"Hiring the Best Corrections Officers"

No management function is more critical to an organization's success than the hiring of people who will go on to become competent, motivated and productive employees. In annual report after annual report, of corporations and governmental organizations alike, you will find essentially the same comment, "Our employees are our most important asset." The fact of the matter is that employees **are** an organization's most important asset, and failure to get the best employees can have dire, if not disastrous, results. It is ironic and surprising, therefore, that almost universally, so little time is spent on the employee selection process of fitting the job candidate to the job, and so little training is given to those doing the selecting. Corrections and law enforcement are not exempt.

Hiring is a complex, difficult, time consuming, and generally unrewarding task at best. Selecting someone for a job is probably the single biggest opportunity managers have to influence the development of their organization for good or ill. Yet we tend to want sure-fire formulas for hiring the right person, some process we can put numbers to, crunch through a computer and tell us who to hire. This is especially true with the current prison building boom and the need for employees. Those formulas don't exist—and for good reason. Since hiring is ultimately a matter of predicting human behavior, it is an art and not a science.

Most hiring decisions are made by novices at the game who lack the experience and skills to make hiring decisions on the basis of something other than how they happen to "feel" about a candidate. In fact, most hiring decisions are made within four minutes of the interview. The "halo" effect, where the interviewer sees part of himself/herself in the candidate, is quite common. Job-seekers are taught by professional job search firms how to create this effect. Read the many available books on how to get a job if you want confirmation. This "halo" phenomenon is caused primarily through lack of preparation and training for the people doing the interviewing and selecting. It is important to know that the "Great at Interviews" candidate is not necessarily a fit for the job.

Any smart candidate can be anyone you want him to be for the interview process, and probably throughout the probation period. But sooner or later, if he is not a good job fit, he will revert to his natural personality and performance will become an issue. A lot of things can happen if the person doesn't fit the job—**and all of them bad!** A series of incidents at U. S. Post Offices, and the many "excessive use of force" law suits filed against officers, come to mind.

It is very costly to hire a good employee and have him/her leave. It is far more costly to hire a bad employee and have him/her stay.

The costs for hiring an employee who doesn't "fit" the job can be enormous. Organizations spend great amounts of time, energy and money in a never ending effort trying to train, coach, or motivate low performing employees to a level of merely adequate performance. And yet, all the good management, training, or incentives **will not make** a candidate succeed if he/she doesn't have the characteristics for job success. But the costs can far exceed the tangible costs of hiring, training and turnover. The problem of ineffective hiring goes beyond the disturbingly high proportion of employees who either quit or are terminated shortly after being hired. It extends to the many employees who, while they don't quit and aren't terminated, never make a meaningful contribution to their organizations. For corrections and law enforcement the costs can be even greater through lawsuits filed for inappropriate behavior, and may include physical injury or loss of life. Any time, effort and money spent in hiring the "right" people is well spent!

The world of corrections is changing dramatically and fast. The changes are not unlike those in police departments where the trend toward community policing has changed police officer's jobs and the types of people needed to fill them. The corrections officers' job is replete with conflicting requirements. The modern officer needs to be commanding yet compassionate and fair, adaptable to quick changing situations and yet able to work within the often monotonous daily routine, capable of handling stressful situations but not overreacting to them, able to work as an individual and as a member of the team, and many other such opposing conditions.

How do we find people with these characteristics? The fundamentals of hiring employees who fit the job are the same for corrections as for any other organization. Only the job and the desired personality types differ. The processes for successful hiring are the same.

Hiring, Blocking and Tackling

Any coach will tell you that ultimate success depends on hard work and mastery of fundamentals. If you want to win, you have to pay the price of establishing the basic set of fundamentals and practicing them. The same is true for hiring. The only route to hiring employees who fit the job is through preparation and execution. "In my experience, managers give far too little time or effort to the planning and preparation stage of an interview. It should be no surprise that they do not get the results that they would like."

There are many facets to the hiring process: defining the selection pool, prescreening, background checks, reference checks, to name a few. This section will focus on one critical fundamental usually missing, or not handled well, in the hiring process: documenting the **<u>real job description</u>**.

The Cornerstones of Job Performance

In several "The New Art of Hiring Smart" seminars we conducted, many with police chiefs and corrections managers, the audience was asked to make a list of what they were looking for in a job candidate. The attendees were then asked which of the qualities, from almost 50 qualities listed by participants, could be determined through the interview process. The answer was always very few, if any. Those areas in which they felt any comfort at all were the non-personality related items such as experience, education, job knowledge and communications ability. It is interesting to note that these non-personality related items can be much better determined through other means such as reference checks, background checks, and specifically designed tests. One shouldn't waste much time on them in the interview process.

What's wrong here? The main problem is not enough people in management know what they are really looking for. Interviewers are primarily guided by their own ideas of what the job entails. This is usually inexact. The items above can have as many interpretations as the people looking at them. And the interviewers usually do not have the training, preparation time or the motivation to find out the information they are seeking. Very few managers have "Hiring" as a high priority item in their performance plan to which they are held accountable and measured accordingly. Indeed, very few managers have performance plans!

In addition, politics is a major problem. Convincing legislatures to fund long term, and ultimately more efficient and effective, hiring processes rather than short term "quick fixes" is a substantial hurdle and one for which I have no answers. Too many politicians, unfortunately, are more inclined to the "glitzy" solutions that look good on TV and in print, and which can get them reelected.

Ultimately, what the employer wants to find out about a job candidate boils down to three things:

1. **CAN** the candidate **DO** the job?
2. **WILL** the candidate **DO** the job?
3. **WILL** the candidate **FIT IN**?

These are the cornerstones of performance, and what you should concentrate on when selecting people for job openings.

CAN the Candidate DO the Job?

The **CAN DO** element can be defined as skills match. This includes special knowledge (industry, product, technical, training, education, certification, experience etc.), special skills (written expression, verbal expression, presentation, physical, etc.) and mental capability. This is classically where we have placed our hiring emphasis. Why? Because it is the easiest area to understand. But there are several traps.

Trap 1. Overemphasis on skills.

There is a definite tendency to concentrate on already acquired skills as the measures of acceptability, particularly such indicators as experience, education, training, etc., and to pay little attention to the other elements of job performance. Every study I've seen on employee turnover says essentially the same thing: when employees don't work out it's rarely because of skills or credentials, but other factors relating to personality (job fit) and organization fit - the Will Do and the Will Fit In factors.

Trap 2. Skills indicators may not be relevant to job success.

It is true that specific skill indicators such as education, experience, training, etc., may be essential in certain jobs such as surgeon, civil engineer, airline pilot and others. But one must be careful that the measurements of such skills are truly relevant to job success or are not unrealistically high. As an example, has someone arbitrarily decided that four years of experience is required? Why not two? Or five? Is it possible that one person may learn in one year what it takes another five years to learn? Has the candidate with five years of experience really had only one year of experience five times? If this type of selection criteria was used in professional sports, a player, no matter how good or how productive, would have to sit on the bench until the required number of years was passed.

The danger here is the potential for focusing on areas with little impact on job success. And when you consider only those candidates with skill indicators in their background, you may limit the candidate selection pool and may wind up with people who have simply been recycled through similar organizations.

Trap 3. Credentials are not the same as accomplishments.

It is also true that just because a person CAN DO the job does not necessarily mean that he/she WILL DO the job. For example, you can formally train an individual on proper telephone techniques and provide the appropriate graduation certificates, but if the individual does not like to talk on the phone, he or she won't!

Trap 4. Highly intelligent people can do anything

It is true that intelligent people can do more things, at least for a short period of time. Therefore, we tend to place a lot of emphasis on such things as academic degrees, educational achievements, training accomplishments, certification, etc. However, research has shown that people perform best when fully engaged in the challenges of the job. That means that unless highly intelligent people are provided with a steady stream of intellectual challenges, they will become a turnover statistic, or can become poor performers or even counterproductive.

Skills, where appropriate, may be an important criteria for job selection. For many jobs, however, skills are only a tie breaker if you have determined that two candidates fit the job equally. The candidate with the skills background then has the advantage of becoming productive earlier. In any case, any number of tests can be administered to determine the skill capabilities, and reference/background checks can determine the accuracy of claimed experience. If it is truly necessary to have the skill at the outset, rather than the capacity to learn it, *test for it*! Don't waste time on it in the interview process.

WILL the Candidate FIT IN?

The **WILL FIT IN** element, or organization fit, is the degree to which the candidate's values, ethics, dress, and attitudes match those of the required position and organization. Various tests and background checks can and should be used to assess such things as honesty, drug use, safety, and tolerance for stress. However, the perceptions and observations of well-trained interviewers are also essential in determining fit in an organization's culture. The interviewer must be very much aware of avoiding the "halo" effect, discussed earlier, and unconscious biases such as weight, race, height, sex, hair style, etc.

WILL the Candidate DO the Job?

The **WILL DO** element, or Job Fit, is the degree to which the cognitive abilities, interests and personality of a candidate match the position requirements.

Cognitive abilities refers to such things as how quickly a person learns, or what type of learning is most effective. It is important to match the job and the required cognitive abilities. People who learn quickly and whose job requires primarily routine tasks tend to get bored quickly. They are usually your earliest turnovers. People who learn more slowly get frustrated in fast paced and changing environments. These, too, are turnover candidates, or worse. There are tests available to measure a candidate's cognitive abilities. You should use them.

Interests, or motivations, refers to a person's working preferences: people, data or things. If a person is not interested in an area, he/she will not perform it well, at least not for long. If an employee loves being with people and hates numbers, you don't assign him/her to a back room creating and maintaining spreadsheets for managing costs of supplies. You make them housing unit officers or counselors. Again, there are tests available to measure a candidate's interests and motivations.

Part three of Job Fit, the core personality, includes the measurable traits that determine situational behavior. Such traits are critical in assessing the candidate's ability to behave as we would like him/her to behave, and critical to job success. These are the traits we are most trying to find out in the interview process and are also the most difficult to assess. This was shown as long ago as 1980 in a *Harvard Business Review* study testing the validity of traditional sales hiring practices among 360,000 people hired for sales positions. The study compared job performance to common hiring criteria: men vs. women, college graduates vs. high school graduates, under age 40 vs. over age 40, whites vs. blacks, and experienced vs. inexperienced. The study concluded that none of these had any bearing on performance; that **success hinges on a fit with the job**.

One more time, there are psychological tests on the market that can help you understand the candidate's personality makeup and how it relates to the job. They can also be effectively used to help eliminate candidates whose personality characteristics are an obvious mismatch, or to narrow the interview focus to the few behavior issues that may remain in question.

So, how do we start?

Understand the Real Job

The hiring process is the most important function any organization performs, and it starts with a journey inward. Before you can go out and select someone for an opening, you need to know what kind of people you're looking for. And before you can decide on the type of person needed, you need to understand what you ***want them to accomplish***. This is not a complex concept, and yet it is the number one problem in hiring today—not enough people in management know what they are looking for! This problem is compounded in large organizations, particularly governmental, where the hiring process is controlled by Civil Service or other such rigid rule making bodies. The ultimate manager with the job opening may not be involved with the hiring process, may have little input in the selections made and is forced to live with, or rectify, the mistakes. And in governmental units, it is sometimes very difficult to rectify the mistakes.

Large organizations tend to have formal job descriptions. This is a start. But there are inherent problems with using these job descriptions as the only basis for hiring:

1. They get out of date, particularly for organizations that are changing, and do not cover new jobs or job conditions caused by change.
2. They are most often developed by people not directly involved with the job openings and therefore do not accurately reflect the job. Emphasis may be placed on minor items, and key items may not be reflected at all.
3. They tend toward the "Super Star" syndrome, setting the qualifications so unrealistically high that its impossible to find a qualified candidate. In all probability, anyone who would fit the description probably wouldn't want the job.
4. They tend to be too broad in scope, in reality covering a wide range of jobs, and are not directed at the specific opening. This is the "one size fits all" philosophy and should not be applied. The actual job for a "Correction's Officer" is different in a maximum security facility from a minimum security facility, a female facility from a male facility, etc. In fact, it will vary from facility to facility of the same type, and in all probability, be different for two officers of the same rank in the same facility. There are many possible reasons for this. It may be as simple as differences in the objectives and expectations of the manager. This is another reason why the immediate manager <u>must</u> be closely involved with the hiring process and any requirement for prior experience should be inspected closely relative to the specific job opening.

Outputs, Activities and Indicators

The responsibility of documenting the <u>**real**</u> job belongs primarily to immediate managers. Only they know what they want staff members to <u>**accomplish**</u>. Notice I did not say <u>**do**</u>! Accomplishments are not the same as tasks. For example, making the rounds in a prison housing unit once an hour is a task. Almost anyone can do that. Making sure that everything is secure, nothing is out of place, nothing unusual is occurring, ensuring everything in the environment has a reasonable explanation, and effectively documenting the results on each round are accomplishments. The first simply demands the ability to walk around. The accomplishments demand attention to detail, awareness of the surroundings, an understanding of the effects of unusual occurrences, the ability to work with words and even a spatial cognitive ability. This is the heart of the matter and is the first step at understanding the behaviors required to do the job—the **WILL DO** factor.

The process is simple, but it demands time and effort, and the desire to really understand the job. We recommend making a series of charts for each job, as follows:

OUTPUT/ACTIVITIES/INDICATORS WORKSHEET

NAME (or POSITION): ________________________

1. Write One Output (Accomplishment) for which this Job Position is Responsible.

2. List the Major Activities (Tasks) Related to Achieving this Output. A. B. C. D.

3. List the Key Indicators (Behaviors) Related to Achieving this Output. A. B. C. D.

Outputs are the end results, or accomplishments, to be achieved. For Corrections Officers this may be such results as providing a safe and secure environment, maintaining prisoner discipline without resorting to violence, or testifying effectively in court. These need to be put into a priority sequence. Every job has many required outputs. Time limitations in the selection process will allow you to focus on only the most important.

Activities are the tasks that produce the outputs. Tasks may include such things as making rounds, preparing reports, inspecting cells, or operating security systems. It is critical to understand what top performing employees **do** to achieve results. This leads to an understanding of their core behavior patterns. If we are going to hire people who will be successful employees, we must select candidates that behave like top performing employees already doing the job. It is equally important to understand the core behavior patterns of low performing employees so the same hiring mistakes can be avoided. Once you list the activities of top performers, you can begin to find out what personality characteristics allow them to behave as they do.

Indicators are the behavior patterns and motivations that make a person act as they do. We must find out the personality characteristics most likely to affect performance on this job. As an example, officers may work under stressful conditions. They must remain in control when under pressure, and not react in an excitable or violent way. Clearly, they must be high on the Stable side of the Emotional/Stable scale. Perhaps not so obvious is the requirement to use persuasion and/or negotiation to influence a prisoner's behavioral decisions. This indicates a high degree of interest in working with people. Build a success pattern using your top officers as a basis, and include cognitive abilities, motivation/interests, and personality characteristics. This can and should be used as a guide for hiring other successful officers.

Once you have an understanding of the key personality characteristics needed, you can start to build the questions for the interview process to reveal the candidate's core personality. Inquiries should be directed at past behaviors. Since personality remains relatively unchanged, the best indicators of future behaviors are past behaviors. This is illustrated by a study conducted by Dwyer, Prien, and Bernard in 1990. "...on average, 'Least Best' officers received over twice as many speeding tickets, were five times as likely to have had their driver's licenses suspended, were nearly three times as likely to have credit problems, and were two and one-half times as likely to have had previous employers say they would not rehire them, when compared to 'Best' officers. ...On behaviors that are clearly related to job performance, 'Least Best' officers were over twice as likely to have been suspended without pay, over five times as likely to have received extended probation, nearly three times as likely to have received letters of concern or reprimand, and eight times as likely to have had an internal investigation conducted on them for conduct unbecoming a law enforcement officer, insubordination, neglect of duty, or unlawful conduct. In summary, 'Least Best' officers were over four times as likely to be guilty of clearly unacceptable behavior than were 'Best' Officers." "Best Officers appeared to have greater need to achieve, to receive advice and instruction from others, to be orderly, and to answer responsibly to higher authorities while having a lesser need to show affection toward others and to act aggressively."

You now have completed the necessary groundwork. You now know what the most important outputs of the job, the activities used by top performers to accomplish objectives, and the underlying personality characteristics you need to look for in candidates. You are now in a position to translate these to effective interview questions directed at behaviors for success. But, without this first step, the other steps make little sense.

Promotions

Promotions should be handled in the same way as the regular hiring process. There is no guarantee that an employee who performs a job successfully can perform successfully at a higher level, particularly if that next level is managerial. The same questions apply. Do you know what the real job is? Do you know what successful people in that job look like? Does the person being considered for promotion look like that? Very often we lose our top employee, gain the worst manager, and other top performing people leave. Employees shouldn't *earn* promotions; they should *earn the right to compete* for one!

Training and Counseling

There are enormous potential additional benefits in describing the job in terms of Outputs, Activities and Indicators. Having listed what good employees do to accomplish the desired end results, you also have a good idea what others are not doing. This can have a dramatic effect on employee performance counseling and on effective training programs tailored to the individual employee's needs. Moreover, having identified the personality characteristics required to perform the job, you can more effectively make a determination if training will do any good for a particular employee. It bears repeating that *no amount of training will overcome a poor job fit!* It's a waste of money.

Recommendations

1. Make sure the goals and objectives of the institution are clearly articulated and understood. Offender programs can not work if they do not have a clear objective and the right people to make them work aren't hired.
2. Get serious about the hiring process. If you're only paying "lip service" to it, you're doomed to repeating past mistakes. Take recruiting very seriously. Always remember, "It is impossible to fly like an eagle when you surround yourself with turkeys!"
3. Put the ultimate responsibility for hiring on field managers and not central office staff.
4. Train all managers on hiring for effect, including techniques for interview effectiveness to discover a candidate's true personality.
5. Use all the tools, techniques and tests possible, including tests for cognitive abilities, motivation/interests, and personality. There are several good ones on the market today. Make sure, however, that any tests are properly validated and EEO compliant. The interview process is usually too short by itself to find out all you need to know about a candidate.
6. Take your time when a position opens. Remember the objective, i.e. trying to hire an effective employee, not just the "best candidate" who applies. The "best candidate" may not be a good performer. Separate style from substance and "likes" from "needs."
7. Institute the process for all levels and use it, including promotions from within.

Playing the Odds

Hiring should not be viewed as a necessary evil that keeps you from doing more important or more satisfying tasks. But without preparation, training and dedication, the odds of hiring effectively are against you. Mistakes may still be made, but continued practice and use of all the tools will move the odds in your favor. Even if you can hire just a few more productive employees and screen out a few more "zeros," the overall effectiveness and cohesiveness of the unit will be greatly improved.

Hopefully, the goals and objectives of the various institutions have been clearly articulated by the leadership so that the process works as it should, and the needs of society are met. One wonders if this is often the case. It is frightening to think that those in control in the Brazoria, Texas, private prison, where inmates were beaten and humiliated, and in Georgia, where black-shirted troopers marched into a facility and did the same, knew exactly the type of people they were hiring.

Charles Dennison is President of The Dennison Organization, Inc., (formerly The Lexington Group) specializing in business process consulting, with an emphasis on people productivity issues, including employee selection and compliance, performance planning, counseling and evaluation, employee development, situational leadership and the art of negotiation. This organization has spent considerable time in dealing with Corrections and Corrections hiring practices. Charles spent 20 years with IBM in various line and management positions, including management development as an internal management consultant. He has been a director of Northern Telecom, Vice President of Business Records Corporation, and Vice President and Co-founder of The Parkside Organization, Inc.

HEATHER WOODIWISS-HL
"Environmental Rehabilitation in Juvenile Detention Facilities"

The concept of *parens patriae* on behalf of minors, established through the courts in 1838, established the system of juvenile justice practiced today. The "state as parent" philosophy paved the way for the state to provide wayward children with the guidance, guardianship, and care they were otherwise not receiving from their parents.

Somehow, somewhere along the line, the doctrine of nurture and family-like care drastically changed to the present "lock 'em up and throw away the key" ideology that pervades the juvenile justice system. The founding principle of rehabilitation has metamorphosed into the establishment of strict rules and regulations. Punishment has become the key ingredient in the juvenile justice stew.

The juvenile justice system is quickly approaching the criminal justice system. Both are a tangled bureaucracy of court officials, probation officers, social workers, police officers, mental health professionals, institutional administration and staff, and many others. These key players utilize varied expertise in administering juvenile justice. The police officers investigate deviant activity and make arrests, the court officials execute the laws, the probation officers make sure the sentences are upheld, the social workers participate in the abuse and neglect cases, and the institutional detention staff run the county-operated facilities. Perhaps the most ironic job title is that of "counselor" within juvenile detention facilities. That title is most likely a remnant of the times when juvenile justice was designed to nurture the minors into reforming their behavior. Today, the title of counselor is reserved for those facility staff who supervise and discipline the minors. The interaction between counselor and juvenile rarely includes the comfort, consolation, care, or gentle instruction one would associate with the definition of the word. The counselors are trained to administer the rules and regulations of the facility; to make sure each established daily routine is followed without deviation; and to execute disciplinary measures when necessary. Providing the minors with much needed counseling comes from other sources. In one particular facility, one psychologist and one psychiatrist are available to the approximately 163 detained juveniles. Volunteers, including mentors, tutors, programmers, church-affiliated groups, and concerned community members, often attempt to fill that void by offering informal counseling.

Some of the detained minors are held within detention facilities on suspicion, not yet convicted of criminal activity. According to the California Juvenile Hall Population Summary Report (1992), on any given day, 55.1 percent of the youths in juvenile hall were in a predisposition status awaiting a hearing.

One issue contributing to problems surrounding the detention arena is the actual physical design of the facilities. By their very design, institutional settings severely constrict the occupants. These restrictions (on freedom, movement, pleasure, stimulus, and personal expression) bear significant relevance upon the detained individual's attitudes, and, in some instances, on behavioral responses.[1] The juveniles spend more time detained within the walls of the facility's living units (cells) than they do in direct contact with staff or volunteers. It can be said with certainty that the actual interior environment created by the physical facility plays a key role in influencing the juvenile occupants. If the founding philosophy of the juvenile justice system was to correct deviant behavior through rehabilitation, then shouldn't the facilities perpetuate this ideal?

The need for dramatic change is evident upon entrance to the average juvenile detention facility. Antiquated and severely stained flooring, somber interior wall hues, windows almost totally obstructed by thick metal screens covered with chipped paint and rust, and pervasive "institutional" smells immediately confront a visitor.

In a 1984 court ruling, a federal judge ruled, among other things, that cells within an Oregon Juvenile Facility were "dirty and unsanitary"[2] (*Gary v. Hegstrom*, 1984). In the face of recent budgetary constraints, a growing number of juvenile institutional budgets have been unable to provide for necessary facility maintenance needs. Tragically, the conditions of confinement have grown worse. U.S. courts have seen lawsuits challenging the constitutionality of these confinement conditions.[3]

The occupants of institutions, including prisons, jails, juvenile training schools and detention centers, camps, ranches, mental health facilities, alcohol and drug treatment centers, nursing homes, and psychiatric facilities, have retained legal service attorneys to protest living practices. Such institutions have been found to be lacking in treatment and rehabilitative services. Also, the conditions of confinement, including filth, inadequate space, light, and ventilation, have proven to be psychologically abusive and even life-threatening.[4]

According to David Lee Lambert, Staff Attorney for the National Center for Youth Law, these conditions of confinement can make institutional occupants more hardened, eventually producing adverse psychological effects which remain with the juvenile even after release from the institution.[5]

Recently, a study was undertaken at a juvenile hall in California to determine whether or not the interior environment within the facility affected the detained juvenile occupants. The study made an attempt to determine if environmental settings in the individual living quarter units within the juvenile hall bore a relationship with depression and aggression among the juvenile population.[6]

The sample used in the study was composed of 108 male and female juveniles. They ranged in age from twelve to seventeen, were in seventh through twelfth grades, and had attended either junior high or high school prior to their detainment. Several different ethnic identities including Caucasian, black, and Hispanic were represented. Only residents who met the study's minimum residency requirement of two weeks detainment could volunteer to participate. No control group was used.

Research methodology was divided into two parts: quantitative and qualitative. Information for the qualitative portion was derived using oral interviews. Data collected for the quantitative portion utilized three distinct instruments for the measurement of the variables: the interior environment of the individual living quarter units (including color, light and textures), depression and depression-related symptomatology, and aggression. Each instrument was individually administered to the juveniles.[7]

Results from the administration of the standardized depression measure supported the hypothesis that the interior environment would adversely affect the occupants. Scores indicated the majority of juveniles, over 76 percent, were depressed. Thirty of those minors' scores reflected they were suffering from severe depressive symptomatology.

Scores from the aggression scale revealed the majority of juveniles (71 percent) were "neutral to somewhat aggressive." Sixteen juveniles fell under the category of "high aggression."

Data derived from the instrument that determined the degree to which the minors were satisfied with the interior environment showed the average response fell into the category of "somewhat dissatisfied." Twelve juveniles were "very dissatisfied" and 18 were only "minimally dissatisfied."

Several significant relationships were found between depression and perceptions of the interior environment. There were also correlations discovered for depression and aggression that, upon further statistical explication, might link them with the environment.

In the qualitative interviews, participants were asked to respond to four open-ended inquiries. They were asked to describe what it felt like to live in their individual living quarter units within the detention facility. They were also asked to discuss any similarities and differences between their personal bedrooms at home and their living units at the juvenile hall. They were then requested to describe their likes and dislikes of the individual living units. Finally, they were asked the following question: "If you could change the interior of your room here at juvenile hall, what would you do?"

Results indicated the most frequent response to the inquiry about how the interior environment made the minors feel was "bored." Of the 108 subjects, 39 stated they felt depressed in their living units. Six indicated they felt happy or good. Other responses included: aggressive, unwanted, stressed and disgusted. One commonly mentioned difference between their residential bedrooms and their living unit environments was decorations. Pictures (both framed or not framed), posters, wall hangings, and miscellaneous personal visual displays were all mentioned as lacking in the detention facility's environment.

The three most disliked items were the color, floor treatment, and window. Ninety-three minors categorized the room color anywhere from "institution green" to "not cheery." Seventy-nine participants stated there were problems with the window. Each window was obstructed by thick metal screens, debris, and rust. Also, several minors stated they would like the window enlarged or more windows added to the rooms. Instead of making unreasonable requests for decorator curtains, miniblinds, or sky windows, the adolescents made rather reasonable appeals.

The last inquiry was perhaps the most telling. The intention of the question was to ascertain the interior variables the juveniles ranked most important to them. Ranked number one among responses was the floor treatment. Ninety-four of the respondents felt the floors should be renovated or replaced. Ninety-three of the 108 participants stated they would like to alter the window in some way so more light would enter the room, the view would improve, their ability to see out would improve, and the window could be opened slightly to allow for the flow of fresh air into the room. The inability to put up decorations on walls, make changes in room size, bed type, artificial lighting and the lack of water closets in rooms were also mentioned. The juvenile residents also expressed their desire to keep personal items such as multiple letters and photographs, hair picks and combs, and cleaning supplies in their rooms.

One minor requested nothing more than one can of Lysol.

It was anticipated by facility staff and administration, juvenile justice professionals, and some segments of society that responses from the juveniles would indicate the subjects' prioritization of entertainment paraphernalia including televisions, stereos, VCRs, and video/board games. However, this was consistently not the case. What appeared to be of more value to the juvenile participants was improvement of the floor treatment from the existing linoleum with holes, cuts, dirt, and paint splattering to a treatment that would not feel as cold to bare feet. Also more valued than entertainment were window modifications. Requests were made to clean the windows, replace current screen coverings with bars or some covering that would not block natural daylight or obstruct views, alter the window's size, and allow residents to slightly open windows for air circulation. The interior color of the walls and flooring were of concern to the majority of residents. According to the juveniles, some suggestions were to, "Make it look bright," and to use "Bright and cheery colors."

Based upon these interviews, the juvenile respondents appeared to value aesthetics, personal expression, and contact with the outside more than entertainment and overall comfort. Suggested changes for the interior environments within the detention facility included, for the most part, basic elements fundamental to humane living conditions.

Data collected during the process also provided ammunition to dispute those common misconceptions held by both the lay public and juvenile justice field professionals with regard to juvenile delinquents. It was predicted that no one would willingly participate in the survey and that answers would be haphazard, with unrealistic demands; this was not the case.

This recent research study indicates that both facility architecture and interior design add to, if not incite, some negative outcomes. If rehabilitation rather than pure punishment is really the goal of our juvenile justice system; if budgetary constraints limit the formal counseling available to the minors in custody; and if the interior environment within the facilities has been linked to negative attitudinal outcomes, then perhaps a cost-effective way to contribute to rehabilitation would be to improve the interior environment within the facilities.

The alteration of behavior and/or attitudes through the use of the interior environment may be a possible way of positively affecting self-esteem, counteracting negative outcomes such as depression and aggression, reducing behavioral infractions within detention facilities, and, most importantly, fostering resolute mental health and well being.

The fact that juveniles used for the purpose of the research study showed positive signs of unselfishness by their voluntary participation regardless of rewards and in their suggestions for room modifications is evidence that rehabilitation is a real possibility. Not yet hardened to a deviant propensity and lacking criminal sophistication, the juvenile delinquents are, perhaps, trainable to proper societal behavior and moral codes.

For years, psychologists, social psychologists, and environmental psychologists have proven the human psyche is strongly affected by its surroundings—whether they be social or physical. Lending further credibility to their claims is continued research in this area. The scientific body of evidence surrounding environmental effects on human inhabitants is only increasing. If the interior environment one resides in affects that individual so as to influence negatively or dictate behavior and attitudes, then it could, if improved, have a positive influence.

Heather Woodiwiss-HL first became impassioned about the plight of juvenile delinquents in 1992 when she took a position at a group home for twelve seriously recalcitrant girls. She went on to obtain an intensive volunteer position with a large California juvenile detention facility; it was there that she conducted research. Portions of her substantive thesis, entitled "The Relationship of Environmental Design to Juveniles' Perceptions of Depression and Aggression," have been published several times. Her ground-breaking research culminated in 1995 with a Master of Arts degree that fused several academic fields, including environmental psychology, clinical psychology, environmental sociology, and architecture. She hopes her efforts will focus more attention, as well as promote additional research, on the affects of poor interior environments on juveniles confined within juvenile detention facilities.

Footnotes

[1] Wright, K. N. (1993). "Prison Environment and Behavioral Outcomes". Journal of Offender Rehabilitation, 20, pp. 93-109.

[2] *Gary vs. Hegstrom*, 1984.

[3] Breed and Krisberg, 1986.

[4] Lambert, 1989.
[5] Lambert, 1989.
[6] It should be noted that the study did not attempt to determine a causal relationship but rather the existence of a correlation between variables. Subsequently, data were statistically assessed through the use of frequency distributions, Alpha reliability and factor analyses, and were tested for correlation and significance.
[7] The first instrument, entitled the Juvenile Detention Facility Perception Questionnaire (JDFPQ), was a nine-item questionnaire developed to assess the degree to which the juveniles were either satisfied or dissatisfied with the interior environment of their individual living quarter units. The responses were arranged on a five-point Likert-type scale. The second questionnaire, the Juvenile Perception of Aggression (JPA), was designed as a measure of the presence or absence of aggression within the respondents. For the purpose of this study, aggression was operationally defined as a high score on the JPA. The JPA was a fifteen-item measure arranged on a five-point Likert-like scale. The third instrument, entitled the Reynolds' Adolescent Depression Scale (RADS), was designed to assess depressive symptomatology as well as depression-related symptomatology in adolescent populations (Kaplan, 1986). The RADS contained thirty items arranged on a four-point Likert-type scale. For the purpose of this study, the operational definition of depression was a score of 77 and above on the RADS.
a. The JDFPQ was a compilation of previous environmental surveys and research (Wener, 1994; United States Department of Justice, 1988; Hughes, 1994). The instrument was divided into the five sections of Interior Design, Color, Lighting, Texture, and Demographics. Each section was composed of individual inquiries requiring responses ranging from very negative to very positive.
b. The JPA was based upon the research findings of Arnold Buss, Ph.D. and Mark Perry (1992). However, the questionnaire used for the purpose of this study was edited to be age-appropriate for the juvenile participants. The final measure was divided into the four sections of Physical Aggression, Verbal Aggression, Anger, and Hostility. Each section was composed of individual inquiries requiring responses ranging from strongly disagree to strongly agree.
c. The RADS was a standardized measure developed by William M. Reynolds and published by Psychological Assessment Resources, Incorporated to measure both psychometric and clinical depression. Response options ranged from almost never to most of the time. A cut-off score of 77 was utilized.

References

Abbott, G. (1938). The Child and the State. Chicago: University of Chicago Press.

Bartollas, C., & Miller, S. J. (1994). Juvenile Justice in America. New Jersey: Regents/Prentice Hall.Breed, A. F. , & Krisberg, B. (1986). "Is There a Future?" Corrections Today, 48, 14-20.

Fox, V. B. (1977). Introduction to Corrections. New Jersey: Prentice Hall.

Lambert, D. L. (1989). Beyond Heat, Light, and Ventilation: Using an Environmental Expert on Behalf of Institutionalized Clients. San Francisco: National Center for Youth Law.

Sandhu, H. S. (1974). Modern Corrections: The Offenders, Therapies and Community Reintegration. Illinois: Charles C. Thomas.

Stalans, L. J. , & Henry, G.T. (1994). "Societal Views of Justice for Adolescents Accused of Murder," Law and Human Behavior, 8, 675-693.

Wright, K. N. (1993). "Prison Environment and Behavioral Outcomes," Journal of Offender Rehabilitation, 20, 93-109.

STEVEN EDMONDSON
"Community Policing"

What is the role of Law Enforcement Officers in today's society? For as many people as you pose this question, you will elicit as many diverse and varied answers. Insiders will tell you that we are merely society's Band-Aids, sticking our fingers in an ever weakening dike that is holding back the rising tide of crime and social disorder. The recently passed crime bill does nothing more than provide more fingers to plug leaks. Ironically, those cities and towns that needed the help the most are the ones that could least afford the matching funds required to obtain a grant.

Many politicians and Law Enforcement Administrators are grabbing onto Community Policing as if it were the panacea for the failed attempts of maintaining order in our society. Community Policing, as we have come to know it today, was dealt a death sentence as soon as it was recognized, labeled, formalized, hailed as a new style of policing and in some cases, mandated into Law Enforcement agencies. This Community Policing has even spawned a cottage industry for those with an entrepreneurial spirit with books, tapes and various training curriculums, with the aforementioned politicians and Law Enforcement executives willing to spend money, usually in the form of grants from the federal government, on anything that shows the world that they have adopted Community Policing into their department. If Bob Peel were alive today he'd be suing these vendors for royalties. Who is Bob Peel you ask? Sir Robert Peel, a 19th century British statesman, is credited with establishing the London Metropolitan Police which in 1829 became the world's first modern organized police agency.

The Metropolitan Police force was guided by the concept of crime prevention as a primary police objective; it also embodied the belief that such a force depended on the consent and cooperation of the public, and the idea that police constables were to be civil and courteous to the people. In that tone, the following quote is attributed to Peel: "Maintain at all times a relationship with the public that gives reality to the historic tradition that the police are the public and the public are the police. The police being only members of the public who are paid to give full attention to duties which are incumbent upon every citizen in the interest of common welfare and existence."

If you were to read that quote today you might think it is a definition of today's community policing. How did we let ourselves fall into a position where Community Policing is being hailed as a new style of Law Enforcement? Any Chief or Sheriff worth his gold stars should have been preaching and insisting his officers be practicing the Community Policing philosophy all along, and not just to line up at the federal grant feeding trough.

True Community Policing is nothing more than an attitude carried by an officer who is willing and able to do whatever it takes to resolve a situation to a successful conclusion. Often this means including the citizens in the problem solving process. In order for this to happen, a Law Enforcement Administrator must provide an atmosphere that allows and encourages an officer the freedom and autonomy to seek out remedies and solutions, even those not traditionally within the recognized realm of law enforcement.

The specialized programs that have popped up across the country under the guise of community policing such as bike patrols, trading cards, walk & talks, ride-along and block parties are just that—programs. Granted, they may further the cause of community policing and are certainly great public relations tools, but they do little to advance the core message of community policing, that being a shared responsibility between the police and the citizens for the general welfare of the community.

A new variation of community policing being practiced by agencies in Maine, one more in line with Sir Robert Peel's philosophy, is called Enhanced Neighborhood Policing (ENP). The goal of this campaign is to mobilize members of a given community or neighborhood for the purpose of sharing the responsibility of identifying problems and devising solutions. This effort begins with the premise that the people who live in a given neighborhood know best what is important to them. The age old practice of a police officer rolling into a neighborhood and sermonizing the citizens with the pat crime prevention lecture has proven to be ineffective at best. ENP provides an opportunity for the citizens to establish the priorities and then take appropriate action

After the citizens have mobilized (often the toughest part of ENP), organized and established their goals, the officers working with that group can take a step back and change their role to that of advisors and as a conduit to the resources and agencies that are needed to address the identified problems. The ideal result of this approach would be that many of the minor, time consuming complaints that have historically been handled by the local police, would be resolved through a problem solving process at the neighborhood level and thus free up the police for more significant issues.

An additional benefit to the officers is the exposure and training received in fields often ignored in traditional law enforcement training such as public speaking, problem solving and organizing meetings. Along with a socially heightened and civically responsible citizenry, a department gains an officer with unique and beneficial skills.

The philosophy of this approach can best be summed up by a mission statement that has been adopted by many Law Enforcement agencies across the country in one form or another. It states: It will be the mission of this department to work with all citizens to preserve life, maintain human rights, protect property and promote individual responsibility and community commitment.

Was Sir Robert Peel a visionary or are we just slow in catching on? I guess the old adage is true; what once was old is new again.

COMMUNICATION

There is probably no profession more visible to the public and that elicits such a wide variety of emotional responses than does law enforcement. Despite this visibility and notoriety, the work of law enforcement officers is often shrouded in mystery, clouded by misconception and simply misunderstood.

It doesn't take a rocket scientist nor should it take a police administrator to figure out that a good portion of the citizenry are starved for information and news about the police and their activities. All too often, police departments work behind walls and shroud their activities under veils of secrecy. I firmly believe this is a major contributing factor to the animosity and adversarial feelings that often exist between the police and selected factions of society. In this era of re-discovering community policing, success hinges on the ability of the police and the public to share in the responsibility of taking control of a given situation. This cannot be accomplished if the police are not willing to open up to those who have the most at stake.

In my two decades in this work, it has become painfully apparent that a good many citizens don't have the first idea of just what it is we do and more importantly, why we do it. Some feel that we are chained by legislative and constitutional restraints while just as many feel that we possess an all encompassing power. Regardless of where you fall on the awareness scale, the bottom line is that Law Enforcement agencies have done a poor job in truly communicating with the public.

I use this condemnation as a segue to share information on a unique and innovative approach to addressing this communication problem. In 1992, the owner/publisher of our hometown newspaper asked the police department to provide information on our activities that he could publish as a regular feature. My first few submissions were nothing more than a compilation of our calls for the week, i.e. accidents, burglaries, assaults, etc., in a police blotter format. It wasn't long before I recognized an opportunity to take a particular incident, event or crime and expound on the specific law or police procedure involved in the handling of that case. This extra narrative was born out of frustration in witnessing what appeared to be a lack of knowledge of the law and police procedure and the lack of concern to people's own well being and that of their neighbors. It was this apathy and ignorance that has spurred my continuing efforts in using journalism to share information with the citizens.

As the weeks passed, I dropped the police blotter approach and focused strictly on issues and events that I felt had some effect on the lives and property of the local residents. Domestic violence, traffic accidents, property crimes, drunk driving and crime prevention were just some of the topics addressed in my column. My writing style also reflected an attempt at reaching the masses as I intentionally avoided using police jargon and the robotic delivery that often plagues conventional law enforcement journalism. If no one understands your message or takes the time to read it because it's too technical, then you've failed at communicating.

I don't mind saying that my motives were not totally unselfish. Besides my ego getting its weekly boost by seeing my work published, albeit on a small scale, my truest desire was to make my and the rest of the officers jobs just a little easier. It had been my hope that by revealing and sharing this information, the local citizens would become more responsive and act more responsibly with the end result being less demand for our services.

When this newspaper ceased publishing two years after its first edition, I sought out other means of continuing the dissemination of information in my town. Less than two months later, the Managing Editor of the local commercial newspaper with a circulation of 13,000 called and asked that I continue writing my column for him as a regular feature.

Long story short, three years and 110 columns later, my journalistic efforts to make life a little safer and law enforcement a little less mysterious continue. Besides writing about current events and situations that could alter the peaceful existence of residents in the area, I also brought the readers inside the patrol car and police station for a peek of the inner workings of this most visible but least understood occupation. I don't mind saying that it was in great part due to my column that I was invited to contribute to this book.

Some of you may wonder how a newspaper column written by a cop fits into a book on issues surrounding corrections, offender programs and other restorative justice efforts. Earlier, I referred to the role of police officers as holding back the tide of crime and social disorder. When the dike fails, it is the law enforcement officer that is the first to be called and bears the brunt of the effort in cleaning up the proverbial spills. It is the police that act as the conduit within the criminal justice system and that are the one consistent presence from the time a crime is committed to trial and incarceration.

It is our methods and actions that have of late come under scrutiny by the public, and in many cases deservingly so. If there is no trust and faith in the law enforcement officer by the public, then the criminal element will have the upper hand. Each week I take a little piece of this job and explain it so that the public will have a better understanding of just what it is we do and why we do it. It is incumbent upon all citizens to take an active role in the general welfare of their community, or at least in protecting themselves and their property. I use my column as an impetus for citizen action.

I firmly believe that the true threats to a peaceful existence in our country are not crime, poverty or war. The enemy among us is the enemy within us, and that is apathy and ignorance. I wage war against these enemies each week with my column as I use the written word to inform, educate and sometimes entertain the citizens of Mid Coast Maine. I do so because an informed society is an enlightened society; and an enlightened society produces the warriors willing to do battle against the enemy within us.

PROGRAMS

In keeping with the overall theme of this book, I want to share information on two offender based programs being used in the Mid Coast region of Maine that are going a long way in restoring dignity, minimizing emotional and financial trauma, providing accountability and saving money to local governments.

Sagadahoc County, Maine, made up of 10 communities along the mid coast area with approximately 35,000 residents, is geographically the smallest in Maine. It also holds the distinction of being the only one of Maine's 16 Counties without its own jail. In Maine, the Counties are tasked with housing all prisoners sentenced for up to one year. As a result, all persons incarcerated in our County, whether they are serving time for a post conviction sentence, awaiting trial, pre-sentence, bail violations or probation disposition, have to be shipped out and housed in neighboring county facilities. As you may guess, they don't do it for free. The cost of boarding prisoners ranges from $60 to $70 per night for each one. For a resource poor county, it becomes substantial rather quickly.

Being a law enforcement officer, my sympathies rarely lie with people convicted of committing crimes. But as a closet humanitarian, I have become aware of the dynamics involved in people's lives that may have contributed to the act which landed them in this situation. I also recognize the financial and emotional trauma placed on families of those incarcerated.

The plan being phased in by the Sagadahoc County Sheriff's Department is to house selected prisoners in a rarely used National Guard Armory within the County lines. Already being used as temporary housing for drunk driving offenders serving weekend sentences, the County has developed a plan to expand its use of the armory to cut the cost of housing prisoners in the neighboring counties. The work release center, as it will be called, will hold up to 15 non-violent offenders. Anyone serving a sentence for a drug conviction or sex offense will not be eligible. Those that are must pass a rigorous screening process in order to qualify

The benefits of this program are many. For the taxpayer, the County will realize an annual savings of $30,000 to $100,000. This will be realized from the $40 a day it will cost to house a prisoner at the armory as opposed to the $60-70 a day charged by other Counties. Additional savings will be realized from the 17% of the prisoner's pay checks that will be kept by the County for administering the program. This brings up another of the benefits of this effort. Prisoners who are employed will be able to keep their jobs, in fact they will be required to maintain employment in order to stay in the program. For those that are unemployed at the time of incarceration, they will be assigned to a public works program with the hope of finding permanent employment.

Under the work release program, prisoners serving a sentence at the armory would be released each morning to go to work and return each evening immediately after. Breakfast and supper would be served in the armory and prisoners would sleep in a basement bunk room. Contact with family and friends would be limited by the same rules as those for people held in the county jail. On weekends, the prisoners would be required to clean the areas they use within the armory.

Local District Court Judges, who would be the primary sources of filling bed space, hail the program as an opportunity to break the cycle of unemployment caused by incarceration which often leads to recidivism.

The dictionary defines dignity as worthiness and self-respect. Is it not true that the lack of self-respect is a leading contributor to anti-social behavior? Is it not true that one of the goals of incarceration is to rehabilitate? And is it not true that earning a paycheck maintains a man's dignity? Trust me, a little goes a long way.

Finally, I want to share information on a program that shows promise in dealing with that segment of society often relegated to the leftovers of our efforts.

There are a good many people who consider the term "juvenile justice" an oxymoron. Victims of juvenile crimes will tell you that they have received little or no justice in the way of reparation. Law Enforcement officers who continuously deal with the same offenders will tell you that there is little or no justice when they feel there is a lack of or insufficient punishment or sanctions against these offenders. And in many instances, even the juveniles themselves and their families will tell you there is no justice when they are unable to find appropriate support services to get their children back on the right track. I have seen the young victims of yesterday become today's offenders.

Although there are many dedicated and skilled advocates working for and towards a comprehensive system that would provide prevention, restoration, rehabilitation and accountability to juvenile offenders and the people who are affected by their actions, institutional obstacles have made it difficult to offer and sustain those programs that could do so much in the way of righting wrongs.

How did we let ourselves get into this position and what do we do about it? The answer to the first question is the almighty buck, or more accurately, the lack of it. A good deal of capital is needed to employ staff, purchase equipment and house programs, and to the surprise of no one, the State doesn't have it. The other primary funding source for such efforts has been federal grant money. But with the tightening of the federal belts, even that pool is getting more shallow.

Another of the roadblocks that I have witnessed is the inability of community based groups to break the stranglehold that certain State agencies have on what they consider their bailiwick of juvenile justice. Many of the individuals working within the system agree that it could be better, but are hesitant to let anyone else have a crack at it. Without the cooperation, or at least the blessing of these agencies, non-governmental efforts are doomed to failure. Politics; go figure.

I would be remiss if I didn't mention perhaps the biggest obstacle to a viable alternative and that is you and I. A lack of interest and participation by citizens of a community is the death knell of any effort or attempt at improving an admittedly inadequate system. Invariably, only those most affected by the problem are the ones who contribute to the solution. Many an effort to produce alternative services to juveniles has been shelved by a lack of participation.

Parents of kids who have managed to avoid the pitfalls of youth and have yet to be introduced to the juvenile justice system should thank their lucky stars; I've seen the pain and anguish from parents of troubled children who learn there is little or no help out there.

It's ironic that what little assistance there is usually ends up expended on those juveniles who have crossed so far over the line that the chances are remote they can ever be pulled back. It's the youths who are on the edge who can be pulled back, who often are reaching out for that safety line to be pulled back, who show the most promise from early intervention. They are the ones offered the fewest options.

I realize I've painted a pretty dark picture on the subject of juvenile justice, but I am also confident that change is possible, and in some cases inevitable.

I do want to close on an optimistic note with mention of an attempt at providing the missing pieces to this puzzle. Several communities within the Mid Coast region will be adopting a program that has shown positive results in other parts of the State. Jump-Start, as it is called and trademarked, is an eight week mentoring program designed for at-risk youths and first time juvenile offenders. It matches up a youth with an adult community member for a series of workshops that deal with issues such as self-esteem, responsibility and community awareness.

Some of the many goals of Jump-Start are to reduce the number of repeat offenders, reduce the time between the offense and the consequences for that offense and to have the youths answerable to their community through community service and restitution. Unlike previous attempts, I predict success for this program, mainly because the key components are in place to make a run at it. The courts, corrections, schools, law enforcement and the community are all on board to do their respective parts.

CONCLUSION

Crimes affect more than just the victims and the offenders within a community. In dollars alone much is being spent to investigate, apprehend, prosecute, incarcerate and supervise offenders. We can and must do a better job at crime prevention, administration, responsible government, training of law and correctional professionals, community participation and citizen involvement. Whichever area strikes a chord with you, do your part to make your community whole.

Lt. Steven Edmondson is a 20 year veteran of the Topsham, Maine, Police Department. Besides being a regular columnist for the local newspaper, for which he has earned State-wide honors, Steve has been active with several local social service organizations, including serving on the Boards for Domestic Violence, Child Abuse and Sexual Assault agencies. Steve has a degree in Law Enforcement Technology and has attended the Delinquency Control Institute at the University of Southern California and is a 1990 graduate of the FBI National Academy.

JOANNE PAGE
"Testimony on Police Brutality, New York City Council Hearing, September 11, 1997"

Thank you for the opportunity to testify at this hearing. I speak to you both from personal experience and as Executive Director of The Fortune Society.

My personal experience ranges from working in prisons as a volunteer at the age of 18, to practicing criminal defense law, to teaching police officers, to serving on commissions and boards with police chiefs and experts on policing. The passion with which I approach this issue is drawn from those experiences as well as my bone-deep knowledge, as a child of Holocaust survivors, of the human damage that is done when the forces of government act savagely and are allowed to do so.

I also speak as Executive Director of The Fortune Society. Fortune is a 30 year old advocacy and service organization committed to educating the public about prison conditions and criminal justice issues, and helping ex-offenders and young people at-risk avoid further criminal justice involvement and return to their communities as constructive citizens. Approximately 2,000 such individuals pass through our doors each year, and issues of police brutality and brutality within correctional facilities surface all too regularly.

I would like to begin my testimony with my experience as a criminal defense attorney with the Legal Aid Society in Brooklyn between 1980 and 1983. I will start there because the issue of police brutality did not start with the Abner Louima case and will not end once the prosecution of those accused of his torture has been completed. Police brutality surfaced many times during my representation of clients at Legal Aid. It was so common an issue that I quickly learned, as a young attorney, to identify such cases simply by looking at the initial court papers.

The stereotypical police brutality case set forth an underlying basis for the arrest such as disorderly conduct, resisting government administration, fare beating, or trespassing. These charges, by themselves, usually called for no more than a summons or a warning and, if prosecuted in court, would usually end with an Adjournment in Contemplation of Dismissal (ACD) or with a plea to a violation rather than to a crime. However, the charge providing the basis for the arrest would be coupled with charges of resisting arrest and assault on a police officer. The injury to the police officer often would be to his hands. The defendant would be bloody and battered.

Such cases did not come through the courts every day, but they did come through with painful regularity. The officers involved in these cases were known to everyone in the court system by name and by reputation. Not many officers brought their arrestees in beaten and bloody, but those who did were never, to my knowledge, sanctioned for this behavior. In fact, the reverse was true because the criminal justice system protected them, allowing their abuse to continue. Their victims were victimized twice: once by being beaten by the police, and a second time by being prosecuted through the criminal justice system.

Many instances of police brutality stand out in my mind. All of the victims were black. One was a young girl who tried to use a school subway pass at the wrong hour. She was warned not to do so by a police officer and, when she tried to do so again, was pressed against the grating at the Nevins Street subway station, facing over the tracks, and was beaten and punched about her head, back and kidneys with the police officer's fists and his radio.

Two nurses walking by were horrified and complained at the police station. They eventually served as witnesses in her trial, when she was prosecuted for assaulting the police officer. The fact that this was police brutality was recognizable immediately. The victim was a shy, strictly raised West Indian child who was an honor student and had never been in trouble with the law. The injury was to the police officer's fists. The witnesses on the girl's behalf were independent and impeccable. The young district attorney on the case, when told by me and the judge what was happening, went to his supervisor to have the case dismissed. He came back with tears in his eyes, saying that he had been ordered to prosecute it.

The case was dismissed at trial. The police officer was never disciplined. The girl went on to college and, years later, I heard from her brother that she still has nightmares of being pressed against the grating above the subway tracks and being savagely beaten by a police officer almost twice her size.

There are other cases that I could describe. There is no need for me to do so, because any defense attorney, prosecutor, judge, or court employee has seen many cases like this one.

The torture of Abner Louima shocked New York City and the nation, catching the attentions of the media because of the bizarre means by which his injuries were inflicted and because of the sexual overtones to his torture. If not for those factors, Mr. Louima's torture would have likely received little or no broad media or political attention, because instances of serious injury due to police brutality are abundant and largely ignored. Mr. Louima's case shares fundamental characteristics with more typical and widespread instances of police brutality, and this commonality is important to set forth:

- Mr. Louima's beating allegedly occurred in the presence of other police officers and without interference by either those officers or their superiors. In effect, police officers and their commanding officers are said to have looked the other way while the abuse occurred.
- Abner Louima, the victim of a vicious assault, was treated as a criminal. He was charged with assaulting a police officer and his medical care was compromised because he was in custody. (In fact, he was chained to his bed for four days in the hospital until the charges were dropped.)
- Initial efforts to file police brutality charges were ignored.

- Police officers were reluctant or unwilling to come forth to testify against criminal behavior by their colleagues.
- Those police officers who did come forward are now stigmatized and at risk because of their compliance with their own oaths of office and their acceptance of their responsibility to uphold the law.

Abner Louima's case is not an isolated incident but part of a larger pattern. The pattern must be recognized in order for it to be ended.

I want to talk about one more case because, for me, this case illustrates the price of permitting the existence of a police culture and a criminal justice system that look the other way when those who are trusted to be the agents of the law violate that trust by committing savage assaults and then are protected while their victims are treated as the criminals.

Recently, one of the employees of The Fortune Society came to me for help. His son had been arrested and beaten by the police. The underlying incident serving as the basis for the arrest was an accusation that he was playing his radio too loud. I spent the night in court with the young man's father as he waited for his son to come through arraignment. I watched a man who was a leader in his community and a human service professional go through pain and rage and helplessness as he waited to see how badly his son had been beaten and what crimes his child, the victim of a vicious assault, would be charged with.

The price of police brutality can be measured in dollars, calculated in part by looking at the millions of dollars spent each year to settle civil suits by the victims of police brutality. It can be looked at in terms of risk to police officers who patrol communities whose attitudes toward the police are shaped by the rage and pain fostered by unchecked periodic assaults on their children. I would suggest that the price be measured in the legion of parents who fear for the safety of their children at the hands of police and who have, themselves, experienced the shame and rage and helplessness of being treated with disdain and the threat or reality of criminal assault by police officers who are trusted and violate that trust.

There will always be a percentage of any population that is willing to step outside the law and do damage to other human beings. When such individuals are police officers, the City's leaders and police management are responsible for seeing that full effort is taken to prevent such behavior and full effort is taken to address it when it occurs.

I would like to make a series of recommendations regarding each of these points. After the incident with the staff member's son, I participated in a national meeting attended by a police chief whom I had grown to respect over the years. When I discussed this case with him, he said, very simply, "This is bad policing." I asked him what he did in his department to avoid this kind of an incident and he gave two recommendations that I would like to share:

1. Screening and hiring of police officers needs to be oriented toward hiring those who express desire to be public servants and to help people and screening out

those who are looking for adventure or seem to be "cowboys."

2. Leadership of the department needs to be clearly and in no uncertain terms held accountable for strongly and decisively addressing any incidences of police brutality. The issue of police brutality is very much a management issue, and it is essential to have management that begins from a stance of zero tolerance for police brutality and rigorously polices the police to ensure that this occurs. The most rigorous assessment of whether police brutality is occurring and the most consistently proactive response to brutality need to come from the police department.To his recommendations I would add the following:

3. Rules and laws that protect police brutality need to be identified and changed. Among those that interfere with effective prevention of such brutality are the "48 hour rule," protecting police officers from being questioned for 48 hours after alleged brutality has taken place, and the current statutes of limitation on the time period within which prosecution for brutality can occur. Passage of residency requirements needs to be considered, as well as creation of an incentive system to tap role models from the communities most at-risk for police brutality as recruits for the police system.

4. There needs to be a more effective, independent, adequately resourced Civil Complaint Review Board accountable to the community for prompt, fair investigations that will serve as a basis for criminal prosecution in court when brutality is substantiated.

5. Routine and rigorous prosecution of police in court on criminal charges must occur when brutality is found.

6. There must be routine and rigorous independent review of cases that bear the identifying signs of possible police brutality (i.e. defendants charged with resisting arrest, assault on a police officer, and a non-violent crime such as disorderly conduct, but requiring medical attention) at or before arraignment, to identify proactively police brutality and protect victims of police brutality from being further traumatized by being prosecuted in the court system.

7. The police culture must be changed to one where it is the norm for officers to report brutality by other officers, and where such ethical officers are valued and respected rather than stigmatized.

8. Ongoing sensitivity training should be required for police officers and administrators.

9. Recognizing the degree to which bias plays a role in fostering brutality and the climate in which it flourishes, an independent training institute should be developed, available without charge to its users, that provides high quality bias awareness and diversity training for individuals ranging from those convicted of hate crimes to persons in leadership positions, to ordinary New Yorkers who recognize bias in themselves and wish to address it. The full range of bias should be addressed, including race, religion, gender, sexual orientation, and national origin.

10. There must be recognition of the importance of vigilantly protecting the

civil rights and the humane and respectful treatment of all New Yorkers, including those in police and correctional custody.

New York is a magical city, and much of its magic comes from the incredible richness and diversity of its inhabitants. We deserve a police force that serves as a model for the country and is characterized by integrity, sensitivity, and behavior that justifies the trust inherent in the role of police officer. We have a police department now where brutality is allowed to occur without sanction and without disciplinary response in the vast majority of cases. We have a police department where good police officers, police officers who would not stoop to criminal activity such as assaultive behavior, either stand silent in the face of such behavior by their colleagues or are victimized themselves if they step forward and speak out against those who violate the trust of all of us. We need leadership in this city that says that criminal behavior by police officers, whether that behavior be theft or assault, will not be tolerated and will be prosecuted to the fullest extent of the law.

The current status quo, where police brutality is permitted and protected, is unacceptable. The cost on all fronts is too high. There have been more than enough credible hearings, reports and recommendations. We know what needs to be done. We simply need to set clear standards, hold police and their management accountable for meeting those standards, and settle for no less than a police force worthy of this City. Abner Louima is New York City's Rodney King. My hope is that the actions needed will be taken to ensure that his case marks the end of a pattern, rather than a moment of professed concern followed by resumption of shameful business as usual.

JoAnne Page joined The Fortune Society in March of 1989 as Executive Director. She graduated from Yale Law School with a Juris Doctor degree in 1980, and worked through 1983 in Brooklyn as an attorney with Legal Aid Society. During 1983, she began working with the Court Employment Project as Director of Court Programs, developing and implementing the alternative to incarceration and detention programs. Her experience in criminal justice dates back to 1972, when she first began teaching and couseling in New York State prisons.

STEPHEN FRALEY
"Mental Health Professionals Should Get Personally Involved"

A social work class from Daemen College last year met with the Criminal Justice and Ethics group in Attica Prison, to which I belong. We debated whether social workers should become personally involved with their clients. The students' training advises against it; I favor that involvement.

Many mental health professionals don't give much of themselves for fear of burnout. Burnout does not result from doing too much, but from fearing that you cannot do enough, and the subsequent inability to separate yourself from the work.

As a peer counselor in prison, I have learned that you can get personally involved with clients, yet avoid being overwhelmed by their problems. Indeed, I live with my clients and can hardly avoid personal involvement.

Mental health professionals who stand out in their fields have always been those who extend themselves to their clients in a human way and beyond the call of duty: people like Carl Rogers, the psychologist who invented person-centered therapy; Mother Hale, who cared for crack-addicted babies in New York City; and Ken Siegel of Cephas, a Rochester-based prisoner rehabilitation program.

Counselors of all kinds can show empathy, vulnerability, and a sense of community without becoming "unprofessional." They don't need to use distance as a defense mechanism, fearing that if they get too close they'll get sucked under with their clients.

A counselor needn't take responsibility for a client's ignoring his or her advice. Neither does a counselor have to come to a client's aid in every crisis.

Social workers must consider themselves and their obligations to their own families. Loving, authentic care does not involve naiveté and foolishness; rather, it is about judgment, maturity, and knowing when to back off.

The problems facing us today are so serious that we need a radical change in the way we intervene in our client's lives. We are losing too many young people to drugs, crime, and violence.

Take me for example. I'm doing life for killing another alienated young African-American man. I could be a successful psychology professor, lawyer, or human rights advocate by now if I had only avoided the lure of the streets. But I didn't, and many others who share my childhood circumstances won't—unless we improve their chances and incorporate them into the larger community.

When mental health professionals resist getting personally involved, what they are saying is that they are satisfied with the status quo—that they'll do what they can as long as it involves no risk to themselves. Indeed, it should be mandatory for all mental health professionals to undergo periodic therapy to address their own issues and relieve job-related stress.

We've been addressing social problems the same way for a long time and the situation is deteriorating. Shall we detach ourselves and fiddle while Rome burns?

That is why I won't accept sweeping generalizations that the Department Of Correctional Services does nothing to rehabilitate us. We must not leave it to DOCS, the institution; rather, we should focus on the people who comprise the department. Individuals can make a difference, regardless of how large and cumbersome their bureaucracy.

For example, I once saw a psychologist for a year, during which time a mutually respectful relationship developed. He was open with me and treated me like a human being, not just a client.

It is really a question of faith and investment. Does the counselor have enough faith in the healing process to get personally involved? That involvement would make the process more effective, thereby giving the counselor more reason to have faith in it.

Stephen Fraley, a prisoner-counselor, earned his B.S. in psychology at the Consortium of the Niagara Frontier (Canisius College) while in prison. He is also senior counselor of the Relapse Prevention program at Collins Correctional Facility. He has spent 17 years in prison counseling, teaching, and writing. Fraley is doing 20 years to life for murder and will be eligible for parole in 2001.

Steven King Ainsworth, "Humor in the Face of Adversity"

GROWTH AND CHANGE AND SELF-RESPECT

Death Row, California

October 31, 1996

*"Yes, we do have access to a small law library here at 'Q.' It has little cages to lock individuals in to do their research. You have to sign up and be escorted over there. It's okay, in fact, I went over there the night of the lunar eclipse to make some notes in regards to my essay. After signing up a week ahead of time, my name came up on that particular night for the 6:00 pm group. I got naked and did my little dance while the guard watched and shook down my clothes, dressed, cuffed-up and was escorted over to the law library, locked in a cage, gave my case citations to a guard who found the right books and brought them to me, did my research in about 2 hours, got naked again, did my little dance, got dressed, cuffed up and was walking back to the East Block, and when I looked up into the night sky....right there above the big rotunda doors, painted with the words 'Condemned Row II-East Block,' was this beatiful orangish disk in eclipse. Quite a sight!! Ironically or whatever, that was only the 3rd time in 16+ years that I was out of my cell after dark! I was moon-*struck!!"

Death Row, Washington

February 9, 1997

"I am always working hard on my spiritual journey, it took me a spell to really understand I was on one and that it wouldn't be easy, but now I know I will constantly be tested and as long as I trust in myself and the Lord, I will be fine!! I have found an inner peace that I wouldn't trade for anything. Nope, if they came to me today and said, we will give you your freedom right now, all you have to give us is your faith and belief, I would have to say No Way!! For at this point I am freer than I have ever been!!"

WENDELL BROWN
"The Case for Lifer Groups"

Despite their concern as to whether criminals are being adequately punished, Americans have shown remarkably little curiosity about what actually goes on in a prison or what prisoners are really like. As a result, prison stereotypes persist that are grotesquely at variance with reality. An example is the image people have of prisoners serving life terms. The logic of the average citizen, who knows that most lifers are murderers, is unassailable: people who commit violent crimes are the most evil criminals; murder is the most violent crime; therefore murderers are the most evil criminals, dangerous and difficult to control. The fault with this syllogism is with the major premise. Most people who commit murder are not of the ilk of Murder Incorporated. They seldom bring to their crime the degree of premeditation of burglars or pickpockets. They are apt to come from a culture that tolerates a certain amount of violence, and usually their crimes were committed in a fit of anger, very frequently when under the influence of alcohol or drugs. Incarcerating people who cannot control their tempers may be wise. But one should not regard them as inherently vicious or brutish.

My first occasion to reflect on these matters came while I, as a "civilian observer," was sitting in the corridor of Walpole prison in Massachusetts where the correction officers had gone on strike. It was a maximum security prison, so most all the prisoners I encountered were lifers, guilty of violent crimes, usually murder. Since they regarded the observers as friends and frequently stopped by to talk, I got to know several quite well. They were serious, witty, insightful, wrongheaded, remorseful, defiant—in short, human. Well, I am a social scientist and I had often told my students that criminals were human beings. What I hadn't expected was that they would be so much like me.

I soon found that, far from being considered the most dangerous prisoners, lifers were generally regarded by corrections personnel as among the least violent, the most cooperative and the most productive persons in the prison. Wardens find it difficult to decide whether to reward lifers for their good behavior by giving them a section of the prison by themselves, or to distribute them among the general population to provide a stabilizing influence. A survey of 41 state and federal penal agencies opted for the second alternative. It found that long-termers were "either proportionally represented or were underrepresented in administration lockdown, disciplinary lockdown, disciplinary status and protective custody."

I never stopped visiting prisons after my monitoring stint at Walpole ended. After a year or two, I began to attend meetings of the Lifers Group at the Norfolk prison in Massachusetts. It was a lucky choice, for this group was as fine an example of the genus "*lifer group*" as existed in the nation. Suffice it to say for the present that I was pleasantly surprised by a number of things about the group: that it was a not-for- profit corporation under Massachusetts law; that it had a bulk mailing permit; that it had an office equipped with computers, filing cabinets, desks and chairs (donated); that its leaders were sophisticated about how to do legal research and how to conduct a meeting. But mostly I was surprised by how much time and energy the lifers devoted to charitable projects that I have termed “good works.”

In 1990, I became president of Life-Long CURE, an organization associated with National CURE (Citizens United for the Rehabilitation of Errants) and dedicated to the concerns of lifers and long-termers in American prisons. The organization soon began to publish a newsletter, with Gordon Haas, a prisoner at the Norfolk prison, as editor. The publication went to more than 700 lifers and long termers and their supporters. Through the lively correspondence which the newsletter provoked, I became aware of how many lifer group members were among our readers. I knew that there was very little research on voluntary organizations in prisons and none on lifer groups. I realized that my newsletter mailing list provided me with an opportunity to fill that gap.

I was aware of the existence of twenty-eight lifer groups. I designed a simple questionnaire asking for basic organizational facts. Then I sought the answers to two questions: 1. the degree of cooperation and good will between the lifer group and the prison administration; and 2. the group’s accomplishments - past and present, and goals for the future.

The questionnaire went to all twenty-eight lifer groups, and I received responses with assurances of cooperation from twenty-one located in seven states. The questionnaire data gave me a good start on acquiring an understanding of the nature of lifer groups. But in the long run, it was the auxiliary documentation that was the most valuable. Brochures, flyers, annual reports, legislative proposals, newspaper clippings and the letters prisoners wrote to me proved to be immensely informative.

Each lifer group is an original creation. No National Association of Lifer Groups exists, and there is no master pattern of how a lifer group should be organized. Of course, approval by the prison administration is necessary. Only one of my twenty-one groups struggled on for a time, more or less sub rosa, without approval and finally succumbed. On the other hand, lifer groups are usually free of direct administrative control. In most cases an important motive for their formation is to create a vehicle to influence administrative decisions.

The phenomenon of lifer groups dates from the 1960’s, a time when authoritarian structures were under criticism from liberal groups. The liberal mood infected some prison administrators who found themselves willing to make small grants of autonomy to lifers, a category of prisoner they regarded as trustworthy. The first of the twenty-one lifer groups in my sample was formed in 1968. Between 1968 and 1975 ten of my groups were founded.

The group membership in my sample varied from 25 to 700, with a median of 103. Many of the groups, particularly the smaller ones, also admitted long-term prisoners to membership.

An important determinant of a lifer group's effectiveness is the attitude of the prison administration—whether it cooperates with the group, merely tolerates it, or consistently opposes its projects and seeks to weaken it. Questionnaire respondents were asked which of four adjectives - cooperative, neutral, uncooperative, or harassing — best characterized the attitude of administrators toward their group. Their responses are presented in Table #1. (Not included is the reply of one group which was apparently sponsored and dominated by the administration.)

TABLE 1

Cooperative	8
Neutral	5
Neutral/Uncooperative	2
Uncooperative	4
Uncooperative/Harassing	1
Harassing	0

The amount of cooperation between the lifer groups and the prison authorities shown by the table surprised me. I think it demonstrates that many of the wardens recognized lifers as a valuable resource for them in managing prison affairs.

• Lifers, Inc. at Graterford in Pennsylvania describes the group's relationship with the administration in these glowing terms:

> *We have been working for the past 13 years to get legislation passed to allow parole review for lifers. This administration has been very supportive of this effort and has given us the lead way to host seminar, legislative conferences, meet with our outside support group on a weekly basis, and allowing us to run our programs to bring attention to our plight.*

The group had the help of more than 300 community volunteers.

• At the Louisiana State Penitentiary at Angola, because of Louisiana's harsh sentencing policies (long sentences, many life sentences, and no parole for lifers), the average age of Angola prisoners is very high. When one adds the number of "practical lifers" at Angola (those with sentences for terms of years they cannot survive, e.g. 99 years) to the number of natural lifers, one finds that about two-thirds of Angola prisoners will die in prison.

Paradoxically, Angola, in the state with perhaps the toughest sentencing laws in the nation, has a very prisoner-friendly administration and one that is extremely cooperative with lifer groups. One Angola lifer group characterized the administration as "fair, understanding, concerned, cooperative, friendly, polite, and committed."

• Lifers Unlimited, Inc. in Salem, Oregon had a membership of 424. It lacks the unqualified administrative support possessed by the groups at Graterford and Angola, characterizing the administration's posture as "cooperative at times." It complained that "prison officials often do not authorize certain projects of the group and remove them from the club's agenda or change the entire concept of the project. These actions are all based on the fact that paperwork 'was not available.'" The fact that the administration controls the group's agenda suggests less over-all autonomy than most lifer groups possess.

The size and complexity of the twenty-one programs differed considerably. Most of them reported a generous amount of community service. Most also had a political component, focusing on legislation affecting lifers. Education and counseling youth at risk were other major concerns. Table 2 shows the variety of programs among the twenty-one groups.

TABLE 2
PROGRAMS OF TWENTY-ONE LIFER GROUPS, BY TYPE

Types of Programs	Number of Lifer Groups
Donations to community agencies (money or services)	12
Political programs	12
Education (prisoners as teachers or students)	7
Family solidarity	6
Counseling for youth at risk	5
Runathons or Walkathons	5
Anti-violence	3
Cultural	3
Senior citizens	3
Anti-drug	2
Self-improvement	2

Good Works. The lifer groups gave both money and hand-made toys and equipment to various social agencies in neighboring communities. Money was raised both by runathons and by the sale of toys and other items. Norfolk reported that its Runners' Club had raised $10,000 between 1987 and 1989 for distribution to local charities. The single most generous monetary gift that of which I have a record was one for $1,000 made by Lifers Unlimited at the Oregon State Penitentiary in Salem to the to the Shriner's Hospital for Crippled Children.

Forty prisoners at Norfolk devoted 30,060 hours to making wooden toys according to a 1990 report. Its program, called "Toys for Tots," donated toys valued at $4,060 to hospitals and agencies providing services to children.

The Oregon toy making program specialized in stuffed animals. The group also had a sizable program supplying playground and therapeutic equipment to children's agencies. The magnitude of the program and the degree of expertise which the prisoners brought to the project is evident in a letter from the Executive Director of the Mid-valley Children's Guild. She asked the lifers to construct the following items: three picnic tables, a balance beam, parallel bars, a sandbox, and a jungle gym consisting of ladder, slide, support for suspended equipment, and support for two swings.

In the files of both the Oregon and Norfolk groups were many letters of appreciation from grateful (and perhaps amazed) agency heads.

Political Activities. The Lifers' Group at Norfolk engaged in a variety of political activities. The group sponsored an annual Legislative Awareness Day at the prison and invited the members of the Massachusetts legislature. Also invited were criminal justice experts and activist friends. Although no more than two or three legislators would turn up, a sizable number of the other outsiders would attend for a lively and informative all day session.

Prisons are required to give prisoners access to law libraries. Lifer groups in prisons across Massachusetts, including the Norfolk group, took advantage of this to do research on legal issues, particularly issues involving lifers. They formulated proposals and wrote memoranda on law which they sent to legislative committees and activist groups lobbying in their behalf.

While Massachusetts permits prisoners to vote, so few took advantage of the privilege that the Norfolk lifers' group persuaded some very reluctant election officials that they must come to the prison and register prisoners to vote. The group then arranged for the orderly appearance of prisoners on the appointed day, and several hundred were registered in a couple of hours. The Norfolk effort was duplicated by other lifer groups in the state.

In Pennsylvania and Louisiana, parole is denied to those convicted of both first and second degree murder. This means that, except for those few receiving executive clemency, all lifers will die in prison. Trying to persuade the legislature to change this law became the principal focus of the lifers groups in both states. They studied parole laws of other states and published numerous pamphlets and other materials aimed at both the legislature and the general public. For instance, Angola Special Civic Project (ASCP) in Louisiana put out a twenty-nine page report entitled *Penal Reform in Louisiana: The Need for Immediate Change*. It contained analyses of sentencing laws in ten states which permit parole for lifers and of the parole laws in Louisiana, and proposed legislative alternatives.

An example of the cooperative relationship between the Graterford administration and its lifer group came when the administration made possible the holding of a legislative hearing on parole inside the prison walls.

Political activity was almost completely absent in the program of Lifers Unlimited in Oregon. The prison administration that controlled the groups agenda may not have permitted it.

Counseling for Youth at Risk. The lifers at Norfolk, Graterford, and Oregon all regularly brought boys and young men to their prisons to acquaint them with the dismal consequences of criminal careers. The Angola group has announced plans to start such a project.

Education and Culture. The Lifers' Group at Norfolk excelled in this category. A College Discussion Program brought students from numerous area colleges and universities into the prison to discuss criminal justice and other issues with the lifers. A Quiz Club pitted prisoners against teams from colleges and organizations in tests of facts, trivial and weighty.

Poetry Readings were organized quarterly in which both inside and outside poets read their work. Prisoner poetry frequently is notable more for earnestness than for literary merit. But at the Poetry Reading I attended, it was quite good.

A Theatre Arts group put on productions every year, always assisted by community volunteers. Most noteworthy was a production of "Man of La Mancha" in which Richard Kiley, star of the Broadway Production, acted as adviser. After a number of performances at Norfolk, the cast went on tour, giving performances at other Massachusetts prisons.

Anti-Violence. Attended by much publicity, Lifers, Inc. at Graterford conducted an Anti-Violence Day in 1992 and repeated it in 1993. One component of the program was anti-crime instruction by ex-convicts in Philadelphia inner city public schools. The lifers launched the program with these words:

> *As perpetrators of violent acts, we have seen first hand how our actions have affected the community. We of Lifers Inc./End Violence Project have made the commitment to take a stand for ending the violence in our lives, within the prison, and hopefully, ending violence as a solution for the younger generation which is so enveloped in this life style.*

The Victim-Offender Reconciliation Project (VORP) brings an offender and the victim of his crime together in the hopes of helping the parties deal with their anger and their guilt. It is an idea that has been talked about in all four prisons. In 1993, the administration at Graterford collaborated with a VORP group consisting of prisoners and community people to co-sponsor a national conference inside the prison entitled "Justice for All: VORP—A Unique Approach to Criminal Justice."

ASCP at Angola has recently launched an inquiry into VORP's feasibility. However, victims have tended to resist the idea of reconciliation. I am not aware that any prison group has a VORP program in operation.

Prisoner Comfort and Welfare. Lifer Groups engage in a multitude of projects to benefit their members and the prison population as a whole, such as dinners and picnics for family and friends, legal assistance, drug and alcohol counseling, parenting and spousal counseling, and selling fast food to prisoners.

The golden age of Lifer groups began to wane in the late 1980's as prisoner-friendly programs became suspect because they were not consistent with a get-tough-on criminals policy. In the 1990's, the programs of both the Norfolk group in Massachusetts and the Graterford group in Pennsylvania were casualties of the new trend.

All Massachusetts programs expanding privileges for prisoners were doomed from the time William Weld was elected governor after a campaign in which he promised to get prisoners back to "the joys of busting rocks." The Lifers' group's programs were terminated one by one—even the toy making program on the pretext that prisoners could not be trusted with sharp tools. Finally the administration closed the lifer's office and confiscated the equipment. Now the Lifers' Group operates an "Ice Cream Shack" and little else.

As in Massachusetts, Graterford's troubles began when a new governor and a new Commissioner of Correction assumed office. In early 1996 I had written a Graterford lifer commenting on the lifer group's "unusually happy relationship with the prison administration." He wrote back saying that "the unusually happy relationship has changed completely. Both deputies of treatment and security have changed and tough new policies have been put in place to eliminate positive programs, leadership and the influence of prisoners. Our organization has been shut down until a review of all activities can be made by the administration." I wrote back sending him a packet of materials, as he requested. He has not written since in response to my letters.

Prisons have again become places for warehousing criminal offenders. For thirty or forty years, some wardens worked valiantly to humanize their institutions. And, in fact, their prisons became more humane, livable places. Permitting lifer groups to flourish was part of that effort.

For humanizing is what lifer groups and similar organizations are about. It is humanizing for a prisoner to interact with a volunteer from the community, to be part of a charitable effort to help someone else, to act in a play, write a poem, or listen to what another prisoner has written. And it is profoundly humanizing to work with others as equals formulating a common purpose and then working with them in furtherance of that purpose.

Groups are an inevitable human phenomenon. And, in prison, as elsewhere, there will be people who aspire to play activist or leadership roles in groups. If there are no administration-approved groups to join and to lead, prisoners will find administration-disapproved ones. Or as Robert Merton would put it, if there are no legitimate opportunity structures, people will find illegitimate ones. It may be, for instance, that underground power centers are strong to the extent that legitimate opportunities for association and leadership are lacking. And some penologists are attributing the rise of gangs in prison to this cause.

Voluntary prisoner organizations are a partial answer to this need for legitimate opportunities for sociability and leadership, including organizations other than lifers. I was much impressed by a meeting of a prison-based chapter of the JAYCEES that I attended. And most prisons have religious organizations and veteran's organizations. These organizations may also humanize, though they have a more limited menu of activities than most lifer groups.

When the present infatuation with punishment subsides, as it will if we are not indeed at the beginning of another dark age, people will begin to talk about creating less authoritarian prisons. And some crazy radicals will suggest prisoner participation in prison management as the only strategy that can lead to truly humane prisons. My experience with lifer groups has convinced me that, when that time comes, there will be many thoughtful and fair-minded prisoners to participate in governance. And when that time comes, this crazy radical will be applauding.

Wendell Brown's educational credentials include B.A. and LL.B. degrees from Cornell University and a Ph.D. from Syracuse University. Most of his professional life was spent at the Bouve College at Northeastern University teaching social science, particularly sociology. He has been visiting prisons since 1971. In the 1980s and early 1990s, he served as an external member of the Board of Directors of the Lifers' Group, Inc. at MCI Norfolk, and then of the Massachusetts Lifers' Organization. In 1990 he became president of Life-Long CURE, a national organization dedicated to serving the needs of lifers and long-termers in American prisons, and served until 1995. This organization is affiliated with National CURE (Citizens United for the Rehabilitation of Errants). Mr. Brown is currently writing a book dealing with prisons and prisoners, with an emphasis on those prisoners serving long terms.

ADRIA LIBOLT
"The Pastoral Work of an Ex-Offender"

Isaac Johnson is talking to a 20 year old man who is in prison for selling cocaine to an undercover policeman. His sentence is three years. Mae Johnson, Isaac's wife, is with him and speaking with another young prisoner, serving life for murder. He also was selling drugs to raise money for himself and his family who were living in a car. These prisoners illustrate a little of the range of those committed to the Michigan Department of Corrections' Youth Reception Center where Isaac and Mae Johnson are volunteers. Several years ago Isaac was one of the prisoners who received visits from Christian volunteers.

The U.S. Census Bureau, in one decade from 1980 to 1990, reports that the prison population more than doubled and grew 15 times faster than the general population. There are many reasons for crime: lack of education, lack of job skills, drug addiction, abuse, and mental illness. But it is the public's reaction to crime and the imposition of mandatory and longer sentences that accounts for most of the expansion in the prison population.

James Q. Wilson, from the University of California and author of several books on crime, justice, and morals, proposes that increase in crime may also indicate a spiritual crisis. His study found an inverse correlation between the level of spiritual activity and the level of crime. The more spiritual activity, the less crime; the less spiritual activity, the more crime. If this is so, then volunteers who bring spiritual guidance are an important resource for our prisons.

There is an historical justification for a spiritual presence in the prisons. Early in the development of penitentiaries in the 1700s, the Quakers were concerned with the treatment of their inhabitants and made attempts to reform them. Despite these early efforts, spiritually oriented volunteers have not kept up with the number of prisoners incarcerated.

Michael Quinlan, the Director of the United States Bureau of Prisons, believes that volunteers in the religious sector make the greatest impact of anyone on the lives of prisoners. He claims a need for 62,500 volunteers, equal to the number of prisoners in his population. Volunteers are needed to visit prisoners, but spiritual communities are also needed once prisoners are released: over 80% of ex-offenders never find a spiritual home.

Further, volunteers, in times of scarce resources, provide many services which add few costs, provide moral instruction to those incarcerated, and the possibility that they will turn prisoners around.

The volunteers who visit the Reception Center appeal to the prisoners whether they are holding worship services or seeing prisoners individually. Their appeal may be partly based on the "no-nonsense" beliefs held by these volunteers which include accountability for one's actions, faith that past behavior can change, forgiveness of others, and a vision for the future which establishes conditions that either help prisoners adjust to a Christian life in prison, or restores them to their communities. Even more significant is the relationship the volunteers develop with prisoners. The fact that someone from the community and church would care enough to visit them has a powerful impact on them.

Biblical mandates which motivate these Christian volunteers are compelling. Jesus, faced with the opinion that one should not be seen eating with the sinners and the tax collectors said, "It is not the healthy who need a doctor, but the sick. I have not come to call the righteous, but sinners." {Mark 2:16} Hebrews 13:3 urges Christians to remember those who are in prison. 2 Corinthians 5:17-19 advises humbling oneself and reconciling oneself to others, "not counting their sins against them." Prisoners, keenly aware that the line drawn between themselves and others is not as clear as some think, are grateful for people who treat them as brothers.

Christianity is supposed to be inclusive. Jesus, in Matthew 25:36, says, "I needed clothes and you clothed me, I was sick and you looked after me, I was in prison and you came to visit me." For years churches have sent people to remote places, but neglected prisoners. Dietrich Bonhoeffer, himself a prisoner who ministered to others in a Nazi prison, cautioned Christians to actively love those among them. He said, "He who loves his dream of the community more than the Christian community itself, is a destroyer of it." Initially, volunteers often find the prison to be a "foreign" land; they are not always prepared for the spiritual hunger and longing of the prisoners, and conversely, their own experience of spiritual fulfillment when they visit prisoners. Christian communities often do form in what seems to us an unlikely environment.

James Skillen, Director of the Association for Public Justice, cites another reason for Christian volunteers. Our criminal justice systems define justice in terms of guilt or innocence and release or punishment. His contention is that we should not stop there. Just avoiding crime is not enough; we need to actively seek justice. Skillen believes that God wants people to be reconciled and have order restored. Mature, Christian volunteers who are well-trained understand that our preoccupation with punishing offenders will not bring anyone peace. They come with a faith that there is always the possibility of grace for the most unlikely prisoners, and that they may be the vehicle for that transformation. Their visits show prisoners that they are valued and give them hope with a vision beyond the grim reality of their sentences. It is not that prison employees are not concerned with prisoners' amelioration, since many of them work hard on programs which help prisoners develop skills and overcome erroneous thinking processes, but their time is quickly consumed by the practical maintenance and schedules of prison operations. The context from which Christian volunteers approach prisoners is expansive; their perspectives as well as their relationships with prisoners have the potential to enlarge prisoners' beliefs and develop their spirituality. There is at least one volunteer who can attest to this.

Several years ago Isaac Johnson was himself sentenced to prison. I first met Isaac when he had reached minimum security level in Corrections. He stood out because of his winning personality. He led small Bible groups with prisoners—activities which did not endear him to the staff. Without always intending to, prisoners with special gifts of charm and leadership often upset the prison routines and may be seen as manipulative. Isaac himself received visits from concerned Christians in the community who had taken an interest in him and his family.

While on parole, Isaac appeared at a Sunday worship service where I attend church. His first thought was, "What is the deputy warden doing here?" He had remembered me as the person who asked the staff to remove the flimsy, bedraggled curtains which were fire safety hazards—not exactly the way I had hoped to be remembered. Our Corrections rules did not allow me to have contact with him.

His greatest challenges occurred while he was on parole. The severity of prison life gave way to a harsh transition to the community. Initially, almost his entire paycheck supported children he loved but was not permitted to see. Various members of the church gave Isaac support as he struggled to overcome a prison record while establishing himself in a world with which he was no longer familiar.

After he had paroled, Isaac volunteered to visit male prisoners under 21 years old in the Reception Center in the Riverside Correctional Facility in lonia, MI. For 6 years he has been coming to the Reception Center on a weekly basis and often twice a week. Isaac and his wife Mae lead worship services and Bible studies with the young male prisoners. They have begun a one-to-one program on Saturdays. Their prison ministry attracts others from the church who assist Isaac and Mae. Prisoners cry while Mae and Isaac sing, pray, read the Bible, and worship in the Reception Center. The prisoners tell me that their lives have changed significantly because of the Johnsons' work. Prisoners find Isaac attractive, and he is charismatic. No one would know, unless he told them, that he grew up with an alcoholic, abusive father, unchurched and illiterate. By the time he was 7 or 8 years old, he had run away from home.

What accounts for Isaac's return to this bleak environment with such painful memories? He says, "When a person has been forgiven much, much is required." He received visits from a person who valued him and led him to a church that helped and encouraged him. The young males in the prison want to hear about him, about how he has changed, and whether it is possible for them.

It is possible to be cynical about change occurring in prison, and I share some of this skepticism. Perhaps, for some prisoners, Isaac and other volunteers simply offer entertainment in the face of the numbing idleness and boredom of prison life. Several years ago the Reception Center employees made plans to honor our volunteers with a dinner. The Gideons generously distribute to the prisoners every few weeks small New Testaments with thin white paper. I had been pleased that so many of the prisoners seemed to be requesting Bibles. On the night of the dinner, one of the unit officers came to me and said, "The prisoners are smoking the Bible. One is halfway through Proverbs." I was reminded that the Bible is not only a great book but contains good paper for contraband cigarettes. Another employee speaks about the young, angelic faces of the prisoners at an evening worship service and their swearing mouths as they return to their cells. Such incidents make one dubious about the long-term impact of Christianity on behavior in the prison—though the staff hope for those rather pragmatic results. But some objective measures for the value of volunteer programs may exist. One study suggests that the overall failure rate for adults after prison is 75%, and for juveniles 85%, while the success rate for prisoners who are seen by volunteers is 60-80%! Charles Colson, an ex-offender who became an enthusiastic Christian in prison, provides many examples of the lives around him that changed as a result of Christian volunteers. More direct evidence of the need for and appreciation of ministry such as Isaac and Mae's is found in the many letters they receive from the prisoners they see.

One prisoner, Daniel, writes: *I'm writing to you to let you know I appreciate you and your wife, Mae, for coming out on Thursdays, some Saturdays, and Sundays to our Reception Center here at Riverside. I have only been here for about 2 weeks and you already hold a place in my heart because you guys show that you really care about prisoners and want to help change their ways before we get out of our prisons. After my last arrest on Nov. 16, 1995, I knew I had to change my life. I just didn't know how or when. But on Nov. 27, 1995, I let God tell me what to do with my life and how to do it. Even though God has a plan for me I don't know exactly where to start. I can see myself helping prisoners to learn about Jesus Christ and make the rehabilitation to Him. But I don't know where to start. I need to get myself in a good church but don't know what religion I should go to. I'm not quite sure if I have a place to stay because I don't want to live with my father because he lives in the country and I have no car to get to work. I don't want to live with my mom because she lives in a duplex with my brother, 2 sisters, my sister's son, and her new husband, and a baby boy due in 1 1/2 months. So I'm trying to find a place for Christians so I can stay around people that live for God and only for God. Do you know of any places?*

A prisoner named Tony writes about his frustration:

I'm 18 years old. I joined a street gang when I was 12 years old....when I was young and dumb. I'm trying to put everything behind me so I can start a new life—you did. I'm tired of being locked down. My family and people is suffering. I'm killing my mother, just breaking her heart. Just because I'm trying to get life right and right with God it does not get any easier. I just wrote to get some advice and maybe you could spread your story with me please. What you are doing is a good thing, both of you.

Isaac Johnson is an unusual person. But there are many Daniels and Tonys who need people like Isaac and Mae giving them spiritual direction and options which may lead them back to the prison—this time to help others. In any case, volunteers add a dimension to our prisons by enriching the lives of the prisoners within.

The views presented above do not necessarily represent the views of the Michigan Department of Corrections.

Adria Libolt, Deputy Warden, Reception Center, Riverside Correctional Facility, received a B.A. from Calvin College in Grand Rapids and a Master's Degree from the University of Michigan. She was a contributor to Frontiers of Justice, Volume 1: The Dealth Penalty.

LOUIS OSEI COTTON
"He's My Brother"

There is a vast difference between a state prison system and the federal prison system, and I quickly recognized this upon entering the Kansas Department of Corrections for the first time. I was shocked beyond words at what I saw.

I had served a number of years in the federal system; on the whole, I had found cleanliness, good food, unity among convicts, programs that allowed you to learn and upgrade yourself and to share that knowledge, and those skills and talents with each other and the outside world. I enjoyed learning about things that would help me later down the line.

One of the few encouraging things I found after being at Kansas State Prison for several months was the vast number of talented artists, craftsmen and creative fellows running around in general population, selling their work for little or nothing—2-5 packs of smokes or even less than that, depending just how uptight they were, or how badly they needed the smokes. After asking several questions in regard to the art program, I found that there was none. Basically, the way things were done was if you could paint, draw, do leather or bead work, you simply ordered the supplies or made a deal with one of the other artists, and got busy, but there was a lot of horse trading among fellows for different supplies; art and hobby stuff had become a form of payment or bribery, you name it.

During the following few weeks, I did a lot of research, talked to a lot of brothers that were into the arts, asked a lot more questions, and explained the idea that I was forming in my head. If set up right and submitted properly in an intelligently worded proposal covering every avenue of the project, it would make the administration more likely to consider it for approval.

Prison programs, groups and organizations that I had seen in other prison systems have been an essential and most effective method of relieving prison tension, stress and frustrations among the inmate population. They allow a man to put his thinking and idle time elsewhere, on more positive avenues. Sociologists, psychologists, religious leaders as well as members of the criminal justice system worldwide recognize that when men of any large incarcerated group are allowed to lay around idle, feeling useless, it breeds lots of problems. These problems could be avoided if those minds were allowed to function, making decisions and choices of their own. Attitudes would change, men would be able to use the skills, talents and knowledge they already had, plus that which they could gain from others, and this would eliminate a great part of the negative factors in prison life, producing a healthier and more positive environment. So these prison groups were set up and inmates started to participate, exercising their ability and knowledge and reaping the incentives from these groups. It was a step in the direction of rehabilitation that the system was at that time promoting enthusiastically. These groups generated a lot of self-esteem, and placed a lot of individuals closer to reentering the free society better equipped to deal with what society saw as assets rather than liabilities.

But here at K.S.P. things were slow, the system was backward and programs were cut. In their place lots of methods were used to discourage anyone from starting anything. It seemed that no one really cared, but I felt it could be changed.

My talks in the yard were with artists and creative fellows—I thought they were the best prospects because I had seen their work: leathermen who really did beautiful work, and rock sculptors and top flight yarn workers. I found an older brother who had lived in Oklahoma and worked on the oil rigs all his life, and he could recreate down to the last detail a model scale oil rig out of wood and pieces of rubber from the covering of electrical wires. I found a machinist who was a whiz on the metal lathe, turning out detail scale models of Civil War cannons and other pieces. I had a brother that was a professional cabinet maker prior to coming to prison, and the inlaid coffee table and rocking chair and other things he did were too beautiful to sell. And there was a brother who made walking sticks out of the throw away mop handles with any kind of animal head you wanted on it.

Ours was, in fact, one of the largest gatherings in the yard, outside of gathering for a riot, that this place has ever seen, and I was the center of attention, selling my dream and plans. I spoke of the need for an Art Organization, one that was sanctioned and blessed by the administration, a group that would benefit all of us, providing we ran it like a professional business. I told them that, once set up, it was a must that we give back to society in ways that would help kids, because this was the thing that was mostly looked at by the administration and society, from whence our main support would come. And they accepted the idea and agreed on a plan, and the race was on, because I had sold them the farm!

The Kansas State Prison Fine Arts Society was sanctioned by the warden himself, even though there were stipulations involved. These were: "It had better focus and function in a positive way that reflects on the administration as well as the population as a whole. It had better get plenty of positive coverage from the locals and media, and you have eight months to get this group rolling full blast, or you'll end up doing all the rest of your time in the White House (jail)." That was his promise.

The Fine Arts Society started with a six member Executive Board, and a committee of directors for every phase necessary to handle the work load that was coming up. I was the Chairman. During the next few weeks there were hundreds of letters written and daily meetings. The word had been given to the fellows to start producing. The fat was in the fire—we were beginning to burn!

It's easy setting up a new group compared to revising or changing an old one, so things really went smoothly with the paper work and mode of operation. We had acquired a sponsor who had a gift shop and other outlets and lots of friends interested in being a part of fine arts. We had developed and set up a system for shipping and receiving and keeping accurate tabs on what was sent out by who at what price and when it was sold. Our arrangements with our sponsor were that a reasonable, affordable price would be fixed by the artist, and he could add a 20% mark-up for his efforts. Upon sale, the sponsor was to make out two checks, one to the artist for the work minus 10% that came back to the group treasurer by check, and his 20% came off the top.

In less than five months of operation, there was only one organization in this prison larger in membership and outside participation than the Fine Arts Society. Twice a week, art projects were picked up and twice, sometimes three times, per month, checks rolled in. Suddenly we had no room for our general membership meetings for we had become that large; fellows got upset because their names weren't added to our call-out list right away. Guys wanted to know if we gave art lessons, because they wanted to learn, so we set up classes, brought in outside teachers from different area colleges, and taught the basics of drawing and painting. Then we set up a creative writing class with an outside teacher, and this went over on a grand scale.

The meetings got better and not once was there an incident with disrespect or attitude with our sponsor, guests or teachers, and that surprised me. In fact, I was called to the Warden's office and halfway praised for the way I was keeping a lid on things, and of course I accepted the praise. But really it was the group who deserved the honors.

There was a committee that did nothing but keep abreast of the news, especially the local papers, because we wanted to support youth groups and kids. They had a list of kids that needed help, whose families couldn't afford it, and we always donated money and started funding drives for such kids. I remember the first wheelchair we bought for this little 4 1/2 year old lady, and the thank you note her mother helped her to write. Then there was a little fellow with a rare childhood disease who had a chance with an operation, but it was beyond the family's ability. We came through for them, and the fellows loved doing it, the administration loved it and the local media ran an article, and I made sure the Warden and Secretary of Corrections got a copy!

Often I'm reminded of the statement that former Supreme Court Justice Oliver W. Holmes made in one of his court opinions regarding the ability of man. He said, "The mind of man, once expanded to a dimension of larger and better ideas, will never return to its original size." Well, looking back now at what took place then, I must say that this is what transpired with the fellows of the Fine Arts Society. For once we were able to put aside, if just for a short while, the pettiness, the jealousies, attitudes and dislikes. We were able to overcome the race barriers. We succeeded in overcoming the thoughts and feelings of the dehumanizing and demoralizing treatment that single us out as worthless and uncaring scum.

The K.S.P. Fine Arts Society continued to grow and went on to become one of the most progressive and positive self-help organizations in the Kansas prison system. I will forever be grateful to the many brothers and staff members who saw, understood and assisted in the making and maintaining of this organization.

Now the prisons are full of youth with longer sentences and attitudes with them. There are fewer skills, less education and less respect among them, so the task of trying to get them thinking and acting on a positive level is far greater, which is why the self-help programs are more important than ever. There is a very powerful and dangerous bomb within our midst. It is set to go off at the drop of a pin, unless handled by experts and professionals that care about something other than making money. There are salvageable human beings behind these fences and walls, whose very souls are crying out for a little understanding and more real justice. I am my brother's keeper; I will, if he allows me to, help him to reach a level where he can help himself. Because I love him, I will even pick him up and carry him a part of the way and not shy away from the extra weight. So long as he's about positiveness and unity, he's not heavy, for he's my brother—black, white, red, brown and yellow.

Louis Osei Cotton is an artist, writer and poet, and editor of Caged Freedom [Audenreed Press]. Mr. Cotton has been recognized for his talents and leadership as Chairman of the Fine Arts Society by wardens of both state and federal prisons, as well as by the Governor of Kansas. He is serving a life sentence in Kansas's Lansing Correctional Facility.

Louis Osei Cotton, "Grandma"

MICHAEL TENNESON
"A Music Proposal"

Art and music are two of the most powerful forces known to humanity. What is it that can compel 100,000 people at a music festival to tap their feet to a synchronized beat, that can even alter their collective pulses? What is it that compels so many people to gaze hypnotically into the depths of a painting, searching for a link to the soul of the artist who created it? What are these phenomena, how do they affect us so profoundly, and why? I am an aspiring artist and musician who cannot conclusively answer the questions just posed; suffice it to say that the forces in play are real.

I am also a prisoner who has spent four years in the Redirections Therapeutic Community (TC) studying the literature on maturity, honesty, responsibility, self-esteem, assertiveness and similar concepts. We study these on paper, we talk about them in groups. My peers and I would now like to show the benefits of the purely intellectual lessons we have learned by being given the opportunity to apply them in a real life, practical situation, a "test" if you will. The graduates of this Therapeutic Community have become, for the most part, mature, honest, responsible adults. We should now be allowed the latitude to earn special privileges, like that outlined in the attached proposal.

This proposal could make a very significant contribution towards changing the lives of the persons involved in these earned privileges. It is based on personal responsibility, is funded entirely by the individuals and allows those who participate to master skills that can not only keep them out of prison and off welfare lines, but also give them something to feel proud to have learned. It gives them a tremendous incentive to stay out of trouble and gives them something to live for—the key to getting out, staying out and caring about life, themselves and other people.

It is for these reasons that I am submitting this proposal for in-cell permits, so that eligible inmates can be allowed to purchase, possess and practice musical instruments in their cells, the only way that they can achieve the level of focused study and practice necessary to truly call themselves musicians.

Concerning any propensity for abuse of this equipment, I will simply say that the purpose of rehabilitation is to change the nature of an offender, to teach him to do the right thing, to restructure his thinking so that he can make the right choices. This proposal offers significant rewards and incentives for men who do make the right choices, and offers significant punishments for those who make the wrong ones. None of the equipment proposed herein, sitting in our cells, is going to pose a security threat, not in the context of allowing a man to earn such special privileges. Give a man something to gain...and to lose, something he has paid for and cares deeply about, and you have given that man a powerful incentive to better himself and the tools to achieve it.

A Proposal to Form a TC Music Program

Goals

1. To foster group interaction and cooperation in achieving the long term goal of establishing a musical group.

2. To learn the skills necessary to qualify for a free world music career.

3. To generate "industry standard" quality master audio recordings of original music.

4. To generate a public relations vehicle to educate the public concerning the positive changes offenders can make and the benefits of allowing prisoners earned opportunities.

Proposed Policy for In-Cell Musical Instrument Permits:

Inmates that have met the following criteria will be allowed the special privilege to purchase, possess, and practice certain approved instruments in their cells. The criteria are as follows:

1. Must be an active participant in the Redirections Therapeutic Community, ("active" is defined as a participating member in primary treatment, or in the Genesis Aftercare Program).

2. Must be currently assigned to a TC approved worksite, and maintain at least average work performance ratings.

3. Must not have any Class I, or Class II C.O.P.D. convictions within 18 months prior to their In-Cell Permit Requests, and must remain free of any Class I, or Class II convictions for the duration of their permit.

4. Must not violate any provision of this policy.

5. Must sign Liability Waiver.

This privilege is open to any man within this facility who meets the above criteria. Once a person has applied for and received his In-Cell Instrument Permit he will then be allowed to purchase, possess, and practice the approved musical instruments in his cell during his free-time.

Rules and Regulations for In-Cell Musical Instrument Permits

The following rules/requirements are in effect. Failure to abide strictly by these provisions will be cause for revocation of the permit, and applicable consequences will be enforced.

1. All electric guitars/basses will either he played through a headphone-equipped unit, or they will be played unplugged. No amplifiers with external speakers will be allowed.

2. All instruments will be held to the same volume standards as radio/TV: If it can be heard outside the person's cell—it is too loud.

3. All keyboards/drum machines must be played through headphones.

4. An inmate may only possess three sets of guitar/bass strings at any given time. ALL OLD/BROKEN STRINGS MUST BE SAVED AND TURNED IN WHEN NEW ONES ARE PURCHASED (i.e. one complete set must be turned in, in order to receive a new set; or two sets turned in to receive two new sets, etc.).

A. Strings must be purchased directly from an approved mail-order retail outlet .

B. No lending of strings to another inmate—any inmate that cannot account for all of the strings listed on his permit will he held responsible; The inmate will keep them locked up in his cell, and accounted for at all times!

C. Any inmate found guilty at a C.O.P.D. hearing of using strings as a tattoo implement, weapon, or any other purpose that violates this policy will immediately have his permit revoked and will face applicable charges.

5. Any inmate found guilty at a C.O.P.D. hearing of using his instrument, or any part thereof, to assault a staff member, another inmate, or to attempt to breach the security of this facility will immediately have his permit revoked and face applicable charges.

6. No inmate will take his personal music equipment out of his cell unless it has been approved by his Living Unit Supervisor.

7. Any inmate found guilty at a C.O.P.D. hearing of hiding or smuggling drugs or other dangerous contraband (as defined in the Inmate C.O.P.D. Handbook) will immediately have his permit revoked and face applicable charges.

8. Any inmate found guilty at a C.O.P.D. hearing of hiding or smuggling canteen purchases in his instrument or case will immediately have his permit revoked and face applicable charges.

9. No more than two instruments will be allowed any inmate at one time.

10. Be advised that this is a very special privilege, and no violations of any provision of this policy will be tolerated: Strike one, and you're out!

Proposed List of Approved Musical Instruments and Equipment

1. Guitars—Electric, Accoustic, or Classical.

2. Bass Guitars—(Electric only).

3. Electric Keyboards/Synthesizers—(must be equipped with headphone jack).

4. Headphone-equipped Guitar signal processing units—These are the only amplification units that will be allowed in for in-cell inmate use, and must be equipped for an AC adapter (no batteries allowed in).

5. Factory Supplied Cases (for above).
6. Portable Digital Drum Machines—(Must be headphone equipped).
7. Digital Disk Recorder
8. "Patch Cords"—(for plugging guitar/bass/keyboard into signal processor).

To maintain security and minimize the risks of contraband entering the facility, the following provision applies to all equipment listed herein: All "Approved Musical Instruments" will only be purchased through an inmates I.C.F. Inmate Account, and all purchases will be made directly from the products manufacturer (i.e. Gibson, Fender, Martin Guitars—or—Roland, Kurzweil, Korg Keyboards, etc.).

Liability Waiver for In-Cell Musical Instruments

LIMON CORRECTIONAL FACILITY
LIABILITY WAIVER FOR IN-CELL MUSICAL INSTRUMENTS

I,_______________, DOC#_________, an inmate at the Limon Correctional Facility, in accordance with the special privilege of being allowed to earn an In-Cell Musical Instrument Permit, acknowledge and agree to the following provisions in return for this privilege being granted.

1. That the Limon Correctional Facility hereby grants me the privilege of purchasing, possessing, and practicing certain specified musical instruments within my assigned cell.

2. That the Colorado Department of Corrections, Pikes Peak Mental Health; or any of their agencies, shall not be held liable by me for inmate personal property items obtained through this In-Cell Musical Instrument Permit in the event that these items are lost, stolen, or in any other way damaged due to the negligence of the DOC, the staff of the Limon Correctional Facility, or the staff of Pikes Peak Mental Health.

3. I understand that if I am convicted of a Class I, or Class II violation, or am convicted of any violation of the In-Cell Musical Instrument Policy, my permit may be revoked and I will be required to send out all related items that were acquired through that permit in accordance with DOC policy on inmate property disposal.

4. I understand that if I am transferred to another facility I may be required to send my musical equipment out in accordance with DOC policy on inmate property disposal.

5. I understand that by signing this waiver I am agreeing that I have read it and agree to all the provisions listed herein, and in the In-Cell Musical Instrument Policy .

6. I understand that by signing this waiver I am waiving all claims to any recovery of monetary damages in the event that my musical equipment is in any way lost, or damaged by Colorado Department of Corrections personnel.

____________________	____________________
Inmate signature	DOC No.
____________________	____________________
Date	Staff Witness

Michael J. Tenneson was convicted of five murders (in Colorado and Wisconsin) in 1987, and only spared the Death Penalty because one juror said she had "a gut feeling..." Driven by feelings of deep remorse, his life's goal is to give something back to society through his art, music and writing. For four years, he has been a member of the Redirections Therapeutic Community, at the Limon Correctional Facility, undergoing extensive drug, alcohol and behavioral modification therapy. Mr. Tenneson is conclusive confirmation that even the worst can change dramatically. He says: "Yes, the prisoner must have the true desire for change, but the system must also allow us to earn the tools, education and opportunities that are condusive to radical change."

PAT ALLEN
"Beyond Anger"

There is presently a great amount of discussion as to the treatment of juvenile offenders. Unfortunately, discussion often turns into debate, lines are drawn, and complex issues are turned black and white. What we must keep in sight throughout the discussion, however, is that what happens to our nation's children once they are within the judicial system can never fully repair what happened to them and our society before they got there.

I am a teacher, though not in the typical school setting. My classroom is in the woods. It is a tent, or a forest or river or even an adventure ropes course. The students here are not what you would call typical students. They are either convicted felons, emotionally handicapped, neglected, abused, learning disabled, or, most frequently, some combination of these. Just as the academic content of the classroom doesn't change with the setting, the value and worth of the kid doesn't change with the label. This is the foundation of one of the most successful juvenile programs in the country: Eckerd Family Youth Alternatives, Inc. We teach concepts such as accountability, responsibility, and consequence as they apply to the client's daily life. Future goals, both long and short term, and individual's behavior choices are rooted in these concepts. It is a skewed (or sometimes nonexistent) understanding of these concepts which (in the child's mind) justifies his criminal acts. If we were talking about adults, it would be well to assume that they are responsible for knowing not only the laws of the land, but also for understanding "right and wrong." But these are minors, and it is primarily the responsibility of the parents to ensure that their welfare is looked after. If not, then it becomes the responsibility of all of us. A child's welfare is more than just food and clothing, it includes education, empowerment, and safety.

When minors commit heinous acts such as murder or rape, I hear people asking two questions: "How could a child have done that?" and "What should happen to the child?" These are the questions of the victim, which we all are.

The first question usually receives less attention. From reading the paper or seeing the TV report, who can know what went wrong in the child's past, what complicated set of events and situations created a kid with such horrific capabilities. It is a question in which we know we may never arrive at the full truth. It is an event that can be seen from too many angles for it ever to be described accurately.

With the second question however, there is a set list of options. We merely need to look at the facts of the case and choose one of the options. To many, adult crimes, regardless of the context, deserve adult consequences. To others, all minors deserve the luxury of the protection of childhood.

These are questions that I am quite familiar with through personal experience.

These are the questions of the victim, and they are rarely, if ever, answered in a court seeking to assign guilt and punishment. Here is my experience and how I came, if not to answer, at least to understand these questions.

I was attacked from behind; a hammer plunged through my skull. It was like the sound of finding the pool wall with your head when swimming under water. I fell in a slump. When I came to, everything was silent, and there were thousands of stars in the Alabama night sky. Then a crowd of screaming faces crowded out the stars, but it was still silent. I remember saying, very calmly, "Am I dead?"

To this day, I hate crowds, have trouble enjoying concerts, sit with my back to the wall whenever possible, and sometimes have seizures if I've forgotten my medicine. What I don't have anymore is the hatred and sick stomach every time I open the pill bottle.

Although there was never any indictment or conviction, and I cannot say anyone's name without slander, I know in my heart who it is. I know this not because of facts, or evidence (although there are both). I know it because I must have a person to fill the picture. Just or unjust, there was communication there, and he and I have a lifelong bond made with one swing of a hammer. I don't know him, probably have never met him. But we have a relationship that cannot be destroyed, that of victim and attacker.

I no longer have anger towards my attacker. I don't hate him, and I don't think he should be punished. I know the role of victim, and I have gone through the process of anger and hate and understanding. Of all the injuries I received, it was the hate that was most damaging, and it was self-inflicted, outwardly directed. I can't blame anyone else for choosing hate over forgiveness, but I can proudly take responsibility for surviving the process and changing.

Through that experience and the perspective I have gained from working with juvenile offenders, it has become obvious that our current view of justice is much too limited. Of course, no one likes the complicated answers; they are difficult to implement on a vast scale. And, though we all may have the potential for being just, some will always remain dedicated to hate, and anger.

It seems past time to realize that if we want true justice, for victims and criminals alike, then we must create it before the crime, and be vigilant that we are not substituting vengeance for justice.

Patrick Allen is currently a teacher at Camp E-Ma-Chamee, an Eckerd Wilderness Education facility located in the Florida panhandle. Previous to the teaching position, he served for nearly two years as a counselor at the facility, where he lived in a residential group therapy environment, providing counseling, direct care and instruction to a diverse group of children with a variety of emotional, learning, and developmental disabilities. He has directed a gamut of experiential wilderness activities, including extended canoe trips, backpacking trips, and adventure ropes course activities. He received a Bachelors degree in Journalism from the University of Texas at Austin in 1995. Mr. Allen came to the Eckerd system with approximately six years of prior experience in experiential education.

PAMELA K. WITHROW
"Why Cognitive Restructuring"

In little more than 20 years the field of corrections has come full-circle on the issue of programming for offenders. Until the 1970's, most professionals in the field at least paid lip service to the notion that their primary aim was the rehabilitation of those sentenced to their care. Then a scholar named Robert Martinson concluded—or more accurately was widely claimed to have concluded—that so far as rehabilitation programs are concerned, "nothing works." While corrections agencies kept most of their prisoner education programs, which some studies showed as having value, many other treatment programs were dropped or curtailed, and prisons came largely to be regarded as human warehouses. But over time the recognition grew that separation of the prisoner from the public is not an adequate goal, since most prisoners will be out in a few years, and that releasing an educated but still criminally-oriented person does the community no favor.

So we in corrections are returning to the belief that we have a responsibility to try to help prisoners change for the better, but we now understand that this involves much more than teaching or preaching. Criminal behavior will not be abandoned so long as criminal patterns of thinking and viewing the world are retained. To this end, some in the field are now adopting a variety of "cognitive programs" which offer offenders an opportunity to change the way they think, with the goal of changing how they behave.

These cognitive programs are usually divided into two types—*cognitive skills training* and *cognitive restructuring*. To describe the former somewhat simplistically, it operates from the premise that learning social skills—apologizing, negotiating, or introducing oneself, for example—will cause the offender to change his thought processes related to interpersonal relations: that social skill training will result in a change from criminal thinking to pro-social thinking. (The premise of all cognitive work is that thinking drives behavior, so change in thinking will result in behavioral change.)

Cognitive restructuring, however, is the effort with which I am most familiar, and the one in use at the Michigan Reformatory where I've been the warden for about eleven years. It was selected because the facility houses young adult prisoners, most of whom are first timers, and it was thought that a change effort would be most likely to be effective with individuals relatively early in their criminal careers. We initiated this program for two reasons: first, prisoners wanted something which would help them avoid future criminal behavior (they phrased this as wanting "programs, not warehousing"), and second, I thought such a program might help staff see themselves as having a role beyond merely keeping the lid on, their addressing the problem of burn-out.

Let's look first at the prisoners' issue: in Michigan, as in many other states, newly arrived prisoners go through a reception process where their problems are diagnosed and programs are recommended to address these needs. Academic and vocational training programs are often prescribed, as are therapies to address substance abuse or mental health problems. Most facilities also offer recreational and religious programming and some include music or other arts and crafts.

So a prison sentence may include a complete blueprint for self improvement. The problem is that unless the thought processes which actually drive criminality are addressed, prisoners prepare to leave our facilities well-educated, healthy, religious, work-ready crooks. Parole Boards are then faced with the dilemma of telling offenders, who have completed all the reception-prescribed efforts, that they will not be paroled because they still present a risk to the public—a risk which exists because the attitudes and beliefs which permitted the prisoner to rape, rob or kill are still operating. These thinking processes, while they do present some danger to prison workers, usually are not harmful in the strictly-managed prison environment; but back in the community an unchanged parolee will often commit new crimes rather quickly.

As for the program's benefits for staff, these are two-fold: first, staff can use the techniques for change in improving their own lives. Self-reports indicate cognitive processes have been used to stop smoking, improve interpersonal communication in a marriage, lose weight and change exercise patterns. And the program can indeed be effective in reducing staff burn-out. I've frequently observed a phase which occurs about five to seven years into the careers of persons who have elected to remain corrections officers: the employee becomes sour, depressed, cynical and often either hostile or apathetic. This comes, I think, from the recognition that he or she has nearly 20 more years to do in this job dealing with offenders who have many of the same characteristics as immature adolescents. What had seemed to be a promising career now looks more like a sentence. But since the hours, pay and benefits are pretty good, and half a pension is already invested, the employee elects to plod on with minimal job satisfaction. Involvement in a cognitive restructuring program can provide such employees with new meaning in prison work. In a few cases it may spark return to college and a renewed interest in promotional opportunities. At a minimum, it offers variety in what is otherwise a rather routine work day.

So these are some of the things a cognitive restructuring program can do, but what exactly *is* a cognitive restructuring program? As practiced at the Michigan Reformatory, it involves three phases, and all prisoner participants and most staff facilitators have volunteered to take part. The program (termed **STP**, an acronym for **S**trategies for **T**hinking **P**roductively) is introduced by explaining the concepts basic to the cognitive approach: thinking controls behavior; all people have attitudes and beliefs (which differ for different people); and repetitive thoughts become automatic cycles. It is further explained that changing thinking requires auditing thoughts, and that change is hard work which cannot be imposed by others. Prisoners must want to change, must choose to change, and must put forth individual effort to make initial changes and then continue their efforts over time to ensure these changes become part of a new approach to life.

The program depends heavily on the concepts of criminal thinking developed by Yokelson and Samenow. One of the first steps of Phase I is to give prisoners the list of 36 criminal thinking errors developed by these authors, and ask them for their own thoughts about the list. It is interesting that invariably most of the discussion which ensues does not have to do with whether the thinking errors are properly described, but rather with whether they are in fact *criminal.* After all, from the offender's point of view, everybody thinks like that. A few of the most common, and most dangerous, thinking errors follow:

> Victim Stance—When the criminal is held accountable for his irresponsible actions, he blames others and portrays himself as a victim.
>
> Energy—The criminal's high level of mental activity is directed to a flow of ideas as to what would make life more interesting and exciting.
>
> Anger—The criminal way of life is to respond angrily to anything he interprets as opposing what he wants for himself. Anger is a major way of controlling people and situations.
>
> Pride—Criminal pride is an extremely high evaluation of oneself—the idea that one is better then others, even when this is clearly not the case.
>
> Failure to Consider Injury to Others—The criminal's life involves extensive injury to those around him, but he does not view himself as injuring others. When held accountable, he regards himself as the injured party.
>
> Ownership—When a criminal wants something that belongs to someone else, it is as good as his. He feels perfectly justified in getting his way, and views people as pawns or checkers, waiting to be dealt with as he wishes.

Prisoners meet in group sessions to work on changing criminal thinking; in the group, their progress is supported by the other members. The work of a Phase II group is to listen to a thinking report presented by a member and to ask the member questions designed to help him understand the thinking which supported the behavior described in the report. The entire 1-hour session is devoted to a single thinking report. Following the session, the facilitators document and evaluate participation of the group members as well as that of the presenter.

A thinking report is structured as follows:

•A brief *description* of a specific incident where the prisoner got into trouble (or could have if caught).

•A listing of all the *thoughts* associated with this event. Prisoners are often prompted to "run a tape" of the event in their mind to recall specific thoughts.

•A listing of the *feelings* associated with the event. This sometimes prompts additional thoughts, or permits participants to frame questions if there seem to be no thoughts related to a particular emotion.

•A sentence describing the *attitude* supporting thinking or behavior during the event. Sometimes there are multiple sentences.

•A sentence stating a *belief* supporting the thinking or behavior during the event. This often includes "should" or "ought" terminology.

•Sometimes, *physical responses* are also listed. As with emotions, recalling these responses may trigger additional thoughts or suggest ideas to others for useful questions to ask the presenter.

Each participant will take a turn being the presenter, so there is some reciprocal value to being active; also, because some thinking errors are so common, participants may come to recognize their own errors while pressing another to clarify his thinking. Ultimately, prisoners select target behaviors they want to change and present thinking reports related to that behavior. Patterns, or cycles, of thinking can then be identified, leading to the design of interventions to prevent the cycle from reaching completion.

When participants first enter Phase II, they are given the format for a "relapse prevention plan." They are encouraged to work on this throughout Phase II, and before they can move to Phase III they must present a thinking report to the group about the offense which brought them to prison and present a completed relapse prevention plan directed toward that behavior. Most participants are involved in Phase II for nearly two years before moving to Phase III. Phase II participants live together in a small (75 bed) housing unit.

Once target behaviors are identified, prisoners are asked to "journal" daily during the remainder of Phase II. Journal reports are similar to thinking reports in structure, but they focus on efforts to *change* thinking in selected areas. The change effort may include "thought stopping" (cutting off or redirecting thinking) or bringing in thoughts about how the target behavior will harm loved ones, or lead to sanctions, and may even involve replacing old attitudes and beliefs with new ones. Each prisoner is assigned a "journal partner" who reviews the journal with him each week and helps him continue the process of identifying cycles and evaluating interventions. The journal partner will also help design journal projects which focus on changing attitudes and beliefs.

Journals are a way prisoners can track the success or failure of various strategies. They also provide staff with a measure of the participant's willingness to produce a sustained, focused, effort. When the prisoner feels he has some level of control over a targeted behavior, journaling will permit him or her to move on and address another behavior.

Each quarter, a "treatment team" is held for each Phase II participant. During this session, the facilitators, journal partner, and an officer working the housing unit, will talk with the prisoner about their perceptions of his progress (or lack thereof) in addressing target behaviors—those behaviors the prisoner has said he wants to change. Sometimes lack of effort is so clear that the prisoner is asked to leave the program; if he then claims he wants to stay, a brief probationary period may be offered, during which he'll be monitored for performance on identified objectives. Occasionally a prisoner will be so deficient in the ability to monitor his own thinking, or to present this to the group, that he will be terminated. However, literacy is not a requirement: many participants are low-functioning or involved in special education efforts, yet their ability to communicate their thoughts is unimpaired.

If the correctional system is willing to parole or let prisoners go to community residential placement upon the completion of Phase II, Phase III can be a community-based activity. This is not an option for Reformatory prisoners, many of whom are serving life or long indeterminate sentences; Phase III is conducted at the facility, but outside of the supportive Phase II unit. This part of the program continues the journaling effort and offers weekly group meetings which focus on participants' change efforts. Unlike the thinking report groups in Phase II, these are more interactive sessions, with members offering encouragement and support as participants continue to struggle with the difficult task of self change. Since Phase III involves demonstrating pro-social behavior in a prison environment, participants are doubly challenged.

Does the program really work? The Director of our department, Kenneth L. McGinnis, has challenged us to show that participation results either in reduced misconduct within the prison, or in reduced recidivism as demonstrated by fewer parolees returning with new felony sentences. Grand Valley State University has accepted the charge to research this. Although I did not think that participation in Phase I alone would result in behavioral change, the researchers, led by Dr. Agnes Baro, elected to include a look at this possibility.

Dr. Baro's preliminary research findings (comparing Phase I participants to those in other voluntary self-help programs) have shown a decrease in Phase I participants' misconduct rates, statistically significant when measured by length of segregation stay and in the number of "Disobeying a Direct Order" charges—the most commonly committed misconduct throughout the Michigan DOC. Since the agency automatically adds a week to the release dates of offenders found guilty of misconduct in a given month, expansion of this program department-wide could provide a savings in the cost of housing prisoners. And since high security beds are more expensive, any reduction in segregation stays also has a financial benefit. More time will have to elapse before we can know whether parolees who have gone through the program will commit fewer crimes as a result, but it is at least a reasonable hope that this will be the case as well.

So, with all this good news, is there a down side? Of course. Prisons operate best when there are routines. Change is viewed with suspicion. Anything which appears to be for the benefit of prisoners and which requires additional effort from staff will get close scrutiny and is likely to see some resistance. The Reformatory is the oldest prison in our system, and staff attitudes sometimes reflect that history: "It's just another program;" "You're coddling convicts;" or, "It may work for staff, but prisoners won't be able to use it," ("too dumb, too rigid, too steeped in the criminal subculture"). In addition, participating staff may be accused of "being in bed with the administration."

Then too, since the STP unit is in the oldest part of the prison, and the cells are smaller than those elsewhere, a small day-room with a microwave oven and color TV was created as some compensation, and a private yard with a vegetable garden was developed in a former outdoor exercise area. Even though most staff agree that personal change is one of the hardest tasks any individual can undertake, there is still grumbling about these "perks" for Phase II prisoners.

These are just a few of the obstacles we're still battling. The case managers who deliver much of the program are entry level professionals who are constantly being promoted, leaving shortages in these positions. Work loads increase with these shortages, so cognitive group work competes with the demands of other required activities.

Physical plant issues have also had to be addressed—lack of group meeting rooms, for example. And scheduling was a problem. Since prisoner participants work and go to school mostly during the day when staff facilitators are also most available, arrangements for release from assignments had to be made.

With these negatives, why keep doing STP? Because of the payoff: **We have seen both staff and prisoners grow and change in a positive direction as a result of their involvement in this effort.** Of the original four staff who went to Colorado to learn about cognitive work, I'm the only one remaining at the facility (and I've already reached my career goal); the rest have been promoted. Of staff currently working in the program, one has achieved her Master's degree, two officers have returned to school to pursue bachelor's degrees, a very active participant was promoted at the facility, and others have been promoted elsewhere. One even credits the program for leading to a move to a supervisory position in the Florida DOC—our loss and their gain. Many officers are finding their work more rewarding and look forward to coming to work, rather than dreading it. Staff members who once were terrified of public speaking can now talk about **STP** to large groups, with only mild butterflies. So many staff commented during training sessions that this information should be available to students that two employees have formed a company to promote cognitive work in the schools, in an attempt to forestall development of a "next generation" of criminals.

And we see definite improvement among some of the prisoner participants—in one man, for example, who had such well-developed cheek muscles from clenching his teeth that he looked like he had marbles in his cheeks, and who had hardly ever gone for a six-month period without a segregation stay. This man used STP to get a handle on his anger and was able to qualify for reduced custody. And in another who convinced the Parole Board he had changed and finally made parole.

With some, the change may be less complete, but may yet have impact in the future. For example, a prisoner who manipulated everyone all the time was finally able to see this and know when he was doing it, even though the manipulation eventually forced a move from the prison. And the one who started to get a clear look at himself and bailed out of the program will probably be back, because he didn't like what he was seeing and will eventually decide to work on change.

At least we think he will, because, as we tell all the participants, "You have three choices: change (with the potential to live a positive and productive life—even if that life is in prison), stay the same (with all the consequences you've experienced so far), or die." Those are the only choices, and they are the same choices all humans have. And really, the impetus for offender change is that their experience of prison, what is happening *right now*, is painful to endure and part of a cycle they can only gain from breaking.

While we do not yet have the research findings from Phase II, I'm confident they will be similar to the outcomes demonstrated in an earlier program in Vermont. Those showed that cognitive restructuring is an effective change mechanism both in prison and when paroled. But in the interim we will continue to deliver this program because offenders need to know they have the option of personal change and that the tools for it are available. And we will continue it also so that staff who want to provide more than the functions of basic security have the opportunity to help offenders grow out of criminal thinking and behavior. Since almost all prisoners eventually return to the community, I know of no better way in which we in corrections can contribute to our basic responsibility for public protection.

An expanded article on this program is available; see page 370.

For information on starting a cognitive intervention program, the lessons in Phase I, and the structure for Phases II and III, are contained in the Options manual available through the Information Center at the National Academy of Corrections.

Since 1986, Pam Withrow has administered the 1234-bed Michigan Reformatory, in Ionia, Michigan, which houses nearly 1000 adult males. Her facility offers both segregation and protection housing and serves as an initial placement for young offenders (17-26) serving longer sentences, as well as for youthful prisoners who have been disruptive in lower custody. For the three years prior to assuming her current position, she was the warden at a 400 bed prison. Since joining the Michigan DOC in 1976, she has worked as a Housing Deputy at a State Prison, Administrative Assistant, Prison Camp Supervisor, Analyst in the MDOC research section, and Prison Counselor in the Camp Program.

PAT SNYDER
"A Team Approach, A Holistic Approach"

The North Carolina Department of Corrections believes treatment for inmates will benefit all citizens of the state. The Mary Frances Center (MFC) has taken on the challenge of validating that belief by establishing the first program of its kind for the treatment of female inmates in the State of North Carolina. Not only is the center treating addiction, but genetic and environmental issues surrounding the female inmate population are also being addressed.

The Center is a Total Quality management (TQM) facility, incorporating TQM in its therapeutic community and business functions alike. TQM helps dispel the myth that stereotypical treatment providers and correctional administrators are at opposite ends when it comes to treating inmates. Quarterly stakeholder meetings are held to provide a forum to discuss short/long range goals. This meeting consists of representatives from the Department of Corrections, Divisions of Prisons, Parole Commission, DART, and Key Staff from Fountain Correctional Center for Women. This team approach, focusing on a partnership between the treatment field and correctional field, is helping to teach the women how to take responsibility in their recovery. Responsible decision making is an essential skill in guiding the women to think through a process instead of acting impulsively or reactively. Many women have become trapped in the role of helpless victim as a means of manipulating the system or as a means of not taking responsibility for their needs. This type of thinking on the part of an inmate breeds behavior which will eventually prove to be destructive. MFC teaches each woman to take responsibility for her needs and actions by providing the women with the skills and staff to deal with the problem, rather than running in and fixing the problem for them. For MFC this involves choosing appropriate strategies that will produce positive outcomes for the individual and the community as a whole. The MFC emphasis is placed on taking control of your life in a responsible way, no matter what created your problem, be it addiction, genetics, or environment.

The Mary Frances Center's program is an integrated model incorporating addiction education and treatment with specialized components devoted to enhancing growth through work and study programs. This integrated 365 day model provides individualized levels of care for each woman that is flexible in its continuum of care. The program focus is on the whole person. Other components of the program include focus groups, lectures, education and co-dependency treatment (our belief is relapse is untreated co-dependency). AA/NA meetings are scheduled daily on-site and off-site. Program goals are to abstain from mood altering drugs and establish an effective lifestyle of recovery, and to pursue a higher level of education and job skills.

The program is designed to offer several levels of treatment. The first is the most structured, this level being Assessment and Evaluation, normally lasting 30 days. This includes intensive treatment for addiction.

There are three levels of continuing care; the first is called Level I and is 12 weeks long. During Level I, Vocational Rehabilitation, continuing care groups and family education are added to therapy. Level II, also 12 weeks, offers specialized groups and aftercare groups. Off-site programs and work assignments are introduced at this level. Level III is the last 12 weeks and provides an opportunity for off-site unsupervised activities and family visits.

As each woman achieves a new level of care, she earns extra privileges and more freedom. Level reduction is built into this model. When a woman cannot handle a less restrictive level, she is stepped down to a more structured level of care, and given an opportunity to evaluate her recovery by focusing on the problems that confront her and how she was not able to cope in a healthy way. Women are responsible for developing a plan of action that will assist them in returning back to a less restrictive level of care. This flexibility is a necessary part in developing a strong foundation of recovery and skills to assist them when they leave.

The Mary Frances Center Family and Significant Other Program is another component within the MFC program, to meet the needs of women who have lived in an environment where addiction was present or dysfunction was a lifestyle. Patients and family/significant others will identify familial issues and concerns while addressing personal growth and recovery. The family program works on discharge planning relative to familial issues, and on establishing new behaviors within their relationships with family/significant others that are not enabling. Family Day is held monthly for selected patients. This gives the women time to bond with their children as they are making significant changes in their lives.

We have put together a team of social agencies, local businesses, community leaders and a variety of volunteers. Everyone involved has been educated and trained on our mission and vision. Community support and team building have shown how unity improves quality of services in all areas. This is demonstrated by the energy, professionalism and dedication of those involved on our team. All our resources are enthusiastic about our partnership to help the women and their children. They know they are making a difference in reducing crime and lowering recidivism in our state.

YWCA in Rocky Mount offers a course in survival skill training that prepares the women in several areas. Many women repeatedly share how effective this course is in helping them to develop their community resources and aftercare plan.

Local businesses report women from the MFC are outstanding employees. This is validated by several business leaders writing recommendation letters for these women.

Vocational Rehabilitation assists the women in developing job skills and building confidence in their abilities. They report to us that VR offices across the state are impressed with the women's attitudes, their positive assertiveness, and their dependability.

Prison Ministry supports our mission in bringing assistance on a regular basis for the women and their children. Local churches within 60 miles provide bible study, church services, and a number of other services to the women. They report it is a pleasure to feel they are accepted as apart of our mission.

Recovery volunteers come from as far away as 150 miles to assist the women in their recovery. They provide in-house meetings, take women to local meetings, assist them in recovery contacts, and sponsor individuals when asked. These volunteers assist us in developing resources across the state.

We have over 150 community sponsors that are active at MFC. They provide a number of services, such as tutoring, crafts, entertainment, etc.

East Carolina University and local colleges have become a part of our team. Interns receive training and a valuable experience that will serve them and their future clients well. Exchange training programs assist in the development of our program. Edgecombe Community College in Tarboro provides GED and college courses on and off site. Several women have continued their studies after leaving MFC. They report classes here stimulated them and taught them they can accomplish educational goals in their lives.

SUMMARY

We have a national crisis on our hands. No program or agency alone can make the impact we can if we unite. We have to face the challenge together or we will pay a dear price in the future. It is extremely vital for community agencies, business leaders, and citizens to join this endeavor. Not only can a difference be made in the lives of these women, but in future generations to come. We here at MFC have taken on that challenge by putting together a complete team which is invested in making a difference in the future for us all.

Pat Snyder is the President and CEO of the Mary Frances Corporation in North Carolina. She has worked as a counselor in the areas of substance abuse, family therapy, women's issues, obesity and co-dependency. She has over 29 years of experience and service work with Alcoholics Anonymous, Al-Anon and Alateen, including over 20 years with the Norfolk Naval Alcohol Rehabilitation Center.

BRIAN BALDWIN
"Project Hope to Abolish the Death Penalty"

The name alone defines what it's all about. Hope is about becoming a positive person. Hope is about facing the world and asking forgiveness. Hope is about letting the world know that just because we are on death row, we are not wild animals. Most of us are not innocent of murder, but there are some that are innocent. Guilty or innocent, we stand as one against the death penalty.

Project Hope was started because one guy had been given a death sentence, and this one guy started asking for help; it touched a lot of us. We wanted to help him. Most of us had been here for five or more years, and we lived under the code that "Each man must die alone, like a man."

Five of us decided that as a group we were not like that. We cared for each other. We lived each day together. We shared, laughed, and cried together, so why were we allowing our brothers to die without putting up a fight? Why were we as a group not fighting the death penalty? Were we accepting the state's opinion that we are the scum of the earth? Did we think we deserved to die? The answer was "no" to all of that, so The Committee of Five was started. Word was spread on death row that the guys were trying to do something about the death penalty, so others wanted to join and they were welcomed. The five guys later decided to have a vote on the name of the organization, thus Project Hope to Abolish the Death Penalty was born. I never thought much about actually joining, because I felt like capital punishment was just too big to fight. But the more the guys talked about trying to use collectively our little knowledge of the law, the better it sounded to me. Then I was asked to attend a meeting. I liked what I heard because the guys were being completely honest about their feelings, and making it clear that nobody deserved the death sentence regardless of their conviction. Murder's wrong. It was wrong for the defendant to kill someone, but it is also wrong for the state to kill the defendant.

There are many benefits to having an organization like Hope on death row. First of all, the inmates are not a threat to the officers or other inmates. We meet and we talk. We look for the positive side of life. We study law and apply it to our cases. Our main goal is to abolish the death penalty, and we understand this requires a lot of help from the outside, so we encourage our families and friends to get involved.

When a person comes to death row, he comes in here angry and depressed. He thinks nobody could possibly understand him or care about him. The inmate is put in a very small, 5x8 cell. He's not allowed to go outside with the group for 90 days, so he goes out alone in a dog run, maybe 6 by 9 feet, for one hour. That means he spends 23 hours alone in the cell, stuck with all the negative thoughts he brought in here with him. But since Project Hope was formed things have changed. We speak to the guys as they arrive and we encourage them. We let them know they are not alone and they are not the person the media and court has made them out to be. We let them know that they do not deserve to die.

When I first got here, I was a real negative person. It felt like the whole world was against me. I was not in contact with my family. I was a fresh 19 year old, from out of state and didn't know anyone. The officers were brutal, and my young mind told me I had no fear and didn't care about anything or anybody. But every time some guy was about to be executed it hurt me, because I knew them all, shaking their hands for the last time. It was taking a lot out of me. So when Hope was started, it gave me a chance to let the others know that I really cared about them and that I wasn't a bad person.

Everybody wanted to find a way to end the death penalty and that was what I wanted to do too. Hope has given me encouragement and the positive outlook that death row inmates need. Because we knew we would never get positive media attention, we started our own newsletter. This publication, *On Wings of Hope*, has readers all over the country and even around the world. We tell the public what it's like to be on death row; through it, they get to know us as human beings. In short, we are asking society to forgive us for our wrongs. We are asking people to stand up against the death penalty.

Hope is about learning to live without hate, learning to love regardless of the circumstances, and looking for the positive side of every situation. First, we learn to respect all life. We think about the victims and their families, the pain their families are going through, missing them. We learn that we don't have the right to get angry when the victim's family calls for the death sentence for us. All we can do is hope that they will come to understand that killing someone else is not going to make things right. Our families will be suffering just like they are suffering. We have families and *we* are loved too. I was born poor, black, and loved just as much as anybody else.

I look around and I can see the changes in the other guys since they have joined Hope. The officers here say they would rather work on death row than in any other part of this prison. When it comes time for someone to be executed, I have seen officers decide they can't work here any more. They can't work around the guys and get to know them, then participate in killing them.

We in Project Hope have learned to express our feelings, at least some feelings about seeing our brothers executed. We suffer mental anguish, but we are not given therapy. We have to console each other, even to the point of crying together or hugging.

In Hope meetings, we discuss all of these matters, from top to bottom. We also talk about the mental state a person was in at the time of a murder. I'm convinced that all murders were committed by insane people. That can easily be argued, but I stand firm in my belief just from associating with the guys here, listening to them talk, watching them daily, and wondering, "Did he really do what he was convicted of?" I see a totally different person than the convicted "criminal" that came in here. I see guys that have learned to talk their problems out. I see guys that will admit when they are wrong. I see guys that cry when someone else is hurt or killed. I see guys that will apologize when they have done wrong. It really is something to see a guy on death row apologize then give a hug to the person he has offended. I know because I have witnessed it. I have had to apologize and hug some guys, and it made me feel better.

We have studied the statistics of the death penalty, and have come to recognize that the system is racist, sexist and aristocratic. Per capita, the black race has been hit the hardest. But if you are poor, whether black or white, and accused of murder, you stand a good chance of being tried for capital murder. Of course it depends on who you are accused of killing. It depends on your status in the city or town you live in, too. We in Hope look at the percentage of Americans that support the death penalty. According to the media, it's 70% or more. Of that 70% we wonder how many realize that they are supporting something that could possibly affect their lives one day. Most Americans are poor. The majority of guys here now supported the death penalty, and their families did too. But now they realize that the politicians they were voting for were talking about executing their own family members, not just someone on the real poor side of town, not just someone of a different race, not just the people that were accused of multiple murders and who showed no remorse.

In Project Hope to Abolish the Death Penalty, we study all of these things. Maybe it's because we are forced to think about them, nevertheless it's facts we are dealing with as well as feelings, and I'm proud to be a part of it. I'm proud to say I'm against the death penalty under all circumstances. The death penalty is never right. It does not deter crime. It deters the love and respect for human life.

Project Hope to Abolish the Death Penalty is one of many voices for speaking out against capital punishment. Our families and friends have seen the big changes we as individuals have made. They support us and fight at our sides, because they know our hearts. They know we are not the brutes the media wants society to think we are. They know we are not the heartless murderers the politicians and district attorneys say we are.

Since being a member of Hope, I have met the best of friends, people that visit me and accept me as I am. I have learned a lot from these friends and introduced them to Hope. They have told me they too have learned from Hope and its members. Having an organization like Hope is a plus for the inmates on death row as well as society, because some of us will be released from death row, and we will have a positive attitude. And for those of us who will not be released, Hope has meant that we have learned to work together as a team and to make the best of our situation. Beyond that, it has meant that we could support each other, as well as our families and loved ones, through the hard times. It has been a major step toward our own personal rehabilitation. Furthermore, the members of Hope, inside and outside, have taken a stand together against capital punishment. We encourage you to make this same stand, not because you know someone on death row, but because it is morally wrong to take a human life, no matter who does it. The remorse we feel for our mistakes is with us every day. Because of Project Hope, we have learned to express this remorse, even as we join together, united against the death penalty.

Brian Baldwin has been on Death Row for 20 years. He is the Inmate Editor for Wings of Hope, the newsletter of Project Hope to Abolish the Death Penalty. He is currently taking a Paralegal course, in order to help himself and other Death Row inmates.

DAWNING

First there was darkness,
Deep, black, enveloping, sweetness,
Barely visible were pinpricks of hope ...

Then, they, too, fade into greynesses.
Finally, the rich, velvety cloth of night
Encompasses all of the world.

The world sits waiting, like a bride at the altar,
Waiting, sweating, fidgeting—with hidden anxieties,
Seconds slip by like hours, or years—in darkness.

Then, with a touch of grace and glory,
The horn of victory sounds, as the sun's rays sweep across the sky,
The darkness is again limited to shadows before the greatness of the dawn.

Yet, how many souls slip away in the last seconds of the night?
Their minds heady with the scent of the sweat of their fear,
Do they cry as they despair, "Please God: let there be light."

Karl Chamberlain
Death Row, Texas

EDUCATION AND VOCATIONAL TRAINING

Texas

October 24, 1996

"They let a lot of guys here go work on the cotton farms for real paychecks all day. I was hoping some farmer would come in here looking for more help. I don't know if they would let me,but I'd sure do it. It's been 6 years, 8 months since I earned a dollar. $5/hour sounds like a fortune when you're in jail.

"Prisoners are pretty much like slaves in Texas, since there is no pay for working in prison. Texas is the only state that pays nothing for work. They say your pay is 'good time.' So why ain't I having a good time?"

January 28, 1997

"Last Thursday I worked at the Lynn Co. Stock Show. Yes, that was me shoveling poop from the arena between classes. They had cows, sheep, goats and pigs. It was fun. It's amazing to watch a 50 lb. kid lugging a 1400 lb. calf around the show ring.

"I wonder if professional 'scoopers' belong to a union? I'm considering this as a possible career later, when I'm released. Hmm. Actually it's a humbling experience. Everyone is watching you while waiting for the next bunch of goats and likely judging your speed, technique, thoroughness, etc.

"Well, if they'll let me go to Maine, I'll apply for the job opening as secretary/laborer. I'll need higher wages than your husband is currently receiving, though. My office skills are superb; I can type close to 25 wpm with only one finger, answer telephones, greet visitors, and make coffee. My computer skills and short-hand abilities are non-existent. So you'll have an old-fashioned office. I predict computers will be a short-lived fad anyway. Sort of like airplanes, cars and Coca-Cola."

MY HOUSE

In my house
        there's the whispering spires
        of evergreens,
        the coiling belts of pine
        that kneel in supplication before
        the chiseled visages and sleeping dinosaurs
        of mountain ranges,
        of altars raised to the liquid cobalt
        and cotton-flecked azure skies.
My house
    is warm
        with the strains of jazz
        drifting, wafting, from
        stereo speakers hidden
        in another room;
        with the sparkle of candles
        the silk of her touch
        the splash of light
        in her emerald and plunging eyes
        by the rose and ivory
        of her smile.
In my house
        I have a sink and a commode
        a steel bunk
        a steel table
        a shelf
        photographs
        smiles and memories of
        other people's lives
        taped and fading to a pale blue wall
        growing dingy from tobacco smoke
In my house.

Scott A. Antworth
Maine State Prison

"My House" is excerpted from Trapped Under Ice: A Death Row Anthology (Biddle Publishing Company.

SCOTT A. ANTWORTH
"Higher Learning"

I ran into Jason on the prison's street a few days back. He was carrying his obligatory Maine State Prison coffee mug and heading for the Rec Yard. Jason's a young guy, still a kid really, but he's already got in a few years here at the Concrete Hilton. Like a lot of us, he was barely out of school and only just beginning the business of living when he earned himself a stretch in here.

"Antworth," he says, "I heard you graduated. Good going."

Actually, I wrapped up my B.A. a year ago, but he'd only heard about it recently. He shrugs when I ask what's up with him; after getting a few semesters in with the University of Maine, which offers classes here at MSP, he fell away. He's got time, I remind him (like any of us need reminding), and after so promising a start, he ought to get back at it while the getting's good.

"I think about it sometimes," he says. "But like you say, I still got time."

Talking about nothing, waiting for our cues to go our separate ways, I'm convinced I'll not see him in the Education Department again. I'm enough of an optimist to hope he will return to his studies, but enough of a realist to know that the longer he stays away, the more unlikely it will be.

I don't envy him. I was lucky to be able to get as far as I did when I could. The college program here has been changing through these recent years and Jason faces far greater obstacles than I did back when I had only a few semesters behind me.

The Education Department in Thomaston, the Maine State Prison, is now in its fortieth year. It began with one teacher and a pile of donated, out-dated textbooks. A local high school carried the early students on their rolls and awarded them their diplomas. By the 1960s, MSP had its GED program, and to date more than 600 inmates have been awarded their General Equivalency Diplomas. Not bad for a prison that has a median population of 400 men.

Operating largely autonomously—which is to say, without much in the way of state funding—the Education Department offers basic literacy, GED preparation, a computer lab, and college classes, among other educational programs. While instructors and volunteers have been utilized through the years, the Education Department is composed of only two staff members. That the program runs as efficiently and superlatively as it does is testimony to their efforts.

One of these staff members, Dave MacMillan, began working at MSP shortly before the college program was introduced in 1972. He is currently the Education Department head and recalls when the University of Maine began offering classes in the prison. "It was tough going," he remembers. "The program was polluted by a lot of Vietnam-era vets who enrolled only for the money." These students, who were all covered by federal Pell Grants, found enrollment, then lack of participation, an easy way to pocket their military benefit checks. "Seven hundred dollars a semester could buy a lot of dope in those days. Those were wild and woolly times in Thomaston," MacMillan says, shaking his head. "It took a long time to weed those guys out and make the program what we envisioned."

By the 1980's, the VA caught on and denied eligibility to inmate veterans being schooled on Pell Grant money. In 1994 it was the Pell Grants themselves that got axed, with disastrous effects.

That there is a need for quality education in prison is a point few could debate. While no formal study has been done here, as educational screening is not mandatory, an informal assessment shows that 20% of Thomaston's inmates can be considered at least functionally illiterate. A further 8% read below high school level.

An illiteracy rate well in excess of this country's average, but more reflective of the nation's lower economic strata, from which the vast majority of prison inmates come, is telling. The same social problems found in greater proportions amongst America's "honest poor" (as opposed to prison inmates) are mirrored in the populations of its prisons: histories of substance abuse and broken homes, crime, lower educational achievement, an encroaching hopelessness. The latter, which is rarely addressed in any substantive way, is an essential point neglected at everyone's peril. By ignoring the need for hope, we teach our inmates that this existence is all they should expect. Among those employed by this country's vast corrections systems, precious few work to instill that hope, the spark that may well make the difference.

For Betty O'Brien, MSP's only on-staff teacher, Thomaston proved a pleasant surprise. She found in the prison a position for which she was desperately needed and students who were responsive to her. Betty has an uncanny ability to make her students feel their progress is important to her—and it is. As a result, they instinctively want to please her, to not let her down, and in so doing they begin to discover their own potential.

"If they get nothing else," Dave MacMillan says of the programs offered by his department, "education teaches these guys that there's more to life than being on the inside."

I came to see the Education Department and the prison chapel where most of the live courses were taught as an island. They occupy the same corridor, one floor above the prison's wood industries shop. Clean, air-conditioned, its floors waxed, Education's a sharp contrast to the shadowy, dirty, malodorous cellblocks. The tumult of crashing cage doors and profanity belong to a reality several shades removed from what one finds on that second floor, where intrusion is the near-constant yowl of the wood shop's behemoth of a planer. Its whine can be heard from one side of the prison to the other—and certainly in Education, which is directly above it.

"Don't you find it annoying?" a Marine Biology instructor asked her students, crinkling her nose. "How can you concentrate?" The dozen or so convicts around her looked at each other and shrugged. They no longer notice the din. An Anthropology professor, on her first afternoon teaching in the prison and not knowing what to expect, was making a Herculean effort to conceal her alarm at being "abandoned" in a room full of convicts. She nearly came out of her Hush Puppies when the planer abruptly kicked in. Disarmed by the unexpected normalcy of these classes, the instructors always relaxed quickly enough. It should be noted that once Ms. Talansky settled in, and she did so by the end of that first session, she taught a hell of a class. Her students worked their butts off for those three credits.

No one should be faulted for being anxious their first time coming into the prison. It can be a foreboding place. Being escorted in and having all those doors slam shut behind you, each a reminder that you're now that much farther from polite society and free-world reality, can be intimidating. A recurrent theme, however, amongst those who work closely with us is that they're surprised at how normal most of us seem. Generally speaking, society hears the horror stories and sees the stereotypes, not the individuals who make up such populations as this. We laugh, we cry. We fret over our families and daily stresses. We dream. For the most part, we're men who've seen the failures and repugnance in our own lives and are working hard to reverse them. We do not forget where we come from. It is also true that we're not allowed to forget. We're all very aware of the stigmas attached to our lives, though sometimes the reminders come from unexpected quarters.

Several years ago, a psychology professor with whom I'd had three demanding classes decided he could no longer come into the prison to teach. Actually, his new wife decided that for him. Though he tried to convince her otherwise, and while he himself felt no threat in this environment, she was terrified he would suffer some horrible fate at the hands of his students.

More recently, an ITV instructor teaching Race and Culture Conflict (a class in prejudice, no less) telephoned Dave MacMillan, demanding that she be told for what crimes her Thomaston students had been convicted. She wasn't about to be teaching any sex offenders. Grudgingly, Dave consulted his roster.

"Let me see," he read, "Murder, murder, murder, murder. Nope, they're all killers. Is that acceptable?"

Apparently this did not offend her sensibilities too greatly as she allowed her class to continue. I should quickly add that the instructor in question was not representative of the UMA faculty, which has an impressive roster of first-rate educators. With few exceptions, professors and administrators alike are very supportive of their inmate-students.

Several instructors have returned time and again to teach in the prison. It's not uncommon for some of them to have four and five semesters of experience inside these walls, often teaching students who've attended every one of their classes. As the resources by which the college program was financed began vanishing, some of these instructors took to teaching independent and directed-study courses to classes as small as two or three inmates. These are not the classrooms in which UMA's already-underpaid instructors will get rich.

"I've taken away at least as much as I've given," UMA instructor Jaimee Colbert says. An award-winning author, she found her love for the written word reflected in some of her students. Aside from teaching more formal classes in communications, she has also facilitated two writing workshops here in the prison.

The first workshop, taught through the summer of 1993, resulted in the publication (through the prison industries' Print Shop) of a literary journal called *Rogue's Gallery*. In her forward to the journal, Colbert wrote, "...Hopelessness. This is a word that might ring synonymous with certain attitudes towards prison inmates. But I see the opposite. I see human beings who hit bottom and still have the courage, the hope that each small step they take will help them rise a little higher, move a little closer to functioning as valued and valuable citizens beyond these red brick walls. . . "

In 1993, Augusta's *Kennebec Journal* sent a reporter to do a story on Colbert's live class here, feeling there was a certain human interest quality to it. An intelligent, attractive woman teaching communications skills to a roomful of reprehensible convicts had, I'm sure he felt, all the possibilities of high drama. "If she is intimidated by her surroundings," he wrote, "it doesn't show. And her students appear to respect her so much that a visitor suspects they would defend her against any threat..."

Neither Jaimee nor her students thought much of that bit of sensationalist innuendo—nor could any of us envision an occasion when "defending her" would ever be necessary. That such teachers and volunteers are willing to come in here specifically to work with us is a lesson rarely lost on the prison population as a whole and never lost on the students. If anything, these instructors are treated with deference and exaggerated courtesy born of genuine gratitude and respect.

The threat of blood-thirsty inmates storming the chapel like the Visigoths is a peril that would play well in a B-movie. Classroom reality is the polar opposite. To be fair, this is a prison and ugly things do happen here sometimes—though the ugliest thing I've ever seen in Education was my final exam in Economics.

Through my time at UMA, which is to say the time I've spent in Thomaston as a UMA student, the University became more and more reliant on the Interactive Television (ITV) classroom, broadcasting live classes from UMA's home campus in Augusta to its nearly one hundred distant sites.

The Education Department knew an opportunity when they saw it. Before the advent of ITV, the college program had been hobbled to a degree by its own logistics; "live" courses had to have the University-required minimum of ten students and willing instructors had to be escorted through prison security. Classes had to be scheduled around the prison's existing and sacrosanct timetables. While television learning can never supplant the live interaction of a classroom, the program at Thomaston gained a greater variety and volume of classes it could offer. As its students were included in the rolls of the monitoring sites scattered across the state, the required minimum number of students was no longer an issue.

Actual enrollment has never deterred many inside these walls from sitting in on ITV classes in their cells. For two "jailhouse artist" friends of mine, neither of

UMA Instructor Jaimee Colbert shares a light moment with the author during Speaker-Audience Communication class at the Maine State Prison.

Photo courtesy of: Central Maine Newspapers/Mark Damon

whom were enrolled with UMA, a course in Art History became a Tuesday night ritual. On Wednesdays it was not uncommon to find these guys in the dust and clamor of the prison's Craft Shop, bracketed by equally-scruffy cons, discussing Jan Vermeer, Baroque architecture, or Claude Monet.

"No, no, you're wrong: Rembrandt's use of lighting is clearly Carravagesque..."

The curiosity which draws these inmates to occasionally "sit in" is very much akin to what drew the best of UMA's staff to teach in the first place: a thirst and appreciation for knowledge, to expand one's horizons, to learn and to share.

As with any system, misunderstandings are inevitable. With ITV, they're not limited to instructors and inmates. An Introductory French student on the Augusta campus became outraged to learn she could be seen by "those people" whenever the camera was turned on her class. Mortified that her beauty must be driving "those people" to all manner of lustfulness, she convinced the video technician to avoid her corner whenever the home site class was shown. It never occurred to her that "those people" were far too involved with trying to survive a language course taught on videotape to be frivolously enamored by her. I've seen the young lady in question. She flatters herself.

For the Thomaston inmates, "Interactive Television" was always a misnomer. There never was any true interaction. The courses presented were in fact videotapes of the live classes held the week before in Augusta, and broadcast over the prison's cable system. I took nearly half my courses from the privacy of my cell.

"Every cell is wired for cable," Dave MacMillan recently told a special tour group. "You could see all their eyes rolling over that one," he later told me. Hoping to ease their exasperation, he went on to explain that no public funds were used for this purpose; inmates supply their own televisions. The prison's Jaycee chapter wired the joint for cable twenty years ago. Satisfied that none of their tax dollars were spent supplying society's dregs with color televisions, the tour group moved on, unable to find fault in that particular bit of information—excepting, of course, that inmates are allowed TV's in the first place.

"How can you expect someone to want to stay out when they've got it as soft as they do?" was a question asked of a UMA professor in Criminal Justice, a former employee of the South Carolina Department of Corrections. To such veterans, it's an oft-repeated question asked in ignorance. "When's the last time you've seen the inside of a maximum-security prison?" he asked in response.

True enough. Those that tend to be the most outraged over such perceived amenities in places like this tend to be those who've never been on the inside of one.

"In here," MacMillan told the same tour group, "television is an important educational tool."

If one chooses to look at it in those terms, MSP has potentially hundreds of classrooms. Each cell has the capability of being used in that capacity—assuming, of course, that the inmate occupying that cell has a TV. Assuming, of course, that the inmate occupying that cell has the desire (and, now, the independent financial resources) to learn. For those inmates unable to afford their own television, ITV tapes can be viewed in the Education Department. For 90% of the college enrollees, however, the financial resources vanished with the Pell Grants and the 1994 Crime Bill.

"Don't know how your children will go to college?" the rhetorical question was asked time and again while the sweeping and ham-handed 1994 Crime Bill was being debated. "Send them to prison and they can get a college education for free!" Such detractors, worried as any parent would be over their children's education, thusly gave the impression that inmate students were only out for a free lunch rather than utilizing one of the few rehabilitative programs remaining to them. Financially-strapped inmates were just as eligible to receive educational assistance as their law-abiding and financially-strapped children. It was an abhorrent concept.

Eliminating Pell Grant eligibility for prison inmates was a rider on the 1994 Crime Bill. While ultra-conservatives such as North Carolina's Jesse Helms remained amongst the most vocal proponents, the bill itself was a Democratic one. That prison education is one of the few rehabilitative programs that works was never an issue, at least not in the legislative recesses where such fates are decided. With the climate being what it was (is), being perceived as coddling criminals was political suicide.

"They used fear tactics, telling the people that their kids might not be able to get financial assistance if the Pell Grants were being used up by inmates," Dave MacMillan recalled. "But that was never proven to be the case. "

I remember Dave in the months prior to the ax falling, harried, frustrated, and fighting to keep alive a program in which he believes. He lobbied the state's congressional delegation tirelessly. Few were listening. No one wanted to be seen as "soft on crime."

In the 25 years the college program has operated in the Maine State Prison, over a dozen inmates have earned their Associates Degrees and eight their B.A.'s. Of course, these numbers are misleading because they do not take into account the scores of inmates who've participated in the program and left the prison prior to completing their studies, nor do these numbers reflect those former inmates who've gone on to earn their degrees while free members of society.

Mine was the eighth B.A. awarded here and I may well prove to be the last of Maine's inmates to graduate. Prior to the '94 Crime Bill taking effect, college enrollment at MSP averaged 25-30 inmates. There are currently 3 in the program.

MacMillan and O'Brien worked fast and hard to save the prison's college program from a political demise. In Thomaston, materials utilized by the Education Department, everything from chalk to computer software, were never provided by taxpayer dollars but by the Inmate Benefit Fund (IBF), monies generated by inmates through sales in the prison canteen, etc. for the institution's use. A plan was instigated whereby the IBF would cover two hundred of the three-hundred-dollar-per-class tuition, leaving the student to cover the remaining $100, plus the cost of textbooks. From a free-world point of view, a $100 per class tab is a delicious bargain. For the vast majority of inmates who earn little to no income, it is an exclusionary cost. Being unable (rather than unwilling) is exactly why there are three inmates enrolled with UMA and not thirty. Though salvaged, the program remains in a fragile balance as the IBF is not a static entity; if the funds aren't there when they're needed, the resources vanish. The Maine State Prison in Thomaston remains the only facility in the state with a college program. Increasingly, it's becoming the only facility in the state to have any educational programs at all.

Through recent years, short-sighted cutbacks have decimated the rehabilitative programs throughout the Maine Department of Corrections. Funding, programs, and positions were eliminated wholesale in all areas—education, psychology, counseling—save for security. Such is the reality of a "build more prisons" mindset. A former corrections commissioner decided that Thomaston would be "our education facility," thus eliminating staff positions across the board in Maine's other correctional institutions and allowing what few programs remained there to wither on the vine for lack of support. The flaw in this move lies in that MSP is a maximum-security prison and it is established MDOC policy to transfer out those of lower security classifications. In effect, those closest to returning to society end up in facilities with little or no resources to help prepare them for their transitions.

Currently there is no pre-release instruction in life skills and Maine's handful of minimum and medium-security facilities can offer only a smattering of vocational classes. By all accounts, these are demanding and comprehensive courses—which by no means guarantee employment once the former prisoner finds himself back on the street.

"The last time I was out," Inmate Charlie W., a welding course graduate, recalls, "I went to the Job Service and put that certificate right down in front of the guy. He wouldn't even look at it. It's like because I earned it in prison it doesn't count for anything."

"Man," Charlie adds, shaking his head. "I was proud of that piece of paper. That was the first diploma I'd ever earned in anything."

A society increasingly frustrated and vindictive over its crime rate can angrily question the logic of teaching inmates. Conversely, one could question the wisdom of not teaching them. Statistically, those inmates who've worked to educate themselves while incarcerated have a lower recidivism rate than do their counterparts who've resigned themselves to this existence and the cycle of crime and punishment. Something like 80% of former inmates will again find themselves in trouble with the law. While no statistics are available for recidivism rates among former Maine inmates who put in an honest and ongoing effort with education while here, one fact is established: of the eight inmates who've returned to society after earning their college degrees in Thomaston, only one has again found himself behind bars, and that for a crime that went hand-in-hand with his alcoholism.

"Whenever I go to these seminars and conferences, I run into these people who swear up and down that earning the GED is the single most important achievement in rehabilitation," Dave MacMillan said. "I usually just let them say their piece. The GED is important, but it's only a step in the right direction."

In an information packet given to every new inmate, MacMillan notes that the number of inmates earning their GEDs in the Maine State Prison has been declining in recent years. The explanation for this phenomenon does not lie in lack of interest but in that a greater number of new arrivals have already earned their GEDs in such places as the Maine Youth Center and county jails before "graduating" to this venerable institution. The percentage of new MSP inmates who already possess their GEDs has doubled in the last decade.

What MacMillan finds alarming is that for a great number of these offenders, attaining the GED is their terminal objective. In this regard, both educators who tout the GED as the key to rehabilitation and the inmates who feel they need go no further are riding the same elevator down. Both are equally short-sighted.

Participation in education and other rehabilitative programs is a symptom of positive change rather than change itself. Education is a means to an end, a tool with which lives are rebuilt—and in many cases built from scratch. That "rehabilitation" is an on-going process for an individual is why, I suspect, it fell out of vogue as an institutional expectation years ago. Believing that whole prison populations can be molded into productive members of society through a battery of programs they're forced to take was a fallacy in its inception and it was a fallacy in practice. The key to rehabilitation lies in the motivation and resiliency of an individual, individuals who make up significant percentages of every prison's population.

"In the case of inmates," Jaimee Colbert said, "education is often the only hope of changing behaviors that led them to prison in the first place. Of course (these) programs serve a very special population of inmates, the ones that regret those behaviors and want to make a fresh start. "

"There's an important difference," one of her students recently said, "between guys who go to school in here and 'free world' students. I think that out there they tend to do it by the numbers: get an education, get a job, build a future. We're doing the same thing but we're also doing it with the memory of what our lives were like before and being determined we'll not go back there. "

"As a whole," Colbert adds, "education gives these guys goals they may not have had before and the feeling that they're working towards something, which is something they don't often get in here."

Goals. Opportunities. In and of itself, education is not the solution to our nation's crime problem. The rehabilitative efforts of the individual lends the distinction between becoming a well read criminal and a motivated, productive member of society. An aggregate of these individuals, found in any corrections system, are being increasingly denied these goals, these opportunities. One must then wonder, watching in disgust as prison populations spiral ever upward, how the numbers might have been eased, and lives salvaged, were we not seizing the tools for change from those willing to use them. One must then wonder how many we're throwing away.

"We have an increasingly punitive climate in this country," Colbert says, "whereby building more prisons is becoming the panacea for all that's wrong with the system while ignoring those things that just might help."

In the 1970's, clinician Martin Seligman was electroshocking dogs. A clinical psychologist, Dr. Seligman, in these controversial experiments (Maier & Seligman, 1976), was studying the principles of "learned helplessness." In his experiments, dogs were placed in a chamber where they learned they could escape electric shock (the floor was wired) by jumping over a partition whenever a warning light was flashed. Some of the dogs were shocked no matter what they did, with the result that when an escape was finally offered, they didn't take it. The principles that arose from these and similar studies are generally accepted as being applicable to humans as well. In fact, Seligman's theories are widely used in the study of depression.

What cannot be ignored, or ignored to the detriment of society, is a parallel between learned helplessness and our prison populations. To be fair, society is better served by keeping a number of these individuals away forever. A goodly number will recidivate, returning to the streets to create more havoc, commit more crimes, and again return to prison. These are facts of life. However, we risk sacrificing a significant percentage of salvageable men and women currently incarcerated by denying them hope and the opportunities they are motivated and willing to use. By again teaching these same inmates that no matter how earnest their intentions may be, all their efforts will be for nought, we limit their horizons and may well condemn them to past behaviors. Their motivations (self improvement, family, fear of a wasted life, etc.) may be compelling enough, but so long as they are taught, time and again, to expect no more than this current existence, it will remain a chink in their armor by which their efforts can be consistently undone.

When confronted by current "tough on crime" attitudes and comments, Dave MacMillan is quick to respond. "I'll tell them to do what they want with them (prison inmates). Lock them up, take everything, and give them nothing. Keep them down. But when you're finished having your way with them, you'd better be prepared for what comes back out these doors."

I ran into Jason a few days back on the prison's street, carrying his obligatory MSP coffee mug and heading for the Rec Yard. We got to talking about education and looking for our cues to go our separate ways. With a half dozen semesters behind him, he hasn't sat in a class since the Pell Grants got yanked. He doesn't seem as hot to get back to his studies as he was the last time we talked about it, back when I was a student. He ought to get it while he can, I tell him. It's only a hundred bucks a class.

"A hundred," he snorts. "Where am I going to get that? Might as well be a thousand."

I didn't know what to tell him.

"Take it easy," he said, clapping me on the arm and heading off. He was late for a handball game. He's been doing that a lot lately. Playing handball and hanging out in the Yard.

Scott A. Antworth graduated from the University of Maine while a guest at the Maine State Prison, where he remains incarcerated. He served in the U.S. Army and has been emerging as a writer in recent years, making his debut in print in Biddle Publishing Company's Trapped Under Ice: A Death Row Anthology (1995). He has since been regularly featured in Flying Horse and various other literary journals. He was a winner in the 1997 PEN Prisoner Writing Awards and is currently at work on his first novel.

Gary D. Titus, "The Eyes of Survival"

TEKLA MILLER
"Puppies With a Purpose"

Jamie spent her first fifteen months of life in prison. In the late 1980s, she was one of the dogs in the prison puppy training program for Leader Dogs for the Blind School in Rochester, Michigan. After fifteen months of rigorous training and socialization in this program, the head trainer for the school classified Jamie as a reject because of hip dysplasia. Then they gave her to me.

When thinking about dogs in prison, most people think about the K-9 Units or police working dogs, which are used for narcotics, weapons and explosive detection, for tracking escapees, and as sentries guarding prison perimeters. Service dog programs in prisons are less widely publicized. Their basic goal is to raise puppies within the scope of the protocol set by the various service dog programs. This is only the first phase that prepares them for an in depth training period such as those in the Leader Dogs of Michigan and the Pilot Dog Puppy Program in Ohio.

We discovered that dogs like Jamie also train their prisoner handlers. Jay Worley, Unit Manager, in Ohio, stated, "The benefits for the inmates include development of responsibility, caring, and socialization that may not be acquired in our setting in any other way. There is also the belief that, in part, the prisoners are able to give back to society."

Those involved in other prison dog programs have echoed these benefits. In fact, a veterinarian working with the Michigan program observed that the dogs inspired prisoners in many different ways. These inmates wrote poetry and stories about their experiences and how working with the dogs helped them build trust, responsibility and caring about others. Civilian trainers are aware that matching the human resources available behind prison walls with the needs of the disabled community builds self esteem in prisoners. Before these programs, prisoners did not think they were worthwhile enough to contribute to the community. Prisoners participating in these programs now believe that being locked up does not prevent their making a contribution to society.

The socialization pointed out by Mr. Worley was reinforced by Ms. Dyer, former trainer in Michigan. She reported that the puppies help the socialization process by forging a bond between the prisoners, corrections officers and other employees. The dogs create a nonaggressive common ground everyone can rally behind and talk about without being defensive. This builds a trusting and calm environment. Jeanne Hampl of Washington's Prison Pet Partnership Program reported that during her first year and a half as the director of the program, none of the inmates in the program had a major rule infraction.

One prisoner at Huron Valley Women's Facility said, "Training these puppies is just like being a good mother." Her comment showed us that we could use the program to teach good parenting skills, including nurturing, positive reinforcement, patience, constant care and attention, anger control, and assertive, not aggressive behavior. In addition, through these programs, women and men prisoners, many coming from abusive and dysfunctional families, can learn marketable skills like pet grooming and kennel management that will help them in their reentry into the community.

It is important to understand that puppy programs are cost-effective as well as being educational, and that qualifying for these programs is difficult for prisoners. The work is demanding, including a requirement that the prisoner spend 24 hours a day with the dog.

Mornings come early in prison and the puppies must get up and go everywhere with their prisoner trainers, including job, school, chapel, recreational and special activities, commissary, sick call and yard. In some programs, the dogs also go on visits with the prisoners. Puppies are usually placed in their kennels for count, during meals and when prisoners shower. Prisoner trainers must teach their dogs to lie patiently at their feet when in a classroom, on a visit, in chapel or on their jobs. Puppies learn the proper way to greet other prisoners and employees, and they are often taken to the special needs units or classrooms for pet therapy. Special needs prisoners are those that are mentally ill or in special education classes.

Sensitive dogs like Jamie are wonderful to watch with the special needs prisoners. Once, she was taken to a classroom where one prisoner was crying softly. Jamie walked over to her without being commanded and placed her head on the prisoner's lap. As the prisoner began to pet Jamie, she stopped crying. Jamie never left her until the class was over.

When we started the puppy training program at Huron Valley, Prison Pet Partnership at the Washington Correctional Center for Women was the only service dog program in a prison setting. Kathy Quinn (Sister Pauline) developed Washington's program in 1982 because she wanted to share her knowledge of the benefits of the human-animal bond with others. Quinn learned these benefits when she lived on the streets and befriended some dogs. Today Prison Pet Partnership is a successful and dynamic program employing women inmates to train dogs for people with disabilities. The program has an annual budget approaching $100,000 from various sources: 35% from a contract with the Washington Department of Corrections, grants, and fund raising. Earnings from a related grooming and boarding service offered to the community offset some operating costs. However, free grooming is offered to pets of low income or disabled elderly.

Dogs selected for the Prison Pet Partnership Program live in the cells with the inmates. There are two dogs and two inmates in each cell of a special wing in the housing unit. Though most inmate participants are part time trainers earning $75 a month (they must also hold other jobs in the prison), there are full time trainers who earn $300 a month.

Getting into the program and staying there is not easy. To be considered for a trainer's position, a prisoner must apply in writing, be 90 days free of any major infraction, and meet mental and physical health requirements, like showing the ability to control anger. Once accepted to this point, prisoners must pass a standard exam for Pet Care Technician Certification Level I given by the American Boarding Kennels Association (ABKA). If they pass the exam and after a three-month apprenticeship, they are assigned a dog. Any drug infraction or demonstration that a prisoner cannot take care of the dog means the prisoner cannot remain in the program. Prisoner participants are encouraged to mentor other students.

It does not end there for the prisoner participants. The students must also complete a Companion Animal Hygienist course and are certified after 360 hours of grooming experience. As a result, the pet care industry is provided with needed, highly skilled groomers, trainers and kennel workers. Having a good job is essential to the success of an offender once released from prison, and this program gives the women prisoners just that.

The need for skilled employees in the pet care industry has resulted in a list of employers waiting for the release of qualified prisoners. Few, if any, prison programs can boast about this kind of success.

More than 500 dogs, many mutts, provided by the Humane Society and rescue groups, have been through the program since it began. The dogs must be outgoing and more interested in people than other dogs. It takes about six months to train a therapy dog and eight to twelve months to train service dogs. Not all the dogs make it for one reason or another such as a health problems or attention deficit. Yet if they do not make it, the dogs are "paroled" to good homes of people who have been placed on a waiting list for one of these well-trained rejects like Jamie. The dogs that do graduate to become service dogs provide greater freedom to individuals with physical disabilities.

Though Ohio's London Correctional Institution's Pilot Dog Puppy Program is similar in many ways to the Prison Pet Partnership Program, its goal is to train male prisoners to be Puppy Raisers. Successful puppies will become leader dogs for the blind. Pilot Dog Puppy Program accepted its first set of puppies on October 26, 1994.

The prisoner puppy raiser's job is to care for the puppy, giving it basic obedience training and socialization skills, and to ensure the puppy becomes desensitized to as much environmental stimuli as possible. Pilot Dogs, Inc. provide the puppies. They breed some pups specifically for the program while other dogs are donated from the community. The dogs stay with the puppy trainers until they are about one year old. The successfully trained puppies are released from prison to enter more intense training in preparation for being leader dogs for the blind. Those puppies that do not quite make this cut are given to one of the patient people on a list waiting for a reject.

Mr. Worley reports, "On an institutional level it is our goal to instill in the inmate participants a sense of responsibility and purpose. The regimen required to raise a puppy properly demands discipline while offering positive feedback through visible progress of the puppy."

Prisoner participants are selected from a pool of volunteers who must submit to a rigorous interview. First consideration is given to prisoners who have had prior animal experience and a positive overall institutional record. As in the Prison Pet Partnership Program, the dogs remain with their inmate trainers 24 hours a day and share sleeping quarters in a special housing unit. When the pilot dogs reach seven months, they are taken home with volunteer prison employees. These volunteers introduce and desensitize the puppies to environments not found in prison, such as heavy street traffic, large stores/malls, restaurants, wild life, lakes, houses, apartment buildings, and to riding long distances in automobiles and buses.

No institution money is used for the Pilot Dog Program. The London Correctional Institution's administration used existing structures and/or supplies to set up the program. Day to day operation of the program requires only the items (food, leashes, collars, bowls) and veterinary services supplied by Pilot Dogs, Inc. Employees purchase toys, treats, flea shampoo, and other incidental items for the puppies. Like Prison Pet Partnership, this is a cost effective, educational program inside a prison that also provides benefits to the community.

Mr. Worley found, as others have, that the dogs gave employees and prisoners something in common to share. Such sharing lends itself to a less hostile environment. Speaking of sharing, programs like these cannot succeed without community support and volunteers who work with the dogs in community settings where prisoners cannot go. They also help increase public awareness about positive prison and service programs.

The women inmates at Huron Valley Women's Facility outside Detroit, Michigan christened my golden retriever Jamie Newbarker. They named her after Jim Neubaucher, a journalist who wrote about the disabled for the *Detroit Free Press Newspaper*. Though he and many others were avid supporters of the puppy training program, the Michigan Department of Corrections closed it down because of budget cuts forced by increased prison populations. The closure drew outrage from the community. Concerned citizens who understood the many benefits of the program sent donations, a goodwill gesture never seen by the department before or since. Despite this, they have not reinstated the program in Michigan.

When Jamie became Huron Valley's first reject, the women prisoners took it as a personal failure. After a few days of brooding, they decided this would not defeat them. So on their own initiative, they encouraged the Leader Dog School to use Jamie's picture on the certificate they give to puppy raisers. The prisoners also began sewing the bandanas worn by leader dog puppies that say, "Future Leader Dog." For the first time in most of their lives, these women prisoners learned from Jamie that a failure can become a success.

These puppy training programs teach demanding employment skills while insisting that prisoners demonstrate responsibility and accountability. The dogs and prisoners educate each other. A prisoner from the Washington program described this best when she wrote, "This program has given me a purpose in life and helped me to realize that I do have self worth and can help others. Had it not been for my involvement in this program, I would still be using drugs and not caring about anyone or thing, least of all myself. Being able to see the joy in the faces of the people that receive our service dogs has given me a reason to continue on with life."

Tekla Dennison Miller attended Cazenovia College, UCLA and Oakland University in Michigan. She worked as a probation officer and a halfway house agent in Detroit, was supervisor at the first women's prison camp in Michigan, and warden at Huron Valley Men's and Women's Prisons. Ms. Miller was the first warden in Michigan to manage two maximum security prisons simultaneously. She is the author of The Warden Wore Pink [Biddle Publishing Co.], a contributor to Frontiers of Justice, Volume 1: The Death Penalty, and co-editor of Frontiers of Justice, Volume 2.

Gary D. Titus, "A Drink in the Desert"

CLAUDIA WHITMAN
"The Wild Horse Program"

W.H.I.P. is the acronym for Colorado's Wild Horse Inmate Program, an eleven year old example of a unique partnership between the Colorado Department of Corrections, and the Bureau of Land Management. That same acronym could be used to describe the program: Watching Horses Instruct People.

Tony Bainbridge, who started W.H.I.P. in 1986, is a man who lives to work with horses. He has always been a professional horseman, and in the course of his career, he had done some breaking and training for the American Humane Society and another organization called NOAH. He was living in Nevada, training horses, when he got a call from NOAH and was asked to come back to Colorado to help work with the Mustangs it was adopting from the Bureau of Land Management. They asked him to build pens and design a curriculum that would enable them to train inmates to work with the wild horses. A retired Corrections security commander, Jim Like, who is also a bronco rider, volunteered to help Tony (who had no experience in Corrections) set up a program that would work for prisoners. Together, they designed and implemented the program, using the time proven method of trial and error, and, as Tony recalls fondly, "He got me through the rough spots that first year." The Mustang, which is any feral horse, shares a long history with the settling of the American West. As the brochure for W.H.I.P. states, "These noble creatures carried cowboys up the Chisholm Trail, mountain men through the Tetons, trappers into Oregon, Native Americans into buffalo hunts and settlers from the east coast to the west. Now, Mustangs are helping troubled men make a new beginning with an old craft—horse training."

The program is impressive, from the moment you descend from the Canon City visitor's center, past the many buildings that house everything from maximum security and death row, to various medium and minimal security facilities, a dairy farm, and a furniture factory. By the time you arrive at the horse facility, located in the most rural part of the 5500 acres of East Canon Facility, you are confronted by lovely old stone buildings, regal cottonwoods, eight round corrals and a host of other holding and training pens. There are horses everywhere. Some are milling around in pens, obviously recent arrivals. Others are tied to a hitching post in front of the main building. Others are in the round pens, embarking on their education in conjunction with a prisoner who has charge of that horse from beginning to end, ideally a 90 day period which culminates in the adoption of each horse by someone who has preselected it and is paying for the feed and training. It is a great deal for everyone involved. There are currently some 40,000 wild horses running free in the western states. Given the competition for food and the encroachment on open spaces by development, this number is too high to maintain a healthy herd. Rather than allowing for attrition through sickness and natural selection, the B.L.M. rounds up a certain number each year and sends them to the handful of adoption programs that currently exist. W.H.I.P has received and trained about 4500 horses since 1986, or approximately 450 a year. There is a waiting list for adoptions, across the entire country. The new owner pays only $740, which includes 90 days of training, food, and the $125 B.L.M. adoption fee. A horse trained at the prison can be returned at any time for further training, can be boarded for only the cost of feed, and can have special training corresponding to the needs and interests of the new owner.

The program is filled from a pool of prisoners who have volunteered their services and been carefully screened. Before being eligible, the man must be part of the Four Mile Program, which is a minimum security set up, meaning that the person has to have demonstrated a certain amount of trustworthy behavior. Typically, people in the program will be getting out of prison in the foreseeable future, and will be leaving with real skills and knowledge in the areas of horse training, equine science, horse-shoeing, stable management, fence building, and maintenance of equipment. Two hundred hours of classroom and practical instruction are presented in several phases. If the men survive the early days, where they have to overcome fear of horses, lots of grunt work, and taking orders, to name a few challenges, they stay in the program for anywhere from three months to three years. Most have little or no previous experience with horses. The bottom line is the development of a good work ethic.

Tony is very clear that rehabilitation is not what the program is about. He explains this by saying that if everyone who participated got better and stronger and became a healthy person, then maybe he could use the word rehabilitation, but that this is not at all the case. "We can't turn around the guy who has problems with authority. We have one of the best programs in any prison, and yet, in order for it to be a real rehabilitation program for me, you would have to be able to put anyone in it and get success." Some people just can't cut it. Some are "gangbangers" and don't do well if they are not in groups. Some can't follow orders. "They ball up", he says. "If they don't want to help other inmates, it can get ugly. The group will eliminate them. People can get hurt working with wild horses, and if they can't follow the chain of command, there will be problems."

Tony goes on to explain that the basis for W.H.I.P. is that they are there to train horses, not just to care for them. Through this objective, a person builds self esteem, learns a trade, takes pride in what he is doing, learns to work on a team. "A lot of people come here not caring what people think about them. The horses have an effect on them. They get attached to the animals. They can see accomplishments quickly. One thing that is really helpful is that horses are honest. If they are going to kick you, they will just do it. They have no racial or gender preference."

"Our mission statement is clear and simple. We would like to send an inmate out of the program with a trade. We want him to know what he is doing in all aspects of equine management and training. We want to produce horses that won't hurt anyone. Here at the prison, we want to maintain a safe, healthy place for horses. We

Colorado's Wild Horse Inmate Program

want to assure a good future for each horse."

"The Wild Horse Program is the inmates' program. Without them it doesn't work. Two thousand inmates have been through here in eleven years. You start out with what seems like the worst possible scenario: wild horses and inexperienced people, many with a poor attitude and few successes behind them. If things go wrong, they can really go wrong." He goes on to explain that, fortunately, this has not generally been the case and that the program stays around because there have not been a lot of injuries. When he started, he knew what he wanted to do, but he did not know how to teach it. Over a period of time, he realized that a lot of the actual teaching could be done by team trainers: prisoners who had progressed to the point where they could teach the others. Now, out of a group of up to 28 inmates, he has three team trainers. These people make $2.50 a day instead of the $2.00 that the others make. They work directly under Tony or Brian Hardin, who has been with the program for about 6 years. The first day an inmate is in the program, he has to clean the pens, which gives both him and the staff a sense of whether he is going to be able to follow an order. Pretty soon, he is put on a horse in one of the small round pens, and he is basically left alone with the horse, having been told that he has to stay aboard. "Usually a guy wants to get off after a while, but we make him get right back on," Tony chuckles. This gives him a chance to get to know the horse. The next step is to learn to halter break.

The wild horses, who have come directly from holding pens after their capture, are put in a narrow chute with panels that slide across, so they are in single file. One guy gets up above the horse and eventually manages to slide the halter on. Since the horse has had little or no physical contact with humans, it is quite alarmed by this procedure. Next, a thick rope is attached to the halter and four prisoners grab onto it. The latch is released on the gate and the horse bolts for freedom. The four prisoners hold on for their lives while the horse drags their feet through the dirt. Their job is to keep him facing directly at them, so he can't turn and kick, and to hold on to him. The horse is generally frantic, rearing a lot, trying to get away, sometimes even falling in the deep, soft dirt, in his effort to escape. The man in front then begins a process called "sacking," which is to take a small blanket and lightly hit the horse with it until he realizes that it isn't going to hurt him, whereupon he calms down rapidly. The same process is repeated on the other side, since horses don't transfer information learned on one side to the other until they actually experience it there. Amazingly, in a matter of minutes the horse is quite calm, and he is turned loose to return to his buddies. The next day, a similar series of activities occur with a rope, and both inmate and horse learn to respect, not to fear each other. Very shortly thereafter, the horse learns to be saddled and bridled and then the riding part of the training begins.

By and large, the inmates learn from each other, from their team trainers, and from watching Tony and Brian do the various tasks with tremendous skill. Each inmate may be working up to seven horses at any one time, and each horse, when it goes to its new home, leaves with papers identifying the trainer. That trainer also receives a $25 bonus when his horse is adopted. The program pays for itself through adoption and training fees. The prison complex grows much of the hay. Saddles are made in a prison workshop in Buena Vista. Chaps and boots and any other necessary equipment are provided for the prisoners. Besides the ring work, there are miles of trails on the grounds, where prisoners can ride as long as they are accompanied by staff. There is also a library full of books and videos on all aspects of training and management, so an inmate can become familiar with other styles and philosophies of training.

Rick Slagle, a team trainer for nine months, has been in the program for over a year. He will be up for parole in a few months, and he hopes to continue training Mustangs when he gets out. He says that before he got involved with W.H.I.P. he had no goals. Now he knows what he wants to do with his life. Colby Blades, also a team trainer, has been part of the program for two years. He had ridden before going to prison but knew nothing about training. He will be up for parole in a year and a half, and when he gets out he plans on being a farrier. He will serve a minimum of five years. Before his incarceration he worked in the oil fields, but he has no interest in going back to that life. He says, "Working in the horse program gives you something to look forward to every day. It is easy to get down and discouraged in prison, but when you work with horses you get a real sense of accomplishment. It is easy to lose self esteem, and sometimes you are treated in a demoralizing way in other parts of the prison, but here that is not so. As a team trainer, I have to earn respect from the other prisoners, and that has been a real challenge."

Ian Rendon has been in prison for three years and has spent seven months in the program. He is due to get out in a few days. He says that prison has been a blessing in disguise. "It gave me a chance to look at myself and where I stood. I came to prison and had a lot of time to think. I look at the whole thing as a valuable experience. I have a wonderful, supportive family, and I am paying them back by changing my life around." He also hopes to work with horses when he gets out. He says that the amazing thing about the horse program is that you are outside all the time, and you almost feel that you are free. Tim Pappe, who Tony describes as having "great hands" for working with horses, is also due to be released in a few months. He has developed a great love for horses and hopes to continue working with them in his leisure time, but he plans to go to school. He claims that more than anything else he has learned patience through being in the program. Rene Zavala Arana is a Mexican national who has only been in the program for 4 months. He had worked with horses a lot back in Mexico, and for twenty months prior to joining W.H.I.P, he always worked but was inside, which was terrible for him. He loves the chance to be outside and to be around horses again. He understands very little English, and several of the bi-lingual inmates seem to enjoy translating for him and helping him to understand directions and conversation.

At lunch time, we sit in on a meeting where Tony talks about activities for the afternoon. Everyone appears relaxed. Of the 21 people present, there is quite a mix of ethnic backgrounds and no apparent tension. People feel free to discuss any concerns. Everyone is on a first name basis, even with Tony and Brian. Tony stresses the safety of the horses as a primary feature at all times. "You want to rodeo, you get out and rodeo. We break horses here." As things start winding down, later in the afternoon, we see a couple of guys riding horses that are bucking a bit. There is a lot of laughter and comradeship. Brian notices my quizzical expression and says, "Hey, they have to have some fun. They can't just work all the time." Tony sums it all up when he says that he is one of the fortunate people who got to do what he wanted most, working with horses every day. He sees the Wild Horse Program as an opportunity for all involved to do a really good job, and the "rehabilitation," such as it is, comes as a side product of this good job. "A lot of people come in here as kids and they go out as grown ups, grown ups with good skills, good attitudes, and a good sense of self esteem."

The only downside that can be noted is that after all this progress in self esteem and good work habits, not all inmates will then be released. After their two to three years in W.H.I.P., if they still have more time to serve, they have to leave the program because it is Department of Corrections policy, and it is likely that they will not find any other program in the prison of comparable vitality. Instead of a straight progression in skills and responsibility, as preparation for a successful free world life, they may then be re-subjected to the more traditional and often non-progressive approach that permeates prison life. Tony laments this but he has no control over DOC decisions.

One can only hope that the "grownups" the horse program has helped develop will be able to hold onto their memories of success, both in the personal as well as the horse realm, so that they can meet the challenges of ongoing prison life or a return to the outside with a new paradigm working for them. Tony and Brian are strong models, and though they claim they stick to horse training as their goal, their mentoring function is omnipresent. Likewise, the horses give beauty, excitement, challenge, and love to the whole experience. They, too, are mentors. And perhaps this element is one that can make the necessary difference for lasting success. Tony has no numbers or statistics, but he hears his guys are getting out of prison and making it out there.

Claudia Whitman is an artist who divides her time between Colorado and Maine. She co-edited Frontiers of Justice, Volumes 1 and 2, and works with Equal Justice, U.S.A. as a member of the editorial board on their upcoming book, Saga of Shame. She is a penpal and visitor to prisoners across the country, and takes on special projects to support these friends. She is a lover of dogs and horses.

JENNIFER R. WYNN
"Rebuilding New York, One Life at a Time"

Founded in 1989, the New York City-based, nonprofit organization, Fresh Start, Inc., offers vocational training to inmates on Rikers Island-the world's largest penal colony. The areas in which Fresh Start provides vocational training, culinary arts and publishing, were selected because of the vast employment opportunities that exist in these fields in New York City.

Our Mission: Fresh Start's mission is to help break the cycle of recidivism by providing offenders with the tools they need to stay out of jail for life. For our population, mostly men who commit crimes to feed their drug addictions or who sell drugs as their only perceived way to make a living, assistance in helping them get and keep legal jobs, and access to appropriate substance abuse treatment programs are the most important tools we offer.

Fresh Start conducts three-month training programs in both culinary arts and publishing for up to 30 inmates, approximately 15 per class. Inmates learn about the training through fliers posted in the dorms, and sign up in the Programs Department. Approximately 200 of the 1,200 inmates in the jail in which we work express interest in joining the program, but only a select few, the ones who are able to successfully convince Fresh Start interviewers that they have a sincere and deeply-felt desire to stay out of jail, are chosen. Besides instinct, which comes from knowing the inmate population well, the objective criteria we consider include: whether the inmate has held a job in the past, can read and write at the 7th grade level, does not have a history of committing violent crimes and, if substance abuse issues are revealed, is willing to enter a substance abuse treatment program upon release. Eye contact, politeness, articulateness and maturity-the qualities that will engage a potential employer on the outside-are the traits we look for in the one-on-one interviews we conduct with each applicant.

The typical participant is a man in his mid-thirties who has a history of petty criminal activity, usually drug-related. Most likely he is Black or Latino, as are 95 percent of Rikers inmates. In and out of jail since his mid-teens, he is basically doing a life sentence, one six-month bid at a time. Occasionally we accept men in their late teens or early twenties, but find we are more successful with the older inmates, men who have hit bottom, are willing to face reality and ready to change their lives. Young offenders, on the other hand, often view jail as a one-time rite of passage, not recognizing that it is a pattern which, if not interrupted, will continue. The recidivism rate of New York City inmates is a whopping 85%.

The program itself is run as a workplace; trainees are held to strict standards for attendance, performance, production and professionalism. While the cornerstone of the training involves vocational skills development, additional and equally significant components include groups in Conflict Resolution, Relapse Prevention, Life Skills, Public Speaking and Career Counseling, as well as GED or College Preparatory classes. Coupled with hands-on vocational skills development, these groups form a holistic program, working on the "whole" individual with the goal of improving a trainee's prospect, not only of gaining employment, but of keeping it. Our typical trainee often has no trouble getting a job, but a poor workplace ethic or an unconquered addiction will cause him to lose the job within the first six months. It is for this reason that we emphasize enrollment into a drug treatment program immediately following jail for those with a substance addiction, and that, on the inside, we hold trainees to the same standards as employers do on the outside.

No more than three absences during the three-month period are permitted. A trainee will be terminated for this, as well as for substandard performance, or a poor attitude toward either instructors or fellow inmates. Failure to meet deadlines, to turn in assignments or consistent low grades on tests are also grounds for termination. Typically, two to three trainees are terminated within the first two weeks for any of the above reasons, which usually leaves the team feeling more empowered to get the job done, and more serious about the program.

<u>The Culinary Arts Program</u>: The culinary arts segment of the program is taught by a former New York City chef, who currently works as a teacher for the city's Board of Education in an alternative high school on Rikers Island. Each week, two classes are taught by four-star chefs from leading Manhattan restaurants, which opens new worlds and potential employment opportunities to the trainees. Initially, some chefs are reluctant to come to jail to teach convicted felons, knives in hands, how to truss a chicken, but in the end most chefs find the experience tremendously rewarding. Some of the volunteer chefs have hired Fresh Start graduates as pot washers and prep cooks in their kitchens, and most have volunteered steadily for Fresh Start since its inception in 1989.

The curriculum begins with Kitchen Safety, Sanitation and Knife Skills and covers all aspects of food preparation and cooking techniques. This prepares graduates of the program to pass their New York City Food Handler's test and receive the Food Handler's license upon release. An underlying goal of the program is to use food preparation as a way to build self-esteem, to teach cooperation and to learn about short- and long-term goal setting, all of which will be needed on the outside. To prepare meals successfully, kitchen crews must operate as teams. For many Fresh Start trainees, their first taste of professional success is experienced in the program. The rewards of seeing a perfectly prepared soufflé emerge from the oven cannot be overstated.

The long-term goal of the food trainees is to prepare a five-course meal for the 100 family members, friends, staff and corrections employees who attend their graduation. All skills and behaviors learned throughout the course must be put into practice during the final week of the program, where menu planning, prepping, cooking and team playing all come into play. Despite the typical setbacks that are part and parcel of working in any correctional facility, Fresh Start trainees have always succeeded in preparing memorable graduation banquets.

More importantly, many have succeeded in landing jobs in the food industry as prep cooks, institutional cooks, pot washers and cake decorators. A few have become executive chefs in corporate kitchens, and many supplement their income with catering work.

The Publishing Program: Like the culinary arts program, the publishing program is modeled on a workplace environment, in this case a newsroom. Trainees' long-term goal is to produce a magazine in twelve weeks. The class is taught by a professional journalist, supplemented with visiting writers, editors and novelists. Each trainee takes on the role of staff writer, conceiving feature stories, service pieces, short stories, humor or entertainment. The magazine, called the Rikers Review, is written primarily for New York City Department of Correction inmates and a small but growing list of outside subscribers. Approval for its sale in jail commissaries is pending, which will bring the magazine to a new level of professionalism and greatly increased readership.

The mission of the magazine is to inform, inspire or entertain the inmate reader. Compelling stories, such as "Confessions from a Former Drug Dealer," and useful service pieces, such as "How to Be a Dad from Behind Bars" or "Your Guide to Legal Work on the Outside," are examples of how trainees use their experience, knowledge and research to help their fellow inmates.

In addition to learning how to organize their thoughts on paper, trainees also learn keyboarding skills and the basics of computers. A requirement of the course is that each trainee word-processes his own work. As in the cooking program, the project of producing a magazine affords an opportunity to introduce the concepts of team playing, meeting deadlines and setting and reaching short, and long-term goals. Once the articles are written and re-written according to the editor-in-chiefs specifications, the magazine is laid out by a graphic artist, using illustrations provided by the trainees themselves, or by jailhouse artists to whom the trainees have "subcontracted" work. The final phase of the program is the printing of the Rikers Review, which is done in the D.O.C. print shop located in the same jail in which the trainees are housed. During this process, trainees are exposed to yet another aspect of publishing, printing on state-of-the-art equipment, and experience a great sense of fulfillment in seeing their project to completion. For many, a printed by-line over their story, something just weeks earlier they never thought they'd achieve, is a great self-esteem booster. At the end of the program, many trainees remark that if they can learn to write for publication and meet a deadline, they can do anything. It is a small step, but often a first step, in the right direction.

At graduation, as the cooking trainees unveil their five-course meal, the publishing trainees unveil their magazine; copies are placed on each chair for family members, friends and correctional staff to read. Some trainees are so inspired by the writing class that they continue to write for publication on the outside. To date, of the approximately 90 graduates, two have had lengthy op-ed pieces published in major New York City newspapers, for which they were each paid $200 and had their pictures appear alongside their stories; one has completed a novel; one is the editor-in-chief of his college literary journal; many have had "Letters to the Editor" published in city papers; two regularly perform their poetry at readings; and another five have had small pieces published in a national glossy magazine for prisoners.

What makes Fresh Start unique is that the program continues after jail. The same counselors and instructors who worked with the men on the inside are available to them on the outside. Because the program is small, bonding between participants and counselors is possible, and is sometimes the only reason an inmate will contact Fresh Start once he is released. He may not want or need our services at the time, but he'll stop by to say "hello" to his favorite instructor and then, maybe a month or even a year later, will knock on our doors in need of a drug program, housing, clothing or a job. From helping graduates find employment, housing or drug treatment, to assistance with cleaning up their rap sheets or studying for their GEDs, Fresh Start's doors are always open to its graduates.

To assist graduates in staying out of jail, a post-release support group called "Jails Anonymous" (JA) is held once a week for two hours in Fresh Start's offices. In this confidential forum, facilitated by a professional counselor, graduates discuss and find support for the difficulties they face in rebuilding their lives. Coping with the stigma of being an ex-offender, battling an addiction, relearning how to be husbands and fathers and avoiding the streets are just some of the other issues addressed. JA succeeds as a support group because the men often know each other from the inside, can identify with their shared hardships and, because they helped each other in jail to graduate from the Fresh Start training program, often have a vested interest in helping each other make it on the outside.

The final question: Does the program work? can best be answered statistically. While only 15% of New York City offenders will stay out of jail, for 60% of Fresh Start graduates, freedom and dignity are a new way of life.

Jennifer R. Wynn, program director of Fresh Start, also serves as editor-in-chief of the Rikers Review. Prior to joining Fresh Start, she served as managing editor of Prison Life magazine, a national glossy magazine for prisoners. Ms. Wynn has had numerous freelance articles published in New York City newspapers and national magazines, and is currently earning her Master's of Arts degree in Criminal Justice at the John Jay College of Criminal Justice. She holds a BA in English from the University of Colorado and lives in Manhattan.

HIDDEN TREASURES

Concentrate and you shall hear them speak.

Books.

A new world, an old thought brought anew.

The great mind builders of yesterday
continue to orate a powerfully compelling seminar.

Wisdom, knowledge and courage are precious gems —
which guide you on an unrelentless path of discovery.

If the eyes are the mirror to the soul
then,
books are the keys to life.

Unlock the treasures and
leave no mystery unsolved.

Books,
from their pages comes sheer ecstacy.

Willie Christopher Tucker
Bostick State Prison, Georgia

MELBA R. CONWAY, MEd
"The Rehabilitative Benefits of Multicultural Education, Literacy and Literary Therapy"

The failure in this country to adequately address educational needs and cultural diversity has disabled our society and clogged our penal systems. As tools for social action, multicultural education, literacy education and literary therapy embrace issues of personal empowerment, socialization, race, and gender; their benefits emphasize the need for change in the education and rehabilitation of juvenile and adult adjudicated populations.

We live in a society of tough guys. There are tough guys in prison and there are tough guys who want to put more people in prison. We don't need any more tough guys—hard on the outside while lacking inner strength, courage and compassion. People, whether prisoner or jailer, subjected to the dehumanizing extremes of institutions focused on punishment will not be bettered by further brutalization. Neglect and abuse by a marginalizing society have helped create the troubled and troubling criminal. More neglect of basic needs and "therapeutic" abuse will do nothing to create a capable human being or a productive citizen.

Impacting the under evolved human side of people is crucial in connecting them to themselves and to a society which has at once abandoned them and is fearful of them. We need to educate and elevate. Awareness of self and purpose in life are ultimate goals for rehabilitation and reentry into the family, the workplace, and the larger community. Multicultural education, client centered literacy instruction, and literary therapy are strategic in furthering these outcomes.

<u>Multicultural Education</u>

The efficacy of rehabilitation in our nation's penal institutions is in part contingent upon how the racial and ethnic makeup of the imprisoned is addressed. Articles, speeches, and books have been written about the glaring disparities of the racial percentages of the country as a whole and the racial percentages of those who are arrested, locked up, and on probation. When we are looking to provide positive programming in correctional institutions, it is imperative that we acknowledge the societal, economic and educational inequities that have created this situation.

While the overt racist realities of society and the justice system persist, positive programs must acknowledge the diverse prison populations they are attempting to rehabilitate. In literacy instruction and literary therapy, the history, literature, and sociological realities of African Americans, Latinos, Native Americans, and other racial and ethnic minorities constitute some of the most effective reading material. The use of culturally inspired poetry, short stories and books can help develop positive ethnic identities and cultural competency. This basic principle must not be overlooked when implementing positive programming in prisons.

Literacy

A high percentage of prisoners have inadequate academic skills. This lack of educational achievement can be attributed to many of the same factors that plague more traditional students in public schools: untreated physical conditions; learning disabilities; psychological trauma; low intelligence; infrequent school attendance; and poor instruction. It is very likely that these adversities have been intensified in the lives of prisoners, both before and during incarceration. Ameliorating these conditions in prison settings is merely a precursor to authentic literacy.

Reading specialists have become increasingly vehement about focusing attention on the reader, his language, and experiences rather than on using a one size fits all methodology and curriculum. This is of great importance when working with juveniles and adults in prison settings. A rudimentary knowledge of the complexities of regional and ethnic dialects is enough to discourage classic phonics instruction. Consequently, the most effective approach is to de-emphasize phonics and worksheet/workbook exercises and to emphasize the reader, the informed selection of appropriate literature, and the reader's culture. Consonants; the long sounds of vowels; common prefixes and suffixes; and syllabication will suffice for "skills" instruction.

Assessment of the reader is the foundation of literacy instruction. Who are the particular flesh and blood humans sitting in front of us? What are their academic capabilities? Equally important are their attitudes toward learning; family, socio-economic and linguistic backgrounds; and life experiences. This information represents the challenges and opportunities for literacy instruction.

Basic functional literacy is the goal for many institutions and for many inmates. The very real need to read a newspaper, to get and keep a job, to be able to follow written instructions, and to fill out the multitude of forms and paperwork facing today's citizen must be addressed. But basic functional literacy is not equivalent to enhanced human connections.

Literary Therapy

Passionate learning takes place when it comes from and is connected to our own experience. Inmates have powerful concerns, dreams, and expectations. Literary therapy encourages a profound literacy that taps into powerful inner dimensions and abilities to bring forth a newly empowered individual capable of interacting with the world in new ways.

Literary therapy is the use of literature to effect change. It is the coupling of literature with cognitive and humanistic therapies. Through the use of poetry, short stories and longer works, self awareness, insight, cognitive restructuring, and socialization can be enhanced. Research underscores the therapeutic value of literary therapy with both adjudicated and minority populations.

Literary therapy provides the opportunity to see one's own story through the story of another, to construct one's own narrative. This invites interpretations and analysis that have not been evident before. It is used to create dialogue between the literary therapist and the students, to promote ethnic identity, to explore issues relevant to the students, and as a means of promoting verbal and written expression. When we are able to see ourselves in the experiences of others, new perspectives and alternative reactions present themselves. Immediate emotionality is filtered so that cognitive examination is more likely to occur. Order can be made of what previously was perceived as chaos.

Literary therapy involves the integration of content, process, and affect. These facets are not independent, but are intertwined from beginning to end. For the purpose of illustration, I will attempt to treat them separately.

<u>Content</u>

The effective literary therapist selects literature whose author has something to say to the specific group of clients he or she is working with. Race, ethnicity, gender, themes, genre, and level of difficulty are to be considered when deciding what poetry, short stories, and excerpts to use.

In my work with male offenders, I rely on the magnificent work of Jimmy Santiago Baca. Baca's first hand knowledge of being incarcerated, in both Arizona State Prison at Florence and San Quentin, is unquestionable when one reads his poetry and essays. Baca's reflections speak directly to inmates and invite them to examine and discuss what has happened and what continues to happen in their own lives. On a daily basis Baca had to choose between the pen and the shank. Other inmates need to know that that choice exists. When walking into a new group of prisoners I can ask for no better weapon than one or more copies of Baca's <u>Immigrants In Our Own Land</u>. Some of Baca's poems are requested over and over because they resonate so powerfully with the yearnings, regrets, and basic realities of inmates. After one session the participants understand themselves and one another on a different level. This has been my consistent experience.

Luis J. Rodriguez is another wonderful source of literature consistent with the experiences of many prisoners. Rodriguez was a East Los Angeles gangbanger in the sixties. His eloquent autobiography, <u>Always Running</u>, is a plea to his own son and to other young men to stop running, to leave *la vida loca* for a more meaningful existence. <u>Always Running</u> never preaches; instead it is the account of Rodriguez's failure to find acceptance in the larger society, the lure of gang life, his violent and illegal activities as a gang member, and the struggle to leave the gang behind. Rodriguez's compelling voice reaches inside and grabs hold.

Langston Hughes, Maya Angelou, Sherman Alexie, Patricia Preciado Martin and many other authors provide dynamic content for use by the prison literary therapist. The crucial consideration is always the clients when selecting an author and literary work that will touch and expand their minds and souls.

<u>Process</u>

Literary therapy is about processes—reading, listening, speaking, writing, thinking, feeling and changing. Even functionally illiterate participants benefit from hearing stories and poems. Being read to is often a foreign and pleasurable activity for inmates. Hearing a selection being read can make otherwise too difficult material accessible while increasing understanding and appreciation of literature. We know that people who have been read to a great deal as children are usually better readers themselves.

Because the literary therapist has chosen literature that is relevant, discussion is often spontaneous. In some cases, perhaps with a volatile issue, written responses are very appropriate. These can be kept private, shared with just the therapist, or read aloud to the group. Another advantage of starting with written expression is that often more thought goes into the written response. Many times participants want to keep what they have written because of its relative permanency. Also, when written responses are read aloud to the group there is an accepting audience for not just one's thoughts but for one's writing. This can have long lasting effects on how the inmate sees himself as a thinker, speaker, writer and human being.

Affect

The listening, reading, and discussion of literature as it applies to actual experiences provoke the therapeutic process. In a group setting participants become involved in the literary selection, their own lives, and the dynamics of the group. The skilled literary therapist will emphasize certain aspects of the selection, encourage exploration of the significance of these in the lives of the inmates, draw out difficult memories or feelings and provide support for the timid or reluctant participant. Inmates are able to identify with group members through commonalities revealed by the poem or short story and their reactions to them. During these discussions there is a tendency to suspend negative labeling and prescribed outcomes. New ways of seeing oneself and one's life emerge, as do new outcomes for what once felt predetermined. In the safety of the literary setting inmates can experience life events similar to their own, identify with characters, and investigate possible solutions to seemingly unsolvable difficulties.

Conclusion

The cultural diversity represented in our penal system requires culturally sensitive programs and practitioners. Literacy instruction must go beyond functional literacy. Luis J. Rodriguez defines real literacy as being able to take part in the various aspects of society, comfortably and with assurance. Literary therapy as described here is the potentially revolutionary interaction of the mind and heart of a human being with galvanizing literary works.

The skilled literary therapist is a catalyst. He or she combines a thorough knowledge of multicultural history and literature with expertise in literacy education and an understanding of therapeutic processes. By bringing to the surface long dormant strengths, thoughts and feelings, the skilled literary therapist promotes cognitive restructuring, personal empowerment and enhanced socialization to adjudicated populations. This is a powerful method for bringing about new connections and new behavior.

Jimmy Santiago Baca, a mestizo from New Mexico, was basically illiterate until he went to jail. There he began the long, tedious, ultimately life changing process of teaching himself to read and write. Poetry workshops in Arizona State Prison at Florence opened a new world to this man who is now a nationally recognized poet and essayist, a participant of Bill Moyers' nationally acclaimed Poetry Festival. In Working In The Dark Baca speaks most eloquently of being on the fringes of society, of the power of language to bring one knowledge of self and access to the larger world. We need to listen to this man and then to act.

Melba Conway is a Master's level reading specialist. Her areas of specialization include multicultural American history and literature and literary therapy. She has worked with at risk adolescents in culturally diverse settings for twenty five years. She has vast experience with abused, abusing, and gang affiliated young people. Ms. Conway is founder and president of Many Voices, a diversity education consulting company which focuses on adjudicated populations.

Suggested Books

Jimmy Santiago Baca

- Immigrants In Our Own Land And Other Early Poems
- What's Happening?
- Working In The Dark

Luis J. Rodriguez

- The Concrete River
- Always Running

Sherman Alexie

- Old Shirts and New Skins
- The Business of Fancy Dancing

Maya Angelou

- I Shall Not Be Moved
- Wouldn't Take Nothin' For My Journey Now

Langston Hughes

- Selected Poems

Patricia Preciado Martin

- Days Of Plenty, Days Of Want

Milton Meltzer

- A History In Their Own Words—The Black Americans

Julian Samora and Patricia Vandel Simon

- History Of The Mexican American People

RUBEN RODRIGUEZ
"Industrial Training Programs"

I first went to prison in 1968 at the age of 16 for selling drugs and the possession of hypodermics. My last incarceration in 1981 landed me a 15 year to life sentence. I did always look to educate myself and participated, to some extent, in academic and vocational programs, but I was still in a negative frame of mind.

The optical program at Wallkill Correctional Facility did not present itself to me until this last incarceration. Inmates were chosen for this program depending on their institutional records and how well they did on a mathematics exam. Afterwards, the inmate was given class instructions for three to six months, then moved up to the shop and the actual making of eye-glasses.

I always found this an interesting program, because I saw it as the most productive, progressive and realistic means of preparing for my eventual return to society. As this program went from serving state run facilities to providing glasses for Medicaid clients in upstate New York regions, I started to view the program from a more goal oriented perspective. I saw the optical program as a fall-back means of employment in the event I could not land a job in the counseling field, which is what I really wanted to do. So the optical program became a serious objective in terms of a personal goal.

Another interesting program is the Industrial Training Program, a temporary release, or furlough program. Basically it consists of working at a warehouse in Albany where the products produced in all correctional facilities are stored and shipped. Qualifying inmates are transferred to a facility from which they are transported between the prison and the warehouse five days a week. Participating inmates are paid from $2.00 to $3.50 per hour. Furloughs consist of leaving the warehouse on Fridays and returning to prison on Sunday nights.

The furlough program affected me tremendously in that it showed me how business is run, and allowed me to put my training to use. It definitely prepared me for release, because it put me in contact with the outside world while at work and on furlough. It also helped strengthen family ties. It helped me to gradually absorb the changing world after being away for a period of thirteen years.

Life for me today has taken on more meaning. I am working as a counselor at The Fortune Society. I see life in general from a much more positive perspective, and I feel as if I have a lot to look forward to. I'm proud of my achievements, and my sight is set toward the future because, with God's grace, there's still more that I want to do.

Looking back, I can say that prison is a horrible experience for anyone. But prison did a lot of good for me in that it provided the time and opportunity to educate, train and prepare myself for a greater chance at making it out here in the free world.

Prison programs are often not geared toward providing realistic skills. They are not as up to date as they need to be, and today there are more and more programs being taken away. But while prison programs can be improved, I personally believe it's up to the individual to do the best with whatever little there is available to him. The opportunity to educate, train and improve one's life can be found in prison, but the individual has to be ready to make the necessary changes it requires.

With me, it began when I started to see what AIDS was doing. When I realized that my life was going nowhere, and, but for the grace of God go I, I educated myself on AIDS; in the process, I discovered I have potentials I could explore, i.e. writing, a caring compassionate nature, and a good ear for listening. My philosophy on prison programs is they work if you work them. Inmates need the opportunity to prepare for re-entry into society, and they need to grasp that opportunity to be all that they can be.

Ruben Rodriquez, born in Puerto Rico, came to New York with his family when he was about six years old. He grew up in Brooklyn, went to school, and got trapped in the world of drugs. He has served many years in New York state prisons, and has always had the support of his parents. Now he has a career at The Fortune Society as a general counselor.

ART BESSE
"Industries: Mobile Home Repair"

I

Wisconsin, like most states, is experiencing a burgeoning prison population. The state's prison population in 1985 was approximately 6,000 inmates; by 1995 that figure had leapt to 10,000 inmates. It is projected that 17,500 persons will be incarcerated in the state system by 1999, a nearly three fold increase in fourteen years. The issues that arise from this situation are dramatic. Wisconsin taxpayers are paying millions of dollars to house, feed, and clothe an ever growing population. As (re)habilitation dollars shrink, compared to the population, inmate idleness increases along with the associated security concerns. The bottom line is: Wisconsin taxpayers want relief from the costs of incarceration <u>and</u> insist that criminals spend time in prison for their offenses. Wisconsin taxpayers want offenders to <u>contribute significantly</u> to the cost of their own incarceration, provide support for their families and meet other court ordered obligations.

Which brings us to 1995 and Wisconsin Governor Thompson's Inmate Work Initiative. Governor Thompson wants far more of Wisconsin's inmate population working and contributing to the cost of their incarceration, requiring that new sources of work be identified. Department of Corrections Secretary, Michael Sullivan, created an Advisory Committee of Corrections personnel, private business and labor union representatives.

According to the Program Statement of the Advisory Committee: "The need for meaningful work for incarcerated persons is undeniable. The concerns of private sector business and labor are understandable and legitimate. This work group has been tasked with identifying a niche within which prisons can provide inmates with meaningful work that will prepare them for release, transition them to jobs in the community, and enable them to be contributing members of the community in which they live, be that in prison or at home."

This advisory committee established the following goals for the Work Initiative:

- **To save Wisconsin taxpayers money through the use of inmate labor**. All inmates earning a wage should return a portion of their earnings to the state for their room and board and services. Inmates assigned to full-time programs, or otherwise unavailable for work, should be required to participate in community service projects.
- **To require all inmates to work for their room and board**. All inmates should have a primary, full-time assignment that reflects their primary need: school, treatment or work.

• **To develop a balanced program of work that will**

a) enlarge the role of prison industries and its contribution to the self-sufficiency of the Department of Corrections,

b) provide goods and services to the prisons and other state agencies that will reduce overall government expenditures,

c) establish private sector relationships that will provide employment, work training, and job placement services,

d) support community non-profit agencies by providing volunteer inmate labor, and

e) maintain institution operations through meaningful employment of inmates in institution jobs which require effort and performance expectations comparable to private sector employment.

• **By the year 2000**, it is expected that 2,500 inmates will be involved in these activities.

• **By the year 2000**, it is expected that the prison system will be 25% self-sufficient.

• **This will be done** in a way that will not compete unfairly with Wisconsin businesses or take jobs away from state citizens.

Falling within the objective of supporting community non-profit agencies, one of the Wisconsin Department of Corrections' most outstanding community service projects—the Mobile Home Recycling Project—spans both minimum and secure facilities. The project is a joint effort of the Bureau of Correctional Enterprises, the Foundation for Rural Housing, Inc. (FRHI)—a statewide non-profit corporation—and the Wisconsin Manufactured Housing Association (WMHA). Inmates at three facilities totally rehabilitate used mobile homes donated by the WMHA and its member organizations.

The project has been recognized for its creative partnership linking together the public, private non profit and private business sectors. The Mobile Home Recycling Project has been cited as one of four exemplary programs in the nation by the American Correctional Association. Additionally, the Wisconsin Manufactured Housing Association received the Summit Award from the American Society of Association Executives for its role in the project. The Foundation for Rural Housing, Inc., received the Fannie Mae Foundation Award of Excellence.

News coverage for this project has all been positive. Several newspapers have issued articles on the project and a local TV station traveled 70 miles to cover the story on the first completed mobile home at one of the centers.

II

Both ingenuity and serendipity led to the inception of this project. Wisconsin Manufactured Housing approached the Foundation for Rural Housing, Inc. with the offer of older mobile homes available for donation. Fortunately, this followed a presentation by staff of the Department of Corrections (DOC) to a state wide association of private-non-profit agencies including FRHI. The presentation was for the purpose of expanding the DOC's already considerable community service program utilizing inmate labor. The fortuitous juxtaposition of these events contributed to the birth of the project.

This innovative project ultimately was initiated through a federal grant developed by personnel of the FRHI and the DOC. The initial 18 month start-up grant of $237,125 from the U.S. Department of Health and Human Services, Office of Community Services allowed the repaired mobile homes to be given at no charge to people living in penury (average less than $4,000 per annum, per person) and often homeless families. Grant funds covered the administrative and service costs of the FRHI and material cost, i.e., new furnaces, new plumbing fixtures, shingles, paint, etc. DOC has donated its services. WMHA through its member organizations has donated the mobile homes. Start-up was feasible without this grant, however the grant provided an ideal beginning by allowing for the mobile homes to be given to the poor at no charge.

III

The FRHI has the overall administrative responsibility for the Mobile Home Recycling project. Key responsibilities of FRHI include identification of mobile homes for recycling, acceptance of the mobile home titles, payment and authorization for purchases of repair materials, arrangement for transporting mobile homes, mobile home site selection, arranging financing and identification of potential mobile home recipients. Because of FRHI's extensive administrative role, the administrative role of DOC has not been substantial, taking perhaps 10% of a central DOC staff's time. This position is charged with community service development as part of the Governor and Secretary's Inmate Work Initiative.

WMHA, through its CEO and member agencies, is responsible for the donation of appropriate mobile homes. An appropriate home is one which, without prison labor, would be too expensive to repair, however it can be rehabilitated at a materials cost of about $5,000 per home. A likely alternative for a mobile home in this condition would be landfilling, an environmental and social waste. Wisconsin has a surfeit of mobile homes which meet the "appropriate" definition. DOC's role is to repair the mobile homes. Inmates are first trained in one of DOC's vocational training programs such as building services and then put to work applying their new skills. The goal of the building service program is to introduce students to the building service trade and prepare them for job entry upon release from the Department of Corrections. Students learn to repair and maintain physical structures of commercial and industrial establishments such as factories, office buildings, hospitals and apartments using hand tools and power tools to replace defective electrical switches and other fixtures. Participants paint structures and repair woodwork with carpenter's tools, repair plumbing fixtures, repair plaster and drywall, and build a shed and other out-buildings. DOC provides the inmate wages, teacher/trainer, on-site supervision and security. It also provides the administrative oversight staff time for its share of the partnership, and manages the repair scheduling.

Part of the reason for the recycling project's success is the existence of an ad hoc oversight work group. The group is made up of representatives of each of the major partners: the Foundation for Rural Housing, Inc., the Wisconsin Manufactured Housing Association, the Wisconsin Department of Corrections, each of the three correctional sites where recycling occurs and Steenberg Homes, Wisconsin's largest manufacturer of mobile homes. The work group meets on an as-needed basis addressing such issues as fund raising and coordination.

All of the partners have the responsibility to raise funds for the project. For instance, DOC has provided older workers as construction aides financed under a federal Older Americans Act grant and has involved local community action agencies to provide weatherization funds channeled from the federal government through the state. Weatherization funds have paid for costly items such as furnaces and have also provided for energy audits. FRHI has used Housing Cost Reduction Initiative (HCRI) funds from the state to help with closing costs. DOC and FRHI have successfully solicited the donation of building materials such as paint, electrical fixtures and plumbing supplies to further bid-down the price of the project. It should be noted, however, that continuing the project is a day-by-day budgetary struggle.

Since the end of the federal grant, the project has continued at a slower pace. Eventually we hope to make the program self-sufficient. One of the three sites has switched over to construction of stick-built housing. Between April, 1995 and April 1997, nine homes have been completed. The repair materials are now paid for by the families who will receive the homes. The average income of recipient families is slightly higher than before and each placement is worked out with a local lender. There are many families who would like the mobile homes but cannot finance $5,000 and/or find the park/land on which to site the mobile home. To reiterate, the real dilemma has been in the cash flow for materials and covering the staff time of FRHI working with the families.

IV

These arrangements are a win/win/win for the partners. Rural Housing carries out their mission by providing low cost housing to very needy families. Manufactured Housing members provide a popular public service, receive a tax benefit from the donation and save land fill tipping costs. Corrections addresses the inmate idleness issue and performs a valuable community service by diverting waste from the landfill and providing low cost housing for the poor.

During the 18 months of the grant, 31 homes and one transitional shelter for a Community Action Agency were provided, as well as three mobile homes used as workshops at the prisons. Over 66 inmates were trained in the 18 month period. The skills that they had learned as part of the program in the three correctional facilities were applied to a visible product. Not only did that represent realistic employment, but pride was developed in assisting others. The work done was excellent and the materials cost was about $3,000 per home.

Inmates have benefited from this project in a number of ways. One discussed his feelings like this: "Eight hours a day and you're not even in prison as you work on the mobile home!" Another inmate expressed his appreciation for the opportunity to give something back to the community he offended when he stated, "I like doing it for the poor people." Another expressed a common theme in the mobile home project when he stated that the project "gave me a little self-respect about things that I have done." Inmates learn a viable vocational and avocational skill, pay part of their debt to society and make their hours of incarceration more productive for themselves as well as society.

Society in general also benefits in a number of ways from this project. Mobile homes are diverted from the landfill, thus granting longer life to landfill sites. The stock of housing for low income people in rural areas is increased at a reasonable cost to society. Offenders with their new found skills and self confidence are more likely to succeed in the free world and to avoid further criminal and violent behavior. The new home owners benefit dramatically. One perhaps stated it best when she said, "I really love it, it's great to call it my home."

V

Our project paradigm is readily replicable at prisons across the U.S. which are overcrowded and have idleness problems. The project is feasible even in gelid Northern Wisconsin where one of the three sites exists and where temperatures dip to 40 degrees below zero. The work is done out-of doors but in inclement weather can be done in the mobile home itself. Therefore, space should not be an issue at most prisons. Most states have vocational training programs that provide suitable training for this type of project. Wisconsin Manufactured Housing Association is not unique, as similar associations exists in each of the 50 states and are included in the American Society of Association Executives. All states have private non-profit and/or public agencies which are committed to the provision of low income housing and could be recruited for project administration. While Wisconsin received a start-up grant, it was not essential in that DOC could have begun this project without the funds, albeit at a more modest level and based on a modest cost to poor families for the homes. This project can be replicated without substantial outside support. In order to support replication efforts, Wisconsin has developed a short video on the Wisconsin Mobile Home Recycling Project, "Three Way Win: A Mobile Home Recycling Program," which is available on loan. In addition, each of the partner agencies is willing to provide consultation to interested states. An innovative staff with an entrepreneurial spirit is the key ingredient to providing inmates with a valuable rehabilitation opportunity.

Art Besse has worked in program development and management for over thirty years, at both the local and state levels in Wisconsin. He was the executive director of Northwest Wisconsin Community Service Agency in the tumultuous '60's. Mr. Besse has been with Wisconsin Corrections for fifteen years while also heading up his own consultant business where he is a speaker, trainer, facilitator and program developer.

Billy Hughes Jr., “Mare and Foal”

BILLY G. HUGHES, Jr., CPL
"Paralegal Degree Program/Braille Program"

When I walked onto Texas Death Row in 1976, almost 22 years ago, the last thing on my mind was education, but mine had only just started. I was walking around shell-shocked over what had just happened to me: a three day trial and the State of Texas wanted to kill me! I had trusted in the law and been naive about the courts and the way justice clearly works. It only took a few days to realize that I did not know anything about the legal system. I quickly learned that the other prisoners didn't have a clue either.

Here I was, 24 years old and beginning to realize I didn't know anything about the situation in which I suddenly found myself, or about life in general. I felt that I should be like a sponge and soak up everything I could from all the books, television, newspapers, and the people around me. My self education was beginning and I was determined to learn all I could, and I am not referring to 'how-to-be-a-better-criminal' education.

There are several points I should make about getting an education on Death Row. The mind set within the institution was that nothing should be wasted on dead men. We were not to get dental work (like false teeth so a man could eat), no physical or mental help, no medical care to speak of, no access to a law library or legal assistance, and, God forbid, no schooling. The men on Death Row in Texas weren't even allowed to do art work or crafts back in the 70's.

In the early 80s the RUIZ lawsuit was found in favor of inmates in the Texas Department of Criminal Justice (TDCJ). Changes were ordered by the Federal Court and things started to improve for the prison population. General mental health and overall conditions improved and Death Row Inmates were able to start taking some high school equivalency classes. It was good to see over 100 Death Row Inmates earning their GED's before TDCJ shut the program down again.

To make educational matters worse, nationwide, the Federal Pell Grants were taken away from all inmates a few years ago. Prisoners aren't allowed to get ahead or to improve themselves so they can return to society with a better chance of staying out of prison. Now, in Texas, if a general population inmate wants college, he or she has to agree to pay for the courses. The Catch-22 is that prisoners in the TDCJ are not paid, not a nickel, for working. The men and women have to use any money they get from families and friends, or from crafts they make and sell. Needless to say, the number of prisoners going to college in Texas has dropped dramatically.

Yet there is hope for education and self-improvment. Death Row inmates still can and should strive to better themselves and their situation. Coming to Death Row in this country is as low as a citizen can fall, but the Death Row inmate should quit hanging his head. He needs to look up, have hope, pride, and feel worth. There are only two directions off Death Row, into death, or back into the world of the living and a future. Education can be a driving force and key to leaving the row alive.

Every Death Row inmate has ended up where he is because of not understanding the law and the court system. 99.9% of death row inmates, as well as their families and friends, did not know what they were getting into or how things work at trials. Faith in their attorneys and the law has put more men and women on death row than evidence, and it has gotten them killed too. So understanding the justice system should be the first and foremost educational concern of Death Row Inmates. But where do they look and how do they get started?

The answer is Paralegal Studies. We are very fortunate that there are a number of excellent correspondence courses available. There are associations and schools in different parts of the country offering paralegal/legal assistant training, certificates, and even specialized degrees. Every Death Row inmate has access to these programs because they are by mail. These paralegal studies are geared to educate and train prisoners about the legal system, be it civil or criminal law.

A paralegal course should include text books, lessons, instructions, and an instructor who works with each student. The cost of study can vary from course to course, from school to school, but the best price range is in the $600 to $800 dollar area. The total course should cover and explain the laws of the state the Death Row inmate is in, the state process for appeals and the process for habeas corpus. We need to know about legal research and writing, legal briefs and petition filings, and how to spot and bring out points of error. It is especially important to learn about post-conviction remedies available through the state and Federal Habeas Corpus. These paralegal courses are worth their cost in providing understanding about what is happening in our appeals. It lets us help ourselves and gain some peace of mind. Names of paralegal schools and their addresses can be obtained free of charge from Distance Education and Training Council, out of Washington, DC.

Besides paralegal studies, there are hundreds of schools and colleges offering correspondence courses. Someone on Death Row can learn about and study art, computers, religion, music, languages, writing, and earn college degrees in any number of subjects. Addresses for these schools and colleges are available free of charge from Distance Education and Training Council. Another form of education that is worthwhile is one that can help others.

Braille transcribing is a course open to interested people, Death Row inmates included. This is a correspondence course available free of charge from The Library of Congress, National Library Service for the Blind and Physically Handicapped. Braille is a completely different written language, and there is a great need for Braille transcribers by all sorts of services and agencies for the blind across the country.

The course to become a Braille transcriber is nineteen lessons long and takes well over a year to learn. Anyone wanting to take the course will need a brailler which can be purchased or furnished by some organization or service for the blind that wishes to sponsor the student's study. The direct Braille slate is also needed; it is made of plastic and there is a stylus for punching the raised braille dots. A special stiff paper is used for the braille transcribing.

Learning to Braille helps in many ways. It keeps the mind of the Death Row inmate busy, helps Braille organizations offer more services, and provides someone who is sight impaired with more material to read. In the long run, everyone connected with Brailling is helped.

The men and women on the Death Rows in this country do not have to sit and wait and let their minds vegetate. Every living human being needs encouragement and love, and Death Row inmates are no exception. Given the chance, even the lowest of the low in this country can be productive. With any kind of education these men and women can grow and learn to use, not lose, their minds.

Billy G. Hughes Jr. has been on Death Row at Huntsville, Texas, for 22 years. A farrier and horse trainer by trade, he has published Horseman's Travel Guide from prison and continues to write and draw for horse lovers nationwide. In addition to being a writer and artist, Mr. Hughes, since coming to Death Row, has earned two college degrees, become a Certified Paralegal, takes courses in Bible Studies and numerous other subjects, as well as becoming a Certified Braille Transcriber. He designed and painted the artwork for the covers of Frontiers of Justice, Volumes 1 and 2. As this book goes to press, Billy Hughes is facing a May 7 execution date.

References

1 Academy of Paralegals, Attn: Dr. J.D. Kallmyer, President, PO Box 953, Harve de Grace, MD 21078-0953

2 Distance Education and Training Council, 1601 18th Street, NW, Washington, DC 20009-2529

3 The Library of Congress, National Library Service for the Blind and Physically Handicapped, 1291 Taylor Street, NW, Washington, DC 20542

4 American Printing House for the Blind, Inc., PO Box 6085, Louisville, KY 40206-0085

5 Howe Press, 175 North Beacon Street, Watertown, MA 02172

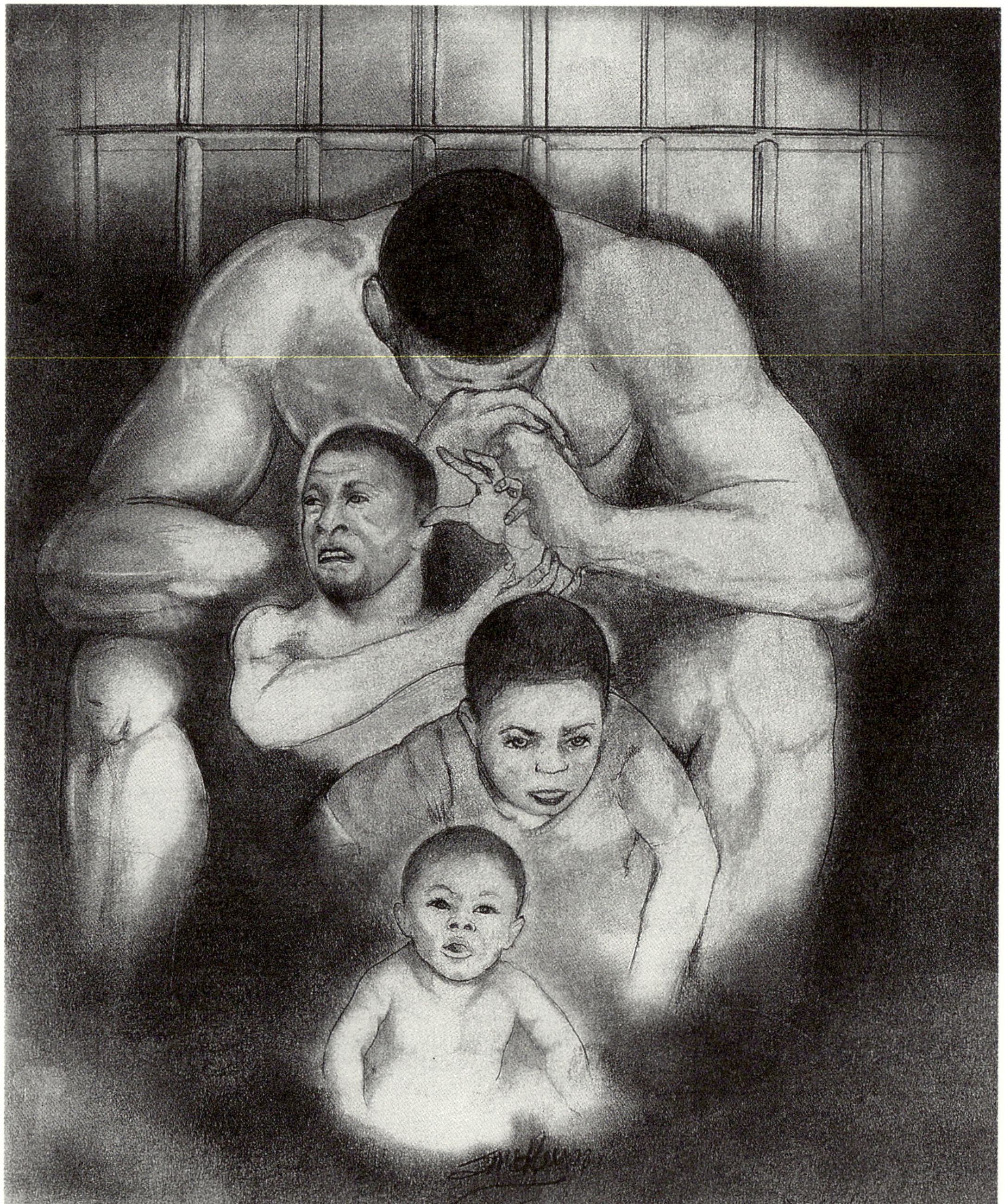

James Lee, "Programming"

CHILDREN

Death Row, Washington

March 1, 1997

"I myself probably get more visits than most of the other guys on the Row, for my family lives closer, matter of fact my brother and his family live only 10 miles away from the prison, so I am very lucky!! It is still very hard for them to come and see me, for it hurts them to see me in here, but I do encourage them to visit as much as possible. My nephews think the world of me, and they are so smart. It's hard though at times, for they know why I am in here, and when they get to asking questions, it's hard to help them understand I don't have no solid answers as to why, and never will!

"You asked if the visits here are drastically limited? Yes, they are, out here in IMU it's all non-contact, but out in SHU, if I jump through their hoops of fire I can get contact visits with family members, and friends that knew me before the crime, but there are so many hoops to get through that it is almost impossible. Out of the four years I have been here I have only been able to get my mother and my brother approved for contact visits! And I can never have contact with any of the kids as long as I am on Death Row. For some reason they feel we would hurt our own family before them?!

March 27, 1997

"Yeah, my nephews are great. I have gotten very close to them since my brother and his family lived right here in Walla Walla when I got here. I love them all very much. It's cute because Dominick, his biggest obsession is bailing me out and having me shave his head, for lots of the time I got my head shaved! And of course I have to teach them how to play (Mary had a little lamb) on the telephone key pad. He truly thinks that's the cat's meow!!"

DENISE QUARLES
"Our Children Do Time With Us"

Eight year old Trevor's behavior has changed considerably for the better during the past year. Prior to that time he had been a problem for both his grandmother and for school teachers. Out of shame, his grandmother had told him two years ago that his mother Susan was in a hospital. In fact, she began serving a lengthy sentence for Second Degree Murder for killing her physically abusive boyfriend. Trevor could not understand why he was the only child in his neighborhood whose mother was not living with her children. He worried about her—the extent of her illness, whether she was going to die and if he would ever see her again.

About one year ago Susan told her mother, Trevor's guardian, that it was time to tell Trevor the truth that she was in prison. She also told her she had informed Scott Correctional Facility prison officials of her interest in participating along with her son in the Children's Visitation Program. Susan missed her son a great deal and could not imagine not continuing to see Trevor and hold him. Like her son, she too had displayed behavior problems after the abrupt separation from him when she was sentenced to prison. She was angry at the predicament she was in and often wondered why she had not terminated her relationship with her abusive boyfriend many years ago. It seemed that she was angry with almost everyone she came into contact with in prison, as well as being angry at herself. Susan had received misconduct citations from prison staff for Insolence, for cursing at them, and for Disobeying A Direct Order. She also did not want to attend school classes which would assist her in preparing to pass the GED exam. Her counselor told her that if her behavior and attitude did not improve, she was jeopardizing any opportunity she had to have the warden award her credits which would reduce the amount of time she would have to stay in prison before she could be considered for parole.

Susan finally began to realize that she was not making the best of the predicament in which she found herself. She summoned up the courage to be truthful with her son by telling him that she had committed a very serious crime for which she was being punished by serving a prison sentence. To the extent she could, she wanted to parent her child, even if from a distance. Although Susan's mother could not financially afford to transport Trevor to the Scott Correctional Facility on regular visiting days, Susan and her son were able to participate in the Children's Visitation Program which provided the opportunity for a monthly visit between them, along with other prison mothers and their children.

Children's Visitation Program day is a big day for mother and son, one which the two of them look forward to each month. It is the day they are able to spend some quality time together talking, playing games and just holding each other. A volunteer with whom Trevor has established a trusting relationship over time drives him to the prison where he is searched after entering a security gate, just as are all visitors to any Michigan prison. He had previously been informed that the search is a requirement to ensure visitors are not bringing in inappropriate items. Despite this explanation, his young mind does not fully comprehend the purpose of the search, but he accepts it as part of the requirements necessary when he visits his mother. Each time Trevor visits, he is escorted into the visiting room by prison staff. His face lights up with happiness when he sees her there waiting for him. In between the special monthly 3-hour visits, he desperately misses his mother; although he knows she is being punished for having done something "real bad," he still finds it difficult to understand why he cannot see her every day. Susan continues to try and explain to her son that she will one day come home after her term of punishment ends. She realizes that it may be impossible to get her son to accept her daily absence from his life, but at least she can try to influence him positively through the frequent letters they write to each other and through the visitation program which is helping her to improve her parenting skills. She is also pleased that Trevor's behavior has greatly improved in the last several months. He knows now that she is not ill, that she loves him and that she will return home one day.

The Michigan Department of Corrections began the Children's Visitation Program in 1986 at the Huron Valley Women's Facility (later closed and replaced by the Scott Facility). Initially the program was proposed to then Warden Tekla Miller by an advisory board which was established as a result of a consent decree following the filing of a federal class action lawsuit. Female prisoners had alleged a lack of parity in programming for female versus male prisoners. Three of the board members (two social work professors from the University of Michigan and one representative of the Women Lawyer's Association) presented information from a study of children of incarcerated single mothers which indicated that the children were at the highest risk to suffer from depression, to get involved in crime and to display violent behavior.

A technical assistance grant was received from the National Institute of Corrections so that input from a prison parenting consultant could be obtained. Warden Miller received approval from administrators of the Department for implementation of the program, and volunteers and the advisory board obtained grant funds through the Skillman Foundation, a philanthropic organization headquartered in Detroit. The funding was administered by the Michigan Council on Crime and Delinquency, an agency devoted to development of effective solutions to crime and victimization. Board members and prisoners had input into the development of the program which initially began with 10 children of prisoners who participated in a three hour structured visiting session with their incarcerated mothers. During the visiting period, prison staff who had volunteered to assist with the program, as well as a Children's Visitation Program employee, would observe the interactions between the prisoners and their children and organize some group play activities.

Unlike during regular visiting periods, a uniformed corrections officer was not present to monitor the visitation. It was determined that a better degree of normalcy for the children could be achieved by not having a uniformed corrections officer present. After each visit there were two debriefing sessions held, one for the prisoners and one for the children, to discuss issues relating to the visit and interactions between mothers and children. Program staff assisted the participants to work through difficulties with having to say good-bye to each other at the end of the visit.

Tekla Miller states that the program was successful in helping to improve the behavior of both prisoners and their children. Through debriefing sessions, the participants were able to resolve some of the emotional difficulties resulting from the separation of parent and child due to incarceration. Also, the parenting class required of the prisoner participants, as well as the constructive visiting activities, helped them learn how to effectively interact with their children. Ms. Miller stated that when the other prisoners began to see the benefits of the program, they became enthusiastic about it and participation substantially increased. She indicated that one of the most telling comments made by a prisoner program participant was that for the first time the prisoner had sat down and actually spent time talking to her teenage son.

Due to prisoner acceptance, the program continued and increased to 60 mothers and 120 children at the Scott Correctional Facility. A coordinator of the program was hired by the Michigan Council on Crime and Delinquency and volunteers/drivers were trained by the Council staff. These volunteers were matched with the children in an effort to build trust and to establish a relationship between them. Typically the volunteers transported up to 30 children per week. Enrollment in the program was considered a privilege and a prisoner's acceptance into it was at the discretion of the Council staff. The number of participants was limited only by the availability and capacity of the prison visiting room. Additionally, the prisoner participants had to comply with the mandatory requirement to attend parenting classes and support group sessions as well as to refrain from any physical discipline of their children and to comply with prison visiting rules. The visiting periods continued to consist of story telling, mothers helping children read and draw, program staff organizing meaningful group play activities, and debriefing sessions at the conclusion of the period. Whenever clinical interventions were deemed necessary by the program coordinator, the interventions were carried out in consultation with the prison psychologist.

Unfortunately, the Children's Visitation Program ended as of November, 1997 due to the lack of funding. The warden of the Scott Facility and the Council Executive Director are now looking for other funding sources for what has proven to be a successful and meaningful program which provided positive mother/child interactions, and one which hopefully over time will prove to reduce recidivism for the prisoners and to prevent criminal behavior in their children. Warden Joan Yukins stated, "The Children's Visitation Program provided an opportunity for meaningful interaction between prisoners and their children and sometimes provided the forum for reconciliation between estranged parents and children." She also indicates that she has witnessed program participation having a positive effect on the behavior of prisoners during their incarceration.

Programs such as the Children's Visitation Program help reduce anxiety in the children of prisoners, in part because they are comforted by the knowledge that their mothers still love them and care about their well being. Sometimes they are able to bond with their mothers in a more meaningful way than they had prior to their mother's incarceration. For the prisoners the program is a positive influence because they come to realize the degree to which their children need and love them. This can be a catalyst to help them improve their behavior in prison and to take advantage of the various rehabilitation programs offered in preparation for their eventual release and reunification with their children. Female prisoners who are mothers oftentimes say that the most difficult aspect of incarceration is the separation from their children. As one program participant stated, "Our children do time with us."

Denise Quarles is a Regional Prisons Administrator who supervises the wardens and oversees the operations of 16 prisons for the Michigan Department of Corrections. She has over 26 years of experience with that agency for which she has worked in many positions which had previously not been held by females: 1 of 2 females to first supervise a male felon probation caseload, manager of a half-way house for male prisoners, Assistant Deputy Warden of a male maximum security prison and manager of a male prisoner reception center. During her career she has served as the warden of four prisons containing male and female prisoner populations of various security levels. Ms. Quarles also served in the capacity of Deputy Director of the Bureau of Field Services, which bureau operated the state's parole and probation services, half-way houses for prisoners and alternative to prison incarceration programs. While holding this position, she was responsible for the development of several new programs which were alternatives to prison incarceration for probationers, parolees and half-way house prisoners such as probation detention centers and technical rule violation centers. She has bachelor and masters degrees in sociology.

James Lee, "Lost My Biological Love"

JUDY BRISCOE
"Resocialization: Teaching Accountability, Social Skills and Victim Empathy"

For the last several years crime has been consistently rated as the public's number one concern, but more particularly, juvenile crime has had the public perplexed and fearful.

It is important to keep in mind several things about the potential juvenile crime challenge. First, *the vast majority of juvenile offenders are not violent predators.* They are neither violent nor incorrigible, and the juvenile justice system needs to be able to address the entire range of at-risk, delinquent and criminal youth. Solutions must span the entire spectrum—from prevention to early intervention to swift and sure punishment for chronic/violent offenders.

Public concern about crime has been influenced by several factors: first, by the ever increasing politics of crime by national, state and local leaders; second, by the reporting, exaggerating and sensationalizing of crime by the media; and third, by the failure of academicians, criminal justice experts, and policy makers to agree upon how best to manage crime. Whether that concern is perception or reality is not important. What is important is that policy makers not be infatuated by *sound bites* and expedient *get tough* approaches, but work toward a rational, comprehensive approach to delinquency prevention.

Society must invest more time, money and effort in both public and private crime prevention efforts that encourage responsible, caring, pro-social adult role models becoming involved in the lives of at-risk youth. Society must place a priority on educating its children and instilling those values that make them responsible citizens. Communities must identify those factors that place children at risk and then mobilize forces to eradicate bad influences and build or strengthen those factors that provide protection and hope. Economically-depressed, crime-ridden neighborhoods must be revitalized so that youth can experience hope and dreams for a better way of life.

Juvenile justice professionals must argue vigorously to maintain separate juvenile and criminal justice systems. Legitimate public concerns justify imprisoning dangerous, repeat offenders; however, research shows that housing juvenile offenders with adult felons is not the answer to decrease the rate of violent crime. Youth who get into trouble with the law need adult guidance, and suitable role models won't be found in prison. People must understand that the development of children and youth is a process that allows for learning, growing, changing and maturing. Just as youth are vulnerable to negative influences, they are just as likely to be amenable to positive influences if adults can figure out how to reach them, or recognize they must be reached. Citizens must maintain hope for rehabilitation; for without that, society will surely self-destruct.

In the last twenty years, social order has changed dramatically. An increasing number of children are living with only one parent, and that parent often depends on government assistance or works two jobs to keep food on the table. People have become more transient which precludes establishing roots and having access to extended families and long-term friendships. Neighborhoods are no longer stable, and many are violent and poverty-ridden. For people with economic means, burglar alarms, fences, and private security systems keep them safe; for people without means, violence is a fact of life. More children today are born into poverty to unwed, uneducated, young mothers who don't understand the basics of nurturing a child, much less what it means to be a teacher or role model. Poverty can create a sense of hopelessness which becomes a self-fulfilling prophecy. The church is no longer a focal point and children grow up without a spiritual connection and with no sense of right and wrong. Reverend Eugene Rivers III, who established a youth ministry in inner-city Boston, developed a ten-point plan "to save children," and "mobilize churches to combat youth violence and despair," based in part on his conversation with one of the neighborhood's most notorious drug merchants. At the end of a long and complicated discussion of why so many of the community's children had fallen prey to drugs and crime and violence, the drug dealer cast a cold eye on Rivers and his fellow ministers and declared plainly, "I'm there, you're not."[1]

Many professionals and practitioners have known intuitively for some time that violence begets violence, but until recently, there have been few scientific studies that have shown the correlation empirically. One exceptional longitudinal study completed by Cathy Spatz Widom, professor of criminal justice and psychology and director of the Hindelang Criminal Justice Research Center at the State University of New York at Albany, was entitled *The Cycle of Violence*.[2]

Widom's study tracked 1,575 cases from childhood through young adulthood, comparing the arrest records of two groups: a study group of 908 substantiated cases of childhood abuse or neglect and a comparison group of 667 children, not officially recorded as abused or neglected and matched to the study group according to age, race, sex, and approximate family socioeconomic status.

Some of the findings were that:

- Those who had been abused or neglected were 53 percent more likely to be arrested as juveniles;
- 38 percent more likely to be arrested as adults;
- 38 percent more likely to be arrested for a violent crime.

It further showed that abuse and neglect cases were more likely to average nearly one year younger at first arrest; commit twice as many offenses; and were arrested 89 percent more frequently.

A more troubling conclusion was that a child who is neglected is just as likely as a child who is abused to be arrested for a violent crime. *And unless there is neurological damage from the abuse, neglect has a longer term, more damaging impact to the development of a child.* (Italics mine.)

Preliminary Phase Two findings of Widom's study, based on follow-up interviews with 500 study and comparison group subjects, indicated other negative outcomes to be as common as delinquency and violent criminal behavior, including mental health concerns (depression and suicide); educational problems (inadequate cognition, extremely low IQ, poor reading ability); health and safety issues (alcohol and drug problems); and occupational difficulties (lack of work, employment in low-level service jobs).

What do children need? They need, first of all, to be born healthy. Pre-natal care, which is extremely important, should be treated as a public health issue. Children need to be nurtured so they are well loved, well fed, immunized against childhood diseases, read to, touched, taught right from wrong, encouraged creatively and allowed to bond. The Carnegie Corporation of New York studied the importance of the first three years of a baby's life in terms of brain development. We now know, for example,

- The brain development that takes place before age one is more rapid and extensive than previously realized;
- Brain development is much more vulnerable to environmental influence than ever suspected;
- The influence of early environment on brain development is long lasting.

The Carnegie study identified many risk factors in a child's life; e.g. personality, physical health, family, social/peer influence, neighborhood, community, school and individual interaction with the environment. Risk factors are often multiplicative, not additive, in their effects. "When children showed only one risk factor, their outcomes were no worse than those of children showing none of the identified risk factors. But when children had two or more risk factors, they were four times as likely to develop social and academic problems."[3]

To help ensure that children are properly nurtured, communities can replicate a program that began in Hawaii, called Hawaii Healthy Start. This program has social workers go into the hospital and interview mothers shortly after they have given birth. If the mother agrees, a risk assessment is administered to determine whether the mother might be at risk for abusing or neglecting her child. If the risk assessment indicates the possibility of abuse or neglect and the mother agrees to participate in the program, a home visitor schedules a time to meet with her once she leaves the hospital. The home visitor teaches the mother parenting skills, helps her access government services for which she is eligible, and establishes a relationship with a primary care physician for the baby. That family is monitored for the first five years of a baby's life. Among those mothers who agreed to participate, child abuse and neglect was averted in 99.7 percent of the cases.

To ensure that children are prepared to learn, pre-school programs should be available in every community. The High/Scope Perry Preschool Project Study Through Age 27 assessed whether high-quality preschool programs could provide both short and long-term benefits to children living in poverty and at high risk of failing in school. The study followed into adulthood the lives of 123 such children from African-American families who lived in the neighborhood of the Perry Elementary School in Ypsilanti, Michigan, in the 1960's.

Findings at age 27 indicated that in comparison with the no-program group, the program group had:

- significantly higher monthly earnings (with 29 percent vs. 7 percent earning $2000 or more per month);
- significantly higher percentages of home ownership (36 percent vs. 13 percent);
- a significantly higher level of schooling completed (with 71 percent vs. 54 percent completing 12th grade or higher);
- a significantly lower percentage receiving social services at some time in the previous 10 years (59 percent vs. 80 percent); and
- significantly fewer arrests (7 percent vs. 35 percent) with 5 or more arrests for crimes of drug making or dealing (7 percent vs. 25 percent).

A growing body of empirical research supports the efficacy of church-centered approaches to battling crime, delinquency, and other economic and social problems. "Just as the density of liquor outlets in a neighborhood correlates with negative phenomena, the density of churches correlates with positive ones."[4] "Several recent econometric studies find that controlling for all relevant individual characteristics (race, gender, education, family structure, etc.), urban youth whose *neighbors* attend church are more likely to have a job, less likely to use drugs, and less likely to be involved in criminal activity. In other words, church-going has what economists term "positive externalities." In this case, church-going affects the behavior of life prospects of disadvantaged youths whether or not they themselves attend church."[5]

There is no *one* program to fit every community or every situation. An array of programs along the developmental continuum where there is citizen investment have the most promise for success. Children must have a safe and secure environment in which to grow and mature. Even impoverished youth living in crime ridden neighborhoods tend to make it if they have an adult parent, teacher, coach or clergy to protect and guide them. Youth who commit the worst crimes have almost always been raised without adult care and supervision. The presence or absence of a positive adult mentor is a principle element in whether or not a teen is able to oppose criminal conduct.

II

The Texas Youth Commission created the Office of Delinquency Prevention specifically to provide information about programs as well as the latest research on issues relating to early childhood development, adolescence, family problems, juvenile justice, and delinquency prevention.*

The Texas Youth Commission (TYC), the agency that handles the state's most seriously disturbed and delinquent youth, is the ultimate sanction in the juvenile justice system. In 1996, 36 percent of the youth were committed to TYC for violent offenses; a 356 percent increase since 1988.

In 1995, TYC began implementing a research-based therapeutic approach that utilized the best, most effective elements of various treatment modalities. This treatment program, called *Resocialization*, is based upon the premise that youth have been "socialized" to a delinquent/crime-prone subculture, must be held accountable for their behavior, and must be helped to understand and to develop the skills and empathy necessary to become positive, prosocial individuals. *Resocialization* uses a variety of interventions that emphasize therapeutic community concepts and cognitive-behavioral interventions in a continuum of care context. It is based on the philosophy that children are not born delinquent and that delinquency is learned behavior that is influenced by early family relationships, social environment, biological factors and subcultural norms and values that justify criminal behavior.

The *Resocialization* Goal is to involve youth in a positive social contract. For example:

- Members of society agree to uphold certain rules of behavior for the good of all its members.
- Individuals must be accountable for their own actions.
- Reparations should be made when harm has been caused intentionally.

The five phases of *Resocialization* were designed to take approximately 12 months to complete. Phase I, the *Orientation/Control Phase*, takes about one month and relies primarily on external controls. Youth adjust to program norms, learn the rules, are introduced to the core program concepts, and experience a safe environment.

Phase II, *Discomfort/Motivation Phase*, takes about two months. Youth recognize how thinking errors are used to justify hurting others; confront their delinquent need gratification; recognize critical life events that have led to delinquent lifestyles; and identify unmet needs.

Phase III, *Hope/Positive Expectations Phase*, takes about three months. Youth recognize that choices change lives, experience the effects of positive reinforcement for prosocial attitudes and choices; accept responsibility for their own choices and understand the impact those choices had on their victims; and recognize the connection between values and behavior.

Phase IV, *Personalization/Experimentations Phase*, takes about three months. During this phase, youth practice new ways of getting needs met in prosocial ways;

assume greater leadership responsibility; increase their use of coping skills; and begin efforts at restitution.

Phase V is the *Integration/Maintenance Phase* during which time the youth are on parole. At this point, youth recognize high risk situations, practice realistic relapse prevention strategies; consistently self-interrupt their delinquent offense cycles and thinking errors; develop and implement realistic success plans; and understand and experience family support.

Each phase has objective criteria and youth must demonstrate mastery of the skills required in each phase. Workbooks are available, homework is assigned, staff are trained, curriculum-driven groups are consistently held and controls are in place for verification and documentation. Education, discipline training and work, three cornerstones, are complementary to the *Resocialization* program.

In addition to the *Resocialization* program to which all youth have access, the Texas Youth Commission operates four specialized treatment programs: capital offender program for youth who commit murder, sex offender treatment, chemical dependency treatment, and programs for youth with emotional disturbance. Of all the youth who are committed to the agency, approximately 80 percent have a need for one or more of the specialized treatment programs. Unfortunately, TYC only has resources to provide the specialized treatment to approximately 30 percent of the youth with special needs.

All TYC treatment programs are designed to hold youth accountable for their own delinquent behavior. Their willingness to hold themselves accountable depends upon their acquisition of sufficient internal control and prosocial skills for need gratification. Through accurate assessment, provision of a therapeutic environment, appropriate intervention, effective skills training and meaningful community support, TYC attempts to remove youth's justification for continued delinquency and provides the tools necessary for lasting behavior change.[6]

*There is a tremendous need for this information, as evidenced by the requests received from all over the world. The address for the Prevention Web site is <www://tyc.state.tx.us/prevention/>

An expanded article on this program is available; see page 370.

Judy Briscoe is Chief of Staff and Director of Delinquency Prevention at the Texas Youth Commission and has over 20 years experience in juvenile corrections. Judy has a Masters Degree in Criminal Justice Management from Sam Houston State University and a Bachelors Degree in Public Administration from St. Edward's University. She is a member of the Board of Governors of the American Correctional Association, the Board of the Texas Institute of Children and Youth, and the Executive Committee of the Board of the Council on Offenders with Mental Impairments. She also serves as a peer review consultant to the National Institute of Justice. Judy is past president of the Texas Corrections Association and past chairman of the Interagency Council on Sex Offender Treatment.

References
1 Preventing Crime, Saving Children: Monitoring, Mentoring, & Ministering (Council on Crime in America, February 1997), p. 20.
2 Widom, Cathy Spatz. "The Cycle of Violence," National Institute of Justice Research in Brief, October 1992.
3 Starting Points. Meeting the Needs of Our Youngest Children. The Report of the Carnegie Task Force on Meeting the Needs of Young Children, 1991.
4 Preventing Crime, Saving Children: Monitoring, Mentoring, & Ministering, p. 21.
5 DiIulio, Jr., John J. Director, The Brookings Institution and Princeton University, February 28, 1996. "Fill Churches, Not Jails: Youth Crime and 'Superpredators'" Statement Before the United States Senate Subcommittee on Youth Violence. [Online] Available: John DiIulio Testimony <http://www.brook.edu/pa/hot/diiulio.htm>Reyes, Linda, Ph.D. "Resocialization Approach." Texas Youth Commission, June 1995.

CYNTHIA LANCE
"Learning Center for Public Housing Children"

Chicago police officers are sending a loud and clear message to the young residents of a public housing development. The message: we care about the future of children in public housing.

Several programs have been instituted for the school-aged residents who live in Robert Taylor Homes, a public housing development on Chicago's South Side. For several years, the children have had an opportunity to learn to play golf, fish or participate in a little league baseball program. Many also can attend a safe summer program and participate in a summer fitness program.

Of all the activities open to the young residents, perhaps the most popular is that of learning computer skills at the Robert Taylor Learning Center.

Children seem to be drawn to the housing development's computer lab because they are curious and anxious to explore this technology. Children come diligently, despite the obstacles they sometimes face traveling to the Center. Young residents often travel through rival gang turf as they go from building to building in the huge Robert Taylor complex. Even as they go to and from school, the gunfire that resounds throughout the development serves as a reminder of the deadly gang activity that surrounds them. But these children will not let anything, not even stray bullets, keep them away from their warm, safe haven at the Robert Taylor Learning Center.

The Robert Taylor Learning Center is a dream come true for Commander Michael Tolliver of the Chicago Police Department. Tolliver commands the department's Public Housing Section, located in the heart of the Robert Taylor public housing development. Robert Taylor Homes is the largest public housing development in the United States, with 28 buildings that contain 4,227 dwelling units. Those dwelling units are occupied by 12,645 residents.

Tolliver believed that it was time to reach out to this community and increase the quality of life for the residents, especially the youngsters who live in the Robert Taylor Homes. He envisioned a place where children could escape street violence after school, if only for a few hours. At that place, they could safely come to complete their homework and learn basic computer skills.

Tolliver decided to convert a first floor room in one of the buildings into a computer lab for the residents of the housing development. With help from the Chicago Housing Authority (CHA), steps were taken to transform the room into one that would be conducive for learning. CHA improved the ventilation and the electricity in the room, and donated air conditioners and additional supplies.

Tolliver also requested assistance from the Department of Housing and Urban

Development (HUD). HUD enthusiastically donated several computers which contributed to the 50 workstations that were built in the center. Finally, in August 1996, the Learning Center was introduced in the Robert Taylor housing development.

Since its inception, several resident children race to the Learning Center after school in order to practice computer skills. Rarely will you find a computer that is not in use. The children improve their math and reading skills while "playing" with the Math Blaster Plus and Reading Readiness programs. We are constantly working to improve the computer lab," Tolliver said. The DIGEX Co., a business Internet carrier, donated its services to the Learning Center shortly after the program's first anniversary. All of the computers now have access to the Internet.

Odum Carter, 11, has come to the Learning Center almost daily since it was established. "I like coming here to work on the games, look at the Internet, and see what movies are coming out," Odum said. He has become well-versed on the Internet, and is able to assist the other children in gaining access to it. Odum is a student at Beethoven School, and does his homework at the Learning Center. His grades have improved since he started coming to the Learning Center. "If I didn't come here, I would probably get in trouble outside," Odum said. Some of his friends also come to the Learning Center, and he encourages others to attend as well.

Angela Falls, 13, has also attended the Learning Center since its inception, and has taught herself to type and gained basic computer skills. Also a student at Beethoven School, she recently completed her science project on a computer at the Learning Center. "I did my science project on the effect that vinegar has on plants," Angela said. "I typed my research on the computer here." Although they have a few computers at her school, she could not complete the project there because she says "they don't give you enough time." She received an A on her science project, and has seen her other grades increase from C's and D's to A's and B's.

On any given day, you can see the enthusiasm in the children's faces as they rush through the door, book bags in tow, to get to a computer. Children 12 and under are able to use the computers until 6 p.m., and older children can stay in the lab until 9 p.m. Not only are they given the opportunity to learn computer skills, but they are also provided a warm and safe environment with officers who demonstrate a genuine concern for them.

The police officers assigned to the Public Housing Section are a great force behind the Learning Center. Many officers have donated their own money for school and computer supplies for the children and often supply after school snacks for the children's enjoyment. In addition to assisting the program financially, several officers spend numerous hours in the Learning Center coaching the children. The officers assists the children with their homework, as well as help them improve their computer skills.

Officer Elaine McKinney has worked at Robert Taylor Homes for nearly a year. She enjoys working in the Learning Center, saying "This is a different type of policing; police officers seem to become more human down here. Kids see us in a different light, not just arresting people. Many youngsters have had negative encounters with the police or have had run-ins with the law. Now they have a better image of local police officers and are communicating better with them."

The children recognize the sacrifices that the officers assigned to the Public Housing Section make for them, and reciprocate by participating in fund-raising events. Recently, the computer students designed and marketed Christmas Cards, the proceeds of which funded a Christmas party for all those who utilize the Center. They also designed and sold Valentine's Day cards and replenished computer supplies with the proceeds.

Commander Tolliver is very proud of the success the Learning Center has had, but even prouder of the youngsters who continue to return time and time again despite difficulties in their families and neighborhood. Recently, Tolliver and his staff sponsored a "Back to School" party for the children, where they were given tee shirts and book bags sporting the Robert Taylor Learning Center logo.

In late 1993 in an effort to bridge the gaps that separate citizens and police officers, the Chicago Police Department introduced its community policing model––Chicago Alternative Policing Strategy, better known as C.A.P.S. C.A.P.S. encourages citizens and police officers, along with city service agencies, to work together as a team to combat chronic crime and disorder. With an emphasis on developing problem-solving techniques and strengthening partnerships, strategies are designed and implemented in an effort to improve the neighborhoods.

Tolliver acknowledges using this strategy as he developed the Learning Center. He felt the center would be one approach to combat problems which plague the Robert Taylor Homes. The Learning Center is, indeed, an excellent approach in accelerating communication and trust between police officers and residents. However, Tolliver's reasons for creating the Learning Center stemmed from his own personal experience, long before community policing was popular.

Tolliver is intimately familiar with the obstacles that residents, especially children, have to face, because he too grew up in a public housing development. He understands firsthand the need for positive activities in such an atmosphere. During the time that Robert Taylor Homes was under construction, Tolliver and his family were living in Wentworth Gardens, another housing project located on the South Side of Chicago.

"I faced some of the same problems that many youth living in a public housing development today face," says Tolliver, adding that programs encouraging children to learn new skills simply did not exist. There was no learning center in his development, and he and his friends relied on Saturday morning trips to the library for "extracurricular" studies.

The computer training program offered to children at the Learning Center is just one of many positive programs designed to support drug and crime prevention at Robert Taylor Homes. "The time and energy young people put in these activities might otherwise be used to surrender to negative pressures and challenges that are part of their daily environment," Tolliver said.

The children have an opportunity to participate in the police Explorers program. This program is a branch of the Boy Scouts of America and concentrates on law enforcement as a possible career option. The young residents meet weekly where activities focus on conflict resolution and exposure to cultural and educational experiences.

There are plenty of positive summer programs available for the children to prevent idle minds straying into wayward activities. "Golf for Kids" is available for residents who are interested in improving their golf techniques. "Hooked on Fishing NOT on Drugs" is a program designed to instill patience and self-discipline in children as they learn to view fishing as a satisfying, confidence-building sport.

Robert Taylor Homes is one of 24 housing developments that compete in the "Inner City Little League." This baseball league, which is sponsored by the Chicago White Sox and the Chicago Cubs, is in its fifth season. "Fitness for Kids" is a jump rope and volleyball program for resident children. The ultimate goal of the program is to compete locally and nationally.

The Public Housing Section is a proud participant of the Safe Summer Program which is aimed to restore a safe, clean, nurturing and supportive environment to residents in and around Chicago public housing developments. The program provides safe recreational areas and activities.

Another one of Tolliver's dreams is in the process of becoming a reality. He is also very concerned about the adult population living in Robert Taylor Homes. Although the children thirst for the opportunities that the Learning Center has to offer, their parents and other residents have been slow to participate.

"In order to be ready for the job force, you have to have computer skills," Tolliver said. Recently, classes were held for adults who were interested in learning the basic functions of computers. "Fifty adult residents started taking classes in a two-week accelerated computer training program," Tolliver said. "Upon completion of the program, they would be eligible to be placed in a job." They were taught how to operate a computer monitor, keyboard, and the proper way to format a disk, as well as other computer functions. In that some of the adults were uncomfortable with their inability to read or learn some of the computer basics, only a third of the individuals completed the course.

Tolliver has not given up hope for the adult residents. More adult computer classes are being planned in the near future. He has also met with several church ministers in the area who plan to send members from their congregations to the Learning Center to better prepare them for job opportunities.

Tolliver welcomed the challenge to work in public housing, and has dedicated much of his time toward making positive on-site changes. Launching the Learning Center has given him immense gratification in his personal life, as well as his career. The dedication that he has displayed will be beneficial to many, even after his retirement. "I just want residents of public housing developments to be afforded the same opportunities as any other citizen in Chicago."

Cynthia Lance has been a Chicago police officer for 11 years. Officer Lance works in the Community Education Section of the Education and Training Division. She instructs recruits and in service personnel in Diversity Management and Chicago's community policing strategy. Officer Lance has also worked in the News Affairs Division of the Chicago Police Department. She attended Roosevelt University where she studied public relations.

TEKLA DENNISON MILLER
"Girl Scouts Behind Bars"

Many of us often feel like sending our children away when they are unmanageable. But few of us want them to go to prison. This is not so in Maryland.

The National Institute of Justice in Washington, DC came up with Girl Scouts Behind Bars and awarded the Girl Scouts of Central Maryland with a $15,000 grant to start this program at the Maryland Correctional Institution for Women (MCIW). The first Girl Scout troop for the daughters of incarcerated women began in November 1992. Though cloning has become a dirty word in our society, the positive outcomes of this program have caused Girl Scouts Behind Bars to be cloned in many women's prisons throughout the United States.

Children suffer when their mothers are in prison. They become victims too. We must remember that when we sentence a parent to prison, we sentence the entire family. As members of a community, we must take responsibility for the children left behind and who had no choice in their destiny.

Surveys show that families are more likely to be broken through a mother's imprisonment than by a father's. According to the Bureau of Justice Statistics, an estimated 80% of imprisoned women in the United Sates have children under the age of eighteen and of that number 75% are single mothers. As a group, children with a parent in prison have been identified for being at a higher risk than other children to be involved in delinquency, criminal behavior, and placement in foster care. They also have increased probability of antisocial behavior, anxiety, depression, aggression, learning disorders, teenage pregnancy, stress disorders and school truancy.

In Maryland alone, it is estimated that three children are affected for every incarcerated mother. The primary goals of Girl Scouts Behind Bars are to reduce the trauma suffered by girls whose mothers are incarcerated and to try to preserve the mother/daughter relationship during incarceration through enhanced visitation and other forms of communications. Correctional officials see the Girl Scout program as a motivating force in breaking the cycle of criminal conduct continuing from generation to generation. And if participation in the program produces better parents who will not recidivate, more power to it.

Other benefits of enhanced visitation programs include the development of socialization skills, tolerance, discipline, trust, anger control and unconditional love. Few inmate mothers entered prison with these. Yet learning these skills will improve their lives and the lives of their children when the mothers re-enter the community.

Girl Scouts Behind Bars is organized much like any troop in the country with the same mission—to prepare today's girls to live successfully in tomorrow's world. The pilot troop in Maryland started with 17 inmates and 24 children between the ages of 5 and 17 years. Two Saturdays each month at the prison, inmate mothers take part in a troop meeting with their daughters. Prior to this, the only time the daughters got to see their mothers was during regular visiting hours. That environment was often frightening to the girls and not conducive to intimacy or positive communication between the mother and child. After the program had been functioning for a while, a volunteer troop leader asked the girls what they liked about the program. One girl answered, "I like to see my mother."

As with many programs in our prisons, Girls Scouts Behind Bars works because of the volunteers. The original program started with a grant, but to continue, stable funding is also needed. Maryland's program has been awarded the National Council of Juvenile and Family Court Judges' Meritorious Service Award for a unique and innovative project. A program recognized in such a manner deserves to be funded.

It is a well known fact that the female prison population is growing faster than the male population. Ninety percent of these prisoner mothers will return to the community. Programs like Girl Scouts Behind Bars help ensure the success of prisoner mothers as parents and stopping the cycle of criminal behavior. Who do we want to return to our communities—the mother who went to prison or the one who participated in a program like Girl Scouts Behind Bars?

Tekla Dennison Miller attended Cazenovia College, UCLA and Oakland University in Michigan. She worked as a probation officer and a halfway house agent in Detroit, was supervisor at the first women's prison camp in Michigan, and warden at Huron Valley Men's and Women's Prisons. Ms. Miller was the first warden in Michigan to manage two maximum security prisons simultaneously. She is the author of The Warden Wore Pink [Biddle Publishing Co.], a contributor to Frontiers of Justice, Volume 1: The Death Penalty, and co-editor of Frontiers of Justice, Volume 2.

PATTY COEN
"Big Brothers/Big Sisters"

Soon after our decision not to have children, my husband and I began to talk about wanting to help those around us that were in need. We had been reading about families that adopt abandoned children and such, but we weren't sure we were ready for that kind of commitment. We both felt very strongly about the fact there were far too many children out there without parents, fathers specifically, to give them the guidance they need and deserve.

My husband made the initial decision to become a Big Brother through our local county Big Brothers/Big Sisters program. Big Brothers/Big Sisters is a national organization that provides adult mentors for youth from single parent homes who have little or no contact with the absent parent. The purpose of having a 'Big' is to help fill this great void in their young lives with a commitment of at least two hours a week.

After my husband's decision, he and I went through about two months of a vigorous and thorough screening process. Soon my husband was told they had the perfect match for him; one day, he brought his new friend home to meet me. I will call him Chris. Of course, with any first time meeting, we were all a little shy, but we all hit it off from the beginning. Chris was 9 years old when we first met him. That was over 3 years ago now.

Chris, we were told, had two older sisters at home and a father who lived far away and whom he had not seen in a few years. As far as we know, Chris's father has relinquished all responsibility for his three children. Chris's mother works full time in her attempt to keep the family clothed, fed, and in school. We learned in time that his mother was very involved with her hobby and often times we would bring Chris home to an empty house, even at 9 or 10 at night. Chris, we learned, was used to taking care of himself. Many times we would call him at dinner time and he was cooking his own dinner, often Ramen soup. His previous "Big" had recently been killed, so Chris had definitely experienced loss and loneliness in his life, even at his early age.

We had also been told he had a condition called Attention Deficit Disorder (ADD) for which he received doses of Ritalin, and a problem with enuresis, or nocturnal bed wetting.

My husband and Chris continued to do many activities together and when I could join them, I did. The three of us got to know each other quite well over the course of two years. After two years, we began to see his problems at home. He had two older sisters, one of whom was very unruly and domineering over Chris. She had had some run-ins with the police and was currently on probation and in a special school. More often than not, his mother never seemed to be around for him. I decided to join forces with my husband. After another somewhat shorter screening,

(Big Brothers/Big Sisters knew us well by now), we became a 'Big Couple'. I felt very strongly that Chris needed to see a marriage that worked, experience how we interacted, and have a non-threatening, non-aggressive female in his life who was there for him. Thus our friendship began to build.

One of my fondest memories of time spent with Chris is when I rented cross country skis for him. We headed out to a local groomed track and skied until after darkness fell. He must have fallen twenty times, but he never became discouraged, and we laughed and laughed that night. He was much hardier than I was, because I had to seek warmth in the hut for awhile. I would peek out the window into the darkness and there he would be, skiing around the track, waiting for my return. The lights of our town lit up our path that night and we both felt very warm inside by sharing a special night together.

One warm summer evening, we pumped up the tires on our spare mountain bike and headed up to an easy trail to introduce our friend to single-track mountain biking. After a few quick lessons, the three of us were off and biking. Chris took to the sport like a fish to water. He was a natural. My husband and I greatly enjoyed watching him attempt something new, somewhat timid at first, then charging up or down the hill like a pro. He never fell once! This being my favorite sport, I enjoyed showing him something new in life.

A very special memory is the night we climbed to timberline, (11,500 ft.) with 3 "masters of the mountains" who taught Chris to "glissade" (slide down a snow slope) for his first time. His anxiety mounted as his turn came to glissade using an ice ax. But once he overcame his fear and let himself slide down the mountain slope, there was no stopping him. On our way home that night, as we hiked out, we found a fresh bear track in the snow and watched the full moon rise over the mountain tops. It was truly a magical evening.

We've included Chris in some of our family get-togethers. He attended my husband's family reunion which included about 40 people, and he was an ordained part of the family by the time we left. He is a friendly, polite young man and related to the family very well. We swam, roller bladed, rode bikes, drove golf carts and had an exceptional and memorable time together.

We've had evening picnics in the mountains and at home. We rock climb together, always stressing the extreme safety required in this sport. We attend his school concerts and functions when invited. We even watched a lunar eclipse with an astronomy professor! Then we attended a lecture at our local college on astronomy, and Chris was the hit of the lecture: he answered most of the questions put forth by the lecturer, putting the dozing college kids to shame.

But, there are also the serious times we've had together. Like the times we haven't been able to walk in his room because the door wouldn't open, due to clothes etc. being piled knee deep. We've spent some serious hours teaching him how to organize his room and live in a habitable environment. Then there are the times his homework isn't done and he needs a little nudge. We've had to say no to more than one visit during a week when he can't get organized and get his homework done. We work with his mom during these times, because our visits are very important to us and to him. We are hoping to teach him self discipline and organizational skills during our more serious visits.

We've made a commitment to have him stay in our home one night per month. We believe this will make him feel a little more at home in our house and know he always has a place to go if the going gets tough. We feel strongly that he knows we are always there for him when he needs someone.

One memorable evening, we were playing the board game "Life." This game is very structured, that is, you always land on the mandatory square, "Get Married." There's no option, no dating period, no time to think it over. After you land on the "Get Married" square, you get little "pegs," representing your kids. There's no divorce in this board game. No "dead-beat dads." Just a by-the-book life. I thought how different this game was from the real game of "Life." Especially Chris's game of "Life." He's already had many disappointments and losses and lonely hours in his life. Yet he is a jovial, happy, joking young man with a great outlook. He has no anger or resentment at this point, yet up to now, the real game of Life has dealt him a bad hand of cards in some respects. And further, he is only one among thousands of children who have been abandoned by their fathers and/or mothers. The real game of Life just isn't fair...

During our time together, we've had many conversations with Chris. Sometimes it's just Chris and I who talk. Sometimes it's man to man and my husband and Chris talk. And other times, the three of us converse on many different topics. When his 15 year old sister became pregnant, we talked about the realities of teenage pregnancy and children raising children. We hope to make an impression on him about how the choices he makes when he is young can impact his whole life. But most of all, we try to express that the upheaval that goes on in his family is not that different from the majority of American families, (a heartbreaking reality). We want him to know we all come from families that have their problems and he is not alone.

Chris has joined my husband and me on a "take your son/daughter to work" day. We are both professionals and college educated so we stress the importance of an education to attain some security within life. He sees the stability we enjoy and we believe this has made a lasting impression on his outlook toward his future. He has stated he wants to be many things in life: a chef, geologist, engineer, to name a few. We are constantly reinforcing that he is more than able to accomplish his goals if he makes a few right choices early in life.

What does this add up to? What message are we conveying to Chris? We believe we are sending a clear message: we have TIME for him: something not many people in his life have done. We lead very busy lives. My husband and I work full time, have aging, even dying parents, and various other commitments, but he is high on our priority list and he knows that. He knows he is very important to us and a major part of our lives. Our conversation on Sunday night is usually, "What night should we see Chris this week?" and "What should we do with him?" If we make a promise to him, such as calling him on a certain night, we make a special effort to do as we said we would. He hasn't had many people in his life he could trust and we want him to know we're different. He can trust that we are there for him. He's that important to us.

Each week, before we have dinner together, we join hands and pray. We all three say a little something and we consistently say a prayer of thanks for our good friend Chris and we pray he will always be our friend. We consistently hug him during our visits, something which seems foreign to him.

Why do we continue our efforts after more than three years? Because we believe we are making a difference, maybe not in the big picture, but definitely in the small picture. Especially in the picture of Chris's life. We believe we will help in steering him away from drugs, alcohol, gangs, skipping school, teenage pregnancy, etc. We are not afraid to talk openly with him about these subjects.

A recent study involving in depth interviews with hundreds of youth around the country was conducted. One-half of the youths were placed with Big Brothers/ Big Sisters and one-half were not. The youth were interviewed two times: when they first signed up with the program and 18 months later. The youths matched with B.B./B.S. were:

- 46% less likely to use drugs.
- 27% less likely to drink alcohol.
- 33% less likely to hit another person.
- 52% less likely to skip school.

There are literally thousands of fatherless, parentless families in the U.S. We live in a society of people not taking responsibility for their actions, including parents abandoning their children. We all have a responsibility to help these kids in any small way we can. We need to provide support and encouragement for these children before our nation is ravaged from the affects of these parentless homes. Big Brothers/Big Sisters meets that need in our society to reach these kids before it's too late. Next time you're wondering how to make a difference in our society which is stricken with violence, remember: Big Brothers/Big Sisters, Big Impact.

Patty Coen's background includes working as an RN for five years in primarily critical care settings. She currently has a BS in Information Systems and has been employed in the Healthcare industry supporting health information systems for most of the last 15 years. Coming from a broken home, she found the greatest influences in her life were those adults who took time out for her. She especially loved being around families where the parents were married and seemed happy together. She spent alot of time with her father in the outdoors, who was a great influence in her life and nutured her tendency towards loving adventure. She has enjoyed climbing many peaks with her husband of 7 1/2 years.

PORTRAIT OF MY MAMA

When I was a young thuggish youth,
I would take from the world.

No one cared.

Really, none dared to speak my name —

I am little Chris.

A lost soul of Africa.

First born to Ruby.

Confused and misunderstood by those that
challenge my right to live as they do,
I constantly rebel,
only to fall prey to an illusion.

When the tears fall in the dead of night,
not a whimper dare be heard.

But the comforting arms of my mama are there,
just like they were in the beginning.

Giving to me
so that I might one day
give to the world.

Willie Christopher Tucker
Bostick State Prison, Georgia

MARY-GARRETT BODEL, M.Ed., MSW

"Brain Building Basics: A Parenting and Literacy Skills Program"

Child abuse and neglect have been regularly identified by professionals in many fields as a significant contributing factor in the subsequent development of violent behavior. There is also a clear link between ineffective parenting, child abuse, and criminal behavior.

Violence is the end result which erupts in response to a combination of factors working together to impact the individual at a particular point in time. Being at risk for violence in any one category isn't sufficient to cause or explain violence. It is a combination of risk factors that results, in the end, in a violent event. Conversely, the reduction of risk factors or the promotion of resilience in any one area improves an individual's chances of breaking out of the cycle of violence and incarceration.

Child abuse exists on a continuum from neglect based on ignorance to willful physical and/or sexual abuse. The National Center on Child Abuse and Neglect estimates that around three times as many children suffer from neglect as deliberate physical abuse.[1] It is common for abusive parents to reveal histories of inadequate and abusive parenting themselves. Much physical abuse is also misunderstood by abusive parents as "discipline," including shaking, pulling a child's hair, burning with a cigarette, taping the child's mouth shut, and invasive sexual behaviors.

A more complete knowledge of child development and better parenting skills will not stop predatory child abuse, but much abuse is based on ignorance, through having experienced abusive parenting and not having learned alternative approaches. Parenting through harsh discipline techniques has been associated with the greatest violence among both youthful and adult offenders.[2]

Maltreating parents have frequently been identified as possessing some or all of the following characteristics: immaturity and dependency, low self-esteem, impulsivity, hostility, isolation and loneliness, anxiety, depression, rigidity, drug or alcohol abuse and criminal behavior.[3] Using the time when a known or potentially maltreating parent is incarcerated to address these issues and build a workable knowledge base about child development and parenting techniques is a good investment from many viewpoints.

Parenting issues and low literacy skills have long been recognized as central concerns when meeting the needs of female offenders. Studies on programming for female offenders have stressed the need to address the unique characteristics of this population.[4] A strong case can also be made for providing parenting education to incarcerated fathers. Families without a father figure have been cited regularly as a contributing factor to children's future involvement in the criminal justice system.[5] Since males are the primary perpetrators of family violence and since absence of a positive male role model is frequently cited as a contributing factor to violent behavior, a parenting intervention that serves to educate fathers while they are incarcerated about their role as "brain building coaches" for their children can serve as a catalyst to increase their positive interactions with their offspring upon release.

Everything we are and everything we do is processed through the brain. The brain is a complex and vulnerable organ. Made of soft matter floating inside a sharp, brittle shell, the brain can be easily damaged by shaking, falls, blows or other violent events. In addition, as a child grows, the stimulation that the child experiences actually enhances, or hinders, the building of brain cells.

Children are born with many more neurons than their mature brain will retain. Through a process known as "pruning" the brain actually loses the neuronal connections that are less used, and forms strong connections in the synaptic circuits that have been utilized the most. Activities that are experienced in an emotionally stable environment and which involve the active interest and participation of the individual are the most beneficial for building the brain. The types of activity that are best for brain building vary as the individual grows. Rocking and hearing spoken language are critical for infants. Toddlers build brain cells by playing with mud, sand and water. Elementary-aged children learn by following a recipe to bake a cake. And adolescent brains mature by learning to understand multiple points of view on a particular subject.[6]

The brain can also, unfortunately, be damaged by exposure to the wrong kinds of stimulation. A child who is raised in a violent household, where there is lots of shouting or hitting, will develop a blunted neurological response that hampers the normal functioning of the brain. Young children, for example, who witness violence in their homes or on the street display symptoms frequently associated with post-traumatic stress disorder; they can't concentrate or focus their thoughts, they have nighttime terrors or flashbacks of the violence, they find it difficult to bond to their parents, they're prone to sudden startling and are overly fearful and apprehensive. These children can then develop a passive and powerless attitude toward the future which leads to heightened risk-taking behaviors.[7]

The brain is also a delicate biological system that is influenced by chemicals in the body. Poor nutrition, drug abuse, and emotional traumas all influence the ebb and flow of chemicals within the brain which can interfere with, sometimes permanently damaging, the brain's normal functioning. Certain chemicals that act on the brain have been implicated in violent behavior pointing to a neurochemistry of violence. For example, lower levels of the neurotransmitter serotonin are regularly found in persons who commit explosive, violent attacks or in violent forms of suicide. High levels of the hormone testosterone are also implicated in aggressive acts.[8]

Traumatic brain injury is also regularly implicated in violent criminal behavior.[9]

Brain injury that damages the prefrontal cortex where impulse control, morality, and cause and effect thinking are modulated, may be particularly significant.

"If abuse and paranoia are combined with brain damage that diminishes the individual's capacity to control or to modulate his violent impulses, a very dangerous person can result."[10]

Dr. Prothrow-Stith and Sher Quaday of the Harvard School of Public Health provide the following profile of a child at high risk for violent behavior. They also note the relationship between brain injury and impulsive violent behavior.[11]

Individual Characteristics:
- Low IQ
- Poor verbal skills
- Attention deficit disorder
- Poor motor skill development
- Head injury
- Prenatal and perinatal complications
- Antisocial behavior and problems

In their profile of family characteristics recognized as risk factors for violent behavior, the authors point out both criminal behavior and specific parenting practices as significant indicators of future violent behavior.

Family Characteristics:
- Poverty
- Family criminal behavior
- Poor marital relations
- Parental absence
- The following parenting practices:
  - Inadequate discipline
  - Use of corporal punishment
  - Excessive exposure to media violence
  - Presence of guns in the home

Healthy brain development (including proper prenatal and childhood nutrition, abstinence from harmful drugs, protection from traumatic brain injury, and proper age-specific stimulation) is critical for producing children who will be able to choose non-violent solutions to the problems that face them throughout their lifetimes. Dr. Prothrow-Stith and Sher Quaday postulate that children can develop resilience if one or more of the following conditions are met:[12]

Access to an educational environment that promotes constructive coping skills and helps children comprehend how they can actively participate and achieve in life;

Learning or possessing an active coping style that assists a child in becoming involved in activities and positive relationships;

Achieving a certain level of self-confidence and possessing a sufficient level of cognitive competence;

Having a strong, warm relationship with an adult who models positive social behavior.

In the 1993 Summary Report of the American Psychological Association's three year study of violence, they stress that preventing violence must begin early in a child's development; and everyone who comes in contact with that child has the potential to contribute to a child's attitudes toward violence and propensity for violent behavior. They stress that positive interactions with parents and other adults can act as protective factors for children who are at risk for violence.

Correctional settings issues such as poor access of children to the facility, sentencing restrictions and lack of inmate success working in a group or classroom setting make many parenting interventions problematic. Brain Building Basics is a parenting and literacy program designed specifically to overcome these limitations. BBB helps parents learn how to be good brain building coaches for their children from the ages of birth to early adolescence. It shows them how to stimulate and discipline their children in productive ways and how to provide a safe and enriching environment.

BBB uses children's picture books and a simple interactive text to make the complex subject of child development and the growing brain accessible to parents with low literacy skills. Adults who have had difficulty learning in traditional classrooms have a better chance at success if content material is presented in a variety of ways, in a context that is relevant to them.[13] Such functional context education promotes brain building for the parent while at the same time modeling the type of activities that are beneficial for their children. Reading then becomes part of the process, rather than the focus of the program, which presents literacy as a means to an end, something to be desired.

Brain Building Basics uses children's books to present realistic children and issues surrounding child care as focal points for learning. This provides a functional context for parenting and brain building information that can be shared by all members of the group, regardless of the age of their children or their specific familial issues. Using children's literature offers participants a level of anonymity as they are able to talk about the behaviors of fictional characters in a story in a "what if" scenario, rather than disclosing their own weaknesses and short comings. By using the story as the basis for discussions about parenting, participants can look at these situations objectively and analyze without emotion, a rare opportunity for most parents. Reading children's books aloud in the classroom also offers an important literacy building experience for the participants.

Co-Instructor, Marion Guy, who has been working with violent offenders for over twelve years, notes the effect of the BBB experience on men. "The men really enjoy (the instructor) reading to them. It helps them focus on their role as fathers. They begin to share their feelings about their relationships. I've seen them become a positive support for each other, and that rarely happens in a jail."

Brain Building Basics consists of twenty one lessons in a soft back, interactive text written at about the fifth grade level. Each lesson is centered around a children's picture book which presents a variety of children, ages infancy through early adolescence, who face a particular developmental challenge. A pre and post test assessment package is also provided to be used to measure a change in knowledge and attitudes about issues covered in the program concerning parenting techniques and healthy brain development. The program has been most effective taught in small groups in a relatively informal setting—a cross between traditional classroom work and a therapy group.

The Brain Building Basics program has been developed over a three year period working with men, women and juveniles. Formative measurements included the use of pre and post tests to measure a change in knowledge and attitude about parenting practices; group facilitator observations and lesson evaluations; outside observations of BBB sessions; and qualitative reports from the participants. BBB has been successful with women, men and juveniles in changing knowledge and attitudes about issues relating to parenting and in building literacy skills. Single sex groups of no more than ten participants with co-facilitators worked best.

Several participants expressed the desire to get the picture books used in the program for their own children. Participants also regularly expressed their enjoyment in the process and a renewed eagerness to make a difference in their children's lives. We were particularly impressed with the response from the men, many of whom did not realize that they could have an important role to play in raising children. We also found that not being a biological parent did not preclude a participant's gaining from the program, as many are involved in parenting in a variety of ways: raising grandchildren, raising the children of their partner or planning to have children soon. One young participant commented that she was now going to wait to have children because she hadn't realized what a responsibility it was and how much was involved.

When we enhance an adult's ability to parent effectively and stay out of jail, we know we are also improving his or her child's chances of growing to healthy and productive maturity, thereby breaking the cycle of violence and incarceration.[14] In short, "the most important, long term educational intervention program for a child is a well educated, financially comfortable parent."[14]

An expanded article on this program is available; see page 370.

Mary-Garrett Bodel, M.Ed, MSW is the Director of the Violence and Brain Injury Institute dedicated to the prevention of violence and brain injuries. Other prevention programs developed by the Institute include the HeadSmart® Schools program, a national and international program for elementary and preschool children and the Changes, Choices and Challenges program, a developmental program for young adolescents. For further information, please contact: MG Bodel, VBII, 128 S. Royal Street, Alexandria, Virginia, 22314; (703) 299-0699.

Footnotes

1 Tower, 1992.
2 Goleman, 1995; Showers, 1993: Reiss and Roth, 1993.
3 DePanfilis and Salus, 1992.
4 Gwinn, 1992; Carp and Schade, 1992; Lillis. 1991.
5 Showers, 1993.
6 Healy, 1994.
7 Groves et. al, 1993.
8 Jan Volavka, 1995.
9 Volavka, 1995; Pincus, 1994; Prothrow-Stith and Sher Quaday, 1995.
10 Pincus, 1993, p. 867.
11 Hidden Casualties. The Relationship Between Violence and Learning, 1995.
12 Hidden Casualties, 1995.
13 Sticht, 1992; Lancaster, 1991; Dodge, 1990.
14 Dr. Thomas Sticht, July 1995 in Precure, 1995.

References:

American Psychological Association, Violence and Youth, Psychology's Response, Vol. 1, Summary Report of the AMA's Commission on Violence and Youth, 1991-1993.

Bloom, Barbara and David Steinhart, Why Punish the Children?, National Council on Crime and Delinquency, January 1993.

Carp, Scarlett and Linda Schade, "Tailoring Facility Programming to Suit Female Offenders' Needs," Corrections Today, August 1992.

Clement, Mary J. "Parenting in Prison: A National Survey of Programs for Incarcerated Women," Journal of Offender Rehabilitation, Vol. 19, (1/2), 1993, pp. 89-100.

DePanfilis, Diane and Marsha Salus, US Department of Health and Human Services, "A Coordinated Response to Child Abuse and Neglect," User Manual Series, NCCAN, 1992.

Dodge, Kenneth., John Bates, and Gregory Pettit, "Mechanisms in the Cycle of Violence;" Science, Vol. 250, December, 1990, pp. 1678-1683.

Goleman, Daniel, Emotional Intelligence, Bantam Books, New York, 1995.

Groves, Betsy MSW., Barry Zuckerman, MD, Steven Marans, MSW and Donald Choen, MD.; "Silent Victims: Children Who Witness Violence". Journal of the American Medical Association, January 13, 1993, Vol. 269, No 2.

Gwinn, Bobbie, "Linking Inmate Families Together: The L.I.F.T. Program at FPC Alderson," Federal Prisons Journal, Spring, 1992.

Healy, Jane, Your Child's Growing Mind, A Practical Guide to Brain Development and Learning From Birth to Adolescence; Doubleday, 1994.

Lancaster, Alden, "An Introduction to Intergenerational Literacy, Literacy in Context Project," Wider Opportunities for Women, Washington, DC, 1992.

Lash, Marilyn and Jane Haltiwanger, "When Young Children Are Injured," Exceptional Parent Magazine; Tufts University, New England Med. Center, 1994.

Lillis, Jamie, Survey: Programs and Services for Female Inmates, Corrections Compendium, Vol. XIX, No. 2, February 1994.

National Association for the Education of Young Children, Position Statement on Violence in the Lives of Children, Adopted July, 1993, Young Children, September, 1993.

NIH Panel Report on National Institute of Health Research on Antisocial Aggressive and Violence-Related Behaviors and their Consequences, April 1994.

Panel on Research on Child Abuse and Neglect, Commission on Behavioral and Social Sciences and Education and the National Research Council, Understanding Child Abuse and Neglect, National Academy Press, Washington, DC, 1993.

Panel on Violence Prevention, Position Paper, Departments of Health and Human Services, Public Health Service and the Center for Disease Control, February 14, 1991.

Pincus, Jonathan, MD. Neurologist's Role in Understanding Violence, Arch. Neurology, Vol. 50, August, 1993.

Pincus, Jonathan, MD. "The Role of TBI in the Violence Equation: An Interaction of Vulnerabilities, An American Public Health Crisis;" TBI Challenge!, Summer 1994, pp. 4-8.

Precure, Agnes, Cindy Marano, and Antonia Juhasz, "Generations of Consequence: A Status Report on Women and Literacy in the United States;" Wider Opportunities for Women, Washington DC, 1995.

Prothrow-Stith, MD, Deadly Consequences: How Violence is Destroying Our Teenage Population and a Plan to Begin Solving the Problem, HarperCollins, 1991.

Prothrow-Stith, MD, and Sher Quaday, "Hidden Casualties: The Relationship Between Violence and Learning," 1995.

Reiss, Albert and Jeffrey Roth, eds, Understanding and Preventing Violence, Panel Report from: Committee on Law and Justice, Commission on Behavioral and Social Sciences and Education, National Research Council; National Academy Press, Washington, DC 1993.

Roth, Jeffrey, Understanding and Preventing Violence, National Institute of Justice, February, 1994.

Showers, Jacy, Ed.D Assessing and Remedying Parenting Knowledge Among Women Inmates, Journal of Offender Rehabilitation, Vol. 20 (1/2) 1993, pp. 35-46.

Sticht, Thomas and Alden Lancaster, Functional Context Education: A Primer for Program Providers, Literacy in Context Project, Wider Opportunities for Women, Washington, DC, 1992.

Tower, Cynthia, US Department of Health and Human Services, The Role of Educators in the Prevention of Child Abuse and Neglect; User Manual Series, NCCAN, 1992.

Volavka, Jan, MD. et al, Psychobiology of the Violent Offender, Journal of Forensic Sciences, JFSCA, Vol. 37, No. 1, 1992, pp. 237-251.

Volavka, Jan, MD, Ph.D. Neurobiology of Violence, American Psychiatric Press, Washington, DC, 1995.

Zero to Three/National Center for Clinical Infant Programs: The Violence Study Group, April, 1993.

JAMES SMITH & PHILIP TEDESCHI
"Come Join the Circle"

The true leader in the youthful offender intervention field will be the non-obvious helping professional who can organize his or her contributions within the context of a circle.

Most professional youth workers lead careers of quiet desperation. Watch closely, and you will observe the vast majority of helping professionals who work with troubled youth listing on a sea of mediocrity and cynicism. In one corner of the industry there works an overloaded probation officer. She does her job in relative isolation and is ineffective in her efforts at positively impacting the adolescents on her huge caseload. Somewhere in the same town, a county caseworker trudges through each day with problems with families that he barely understands. He never shares his frustrations because everyone he knows is in the same boat. The probation officer and the caseworker rarely speak to one another, with the exception of the occasional court report.

Facing the challenges presented by growing adolescent offender populations, and a rising generation of harder, meaner children, it is clear that our collective efforts for treatment and social well-being are not working. The high-risk youth which now contributes nearly half of the serious and violent crime in our communities frequently appear impenetrable to the efforts to effect change. It appears that our mental models and, more specifically, our management practices are outdated relics based on westernized principles of industrialization rather than humanized principles of socialization. We are trying to do more for less every year. We specialize in our own areas of expertise, stop communicating with others, and compete with each other for territory, information and power. We polarize within the system and quickly forget that we each are the system. We have failed at the most fundamental level of leadership. We have failed to learn to work together.

This article will attempt to outline the critical issues involved in the effective intervention and treatment of high-risk adolescents, specifically the intensive community-based treatment of adolescent sexual and violent offenders. As the pressures on the Juvenile Justice system become greater and the political pendulum swings toward managed care, we are charged to reevaluate the current paradigms that drive the process. It has been our experience managing violent adolescent and youthful sex offenders that new mental health models must be created. Without this reexamination, we will be destined to recreate the failure and recidivism statistics of past efforts.

Introducing Containment Treatment

Facing the dual challenge of participating honestly in systemic thinking around the need for community safety and the needs of a troubled adolescent would lead us to different conclusions than we have achieved in previous generations of professional youth intervention. We would like to propose a form of systemic thinking called containment treatment. The theory and practice of containment treatment creates the most accurate environment within which the *conduct-disordered* adolescent can assimilate new forms of corrective thought concerning his criminality. Containment treatment sets the stage for cognitive restructuring to occur. With containment treatment there is a substantially increased likelihood of long-lasting adjustment of the thoughts, feelings, and behaviors of the criminal adolescent. Without containment, we are likely to continue relying on institutionalized care despite its inability to ready clients for the community, and to continue to see the vulnerable populations in our communities pay the price for this failure.

Containment treatment in theory far exceeds the tenets and demands of "team-building." Teams are inherently fraught with dilemmas such as ego-based competition and hierarchical power structures. Containment redefines the use of power in all relevant organizational structures so that a human circle of contiguous power is formed to effectively treat the child within it. Containment becomes the new environment, the surrogate developmental matrix for the adolescent to grow within until he can be weaned toward interdependence with his personal community.

Defining Containment Treatment

Containment treatment is the integrated, inclusive and thorough participation of the multi-disciplinary helping professionals, community representatives and family members in a circular and systemic containment system. This system seeks to create a new social context for the client to live within. This new environment is designed to embrace healthy social boundaries through a humane process of nurture and accountability. Containment treatment has been successfully applied to the treatment of the client whose diagnostic profile might include conduct disorder, anti-social, oppositional and defiant behaviors, compulsive self-abuse or repeated offenses.

The functional definition of containment theory and practice is hard work, communication, consistency, coordination and compassion. It is the parenting that children never received and continue to require despite their entry into the Juvenile Justice system. Containment is everybody's business.

Containment treatment seeks to create a network that transforms and enhances the nature of each member's "role." In a well constructed circle of containment, a social worker takes on the insight and aptitudes of the therapist, and a parent takes on the authority of the probation officer. Each person learns a new collective perspective on the child's course of treatment.

Who facilitates this set of experiences for a group of professionals who have a young client in their common care? Because containment practice must come from all directions it is ideal when all members come to facilitate the process. But to begin with, it might be the treatment provider, the probation officer, the teacher, or the caseworker. Anyone who understands the principles of containment treatment and multi-dimensional accountability can help others learn to work together.

This process starts in a very common setting: a gathering of people. Someone has to arrange a time and a place for a "staffing" to occur. This requires lots of phone calls and frustrating rearrangements of schedules. Some people will balk or ask why it's so important that we meet each other. Others will be relieved that we are finally getting together. After a couple days of phone-tag and diplomatic persuasion, a containment session is in place. A circle begins to form.

Principles of Containment Treatment

1. The operative feature of Containment Treatment is accountability. One of the most remarkable features of the juvenile justice system is that it actually decreases the intensity and availability of accountability-based relationships in the life of the offending adolescent. The parents have been long since disempowered through their own pathology or, unwittingly, by the system. Probation officers with very crowded caseloads become the point of contact with the adult world for the young person who is slowly losing touch with the mainstream. Soon, the institutionalized teenager, with no significant adult mentors, is released unfettered into the community.

The circle is the regulator of accountability for the youthful offender. This is not just the probation officer's job. A solid therapist who refuses the seduction of the confidential relationship, or a conscientious special education teacher who takes an accurate view of the conduct disordered youth will know why he or she belongs in the circle. They belong there because there will be little or no authentic change or growth in the adolescent client without broad based accountability with other important adults.

In a solid containment network, accountability increases reality based relationships that can serve to move from all sides upon a child's attitude at the first sign of corrosive thinking. This can include an employer, a counselor, a parent, a probation officer or a friend. Containment processes are designed to cause the young person to make every decision with others in mind or to be quickly detected.

2. Containment Treatment is most effective when the use of authority and nurture are in balance. Positions polarize people into two camps: care-givers and punishment-givers. As a result, the young person hears all kinds of different messages, some of them are diametrically opposed. For example, the parent or therapist may minimize the court-ordered probation guidelines because they interfere with other activities. The young person can easily divide and conquer two adults who have not coordinated their agendas. It is a classic scenario.

Containment eliminates this problematic polarity and offers each circle member the ability to give care and authoritative impact to the child. This is vital toward decreasing manipulative thoughts and behaviors. Drawing from the wisdom of the circle, the individual network member can give timely caring and authoritative response to issues raised by the child, as if each member of the circle is standing there at the moment of response.

3. Containment Treatment seeks to exploit the therapeutic value of the "sensation of caughtness" in the client. When language does not quite serve us well we re-invent it just a bit. The "sensation of caughtness" is the feeling one gets when one is apprehended "red-handed." It is a very useful feeling, the breeding ground of healthy shame.

Containment orientation can teach the adolescent offender to set himself up to get caught before something tragic occurs. We teach the young person to warn others of the slightest indications of deviant or criminal thinking. For example, a young person who can say to his mother or father, "If you hear me on the phone in the middle of the night, it's probably drug-related," is likely to abstain from that aspect of drug involvement. This thinking builds on itself and generalizes quickly to many scenes in the young person's life until he has re-thought his behavior patterns.

Caughtness is an opportunity to teach and learn if the issue does not constitute a dangerous consequence. We must look for the "red flags" which can be considered the antecedents of risk. The adolescent sexual offender who appears withdrawn or the violent youth who becomes intimidating needs to feel caught by his containment network and made accountable for sliding toward a relapse. We must catch him before he re-offends. It is highly unethical to gauge progress in the client by simply asking whether or not he has any new victims. A victim should never be considered the measuring stick for whether or not we are successful in our efforts.

4. Containment Treatment requires the first line of interventionists to become proficiently facilitative in relation to the containment network. Effective containment intervention requires the ability and willingness to use the phone, arrange meeting times, drive a car, talk with angry or hurting parents, educate "lone rangers" through excellent example, and share power with others. It is difficult work for phonaphobics and procrastinators. It is also difficult for those who view themselves as the clients' only hope.

Containment treatment of chaotic adolescent offenders is difficult and time-consuming. It is also the most gratifying and safe form of intervention. Proficient facilitation means making contact with others at critical moments without moving toward the seat of power. It is about sharing information and discussing the next decision together with all relevant circle members.

5. Containment Treatment seeks to guide the client toward behavioral change, clear cognitions, and sufficient anxiety concerning his or her potential

dangerousness. What we call thought, feeling and behavior of the adolescent must become the gauge by which we measure progress. Traditional forms of juvenile justice practice often teach the adolescent that there is little connection between cause and effect. It can sometimes take six to nine months before the adolescent receives sentencing for a charge to which he has pled. Due process in the legal sense is nonsensical to the process of learning about why certain forms of behavior are unacceptable and will not be tolerated.

Containment facilitators hope to cause the adolescent to become anxious about his thoughts to re-offend. In fact, we would hope that he would maintain certain neuroses about becoming another recidivism statistic. Along the continuum between apathy and empathy stands anxiety, there to tell us that the child is progressing. If we cannot generate genuine healthy shame and anxiety in the young person, then we have a poor prognosis for long-term change and growth. Normal people become anxious when they contemplate committing an aberrant act. It is a function of healthy shame. Why would we want anything less for the adolescents we treat?

6. Containment Treatment assumes that the client will not readily seek accountability until he or she experiences discomfort from avoiding it or benefits from embracing it. It is a good thing to learn from our mistakes. Devaluing accountability that is demanded by the circle should cause the child some discomfort. We expect that incarcerated adolescents have devalued almost everything that is not tied to survival mechanisms and impulses. They have no reference point to orient to in the form of good memories of how accountability based relationships served them well.

Celebrating little victories for the entire circle to see is vital for the adolescent to begin to value the changes he is making. This offers parents some insight into their child's aptitude that they may not have previously recognized. It would be difficult to overstate the importance of reinforcing the internal and external benefits of a young person voluntarily seeking accountability when before he did not value it at all. This is a great example of a huge shift in thinking resulting from containment treatment.

7. Containment Treatment assumes the interventionist will need to be intrusive on behalf of the client. We fail miserably at asking all the right questions of the young people we serve. We fail because it is impossible to ask all the right questions. When we focus on one area of his life, another will be neglected. However, based on the fact that he must behave safely in the community, we must be willing to ask tough, uncomfortable questions and not be satisfied with the grunts we typically receive in return.

Containment theory makes intrusion a central feature because of the sense of relief it can ultimately elicit in the adolescent. This relief is not the abdication of responsibility or healthy anxiety. The relief is a giving up of the tremendous energy consuming task of keeping secrets and maintaining a facade. A certain form of behavior is more likely to happen if it is a secret. It is a loop of dangerous thinking in the head of the youthful offender. Intrusion as intervention is an act of unsolicited care and authority. We do not wait for an invitation, but assume that we must intrusively approach the adolescent very firmly and carefully in spite of his initial objections.

8. Containment Treatment assumes that trust between the client and the community is not a central variable in the treatment process. How many times have we heard a criminal thinker say to us that he first must trust his treatment providers before he can open up and begin to change. In a sense he is right and in a sense, he is absolutely wrong. Trust is a product of something deeper and more powerful.

Our critics have stated that we de-emphasize the relationship we have with our clients because we value trust far less than other relational constructs. We would respond by saying that we intend to take a higher view of what we are trying to make available to our clients—a shot at integrity that comes from the rigorous process of staying behaviorally accountable for a long period of time until internal changes are evident. Trusting a damaged adolescent on survival mode with telling the truth and therefore being safe is an act of pathetic apathy or complete ignorance. In containment theory, we do not trust our "guts" in determining the likelihood of reoffense or relapse. We can only trust what we can see for a long period of time.

9. Containment Treatment assumes that the client will experience high-risk situations and opportunities to re-offend and needs intensive opportunities for planful forethought and safety planning previous to exposure to community settings. Most adolescents who happen to be in a relationship with a probation officer never talk to another person about their crimes or propensity to commit another. They brood and they ruminate about their condition, but they don't talk about the helplessness they often feel and the powerful rush they feel when offending. When they are exposed to a vulnerable person, they often get psychologically aroused by that vulnerability. The vulnerability is a channel through which they can now discharge their fear of being a "zero."

Containment treatment practice is grounded in the belief that we can repeatedly construct measures of safety long before the client finds himself in a high risk situation. That is why we practice the art of safety planning religiously. It is tedious, repetitious and sometimes really boring. It is paper-intensive and often needs to be done over and over again. Safety planning is a form of thinking out loud over and over again until the adolescent at least understands the measures he must use to be safe.

10. Containment Treatment assumes that the most caring behavior an interventionist can demonstrate toward the client is to prevent him or her from reoffending or relapsing. For every act of emotional or physical violence perpetrated on society by an angry young soul, we lose a little bit of our own integrity and community well-being. We lose our collective sense of safety and develop a deeper sense of insecurity about our neighbors, our friend's children, and the overall direction of our society. We wonder if our children will survive their years in high school without falling prey to some capricious act of cruelty. The offending adolescent sells a chunk of his own mental health every time he hurts another. In the long view, he becomes his own worst victim and eventually becomes a person so incapable of looking honestly at his own condition that others will take charge of him. We are raising tomorrow's prison population. We know them by name. We can predict with relative accuracy where they will be in 10 years unless we change the world they are living in.

Containment Theory Applied

We apply containment theory because it exists as the only accurate treatment environment that creates external conditions to bring about the adolescent's necessary internal changes. The transition anxiety of youthful offenders leaving the structure and predictability of the institutional environment is a common prelude to regression and relapse. Almost all types of treatment designed for high-risk populations (including cognitive-behavioral modification, motivational counseling and relapse prevention practices), are most effective in the containment milieu.

In application of containment treatment, a young offender who is deeply involved in the juvenile justice system will typically have a probation officer, a social worker, a therapist, a guardian *ad litem*, a drug and alcohol counselor, a teacher, a parent or two, residential treatment staff or foster parents, possibly an employer, a coach, a pastor, and a good friend. Getting this group together for a monthly containment "staffing" is not like herding cats; it's worse. But it is worth the effort. What is achieved just in the way of communication is indispensable. The single most obvious benefit of containment meetings is the indispensable information that is communicated. The intangible product of collective socioecological awareness that slowly takes shape around a common language of treatment impacts the adolescent in every corner of his personal community.

Together, after names and titles have been exchanged, the circle sets out to create a corporate sense of the young person's overall treatment plan. This will obviously involve components from every aspect of his life including a sense of whether or not the family or residential setting is going to line up accurately with containment efforts. Oftentimes, the parents are the most difficult to "win over" into the circle and, unfortunately, residential placement staff aren't any easier. If the adolescent's living situation is unstable because the parents or staff are not invested in initial containment efforts, the circle's first job is to influence those parents or caretakers toward full and active participation in the circle. Without it, all efforts at containment treatment will meet with aggravating resistance. The circle will plough ahead but will not reap the harvest it first hoped for. Once this has been done, the circle must learn to work together for the long haul, beginning with the end in mind. What are we seeking to offer this young person? What will we want to see happen as a result of our efforts?

Month after month, the circle strengthens and sees immediate results in the behavioral repertoire of the child; he usually gets worse. The accountability drives him to a whole new level of anxiety and he resists like crazy. He fusses and fumes about every little thing, throws brief tantrums, threatens to run away or sue, or even worse, he just gets grumpy and sullen for a few weeks. His cognitive distortions fly out of him like bats from the belfry. He demonstrates the depths of his learned helplessness and appears to come awfully close to relapsing or re-offending. Interestingly, we have watched many young people appear to be averse to these new conditions and still adjust their behaviors in very positive ways. Something begins to happen in their thinking and we begin to notice that we've had a few solid weeks or months of success.

The circle is dramatically challenged when one of its members must leave because they are moving to Vermont or taking a promotion. The circle must adjust to the presence of a new member and help that person understand what's going on. It seems to go well, although it can cause a few headaches here and there.

Then the adolescent acts out at school or has a blow up at his foster placement. At first, it seems like the whole treatment plan will come unraveled. Again, it remains within tolerable limits and the containment network prevents one more revocation hearing. After about one year, the circle begins to talk about how far the young person has come. The containment efforts have produced a year of relative stability and saved the state a significant amount of money.

Typically, and over time, the circle develops its own sense of identity and accomplishment. We recognize that we've had a lasting impact on a young person's life. The circle is tempted to back off a little, relax, believing that we can live without the intensive involvement for a while. Maybe the guardian is a little tired of dealing with the social worker and we've all gotten a little cranky lately. It is probably a mistake to let things "slide." The circle must stay stronger longer than the adolescent's capacity to sustain any kind of resistance to it. He might have just been holding his breath. We must take the containment milieu as far as we can into the young person's future.

Maintaining the Circle of Containment

How do we keep the circle strong? We utilize a multi-dimensional accountability model. This type of accountability is designed to provide effective treatment to the conduct disordered client. It is important to recognize that working with dangerous clients can be isolating, exhausting and at times an intimidating experience. The creation of a mental model that allows the interventionist to share the responsibility is critical to the outcome. At the heart of this model is the emphasis on shared leadership, shared power and shared limitations. Multi-dimensional accountability recognizes that the ability to effect change in the offender is related to the structural integrity of the circle. Our interactions are guided by a set of principles that help us stay focused and clear about how to relate to one another. After all, this is a group of professional people who should be capable of gathering and tasking and figuring out their differences. Multi-dimensional accountability keeps the circle intact because it empowers every group member to have equal voice, equal power, and equal stake in the outcome.

Conclusions

Containment treatment works. Although we lack the longitudinal studies and empirical data to support that claim, we know from our collective experiences and actuarial findings that it is so. Because this model is defined by the human efforts of its participants, it remains a dynamic and complex event and, at times, flawed. But it is with confidence that we report that the greater the achieved level of effective containment, the greater the prognosis. The stronger the commitment to shared power, shared learning and shared leadership by the members of the offender's circle of concern, the more often positive outcomes and corrective response was achieved. It seems likely that the reason that containment treatment is effective where other models have failed is that containment treatment is the treatment equivalent of the healthy family and extended family system. In the circle, youthful offenders find an abundance of nurturing and authority. It may be valued by them as a safe place to grow and change.

An expanded article on this program is available; see page 370.

James S. Smith, MS, is a founding partner of the Resource Center for High Risk Youth and a co-author of the Resource Study Hall curriculum. He has been working with children, youth and families since 1980. He received his Masters of Science from Avila College, School of Psychology, in 1984, and was the Clinical Administrator at the Emily Griffith Center Home for Boys in Larkspur, CO, and the Director of the Day Treatment Services at the Sycamores in Altadena, CA.

Philip Tedeschi, MSSW, LCSW, is a founding partner of the Resource Center for High Risk Youth and a co-author of the Resource Study Hall curriculum. He has been working with children, youth and families since 1984 and with sexual offenders since 1987. He received his Masters of Science in Social Work from the University of Wisconsin, Madison, in 1987, and became a Licensed Clinical Social Worker in the state of Colorado in 1993. He has been a clinical consultant for several adolescent programs and has developed and implemented sexual offense specific and trauma recovery treatment programs across the state.

ED EARNEST
The Community Intensive Treatment for Youth (CITY) Program

In 1960, at the age of sixteen, I stood before a circuit court judge and pled guilty to five counts of second degree burglary and two counts of grand larceny. The sentence: twelve years and two days. This followed four and one-half years involvement in the juvenile justice system, including three commitments to the state training school where I served a total of three and one-half years.

I was a very frightened youngster when I walked into Draper Prison, but, as I walked down the hall something happened that had a lasting impression and relieved my fears. As I looked around, I saw face after face I recognized. It was like homecoming. The faces belonged to my friends from the training school. It was as if all of us had simply moved from junior high to high school. The training school had accomplished its task—we had been trained for prison life. This was not what the staff at the training school wanted for us, it is just the nature of the institution. Since there was no evaluation by anyone to determine the effectiveness of the juvenile institution in turning children away from crime, the practice of the juvenile system being the feeder system for adult prisons continued. Without an effective juvenile justice system, you can bet on continued growth in the prison population.

During the classification process, I was fortunate to be placed at Draper to serve my time. Draper had a young warden, John C. Watkins, who recognized that over ninety percent of the inmates at Draper were school dropouts with no marketable skills. He realized that their chances of being able to compete in free society after release without education and training was slim to none. He successfully spearheaded a movement to bring basic education and vocational training to Draper. He recruited Dr. John M. McKee, a noted behavioral psychologist, to plan and direct the project. Dr. McKee, in turn, developed a staff of professionals and college students to implement the training.

I was offered the chance to participate in this training program and grabbed the opportunity. Through this program, I passed the GED Test for High School Equivalency. Perhaps more importantly, I was able to interact with college students. This interaction eventually led me to believe I could attend college after I was released.

Release finally came in the form of parole in November 1966 after serving six years of the twelve year sentence. Through the assistance provided by Warden Watkins and Dr. McKee, I enrolled in the University of Alabama in 1967. I worked full time while in college and carried a course load of twelve hours each semester, earning a bachelors degree in social work with a criminal justice specialty in 1973.

During the six years at the university, I reflected on the nine and one-half years I had been locked up and the interactions I had with other inmates and their families. Theory from classes at the university began to blend with experience, and out of this developed an idea that juvenile offenders could be worked with far more effectively and at less cost to taxpayers through comprehensive services and training for these youth and their families in the community. Just as one cannot develop great pianists by sending them to football practice where their hands could be crushed, one cannot train children to succeed in the community by sending them to the artificial environment of the juvenile institution where any identification with the community is eliminated. This thinking led to the desire to develop a more effective method of working with juvenile offenders—a method that would be community based, individualized, comprehensive, non-residential, and data based.

In 1970, the idea was presented to the Director of the Center for Emotionally Disturbed Children where I was employed as a counselor. The Director liked the idea, and from that point it became a team effort involving faculty from the university in the fields of psychology, social work, education (including special education), health, and recreation. In addition to the university faculty, the Tuscaloosa County Juvenile Court and juvenile probation officers were directly involved in the development of this concept. It was agreed by the team that in developing the program model we would do the following: identify the problems to be addressed, establish measurable goals and objectives that related directly to the identified problems, develop a program model that would meet the stated goals and objectives, and develop an evaluation system that would tell us if the strategies employed are meeting the goals and objectives. The outcome of these planning sessions was the development and implementation of the Community Intensive Treatment for Youth (CITY) Program.

IDENTIFICATION OF PROBLEMS Perhaps the easiest part of the process was the identification of the problems we wanted to impact in relation to juvenile crime:

1. Probation officers did not have resources in the community to adequately serve children on their caseload.
2. Too many children were being committed to the state juvenile institutions.
3. Juvenile institutions were basically ineffective in turning young people away from crime, based on the number convicted of new offenses after being released from the institution.
4. The cost to taxpayers to house a juvenile offender in a state institution was increasing.

The identification of these problems led to the establishment of measurable program goals.

PROGRAM GOALS Program goals were established as follows:

1. To demonstrate that 80% of youth enrolled will not be convicted of committing a new offense from date enrolled to the end of one year after exiting the program.
2. To demonstrate that 80% of enrollees would be successfully diverted from commitment to the state juvenile institutions from date of enrollment to the end of one full year after exiting the program.
3. To demonstrate 50% less cost to taxpayers when cost in CITY is compared to

juvenile institutional cost.

Once we had identified the problems to be addressed and established measurable program goals, it was time to develop the program design.

PROGRAM DESIGN In developing the program design, several factors were considered, including the establishment of a specific target group to be served, identification of the general characteristics of the group to be served, the establishment of program objectives, identification of services and training that would be provided directly by the program and those that would be obtained through linkages with other agencies in the community, the development of the staffing pattern, and the development of a long-term follow-up evaluation system.

TARGET GROUP The program will take referrals from the juvenile court and the Department of Youth Services exclusively. Youth referred by the court must be either on suspended commitment to the Department of Youth Services or considered by the court high risk to commit a new crime without comprehensive intervention and to end up committed to the Department of Youth Services.

GENERAL CHARACTERISTICS OF TARGET GROUP With the assistance of the juvenile court we were able to identify the general characteristics of those youth chronically involved with the juvenile court. The youth examined were functioning three to five years below their chronological grade level, had poor behavioral skills, poor social skills, poor employability skills, poor decision making skills, all had home/family problems, and all lacked any involvement in extracurricular school activities or involvement in any legitimately organized activities in the community. While these were the general characteristics of the youth targeted to serve, we realized that the needs of the youth within each characteristic would be different. Thus the need for individualization. This led to the development of program objectives.

PROGRAM OBJECTIVES The CITY Program's objectives include:

1. to identify each youth's strengths and weaknesses;
2. to provide an individualized environment in which the youth can develop the skills necessary for effective living, and
3. to alter the natural environment of the youth so that the newly acquired skills are fostered while the previously learned, inappropriate skills are discouraged.

Once program objectives had been established, the identification of specific services and training that the program would provide followed.

SERVICES AND TRAINING After several planning sessions, it was determined the program would provide the following services and training to youth enrolled.

ASSESSMENT Assessment takes place during the first three weeks of the program and includes academic diagnostic testing, a home visit, completion of parent and youth data questionnaires, collection of school data and observation of behavior. During this period, the counselor works with the youth to establish long-term, intermediate and short-term goals.

SUCCESS PLANNING The Success Plan (treatment plan) begins with the youth's goals and consists of four or more parts, including academic, behavioral, family and group. For each part, a measurable objective is determined. A plan to reach the objective and a means of evaluating the effectiveness of the plan are developed.

ACADEMIC REMEDIATION/GED TRAINING The objective of this academic training component is two-fold, depending on the age and goals of the enrollee. The objective for those returning to public school is to remediate them to a functional level in reading, math and language equivalent to the grade level to which they will return. For older youth, the objective is to develop the academic skills necessary to pass the GED exam, which will allow them to enter the job market, college or technical training.

The program uses an academic system that enables the two teachers and one teacher's aide to identify the enrollee's specific academic strengths and deficits and academic objectives, provide immediate and constant feedback to enrollees, and evaluate progress in meeting academic objectives. Standards are high, which helps enhance self-esteem. The minimum acceptable passing score on a competency exam is 90% correct. Enrollees gain an average of one full year academically for each seven weeks enrolled.

FAMILY COUNSELING SERVICES AND TRAINING There are three objectives in this component: to help the parent or guardian meet basic needs (food, shelter, clothing, electricity, hot water and employment); to help the parent or guardian improve communications and expectations within the family; and to train the parent or guardian in effective parenting skills.

INDIVIDUAL COUNSELING The objectives of the individual counseling component are to help enrollees gain an understanding of themselves and what leads them to get in trouble; to help them set goals and review progress in reaching their goals on a monthly basis; to serve as an advocate for the youth; to help parents and youths identify the areas contributing to their problems, and to develop strategies to overcome these problems; to review behavior; to develop a plan for transition from CITY to school, work, college, technical training, etc.; and to provide support during the five-month transitional follow-up period.

GROUP COUNSELING All enrollees participate in a one-hour group session daily. The group session works to develop basic employability and other life skills. Group sessions also give the opportunity to discuss relevant issues, such as teen sex, teen pregnancy, drugs, crime, perseverance, love, anger, relationships, conflict resolution, etc.

BEHAVIOR CHANGE COMPONENT Youth involved with the court often have developed behavior patterns that interfere with success in school, on the job, or in technical training or college. These behaviors are identified through observation throughout their stay in the program. After negative behaviors are identified, the incompatible opposites of these behaviors are determined. The objective is to increase the occurrence of incompatible opposite behavior (positive behavior) while at the same time decreasing the occurrence of the negative behavior. Theses changes are achieved through contingency management and social and psychological reinforcement. The programs use a point system through which youth earn points for their academic and behavioral performance in recreational and group sessions. Points are offered in exchange for items from a store, time off, and a trip to an amusement park. The awarding of points is paired with social reinforcers and the values of work ethics. This method focuses on teaching new, positive ways of behaving rather than on simply punishing negative behaviors.

SERVICE THROUGH LINKAGES Other services and training that may be needed by the youth and their families, but not provided directly by the program, are obtained through linkages with other community agencies that provide these services. CITY counselors coordinate with outside agencies when needed.

PHYSICAL EDUCATION/RECREATION Each enrollee participates in physical education/recreation one hour per day. These activities include exercise, team sports (e.g. basketball, softball and volleyball) and individual sports (e.g. swimming). Recreation includes both earned fun trips as well as educational field trips, such a trip to a water park or a museum. The focus is on interactive social skills.

MOTIVATIONAL SYSTEM The motivational system awards enrollees for performance through tangible reinforcers as well as social and psychological recognition. The point system is a major component of the motivation system. Staff focus on commending enrollees who are doing well. Various awards and certificates are presented to reward outstanding performance in areas such as attendance, academics and behavior. We also have found that giving youths immediate feedback is motivating as well.

MONTHLY EVALUATION AND REVIEW OF PROGRESS Each enrollee receives a monthly evaluation of progress in reaching the objectives contained in the success plan. If progress is being made, the plan continues; if progress is not being made, the plan is modified. The evaluation is reviewed with the youth, the parent(s) and the probation officer. Each signs the evaluation and each receives a copy.

TRANSITIONAL FOLLOW-UP SERVICES When a youth leaves the program, the youth's counselor is required to have frequent visual contact with the youth. The objective is to increase the probability of the enrollee's smooth transition to the new setting.

STAFFING PATTERN CITY is designed to serve 60 youth at any given time—30 enrolled for services and training and 30 on transitional follow-up. Each program has nine staff: three counselors, one Masters level teacher and one Bachelors level teacher (both certified), one teacher aide, one program coordinator, one physical education/recreation supervisor, and one office manager.

PROGRAM EVALUATION A system was developed with the court system to enable the program to track youth for one year after exiting a program to determine program effectiveness in reaching program goals.

PROGRAM IMPLEMENTATION The initial program was implemented in 1971 at the University of Alabama under a grant from the Alabama Law Enforcement Planning Agency. The program was highly effective; there was an 85% reduction in commitments to the state from Tuscaloosa County and 90% of CITY enrollees were successfully diverted from commitment, 90% had no new felony adjudications and 80% had no new adjudications of any type, and the cost was $28 per day compared with $66 per day in the state juvenile institution.

CITY TODAY

Today there are nine programs operating in Alabama. One was opened August 11, 1997, and it is anticipated that a tenth program will be opened in October or November of 1997. During FY1998 the CITY programs expect to serve over 700 youth and their families.

CURRENT PROGRAM EFFECTIVENESS

With the help of the local court and data from the Department of Youth Services, CITY tracks enrollees for one year after termination from the program. Data collected from the courts show the following results on 231 youths who exited seven of the programs between October 1, 1994, and September 30, 1995. (The eighth program, in Houston County, opened in February 1996.)

These 231 youths had been adjudicated on 470 cases, an average of two adjudications per youth during the period one full year before enrollment. These same youths have accounted for 130 case adjudications (0.56 per youth) one full year after leaving the program—a reduction of 82%.

One hundred fifty-three (66%) have had no new adjudications for offenses occurring from the date of enrollment to one year after termination; 187 (81%) had no new felony adjudications.. One hundred eighty-five (80%) were successfully diverted from commitment to the Department of Youth Services.

The cost per person per day for the 240 CITY program slots in the eight program locations statewide is $43.83, while the cost per bed per day in the juvenile institution is estimated to be more than $140.

These data indicate that CITY is an effective alternative to incarceration for many juvenile offenders, which reduces crime and cuts costs to taxpayers.

CONCLUSION

While the CITY program does not fit well with the "get tough" rhetoric of the eighties and nineties, it is effective in preventing the institutionalization of children, turning children away from crime, and in saving taxpayer dollars.

CITY, after twenty-six years of existence, has a great deal of credibility with and support from the administrative, legislative, and judicial branches of state government. However, I am concerned that both nationally and in Alabama, the focus is on more institutional beds, more bootcamps, and trying more youth as adults at younger and younger ages. While these things may sound good, there is no mention of evaluation of the impact on juvenile crime. I fear the same thing will happen with the juvenile justice system in Alabama as happened with the adult system.

The "get tough" rhetoric began in Alabama with the election of 1974. In 1976, the prison population in Alabama was 3500 and the prison budget was $17.5

million. Today, twenty years later, we have 22,000 prisoners and a prison budget of $180 million. The crime rate in 1996 was much higher and much more violent than in 1976. Imagine the impact had a third of these resources been placed in comprehensive, well evaluated, community based programs. Imagine how many fewer victims there would have been. All of this has taken place over the past twenty years with no mention of outcome evaluation or accountability. It will be a great day in our nation when our politicians become leaders and start looking for solutions to the problems related to youth crime rather than seeing who can "out tough" the other.

In 1962, I escaped from Draper and, after being on the run for nine days, I turned myself in to the authorities. Penalty: loss of nine months good time, isolation for a few days, and assignment to a farm squad. Had Alabama's habitual offender act been in effect at that time, I would have been tried for escape and sentenced to life without parole because of the seven felony convictions I had when I was sixteen. There would be no CITY programs today, and I would not have paid over $200,000 in taxes since being released. Instead, taxpayers would still be paying to house me in one of Alabama's prisons. I was fortunate to be a child of the fifties and sixties instead of a child of the nineties. Today, there is a greater willingness to throw away children who don't fit rather than working hard to find solutions to the problems of those children.

As a juvenile offender, Ed Earnest spent over three years in Alabama's state training school. At age sixteen, he was sentenced to twelve years in Draper Prison. During his six years in Draper, Mr. Earnest earned his GED and came to believe he could attend college after his release, a goal that was realized as he eventually earned a bachelor's degree in social work with a criminal justice specialty from the University of Alabama. When working as a counselor with emotionally disturbed children, he became part of a team that developed the program model that led to the CITY Program, an effective alternative to incarceration for juvenile offenders.

THE RUN AWAY

By choice
By chance
By circumstance, on city streets
In dark doorways, quite discrete
A knowing glance,

A few
words passed
The question asked,
From a two-bit room to the
streets again,
Sweet sixteen come June...

Louis Osei Cotton
Lansing Correctional Facility, Kansas

"The Run Away" is excerpted from Caged Freedom,
Edited by Louis Osei Cotton, Audenreed Press (1997)

Certificate of Achievement

This is to Certify that

Willie Tucker 281918

has satisfactorily completed required coursework in

Substance Abuse II

this 7 day of August 1995

Francis D. Rogers, FA.C.A.P. — Instructor

R. Nelson Brinson — Superintendent

Kenneth E. Kimple — Supervisor

Smith C.I. — Institute

Glennville, GA. — Location

Certificate of Participation

This is to certify that

WILLIE TUCKER, EF 281918

has completed the course

Systematic Training for Effective Parenting

STEP

by authors

Don Dinkmeyer, Ph.D. and Gary D. McKay, Ph.D.

offered by

3-27-95 — *Date*

Bela A. Caldwell — *Group Leader*

CHIEF COUNSELOR

SUBSTANCE ABUSE

Georgia

June 10, 1997

"The reason I had not written is because I've been experiencing, I guess what would be described as, 'pre-parole eligibility blues.' Yes! Next year around this time, I'll be up for parole. The counselors here will do what is called a 'parole summary,' which would include my behavioral record, any participation in voluntary self-help and substance abuse programs, vocational trades or any other personal initiatives. Like my writing of poetry for instance. If these areas were rated on a scale of one to ten, I'd be a ten!

"Here in Georgia Prisons, no one 'makes' you do anything, especially when it comes to offering you a way to possibly rehabilitate yourself. I've learned it's all about taking responsibility for your own actions and consequently using what resources are readily available to assist you in making that transformation, from a life of crime to a life as a working productive citizen in society. I'm ready to give back all that I owe! I never was a real criminal anyways (laughing) I just thought I was.

"I'm enclosing a few of my most recent accomplishments. As you can see, I try to stay busy too."

GEORGE MILLER
"Impact Weekend: An Alternative Intervention Program"

While the primary method of punishing offenders in the state of Michigan relies heavily on incarceration and probation, there appears to be a change on the horizon. In fact, the United States, the largest user of incarceration of any country on the globe, is suddenly finding itself in a crisis, with spending for correctional facilities equal to or greater than the money spent on education. The public finds itself afraid of crime, but more alarmed at the skyrocketing costs of incarceration. As a society, we have begun to ask, "Do we have the right people locked up?" As a result, the term "community corrections" has been revitalized and is beginning to take on a new meaning. In many communities across the United States and here in Michigan, criminal justice professionals are developing alternative sanctions that include partnerships with public and private entities. Furthermore, the local citizen is being tapped as an effective resource in assisting with the rehabilitation of offenders who are ultimately coming back to the community once they have served their "time." With public safety as its number one concern, community corrections has become an effective tool in keeping non-violent offenders from taking up valuable jail and prison space by providing programs that punish, rehabilitate, and reintegrate offenders back into the community whence they came. With the nation's jails being consistently above their rated capacities, alternatives to incarceration for non-violent offenders must be seriously studied.

In Oakland County, two District Court judges determined that there were insufficient programs, besides incarceration, available for drunk drivers. These two judges, like so many of their colleagues today, wanted the ability to respond appropriately to the diversity of offenses and types of offenders coming through the system. In an effort to make a sound management decision, the Community Corrections Division secured data from their Pretrial Services unit to substantiate the need to create an alternative program for first and second time drunk driving offenders. Of the arraignments performed in Oakland County during a six month period, the largest number of offenses were for drunk driving, either first or second time.

The second issue to be addressed was the linking of jail overcrowding as a result of this population. After reviewing statistics for 1996 regarding the total jail population, it was evident that drunk drivers were being sentenced to jail as the only effective means of punishment at the time. Contacting several District Court judges within the county verified that an alternative program was necessary and would be utilized as an alternative to incarceration. Thus, the framework was developed to create what is now called "Impact Weekend."

The final step in this process was to determine who the partners should be, both in creating Impact Weekend and in running its day-to-day operation. Since the disease of alcoholism and the treatment of individuals who have this problem is very precise, it was strongly recommended that a treatment program be brought into the picture for the collaboration of this project. Turning Point Recovery Center, which has had a successful history in dealing with the drunk driving population and is conveniently situated in the center of Oakland County, was asked to participate in the initial discussions. Some consideration was given to housing this program within the jail complex, however there was a problem with limited space and the significant cost factor associated with running a program using government employees. Furthermore, there were several indications that it was time to rethink the balance of public- and private-sector responsibilities. It was apparent that the private sector could create and run the program at a cost that was more reasonable than a government-run counterpart. This collaboration would be the first of its kind within the criminal justice system in Oakland County.

The Oakland County Community Corrections Division, in partnership with the local Mothers Against Drunk Driving (MADD) chapter, Turning Point Recovery Center, an established substance abuse treatment program, and two progressive thinking District Court Judges developed an alternative to incarceration to address the growing need for an effective intervention program for first- and second-time drunk drivers. In the past, judges were limited to incarcerating individuals and then referring them to driver education classes once they returned to the community. Incarceration alone does nothing to help offenders confront the causes and potential impact of their substance abuse behavior.

Recently released statistics are alarming. In 1996, there were 17,274 deaths in alcohol-related traffic crashes, which averages one death every 32 minutes. Persons who drive while under the influence are operating outside of the boundaries of what society deems appropriate and acceptable. The Impact Weekend approaches drunk drivers in a direct, cognitive, and confrontational method.

What has evolved over the last two years is an intensive, three-day intervention/learning experience that begins on a Friday and ends Sunday evenings. Key components include:

- A partnership with the local Mothers Against Drunk Driving Chapter. MADD provides trained volunteers from their organization to present their "victims impact panel" during each session.
- Turning Point Recovery Center contributes a secluded environment for the weekend and trained substance abuse counselors. Counselors provide assessments, education, and an orientation to treatment.
- At regular intervals, case management and follow-up services are provided by the Oakland County Community Corrections Division to both the defendants and their families. For one year after completion of the weekend, trained university interns are responsible for conducting aftercare contacts and providing referrals to participants and their family members.

In addition to the above, a major component of Impact Weekend is the cost.

In lieu of daily jail costs paid by taxpayers, Impact Weekend holds the participant accountable. Participants are charged $175.00 each, paid to Turning Point Recovery Center before attending the weekend. During the past two years, 795 individuals have completed the program, therefore having already saved taxpayers over $162,000 (figure based on an average three day sentence at Oakland County Jail).

Since the commencement of the first weekend, Impact Weekend has continuously expanded, not only in the number of participants, but also in resources. On May 12, 1996, Impact Weekend's one-year anniversary, approximately 250 participants had completed the program. By the second anniversary, that number had almost tripled, with 795 participants. What began as a pilot project between Community Corrections, MADD, Turning Point Recovery Center, and District Court Judges has become a nationally-recognized alternative program to incarceration with participants from 17 district courts in Michigan. Due to the program's success, judicial officers from several other counties in Michigan are also sentencing offenders to Impact Weekend.

Reducing recidivism is a major objective of Impact Weekend. For the purpose of our study, recidivism was defined as any subsequent arrest and/or conviction acquired by the defendant after attendance at the weekend. All new offenses, whether alcohol related or otherwise, were reported. In order to determine these occurrences, a Michigan Secretary of State driving record and Law Enforcement criminal history check is conducted at regular intervals. In comparison to State of Michigan statistics on recidivism rates, Impact Weekend has a significantly lower rate of re-arrest. According to state reports, offenders who are convicted of a drinking and driving charge have a 33% rate of being arrested for a subsequent drunk driving offense within 5 years. Impact Weekend can proudly declare only a 5% recidivism rate, for more than two years. Of the 795 participants to date, 40 participants have been rearrested/convicted of a new criminal offense since their attendance at Impact Weekend. The actual number of drunk drivers with a new alcohol related charge is twenty-five, the other fifteen offenders accrued non-alcohol related charges. This reveals that Impact Weekend has a 3% recidivism rate for the target population of first- and second-time drinking and driving offenders with a new alcohol related offense only.

In analyzing the data to measure the success of Impact Weekend, it is also important to examine the demographics of the population served. Therefore, general demographic information such as gender, age and ethnicity of the 795 participants was collected. Remarkably, these statistics gathered coincide with that of state and national statistics for drunk driving offenders.

Of all participants as of May 12, 1997, 653 were males, which accounts for 82% of the total 795. The number of female offenders who attended Impact Weekend is 142, or 19%. Comparatively, national gender statistics for drinking and driving offenders is approximately 86% male to 14% female.

In addition to gender statistics, the age of each participant was documented and placed in age groups outlined by national statistics for offenders charged with drinking and driving. According to the data collected on Impact Weekend participants, the majority of offenders fall into the age groups ranging from 17 to 38. Again, according to national statistics on age, 63% of drunk driving offenders are 38 years of age or below.

These astounding similarities are also apparent when comparing ethnicity. Impact Weekend compiled data on four ethnic classifications: Caucasian, African-American, Hispanic, and Other which would include, but not be limited to, Asian, Native American, bi-racial and multi racial ethnicities. Of all the participants of Impact Weekend, 91.2% of offenders reported being of Caucasian descent and African-Americans accounted for approximately 3.3% of the group.

In conclusion, the above statistical comparisons demonstrate another important objective of Impact Weekend. This objective is to provide services to the average drunk driving offender. Each participant of Impact Weekend is randomly sentenced to the program by approximately 17 district courts in Michigan. These comparisons confirm that the participants of Impact Weekend are an accurate sample of the national population of offenders who drink and drive.

One final point worth noting: No program or sentencing system can achieve its full potential if it is used with the wrong population. Even with the tremendous success thus far with Impact Weekend, we have noticed what experts call "net widening." This program was designed for first and second time drunk drivers; however, the types of offenses have gradually expanded beyond the targeted population. To correct this trend, the Community Corrections Division has begun to pull the key actors in our criminal Justice system together to re-address our data and policies for Impact Weekend. This goal and mission clarification will result in strong policies that will guide the further development of this intermediate sanction.

George Miller has worked for Oakland County government for the past twenty years. He began his career with the Juvenile Court as a line supervisor in the juvenile detention unit. In 1986 he was promoted to an administrative position with the Substance Abuse Coordinating Agency for the County where he was responsible for developing contracts and monitoring substance abuse treatment programs for the indigent. He returned to the criminal justice field in 1994 after accepting the position of Manager for the Community Corrections Division. In his capacity as Manager, Mr. Miller directs the policies and procedures that increase the range of sanctions and services available in Oakland County for non-violent offenders. He obtained a Bachelor of Science Degree from the University of Detroit majoring in Criminal Justice studies. Mr. Miller also earned a Master of Arts Degree in Guidance and Counseling from Oakland University, Rochester, MI.

NANCY L. KEY, CSW, CASAC
"The Comprehensive Alcohol and Substance Abuse Treatment Program for Female Offenders"

The New York State Department of Correctional Services' Comprehensive Alcohol and Substance Abuse Treatment Program, known as "CASAT," is an intensive treatment program which prepares chemically addicted offenders to transition successfully to the community, and reduces their chance for relapse and return to prison. The CASAT program for women at Taconic Correctional Facility is the largest residential drug treatment correctional facility for incarcerated females in the United States. It has the capacity for three hundred and seventy women and offers a continuum of care and treatment for the chemically addicted female offender. This includes a thirty bed nursery where nonviolent, chemically addicted female offenders reside with their children who are born in prison.

The CASAT program has become a substantive program for a large portion of female offenders in the New York State prison system. Seventy percent of women who enter the prison system have reported drug and alcohol usage. Of all participants involved in CASAT programs throughout the state through June of 1996, 88 percent reported the use of illegal drugs and/or excessive alcohol.

One of the successful participants of the CASAT program is a chemically addicted offender named Anna. Anna entered the CASAT program in 1995 at the age of thirty two. Her criminal history began at age seventeen and since that time, Anna has had over forty arrests for prostitution, pick-pocketing, "boosting" and selling illegal drugs, including two felony convictions for the illegal possession of crack and heroin. Anna's criminal behavior and activities were, in part, to support her drug addiction. In the last decade, prison populations have dramatically increased with offenders who have substance abuse histories. From 1991 through 1995 over fifty thousand individuals have been committed to state prisons for drug offenses.

Anna's last felony conviction resulted in a six year prison sentence, and since her offenses were related to drugs, the judge who sentenced Anna also directed her to get help and treatment for her addiction while in prison. The Michigan Alcohol and Substance Abuse Test, based on self-reported use, history and events, indicated that Anna was addicted to heroin. For 33 percent of the women in the CASAT program, their drug of choice is heroin, while 46 percent primarily abused crack.

The crime Anna was charged for, criminal sale of a controlled substance, was classified as nonviolent. Based on the non-violent offense, drug history, and time frame before her parole board hearing, Anna became eligible for the CASAT program. Offenders who agree to participate in the CASAT program are eligible to transition to the community under the Department of Corrections supervision after completing six months of drug treatment in prison. This is an incentive for most non-violent offenders. If an offender chooses not to participate in the program but the Department of Corrections has identified her via the courts, probation, social services agencies and family members as being in need of drug treatment, then the offender may forfeit the opportunity for early release to the community. Anna chose to participate in the CASAT program, but later confessed that she only wanted to be in the CASAT program to "get to the street" faster, not to work on her addiction. However once involved in the program, she realized she needed help.

Once an offender is approved for CASAT, she is assessed by a counselor who is trained in the field of drug and alcohol addiction. The counselor asks the offender a series of questions about drug usage, length of time using drugs, age at which the usage began, and family history. Most of the women answer the questions to the best of their awareness. Anna completed this questioning during the first week of the program. She reported first using heroin at the age of thirteen.

Each participant receives a week-long orientation where each phase of the CASAT program is explained and the program rules and regulations are reviewed. The participant has the opportunity to ask questions about the program as well as express fears and concerns. Participants are informed that if any of the five cardinal rules—against threats, stealing, sexual acts, weapons, and drug usage—are violated, the result will be automatic termination from the program, and disciplinary sanctions.

During orientation, Anna learned about the three phases of the program—Annex, Community Reintegration and Aftercare. The Annex phase takes place at the prison and lasts approximately six months; once the participant completes this phase she transfers to Phase II, Community Reintegration. In Phase II the participant transitions to a community-based work release facility or treatment program and is required to secure employment and continue drug treatment. In the third phase, Aftercare, the participant is required to work and continue with treatment during her first year of parole.

For 61 percent of offenders in treatment, it is the first time they have been in a structured drug treatment program and they have mixed feelings about the expectations. During the orientation phase, an initial treatment plan with long term and immediate goals is established co-jointly by the counselor and offender. Anna's goals for the first two months of treatment were to remain abstinent from all mood altering drugs, participate actively in groups, attend support groups in the evenings, and learn about the disease of addiction and work on criminal thinking behaviors. Participants in the program have renamed the term "criminal thinking" (behaviors) to "stinking thinking."

Many chemically addicted offenders, even if they were not addicted to drugs or alcohol, would still be involved in some form of criminal activity. Anna admitted that even if she was not addicted to heroin, she would probably be involved in some type of antisocial behavior. Anna commented that she was always drawn to the "deuce," the famous Forty-Second Street area in New York City. She said the lights, people and action were a "high" for her and she was addicted to it. To increase the chemically addicted offender's chance of success in the community as a productive law abiding citizen, both addiction and criminal thinking are addressed in the CASAT program.

During the Annex Phase of the program, Anna was housed in a building exclusively for chemically addicted nonviolent offenders enrolled in the CASAT program. Community living is part of the program and, as such, team-work, organization and structure are integral components. Basic adult daily living skills are taught and each participant must keep her area in order and immaculate.

Anna had lived in various places throughout her life. She lived with an abusive alcoholic father for most of her childhood. They lived in basement apartments, in a one room apartment and a condemned building. As an adult, Anna reported living in shanties, under the subway tracks and in abandoned cars. She remembered feeling cockroaches and rats run over her while getting high in a crack house.

It was difficult for Anna to get used to the stringent guidelines for her prison living quarters. Everyday when she rose, she had to have her room ready for inspection. Her shoes had to be lined up under the bed. Her bed and pillow had to be made to military style. The floor had to be "spit-shined" and her clothes folded neatly and tucked away. There was a small area for pictures where Anna kept a few photos of her two children who had been placed in foster care. After two months of meeting the CASAT program standards for the living quarters, Anna became a "big sister" to new residents on the floor and showed them how to organize their rooms. For the first time Anna had structure and order in her life.

In the morning, Anna attended substance abuse education groups and learned about drugs and alcohol and the effects of each on the body. Anna was street smart and was able to recall every street name for heroin, but did not know what it was made of or its effects. She was surprised to learn about the psychological and physical aspects of this powerful habit-forming narcotic. Anna also learned about health issues affecting women and the characteristics of good health. Preceding the health lectures, Anna did not know about mammograms and her first pap smear test was completed, at the age of thirty, while incarcerated.

Anna was excited about all the new information she learned from her morning groups, but there were many days she said that she wanted to run away and get high. From the groups, Anna learned that this was not uncommon. She also learned about choices and consequences. Anna had a choice to walk out of group, but she realized that the consequences could be harsh. Participants in the program who exhibit negative behaviors, like non-participation, are informed that they can face possible termination if the behaviors do not improve. Anna was made aware that drug usage while in the program was an automatic reason for termination from the program.

In the afternoons, Anna was required to attend substance abuse treatment groups modeled after the Twelve Traditions and Steps of Alcoholics Anonymous. These groups explored the participant's addiction, thoughts, feelings and the path which led her to prison. These groups were difficult for Anna, because she had to sit through feelings of pain, anger, happiness, sadness and boredom without using heroin to escape them. During many sessions, Anna reported that she did not think she would make it, but each day she did, and realized that the feelings, both the desired and undesired, were just that, feelings that eventually passed.

Anna dealt with a lot of pain during the sessions. She remembered childhood beatings and sexual abuse. Anna was molested by her uncle and, as a favor to him, often had sex with his friends. Sexual abuse, rape and incest are common experiences shared by the women in CASAT. To comfort herself when remembering some of the painful experiences, she would roll her tongue around her mouth. This action only triggered another painful memory because Anna had no front teeth. A few had rotted from the drug abuse, and the lack of appropriate dental and nutritional care. The rest of the teeth were forced out by frequent beatings by pimps and so-called boyfriends.

In the CASAT program during group workshops and discussions, Anna learned about relationships. The program stresses that the most important relationship is with self. At first, the concept of a relationship with self was difficult for Anna to understand. She did not trust anyone. The family members that were supposed to protect her as a child betrayed and violated her. As an adult, Anna thought the routine beatings by boyfriends, which left her with broken ribs, a broken nose, and cigarette burns on one of her arms, were done because of her inappropriate behaviors. She also thought that the only way to give or receive love was through sex. The program taught Anna differently. It helped Anna identify her own strengths and limitations in order for her to have a better sense of who she was and what she was able to achieve.

Domestic violence education and information as well as support workshops are offered and highly utilized by the women in the CASAT program. A large portion of the women are victims of domestic violence.

The CASAT program encourages the offender to empower herself and take responsibility for her life. Although Anna experienced a succession of traumas in her life, she was encouraged not to go through the rest of her life pitying herself as a victim. She was encouraged to empower herself and become a survivor. Life is unfair, but using drugs does not change the past. Anna learned ways to make healthy choices through decision-making workshops.

During the evening, Anna was required to attend support groups, including Narcotics Anonymous, where alcohol and drug addicted offenders help each other deal with their addiction through support, and, when needed, constructive criticism and confrontation. Four months into the program, Anna became somewhat arrogant and felt she knew everything she needed to know about the program, herself, and the disease of addiction. Peer members confronted her "stinking thinking" and behaviors and gave her constructive criticism. Anna took a long hard look at herself and her behaviors, and realized her cockiness was a sign of regression.

After two months of all-day drug education and treatment, Anna attended a dual substance abuse education and treatment group one half of the day, and attended school the other half of the day. Anna had enrolled in classes to sharpen her skills to prepare to take the general equivalency examination. Anna's eleventh grade reading average was well above the sixth grade reading average of women in the CASAT program.

Participants who have a high school diploma or GED are allowed to progress to prison work assignments which prepare CASAT participants for jobs in the community. Various jobs are available, including tending to the grounds of the prison and working on a maintenance crew, learning skills such as minor electrical repairs, buffing floors and painting. For participants who want specialized training, there is a food service program in which the inmates learn about food preparation and management. Many offenders who graduate from the food service program transition to the community to jobs in the food industry. There is also a general business class that teaches offenders computer literacy and clerical skills.

Anna successfully made it through the Annex phase of the program and transferred to Phase II—Community Reintegration. The goal of community reintegration is to involve the participant in employment and treatment programs in her community and allow her to utilize the recovery principles and coping skills she learned in the Annex phase.

Due to Anna's estranged relationship with her family and her abusive boyfriend, it was not in her best interest to live with them, so she was placed in a residential drug treatment program in the community. There she took the GED test and passed. She was able to obtain employment soon afterward. Although employed, Anna was still required to attend drug treatment groups at the residence twice a week and to participate in family counseling sessions once a week. Anna successfully participated in all three phases of the program, including Phase III—Aftercare, under parole supervision. In December 1996, Anna completed her entire sentence. Twelve percent of the women who graduate from the CASAT programs return to prison after one year, as opposed to fourteen percent of the general confinement inmates. At the time of this writing Anna is still out in the community, employed and regularly attending support groups, Alcoholics Anonymous and Narcotics Anonymous.

In the field of drug and alcohol addiction, relapse can happen. The CASAT program includes a sixty day relapse program for the women who were out in the community and used drugs. The women participating in Phase II, Community Reintegration, are tested frequently for drugs. Those who test positive are given the opportunity to waive possible disciplinary charges for drug use by returning to the prison and participating in the relapse program. The sixty day relapse program helps participants identify "triggers" and behaviors that led them to use drugs again. The program also teaches the offenders techniques to deal with urges they may experience for their drug of choice. As of June 30, 1996, seventy five percent of the women who participated in the relapse program at Taconic Correctional Facility completed the program and continued on to Community Reintegration.

Another component of the CASAT program which addresses needs specifically for female offenders is the Nursery Program, which is available for nonviolent women who are substance and alcohol abusers and have given birth while in prison. The nursery program allows the offender the opportunity to bond with her child while simultaneously working on her addiction. As with all participants entering the CASAT program, the mothers on the nursery must remain drug free.

The children's well being on the nursery unit is always the greatest concern, hence mothers in the nursery program must adhere to very strict guidelines. The mothers are required to attend parenting classes with their children every morning. During these sessions, mothers learn about child development issues as well as techniques for disciplining a child. Many of the women involved in the nursery program were themselves victims of child abuse and do not realize that there are other ways to discipline children besides beating them. At one parenting session on the nursery unit, the facilitator asked the women how they were disciplined as children. Susan, a twenty-eight year old crack addict serving time for selling drugs out of her apartment, felt there was nothing wrong with beating a child with a thick belt. She described being beaten as a child and remembered one occasion on which she fainted from the agony. She said she was glad the beating took place during the summer recess from school because she was unable to sit down for three days. Susan thought this form of discipline taught obedience and kept kids on the right track. When questioned by one of her peers why, then, did she end up in prison, she replied that she guessed because she did not get beaten enough for the lesson to sink in. This way of "old school" parenting and discipline belief is a common theme for women who participate in the CASAT program. Through the parenting classes, Susan learned positive non-physical ways to discipline her children. She later disclosed that she wished she had been disciplined the way she learned in the parenting classes, not through brutal beatings.

In the afternoons, nursery mothers attend drug treatment groups, while their babies are cared for by offenders not necessarily residing on the nursery unit. The inmates who apply to be baby-sitters are carefully reviewed and their criminal and institutional records are fully investigated for violence charges or convictions and child abuse cases. Any charges and/or convictions of violence makes them ineligible. If an inmate has a past or active case in Family Court for neglect or abuse of children she is also ineligible. The Family Court stipulation eliminates a large number of possible CASAT participants as baby-sitters for the nursery program. Due to the deviant lifestyle, time, and energy the chemically addicted female offenders used to stay high or get money for drugs, many of them have neglected their children and have active custody cases in Family Court or have permanently lost their parental rights.

The CASAT program offers the mothers in the nursery program an opportunity to really experience motherhood. For many of the women in the CASAT program, reunification with their children on the outside will never take place. For those who have not lost permanent custody, the process to get their children back can be arduous and long. Court battles, lack of trust and respect from families and children, employment demands and drug treatment are some of the difficulties they will encounter.

A nursery mother is allowed to keep her child with her in the nursery program until the child is fifteen months old. If the mother is due to leave the prison within three months of the child reaching eighteen months old, then the child can remain with the mother until she is discharged. There are times when a child has to be removed from the nursery due to a mother's behavior on the unit or her lack of progress in the drug treatment groups. Arrangements are then made for the child to be placed with relatives. If there are no relatives to take the child, then arrangements are made for the child to be placed in foster care.

The nursery program is critically acclaimed and has received nationwide attention due to the success of children having the chance to bond with their birth mothers and the mothers receiving treatment for their addiction. Tina, a twenty-three year old participant in the CASAT nursery program, stated that although she had had two other children and loved them dearly, she was too high, when she was not locked up, to see them reach milestones like walking and saying "Mama" for the first time. As a participant in the CASAT nursery program, Tina has experienced many of these milestones with her third child who was born while she was in prison.

Longer sentences for the chemically addicted offenders profiled in this chapter are not the answer. They need programs like the CASAT program to teach them how to empower themselves, through education, drug treatment and vocational training, so that they will return to the communities as productive law-abiding individuals. This will have a positive effect on neighborhoods, schools and children.

The New York State Department of Corrections has saved approximately $153 million of operational and capital construction costs from its seven male and one female Comprehensive Alcohol and Substance Abuse Treatment facilities, since the program's inception in 1990. As mentioned previously, chemically addicted offenders who participate in the CASAT program have a lower recidivism rate than other offenders with or without drug histories in New York State prisons. This saves tax dollars.

With programs in prisons like the CASAT program, our communities will continue to become safer with reformed, law-abiding, employed citizens, like Anna, Susan and Tina, who learned through prison programs to take responsibility for their lives, children, addiction and the paths they choose.

Names have been changed in compliance with confidentiality guidelines.

Nancy L. Key

Nancy Key is a certified social worker and credentialed alcohol and substance abuse counselor in the State of New York. She is a senior correctional counselor for the New York State Department of Correctional Services. Nancy supervises the Comprehensive Alcohol and Substance Abuse Treatment Program for women at Taconic Correctional Facility in Bedford Hills, New York, located in the northern part of Westchester County, sixty miles north of New York City. Nancy is dedicated to ensuring the CASAT program at Taconic provides the highest quality of comprehensive treatment services for its participants. She lives in Bronx, New York.

MICHAEL E. BIBRO
"Substance Abuse Counseling"

My official job title here at the prison is Substance Abuse Associate, though that is something I am rarely called. More commonly I am known as "one of the AA counselors" or a clerk or a "substance abuse teacher." Each of these unofficial names holds a piece of the puzzle as to what I really am, but all are a little misleading by themselves. I like to think of myself as simply a substance abuse counselor. There's a problem with this, though, as the State of Maine has a different view of me altogether. As far as it is concerned, I am an inmate (D.O.C.#36) and that's pretty much that.

Still, thanks to a number of supportive prison staff, I am allowed to provide certain counseling services while under the supervision of a licensed alcohol and drug counselor (LADC), and am the only other substance abuse counselor within the Department of Corrections (DOC). Yes, it's true. For the past several years now, Maine's correctional system has had only one ADC to serve its entire prison population. There was, I understand, an excellent program at one medium security facility, but that was totally wiped out during the budget crunch layoffs several years ago.

The program here was thriving back when I took this job in June of 1991. At that time there were three counselors and myself. Previously there had been four, but one left and the position was terminated. That was when the idea for a peer-counseling position originated. I had been in treatment for several years and was involved in the college program, having aspirations to enter the helping professions one day. All of this was known to my counselor, who was also the program director. She decided that my experiences and aspirations could be put to good use and offered me a job. I jumped at the opportunity and gave my notice at the Wood Shop where I had been working for the previous seven years. Admittedly, I was very nervous about the prospect, having never done anything like it before, but I seemed to be guided by something that made me believe that, somehow, I would do okay.

I feel as though I'm pretty much a natural for this type of work. My opinion has more to do with my life experiences than anything else, and very little to do with anything that I am proud of. What I haven't mentioned thus far is that I am also a convicted murderer. On November 15, 1980, I killed my wife of a little over four years. Previously, I had no criminal record and was not prone to any type of violence, particularly not against my wife. I was 27 years old at the time and I have been incarcerated ever since. I'm looking at another 12 years before I am free.

It was a Saturday night and I was trying to rebound from one of my periodic drug binges. I had been out with the guys drinking, smoking hash, and snorting coke since I got out of work on Friday afternoon. I didn't get home until the middle of Saturday and was greeted by my wife with cold silence. The binge had not been planned, as was usually the case, but neither of us found any comfort in that. She was angry at me, and so was I. Neither of us had a clue as to what was really wrong with me. It wouldn't be for another three or so years before it finally sank in that I was an alcoholic. Because of that, my life had become a contradiction. I was a Dr. Jekyll and Mr. Hyde: hard working, devoted husband and father / drunken, irresponsible fool. I never thought that I would also become a murderer.

When they brought me here, reality hit hard—like a sledgehammer hard. It wasn't so much the sentence I received, nor the prison environment (though both had a powerful effect); what got me the most was an incredibly deep sense of loss. I thought I had hit bottom in this regard while awaiting trial at the county jail, but I discovered that that bottom was a false one. I crashed through it when the door shut behind me in my 5x7 quarantine cell. It was there that the guilt, shame and excruciating pain for the loss of my wife and daughter swallowed me up. And I had nothing to defend myself with; I was stripped of all of my previous identity and was stuck with one that I could not relate to, and which disgusted me.

I didn't want to live but I didn't have what it took to kill myself. Therefore, in my mind I had only one alternative, and that was to rebuild myself and make a new identity—one that I could live with, one that would allow me to live with what I had done. Thankfully, there were plenty of resources within the prison then, and I gradually immersed myself in them.

Aside from the counseling, the most beneficial program for me was the college program. In the early '80's, a Pell Grant was available to any inmate who qualified financially. For many of us, that meant that the cost of a college education would be covered, wholly or in part, by the U.S. government.

Again, I was quite nervous about taking on such an endeavor. I had never thought of myself as college material, but I figured I'd give it a try anyway. What I soon discovered was that I had more potential than I thought. I also found that I had a strong predisposition towards the social sciences, particularly psychology. I got my first A in PSY 101 and it nearly blew my mind. I wanted more—more A's, that is—and I got them. I also got increasingly hungry for knowledge of any kind. It was amazing how much larger and more interesting my world grew, both quite ironic, considering where I was.

Mental health services, for me, were adequate. I cannot speak for anyone else, (those in need of sex-offender counseling I am sure would disagree), and I believe anyone who desired treatment throughout the '80's could be seen on a regular basis. Traditionally, though, this is not something that many men participate in. Voluntary counseling is often seen as an admission of weakness for men in general, and especially for those of us in prison. Even for the ones able to forsake this societal norm and seek out treatment, staying with it is not so easy a task. Those with the most fortitude in this regard are usually the ones who have hit bottom (or come dangerously close) and feel they have nothing to lose. Confronting one's demons is usually daunting, under the best of circumstances; doing it in prison, in the midst of peer pressure, makes this prospect even more difficult. Consequently, men often drop out once the real work begins.

It's unfortunate that the DOC offers no incentive to entice men to enter treatment and stick with it. It is likewise unfortunate that more treatment is not available at Maine's medium and minimum security facilities. The psychological staff, which is based here at Maine State Prison, is probably large enough for this institution; however, they must also attend to the men at two other facilities, one a supermax. My supervisor, the sole staff ADC, is stretched far beyond what is reasonable. He had to draw the line, and consequently the supermax has no substance abuse treatment whatsoever.

Since 1991, the substance abuse treatment staff has been allowed to dwindle down to just one full-time staff state employee. I essentially function as his helper. Despite the shortage of staff, I believe we do a pretty good job. His 24 years of experience in the substance abuse counseling field, and my long-term status as an inmate and prior substance abuser complement each other very well. Each of us has certain unique qualities to draw upon and exchange with one another.

If everyone who needed treatment sought it, the department would be in serious trouble. Statistics vary, but it is estimated that somewhere around 75% of the crimes committed in the U.S. are in some way related to drug use or abuse. Some (inmates, typically) would put that percentage up at around 90%.

Currently at MSP, about 17% of the entire 362 man population are actively involved in treatment. The percentage at a minimum security facility is considerably higher at 69% of their 180 man population. Incentive would be the factor most responsible for this difference, as the prospect of furloughs (not allowed at MSP) and a transfer to work-release function wonderfully as motivators to become involved. Some men participate at this point simply because their release date is near and they realize that stress and the availability of drugs will be greater upon release.

Many men, particularly while incarcerated, don't see this need for several reasons. One very common one is the notion that, since the availability of alcohol and drugs is severely limited, they no longer have a drug problem. Before I stumbled upon a college course in chemical dependency, I was in this category of believers. Like many others, I believed that, if I did indeed have a problem, I would deal with it, say a year or so before the end of my sentence—that would be time enough.

Much of what we do in working with the men who come to us is to help them recognize this sort of thinking as faulty. The point is made, usually repeatedly, that recovery is a slow, on-going, life-long process. Abstinence is a start—it is essential—but alone, it is not enough. Along with it there must be self-awareness, self-honesty, a strong commitment to change and adequate support to accomplish it. We soon realize that none of this happens in the short-term and no magic wand exists to make it come more quickly or less painfully.

Our program consists of basically 3 components: individual counseling, group counseling and education. The latter is mandatory in order for one to be eligible for a furlough. A basic four-hour Alcohol/Drug Education Course is available periodically to men who are interested. There is a weekly Film/Discussion Group that serves this purpose as well. Attendance at six or more of these sessions can fulfill a portion of the furlough eligibility requirements.

Education exists throughout our program; it is on-going. The most fundamental, essential lesson is helping the men to understand what it is exactly that they are dealing with. The "Disease Concept" of addiction is taught because it best explains the power of addiction. At the same time, it allows for some forgiveness (but not forgetting) to take place, while emphasis is also placed upon personal responsibility. Imposing a "guilt trip" on an addict or alcoholic is simply unproductive. It doesn't matter so much how they got that way; of main importance is what they do about it after the diagnosis is made.

The starting point has to be abstinence. This is invariably a very big pill to swallow (no pun intended). Many of the men who come to us for treatment, myself included, have extensive histories of using and abusing drugs. In other words, we have had years and years of practicing all those things we do when we become chemically dependent people. Along with the practice, practice, practice, we have had lots of positive reinforcements implanted in our brains: powerful, visceral, euphoric memories that, over time, tend to overshadow the painful ones. The allure of using again and the prospect of addiction never truly leave us. The worst thing an addict will ever hear, in the early stages of his recovery, is "You can never use again." It sucks, and part of us will never truly believe it. That is why we must not ever lose conscious contact with the memories of the pain of our addictions—this is essential. It is part of the major responsibility that we owe to ourselves and those whom we have harmed over the years when we were sick. Remembering the pain helps us stay well.

Nothing works better at that than AA. MSP has its own group which meets every Sunday in the chapel. The group celebrates its 50th anniversary next year. Although it is a separate entity from the Substance Abuse Department, my supervisor acts as a liaison between it and the prison administration. Both he and I consider it an excellent referral source that we utilize frequently. I also happen to attend for my personal needs. People from the free world attend our meetings—from one to four or five per week—and chair and speak, listen and reap what we reap: they come in to help us and, by doing so, help themselves. "There but for the Grace of God..." many have been heard to say. Painful memories are exchanged, but we also receive hope and inspiration from them, a valuable commodity within these walls. Through them we can come to believe that maybe we, too, can turn our lives around.

It's not easy getting well no matter where you are, but trying to do it in prison is especially difficult. This is compounded if you do not possess any frame of reference to what wellness is to begin with. The nebulous desire to turn your life around, while not knowing where this new direction will take you, can be a frightening proposition. Recognition of this, and having support around it, are necessary if a person is to continue in his program of recovery.

Getting well, when it comes to addiction, means changing the way we think, as well as act, and the people we choose to associate with. It is a lifestyle change of immense proportions. In the context of prison—in the realm of negativity and major peer-pressure—success, on the one hand, can mean failure on the other. Distrust and suspicion abound in prison and it doesn't take much to trigger them. They can occur from something as innocent as declaring your sobriety on your corridor or in your dorm. Declining a joint, for instance, can raise many an eyebrow. Even seeing a counselor or involvement in any prison program can arouse suspicion and ultimately lead to banishment by your peers. In retrospect it is usually seen as the best thing to have happened to you, but, in the meantime, it can be a terrifying thought. Think about it; we're already outcasts from the free world. We all want to fit in somewhere and the prospect of rejection has led many men away from their recovery program altogether.

Substance abuse treatment (and all other forms of counseling as well) is vital if we care about rehabilitation—or just habilitation, as is the case for most of us. Often there is more that needs to be attended to. It wasn't just the alcohol and drugs that led us here. Our individual situations are far more complicated than that. The truth is, many of us used to medicate ourselves from the pain of what really needed to be corrected within us. Few of us became addicts just for the fun of it, while attending too many parties where there were drugs. Usually we're just trying to correct something that doesn't seem right, or trying to feel normal. Then our "correction" becomes part of the problem. In my case, if I had never stopped using drugs, I never would have learned about the obsessive control I had over my anger. I thought I was doing myself (and others) a favor by controlling it; instead, after years and years of stuffing, never resolving, it caused immeasurable harm. I had warning signals galore but I could not see them. I ran and ran and I sank deeper and deeper in a mire and fog.

On the night of my crime I had deteriorated to the point of suicidal homicide. I projected my depression onto my wife and basically concluded that death was preferable to life for both of us. I was very confused, very angry (yet without having a conscious awareness of it) and I was very selfish. I was so in need of help but too ignorant to go after it. I don't know what it would have taken to make me see otherwise. It is something that I have asked myself many times. Certainly "denial" figured into it: denial of a drug problem and denial of my overall psychological condition. But what could have cracked it, I just don't know. It's impossible to help people if they are unwilling or incapable of talking about what's bothering them, and that was true of me. I only know that, looking back, counseling has made a huge difference in my life; I simply wish that I had been open to it and sought it before I needed it so badly. It <u>does</u> work.

Michael E. Bibro has been an inmate at the Maine State Prison since June 26, 1981. His overall term of incarceration for the 40 year sentence he is serving began on November 16, 1980. He has been active in volunteer work throughout most of this period of time and is currently serving as Vice President of the prison chapter of the N.A.A.C.P. and as an HIV/ AIDS Senior Peer Educator. In 1994, Michael earned a B.S. in Social Science. Just prior, in 1993, he married again, a very patient woman, Barbara, the primary person in his life and benefactor of the mixed-bag of lessons he has learned and is learning "one day at a time."

ROD MULLEN
MARK SCHUETTINGER
NAYA ARBITER
DAVID CONN
AMITY FOUNDATION OF CALIFORNIA

"Reducing Recidivism: Amity and the California DOC Demonstrate How To Do It"

The California Department of Corrections (CDC) has the largest number of prison inmates in the United States and has experienced dramatic growth in inmate population over the past decade. The Legislative Analyst's Office (LAO) of the California Legislature recently prepared a report addressing the prison population problem. One of the LAO's recommendations was to expand substance abuse treatment. A decade ago, in contrast, prison drug treatment was considered a failure by the Legislature and by almost all in CDC. How did this attitude change?

How did the Amity/RJDCD Therapeutic Community begin?

In 1987, CDC Director James Rowland called Amity's CEO Rod Mullen. Rowland explained that CDC's rapid prison expansion was not addressing the fact that 70 percent or more of CDC inmates had serious and chronic substance abuse problems. Their substance abuse was the key factor in their violating parole more quickly than other parolees, so that many were "doing life on the installment plan." Rowland asked Mullen to tour several CDC institutions and parole regions and to make a presentation to Rowland's executive staff and Wardens regarding the feasibility and effectiveness of substance abuse treatment for CDC inmates and parolees.

Subsequent to the Amity report, the CDC Office of Substance Abuse Programs (OSAP) and a department-wide CDC Substance Abuse Advisory Panel was formed. In 1989, a report to the California Legislature included plans for a model in-prison Therapeutic Community (TC) and the establishment of two parolee treatment networks.

CDC followed Amity's recommendations that the prison TC be established at a new institution, one that had no history of previous substance abuse programs, and one in which the Warden was willing to give the program an opportunity to prove itself. Director Rowland asked Warden John Ratelle, who had begun his career as an entry-level CDC security officer, if he would be willing to house the model program. Warden Ratelle agreed to house the program if he had the Director's agreement that the program could be terminated immediately if it was not working. Ratelle then visited the Amity/Pima County Jail Program, funded by the Bureau of Justice Assistance (BJA) as a "national demonstration program" in Tucson, Arizona. He viewed a jail pod where 50 sentenced drug offenders engaged in the Amity model, described as a "teaching and therapeutic community" that used ex-addict counselors, a curriculum specifically developed by Amity, and an Amity-developed program of cross training between correctional officers and treatment staff. Participants averaged two prior convictions and four years of heavy drug use. A BJA evaluation revealed that 30 months post release follow-up data indicated that only 35 percent of the 362 program completers had been re-arrested.

Warden Ratelle admitted that he came to look at Amity with a great deal of skepticism. "I've seen a lot of programs come and go, and a lot of them have been 'games' where inmates lay around all day, continued to use drugs, went to meetings occasionally, manipulated untrained correctional counselors, got their day-for-day credit—and then got out and went back to drugs and crime." When he talked to inmates at Amity, he met some "old cons" who had been incarcerated in CDC. They talked about how the Amity program was different than other programs they had participated in. He observed the demanding work schedule, saw that the program curriculum was dealing with "real issues," and that the encounter groups didn't allow inmates to shift the blame for their mistakes to others.

He decided that he was willing to take the risk of starting the TC, since, if the program lowered recidivism only ten percent, it would save the taxpayers millions of dollars over the years. He also knew that the section of the RJ Donovan Correctional Facility (RJDCF) where Amity was to be located had more violence per capita than the rest of the prison. He hoped that the program would reduce violent incidents, which at an estimated cost of $85,000 per occurrence, could alone justify the expense of the program. (These costs included paperwork, medical attention, hearings, investigations, transportation, legal representation, special incarceration in segregated units, and the cost of overtime when entire housing units or "yards" had to be put on lengthy "lockdowns.")

How was the TC implemented?

From the time the contract was awarded, Amity worked closely with Warden Ratelle's staff, OSAP, and security on staff where the program was to be located.

Amity fielded a team of senior counselors and program administrators, all recovering addicts, all ex-offenders, and representing all ethnic groups, with between 10 and 25 years of experience working with criminal addicts. This unusual group "walked the yard," talked to inmates, learned the specific inmate and institutional culture of RJDCF, conducted interviews, met the men who formed the Men's Advisory Council and passed information back to Amity's management about what was needed to mount a successful TC. CDC initially had difficulties screening inmates into the Amity program; the educational requirements for entrance proved too exclusive, and RJDCF classification staff were not experienced with this type of inmate selection. A visit by a committee of the State Legislature to view the program in

November 1990 precipitated extensive and immediate changes in inmate classification when they discovered that the program had only 13 participants five months after funding had been provided legislatively. The next 187 inmates were quickly installed. There were frequent disputes, and some scuffles occurred, as the "Amity inmates" displaced general population inmates from their cells, but despite the tension, no serious incidents occurred.

Warden Ratelle worked closely with the Amity Program Director, and instructed his staff, "We are going to give it {Amity} our full support; we are not going to allow the program to be subverted." His attitude towards Amity's staff was always supportive—even though almost all of them were "experience-trained" professionals, who had been drug users, criminals and had been previously incarcerated. Ratelle's only requirement was that anyone with a record be out of an institution for five years and off parole. He accepted Amity management's verification that they had at least three years of sobriety. He said, "You are the experts at changing these guys; you have proven that. We know how to run a prison. You work with us and we'll support you." All Amity staff participated in the standard CDC week-long security training to learn institutional security procedures and to receive their RJDCF security clearances.

Amity targeted many of the "shot callers" for support. This included inmates serving life sentences, and other long-term inmates who had "reputations" and the respect of the inmate population. Many of these men joined Amity. Those who did not join spread the word that Amity was different; that it was not the equivalent of protective custody; that some "stand-up guys" were trying to get their lives together; that Amity should be respected; that the participants were not "snitches" and should not be "hassled" on the yard. The facility design of RJ Donovan precluded Amity participants from being completely isolated from the general population. Yet Amity wanted participants to minimize contact, as it was well known that the influence of the "convict code" held by general population inmates could significantly reduce the "buy in" needed for Amity participants to progress in the program.

Initially, the plan was for all Amity participants to work together in a new textile mill, which was to be opened by the Prison Industry Authority at RJDCF in 1991. For a variety of reasons the mill did not open until several years later, so Warden Ratelle insisted that the men mix with the general population for their minimum 36-hour weekly work assignment, eat with general population, and share the recreational facilities on the yard. Ratelle felt that this model was more realistic. "If they were on the outside and had a problem," said Ratelle, "they would have to maintain a job and deal with it after work. I don't see why we should make it any easier for these guys." So Amity participants performed their institutional work assignments with non-program inmates (many of whom used drugs), and then most participated in a minimum of twenty hours a week of intensive Amity TC activities, often at night and on weekends in order to accommodate the institutional work schedule.

The Amity program was shaped both by Warden Ratelle's hard-nosed attitude and his support. He insisted that there be absolutely no incentives for men participating in the program. In fact, men who volunteered for the program were not eligible for work furlough, since it would interfere with them completing the required time in program. Because of this, and the program's intensity, Amity developed a reputation as being "serious," which probably discouraged applicants who were looking for an "easy ride." Despite Amity's toughness, the program received from 200 to 500 applications per month for the 10 to 20 program slots that became available monthly.

At a TC in Alabama, Amity consultants had received positive feedback that the "lifers" who were included helped stabilize a program that was severely understaffed and were credible role models for other inmates. Upon implementation of the Amity TC at RJDCF, Amity talked to a skeptical Warden Ratelle about including lifers. Ratelle initially refused, but Amity staff returned to his office after several lifers had approached them expressing an interest in joining the program. Warden Ratelle allowed two lifers to move into the Amity housing unit and become part of the program on a trial basis. These men, one Caucasian, the other African-American, both with convictions for extremely violent crimes, became role models for the remainder of the men. The friendship that they formed became a powerful behavioral message about racial prejudice; their daily demonstration of enthusiastic support of the program, its philosophy, and its staff made it easier for other participants to follow their path. One of the lifers said, "Hey man, I've been in here for a long time and I have respect on the yard. I've been a leader. Problem is that I have been leading these kids in the wrong direction, 'cause it's the only direction I knew. Now that I'm in Amity, I'm still a leader, and those kids are listening to me when I tell them that gangs, crime, and violence is stupid. They need to go out, stay out of prison, get a job, and start supporting their families."

Critical to the success of Amity was the development of a residential "continuance" facility for men who were paroled from the program. The initial contract didn't fund aftercare, so Amity leased a large house to use as an office, and also housed six to ten parolees who had completed the RJDCF program. The OSAP Director wanted Amity to send RJDCF completers to other community-based providers in San Diego. But Amity argued that the program participants said, "We've already been to those places, and we've failed there." They told Amity staff that in order to succeed they needed an Amity facility in the community that was a real continuance of what they had started in the prison. Additional funding was secured and, in 1993, Amity opened a 40-bed facility which allowed about one third of Amity in-prison completers to enter an Amity residential program which built upon the curriculum used at RJDCF. The outcomes clearly demonstrate the critical importance of this linked aftercare in helping the men maintain sobriety, get a job, and keep from returning to drugs and criminality.

In 1992, Warden Ratelle decided to do a surprise urine drop of the entire

Amity in-prison program. He told no one of his decision, neither his staff nor the Amity program staff, so that the results would reflect what was really occurring in the unit. On a Monday, after weekend visitation, he had each cell in the entire housing unit where the Amity inmates are housed locked down simultaneously, and had each inmate give a urine specimen under security officer supervision. "I knew that I had two hundred guys with serious drug problems all living together, and not isolated from the main yard. We were busting guys on the yard for drugs, so I knew that if the guys in Amity wanted to get drugs, they could. I assumed that 25 percent of the people in the Amity program would turn up 'dirty.'" But the results were that only one Amity participant was positive for drugs—marijuana.

"I was shocked," said Ratelle, "but I was very impressed. That was the single most important event for me in convincing me that the program was really working." In the fall of 1996, Ratelle once again had a "surprise" urine screening of the entire unit. Of 214 men tested, there was not one positive test result for any drug.

Results of a National Institute on Drug Abuse study, completed this year, clearly indicate that the Amity/RJDCF program is effective in reducing recidivism. The overall results of this study clearly demonstrate the effectiveness of the combined Amity in-prison and post-prison programs to reduce recidivism to reincarceration.

Former CDC Director James Gomez said, "I think that one of the most important aspects of the CDC/Amity collaboration was the confidence that it gave the Legislature and the Governor to authorize over $100 million dollars to build the largest dedicated prison drug treatment program in the world. And the confidence it gave us at CDC that it could and should be done. It is clear that Amity program's results are going to help shift the public debate here in California about corrections to a more treatment oriented approach."

In terms of the "bottom line," the 1997 LAO report on Prison Population growth determined that if the Amity results could be replicated through an expansion of substance abuse treatment to 10,000 beds over seven years, the state would not have to build an additional 4,700 beds. That scenario would also result in a one time capital outlay savings of $210,000,000 with annual savings of $80,000,000 a year.

But these substantial savings to CDC reflect only part of the cost benefit of Amity at the RJDCF. The Amity Economic Questionnaire, developed by economist Dr. Conn, was administered to men who had both phases of Amity (RJDCF and Vista) in 1995. Information was obtained on criminal activities in the year prior to entering Amity. This data included numbers of crimes in different categories, court cases, public defenders, arrests, jailings, state and federal incarcerations, emergency room visits, children on welfare, and other items. These data were then used to construct estimates of the costs to the public of the criminal, substance-abusing careers of these individuals. Imputations from the National Institute of Justice and other government sources were applied to the actions of these men. The net result is that the average social cost of these men in the year prior to their last incarceration had been over $93,000. On a lifetime basis, each of these men had, on average, accounted for social costs in excess of $1,500,000.

Additionally, most of these men were third strike candidates, with a mean expected cost to the California Department of Corrections of their next conviction in excess of $500,000 each. Similar surveys of men by Dr. Conn who had not yet been to prison found an annual average social cost of well over $80,000.

It is clear that the expenses of an effective prison TC can be recouped, even if only a fraction of those treated can be diverted from returning to substance use and its associated criminal lifestyle. For the men discussed above, if only two stayed out of prison for three years, CDC would save enough to pay for the entire Amity project (200 men in prison, and about 100 in the community) for a full year. With these figures in hand, the question should change from "How much does it cost to provide services?" to "How much does it cost to ignore these men's addiction, violence, and irresponsibility?"

Regarding violence reduction, in 1995 Warden Ratelle stated, "The Amity unit is a safer environment for correctional officers to work in, it gives them an opportunity to be more involved, and there are fewer write-ups—resulting in cost savings for management." He noted there had been no serious incidents of violence at Amity. This, even though "the inmates in the Amity program are some of the most incorrigible inmates in the correctional system, and one of the hardest groups to work with, with an average of at least eight years of prison time, strong gang affiliations, a long history of substance abuse, and violent backgrounds."

Another less quantifiable outcome is what happened to Captain Mike Teichner, known as the "Iceman" over his 20-year history in corrections. When Teichner, then a Correctional Counselor III, was assigned to Amity by Warden Ratelle, he felt strongly that prison rehabilitation efforts were completely ineffective. For the next four years he worked closely with Amity as the supervising correctional counselor in the Amity/RJ Donovan TC. He says now his only problem is that he feels Amity needs to be expanded to every prison in the state. Former CDC Director James Gomez said he wanted to place many two-hundred-bed programs throughout the system, instead of a few larger ones, because he knew that every Warden who had a program at their institution, no matter how they initially felt, would become an advocate for prison drug treatment.

What is the Amity Model?

While an examination of the "Amity teaching and therapeutic model" requires a fuller treatment than the current chapter allows, there are several key elements of the model that can be briefly highlighted here:

<u>Structure and duration</u>. The population in prison TCs typically: began their

drug abuse, criminality and incarceration as teens; have dysfunctional, abusive, and criminogenic families; have little formal education; have inadequate work skills and experience; do not "buy in" to mainstream morality; have little sense of personal responsibility; possess anti-social personality disorders; have neither the attitudes nor skills necessary to take responsibility for their offspring; have almost exclusively negative social and personal relationships; have poor interpersonal and decision making skills; and have never achieved a high degree of functioning in any non-criminal realm of life. In short, they need habilitative, rather than rehabilitative services. Habilitation entails complete cognitive, emotional, and behavioral restructuring. This means that the TC must be highly structured, very intensive, and relatively long term. Amity's model is delivered for as close to 24 hours per day, seven days a week, 365 days per year as prison security regulations and budgeted staffing permit.

For example, Amity has successfully used intensive curriculum based retreats and workshops for many years as an important element of emotional and cognitive restructuring. These often occur in 24, 48, or 72 hour segments, with sleep and meal breaks, and sometimes last as long as seven days. However, security and institutional work constraints resulted in an adaptation: 26-hour workshops at RCDCF, held over two days. These intensive workshops form the backbone for delivery of the Amity curriculum.

While throughout the treatment field there is constant pressure to reduce time in-program, many of Amity's best successes spent as long as eighteen months in the prison TC, followed by a year in Amity's community based TC at Vista. In-prison treatment should last a minimum of nine months, followed by a minimum of six months in community based aftercare, for a total episode of no less than fifteen months. Residential aftercare is more effective in reducing recidivism than non-residential services. Non-residential services, when employed, need to be as intensive as possible and based upon the needs of this population, rather than the more traditional "outpatient services" for a less criminal clientele.

Staffing and Training: Commitment, competence, credibility and congruence are the four "Cs" and key factors in this area. Staff must be highly committed to work in an environment where the "convict code" and institutional security culture are locked in an eternal wrestling match; they must be seen as credible to both security staff and inmates alike; they must be trained in a manner relevant to the unique environment in which they work; and they must be absolutely congruent in their expectations of program participants, each other, and correctional security and parole personnel.

In the early days of TCs, there was no formal staff. "All doctors were patients, all patients doctors." Those who led the TC communities were recovering addicts who were highly motivated, experienced, and had more "clean time" than those they led. All leadership, however, was done from the position of personal demonstration; this made TCs both powerful and extremely credible to participants, as all staff shared the same assumptions and agreed upon the same protocols. As TCs matured, and became more dependent upon mental health funding, staffing characteristics changed, becoming more akin to other health service organizations. The emphasis became more on "individual treatment plans" than upon building a recovering community in which all, including "counselors," were members first. While "professionalization" has benefits, particularly in terms of experience and stability, it can also result in a loss of vitality and credibility. At Amity/RJDCF an "internship program" actively recruits and trains potential counselors from within, increasing credibility. Several Amity in-prison counselors are men who were in the original cohort of Amity/RJDCF participants, who completed parole, trained with Amity and have returned as counselors.

While Amity's results have been influential, around the nation, as correctional agencies issue their requests for proposals, they mostly limit those who can be hired as counselors to those who have formal academic training and/or substance abuse credentials. A good rule of thumb in this area is that requirements should be imposed only when they have demonstrable value in improving outcomes or reducing risks. There are no studies demonstrating that academic training and current drug and alcohol credentials improve outcomes, particularly in prison TCs. In fact, these kinds of requirements often have the opposite effect by imposing irrelevant barriers, the equivalent of a "poll tax," on people who are often the most enthusiastic, able, and most credible to drug abusers in the criminal justice system.

All staff are trained through week-long immersion retreats. In these, staff must learn to do themselves what they are going to ask those they lead to do: self-disclose, deal with difficult personal issues, learn about each other, learn to respect different cultures, become skilled and enthusiastic teachers, and work cooperatively with each other from a common set of shared beliefs about "what works." Staff also "practice what they preach" through regular participation in staff encounter groups. These groups help in resolving issues between staff, keeping morale high, maintaining a sense of staff "community," and demonstrating that the methodology used in the treatment program is part of a life-long recovery process, not just "program stuff" to be jettisoned on exit from the TC.

Curriculum: Most TCs have a set of practices that are passed on from generation to generation, mostly orally. What written curriculum is available is often drawn from other treatment programs, most of which work with a better-educated and more advantaged population. Amity has developed an extensive written and videotaped curriculum that aims to provide guidance for counselors and participants alike in tackling issues relevant to convicted drug abusers. The intensive cognitive, emotional, and behavioral restructuring occurs through the delivery of a curriculum designed to accommodate a wide variety of abilities, cultural backgrounds and learning styles. It has to be interesting, relevant, and interactive—making every student a "teacher."

Cross Training: At Amity/RJDCF all Amity staff attend regular security trainings, and quarterly two and three days trainings are provided for institutional, parole and administrative correctional staff so that the Amity treatment model is understood by all the correctional professionals who work with the program.

The Amity/RCDCF model is now entering its eighth year of continuous operation. It has proven itself able to reduce recidivism of participants to drug use, criminality, and reincarceration. It has proven that a large percentage of men who have been "written off" by society and considered toxic to it, can be reclaimed, and can play productive roles in society. It has proven that there are dramatic bottom-line benefits for taxpayers in supporting such programs. It is our hope that the Amity/RJDCF TC will continue to inspire others throughout the country to replicate its results and improve upon its methodology.

An expanded article on this program is available; see page 370.

Rod Mullen is President and CEO of Amity Foundation of California. Mr. Mullen has worked in the substance abuse treatment field for 30 years, beginning his career with Synanon Foundation, the original therapeutic community in California. He was the Executive Director of Amity, Inc. in Tucson, Arizona for eleven years, during which time he developed or adapted and implemented programs for adolescent gang members, adult IDVUs at high risk for HIV infection, addicts on intensive probation supervision, and the nationally known Amity/Pima County jail program. He is the co-founder of the Amity Foundation of California, and author of numerous articles and book chapters about therapeutic community programs.

Mark Schuettinger is the Program Director of the Amity@RJ Donovan Program (subject of the article). Mr. Schuettinger has been in the substance abuse treatment field since 1983, and is a graduate of the Amity program in Tucson. Mr. Schuettinger has held a wide variety of counseling and management positions with Amity, including management of a multi-faceted substance abuse treatment program for adolescent males and females committed to the Arizona Department of Juvenile Corrections. He has worked at the Amity@RJ Donovan program since its inception.

Naya Arbiter is a board member and co-founder of the Amity Foundation of California, and principal of Extensions, LLC, a private group that provides management consulting and curriculum development for organizations involved in behavioral change and fostering emotional intelligence. Ms. Arbiter is well known nationally and internationally for her work developing curricula and programs for underserved populations, particularly for women who have been the victims of abuse.

David Conn received his Ph.D. in Economics in 1976 from the State University of New

York at Stony Brook, where he specialized in mathematical models of economic organizations. Dr. Conn was a Professor of Economics from 1975 through 1993, holding appointments at Miami University, Ohio State University, Wayne State University, and the University of Arizona. From 1993 to 1997, Dr. Conn was employed as a grant writer and researcher by Amity, Inc. in Tucson, Arizona and the Amity Foundation of California. Dr. Conn is currently employed by the Fromm Group where he is a consultant to non-profit agencies.

References

California Department of Corrections (1995) "California Department of Corrections Overview of Substance Abuse Programs, May 1995," Office of Substance Abuse Programs, California Department of Corrections. Sacramento, CA. Pamphlet.

Condelli, W.S. and De Leon, G. (1993) "Fixed and Dynamic Predictors of Retention in Therapeutic Communities." Journal of Substance Abuse Treatment. 10, pp. 11-16.

Glider, P., Herbst, D., Mullen, R. (1997) Substance Abuse Treatment in a Jail Setting in Community as Method: Modified Therapeutic Communities for Special Populations. ed. DeLeon, G. Ph.D. The Greenwood Publishing Group, NY.

De Leon, G. (1995) "Therapeutic Communities for Addictions: A Theoretical Framewor." International Journal of the Addictions, Vol. 30.

De Leon, G., G. Melnick, D. Kressel, and N. Jainchill. (1994) "Circumstances, Motivation, Readi ness and suitability (The CMRS Scales): Predicting Retention in Therapeutic Community treatment," The American Journal of Drug and Alcohol Abuse, 20(4), 495-515.

De Leon, G., and M. S. Rosenthal. (1989) "Treatment in Residential Communities," in Treatments of Psychiatric Disorders, Vol. II, edited by T. B. Karasu, Washington, DC, 1379-1396.

Graham, W.F. and Wexler, HK (1997) "The Amity Therapeutic Community Program: Description and Approach," In G. De Leon (Ed.), Community as Method; Modified Therapeutic Communities for Special Populations and Special Settings. Westport, CT; Greenwood Press.

Hill, E.G., (1994) "Crime in California," Legislative Analyst's Office. California State Legislature, Sacramento, California.

Inciardi, JA, Martin, SS Butzin, C.A., Hooper, RM, and Harrison, LD ,(1997). "An Effective Model of Prison-based Treatment for Drug-involved Offenders," Journal of Drug Issues (Spring).

Knight, K., Simpson, D.D., and Hiller, M.L. (1996) "Evaluation of Prison-based Treatment and Aftercare: Process and Outcomes," Presented at the Annual Meeting of the American Psychological Association, Toronto Canada, August.

Lipton, D.S., (1995) "The effectiveness of Treatment for Drug Abusers Under Criminal Justice Supervision." U.S. Department of Justice Publication NCJ 157642, Washington, DC

Mullen, R. (1996) "Therapeutic Communities in Prisons: Dealing With Toxic Waste" Prison Based Treatment Programs in America," ed. Early, Kevin. Praeger.

Mullen, R. and Arbiter, N. (1992). "Against The Odds: Therapeutic Community Approaches to Underclass Drug Abuse," in Peter H. Smith (ed.) Drug Policy in the Americas, Westview Press, Publishers, Boulder, Colorado. ("Contra Todos los Pronsticos: Los Enfoques de Communidad Terapeutica al Abuso de Drogas" En Peter H. Smith (ed.) El Combate a las Drogas en America. Trans. Juan Jose Utrilla. Mexico, D.F.: Fondo De Cultura Econmica, S.A. de C.V., 1993).

Mullen, R., Ratelle, J., Abraham, E., and Boyle, J. (August, 1996) "California Program Reduces Recidivism and Saves Tax Dollars," Corrections Today. Vol. 58, No. 5. (pps.118-123).

Nichol, Chuck. (1997) "Addressing the State's Long-Term Inmate Population Growth," Legislative Analyst's Office, Policy Brief. State of California Publications.

Pan, H., Scarpitti, Inciardi, and Lockwood, D. (1993) "Some Considerations on Therapeutic Communities in Corrections." Inciardi, J. (Ed.), Drug Treatment and Criminal Justice, Sage

Publications.

Wexler, H.K. (1996) "Evaluation of Amity Therapeutic Community at Donovan Prison," Center for Therapeutic Community Publications, National Development and Research Institutes. (Volume 1, Number 1). New York, NY.

Wexler, H.K, DeLeon, G., Thomas, G., Kressel, D., and Peters, J. (1997) "The Amity Prison TC Evaluation: Reincarceration Outcomes" Criminal Justice and Behavior: An International Journal.

Wexler, H. K. (1995) "The Success of Therapeutic Communities for Substance Abusers in American Prisons," Journal of Psychoactive Drugs, 27(1) 57-66.

Wexler, H.K. (1995) Report to the California Youth and Adult Authority on the Amity/R.J. Donovan Program. Unpublished Report. National Development and Research Institutes, New York, NY.

Wexler, H.K. and Williams, R. (1986) "The Stay 'n Out Therapeutic Community: Prison Treatment for Substance Abusers," Journal of Psychoactive Drugs, 18 (3), 221-230.

Weikel, D. "In Prison, a Drug Rehab that Pays Off," Los Angeles Times, 1&18) April, 25, 1997.

Winett, D.; Lowe, L.; Mullen, R.; Missakian, E. (1992). "Amity Right Turn: A Demonstration Drug Abuse Treatment Program for Inmates and Parolees," In Carl G. Leukefeld, D.S.W. (ed.) and Frank M. Tims, Ph.D. (ed.) "Drug Abuse Treatment in Prisons and Jails," National Institute on Drug Abuse Research Monograph Series 118; Alcohol, Drug Abuse, and Mental Health Administration. DHHS Publication No. (ADM) 92-1884, 84-98, 1992.

CHARMAINE WHITE FACE
"A Native American Response to Crime"

Despite three centuries of systematic effort to destroy or absorb the American Indian, he shows no sign of disappearing. His culture has been deeply and purposely eroded, yet it persists. We have failed utterly as social engineers—failure from which we as a nation would be well advised to learn, lest we repeat our mistakes on a far grander scale with Negroes and Mexican-Americans, Puerto Ricans and poor whites.

Edgar S. Cahn, Editor, <u>Our Brother's Keeper: The Indian in White America</u>

I

Imagine if you lived in a world where there was no poverty. What if there were no orphans, and the elderly were cherished and looked after as if they were as precious as a new born baby? What if all the men worked and if one went hungry, the others would all give food so everyone always had something to eat? What if the needs of every single person in the community were always considered? What if the children were thought of as a responsibility of every adult to nurture, feed, and cherish? What if human beings could understand the language of the animals, the birds, and even the trees and the grass? What if each young man, as part of his growing up, had to go to talk to God about what he should do with his life...and received an answer? What if there was no such thing as suicide, drug and alcohol abuse, hunger, economic oppression, inadequate education, inadequate housing, and violence against children, women, and the elderly? Imagine if there was no need for prisons.

The kind of world answered in the affirmative to all of the preceding questions is the kind of complex psychological, sociological world of most Native American nations prior to European contact. However, because there was not the 'technology' that gauged people as 'civilized' then, these other aspects of 'civilization' were totally disregarded. A Native American perspective on today's problems of crime and punishment requires imagining a society which contained all of the complex structures which the foregoing questions engender, because crime and punishment are not separate from the whole community but are only a symptom of something more deeply wrong...deep within the whole society.

The history and present day attitude toward crime and punishment in the United States are the separation of crime and punishment as an aberration, not a part of society. All of the components that go into making a crime are not dealt with, and criminals are sent off to prisons, like hiding the dust under a rug. No one talks about it. Everyone pretends it's not there.

The whole process that leads to crime is a thousand times more complex than that. It is too easy and fast to convict a murderer or a thief and automatically sentence him to X amount of time in jail, a certain amount of money for the fine plus court costs, rather than look at ways that might have prevented the crime from happening in the first place.

To consider an analysis of crime and punishment as it relates to Native American people is probably the best way to view the future of crime and punishment in the United States, as Native American people seem to be the "miner's canary" for the rest of the country. The actual numbers of Native Americans living on reservations are so small, when compared with the populations of the rest of the country, that the effects of federal legislation, combined with the destruction of an ancient values system, shows a clear picture of what is happening, or will be happening in the rest of these United States. The rest of America is not exhibiting the results to the extent that they are exhibited on the reservations, particularly the Pine Ridge Reservation in southwestern South Dakota, because the populations, for example of Philadelphia, New York, or Washington, DC, are so large that the total symptoms have not been completely exhibited...yet.

How did the Native American nations lose most of the complex societies they once had? The answers to that one question would require volumes to describe the effect of the imposition of the Euro-American culture upon Native American groups. It is also the effect that has befallen other indigenous populations with contact with Euro-American culture, i.e. Native Hawaiians, Native Alaskans, and other Pacific Islanders.

The consequences on American Indian Reservations are: the highest crime rate per population density of any group in the United States, the highest poverty rates, the highest suicide rates, the highest incidence of alcohol and drug abuse, the highest infant mortality rates, and the highest unemployment rates.

How does this prove that American Indians are the 'miner's canary' for the rest of the United States? Because the values that the United States operates under, (capitalism, consumerism, and materialism), do not put into place any other values, such as the value of inner growth or the value of human lives.

Every human being realizes the transience of exterior things, but we are only taught to replace the thing, whatever it is. How long will a shirt last if that one shirt was the only thing you ever wore? One year? Two years? Five years? How long will your eyes last? Your legs? Your hearing? All of these senses are tuned to the outer world. What about the inner you, the spirit, the loving part, the soul? Where is humanism taught? Where is the spirit nourished so it can grow? Why are people flocking by the thousands to embrace "instant religions," looking for an "instant fix" to fill the void of something that is missing? How strong is your spirit, your soul? It is the permanency of the inner part when all else has been worn out that will be with us during hours of crisis, and into our failing and worn out old age.

The ancient Lakota (Sioux) values of being the best you could be for the good of the whole, considering all people to be as important as yourself, leading by example not words, understanding the effect each individual human being has on other human beings and the entire world and each individual's role in that relationship, all the positive examples and answers to the questions asked at the beginning of this essay have almost totally disappeared. Why? They are not valued anymore. It is more important to be able to be the best producer of things, or to shoot the best basketball, to consider 'me' more important than anybody or anything else, to speak pretty words and hide dishonest deeds, to care little about one's effect on anyone or anything else. But the change in attitude has not brought happiness, or filled the empty place where the growing spirit belongs.

II

In order to understand all the issues involved with a Native American prisoner, the following is a brief narrative of one ex-offender's story.

Jack is presently in his early thirties and grew up in the country near a small village on one of the large reservations. His parents were alcoholic and had been weaned away from the traditional Lakota culture in the Christian and Bureau of Indian Affairs boarding schools. There were no jobs on the reservation and whatever money did come in usually bought alcohol. Drinking alcohol was an almost daily occurrence in Jack's home. He was five or six years of age when he first started drinking.

Jack didn't know a schedule, nor did he eat meals at a certain time. Every morning when he awoke, there were usually people scattered around the house in various stages of consciousness. He saw many things that children in 'normal' environments would never know about in their entire lifetimes. He thought his life was 'normal' because he knew no other kind of life, and all of his friends and relatives lived similarly.

On his reservation, there has been a 90% unemployment rate for the past 30 years. He grew up in poverty, knowing only federal programs such as welfare, food stamps or food commodities, cast-off clothing, housing assistance, and other programs that create a total dependency on federal government assistance. He also experienced physical, mental, and emotional abuse from the adults around him. There was one man in particular who consistently beat him and his cousin in their preadolescent and adolescent years, but they had no one to go to for protection or help. All the adults in his life were drinking buddies with this man.

One day when Jack was seventeen, the man and some friends, who were in the midst of a drunken brawl, beat Jack and his cousin unmercifully. They were grown men and the two boys were no match. His cousin was sent to the hospital with broken ribs and a concussion, on the verge of death. Jack went home and found a gun. He was also drinking. Jack knew where the man lived. He went to the house, knocked on the door, and when the man answered, Jack shot him. He didn't kill the man but he seriously maimed him.

As the shooting was a felony that occurred on the reservation between two Native American people, Jack was charged as an adult in federal court under the

Major Crimes Act. He had a court appointed attorney and was sent to a federal prison in Michigan. He eventually lived in many federal prisons around the country. Jack had never lived anywhere else except the reservation. The prisons were so far away from the Pine Ridge Reservation, and his family was so poor, that for six years he never saw any of his relatives.

Prison was the first time that Jack was around sober people. It was an 'abnormal' environment for Jack. The way of life of mandated respect, everyone having certain responsibilities, consequences for actions, consistent meals and sleeping times, unfortunately for many people like Jack, who grow up in alcohol and drug abusing environments, is totally abnormal.

Alcohol and drug abusing environments are not specific to Native American people. These types of environments, although more the symptoms of poverty, are not foreign to the cities and rural areas of America, and, increasingly, to more members of higher economic strata. These types of alcohol and drug abusing environments may also account for crimes committed by members not necessarily raised in poverty situations.

However, there is another criteria that is never addressed and is specific to indigenous populations, including Native American people, and that is the genetic predilection to alcoholism regardless of economic and psychological conditions. The research has been done and can be found in any medical school library. It doesn't excuse the actions, but it certainly poses questions about medical solutions which could possibly aid in the reduction of crime by Native American people. The US Probation Office in Rapid City, SD, estimates that 90 to 100% of all crimes committed by Native Americans are alcohol related.

III

The federal probation office in Rapid City, SD, processes approximately 200 cases per year. Sixty-three percent of the cases are Native American people from the surrounding reservations. The federal probation office, along with the halfway houses, local treatment centers, local counseling centers, and a community education facility have developed a collaborative program to successfully reintegrate ex-offenders back into society.

Tim O'Daniel has worked in corrections for twenty years. He is the Director of Fresh Start, a program funded by the Jobs Training Partnership Act under the Department of Labor through a private community education facility, the Career Leaning Center. He is also a member of the Oglala Lakota (Sioux) Tribe.

"When a client is on federal probation or prerelease from a federal prison, they're assigned a case manager, a probation officer here [Rapid City], and that probation officer will contact me and arrange to get on the system. We've revamped the program with the help of the federal probation office, and we have identified Jeff Chambers as the Employment Supervisor for federal offenders. Jeff and I work as a team along with Kevin Steinauer, who is the assistant director for Community

Alternatives of the Black Hills, and Jim Menard from Detox. Community Alternatives of the Black Hills is a residential facility that federal offenders are placed in. We work as a team...to help develop the jobs and the training that these individuals need," said O'Daniel. "It's worked out great. The federal probation office has done an outstanding job in trying to help the offenders in getting training and employment."

Jeff Chambers, US Probation Officer, receives the referral from the Bureau of Prisons. He brings the exoffender to Tim O'Daniel and a JTPA Intake form is completed which consists of their work experience and their educational level.

"Probably 65% of my clients will need a GED or a high school diploma," said O'Daniel. "So at the Intake we try to find out what their skills are, what their interests are. Then we set them up with a series of assessments. These include a test of Adult Basic Education, General Aptitude Test Battery, and a career assessment. That allows me to sit down with them and see where their educational strengths and weaknesses are, what their aptitudes are, and then the career assessment gives me an idea of what kind of jobs they're interested in. We do a lot of one-on-one counseling. We place them through a four-day pre-employment training class which is very important. It gives them an idea of what employers look for. They work on applications. They work on enhancing their self-esteem. Probably the best thing about this is we're integrating them with all of our other clientele that come through the Career Learning Center so that they are in with a wide cultural mix of people, wide as far as different types of people and backgrounds. They have a chance to interact. This gives us and them an opportunity to see how well they do interact in the community."

The Fresh Start Program only employs Tim O'Daniel, but he coordinates a collaborative effort by all of the agencies involved to provide training, education, treatment for alcohol or drug abuse, treatment for other behavior disorders, and employment, while helping the ex-offender increase self-esteem.

"The bottom line is, if you get somebody employment, and you get them the counseling that they need to overcome whatever barriers or problems that they face, they are going to be productive members of our community," said O'Daniel. "[The] idea of ending a prisoner's sentence was to give them $50 and a bus ticket...the recidivism rate isn't going to go down by doing that."

Jeff Chambers agrees. "We get a lot of clients off the Pine Ridge Reservation. There's just not a lot of employment opportunities down there for these individuals. So we have a lot of guys that come out of the penitentiaries, or are on probation, that don't have any work experience," Chambers said. "It's always been kind of a guessing game of what we do with guys coming out with no experience and no education, or low experience and low education. What this [the Fresh Start Program] has done is given us an idea, or a snapshot, to see where they're at. Also, what I like about the program, it's designed to what they [the ex-offenders] want to do. The old school always was you had probation officers and courts saying 'You will get a job.' We really didn't assist them a lot in getting employment."

Chambers and O'Daniel also do job development. O'Daniel said, "My line to employers is, "You have to be part of the solution. You can't be part of the problem. You can't complain about the high crime rate or the costs of prisons when you're not willing to hire people that have done their time or that need the chance to go to work and want to go to work."

This past year, the Fresh Start Program has worked with 130 clients and found jobs for 80 within the community. Many other ex-offenders were assisted in areas such as resume writing or were given job leads which they pursued on their own. The South Dakota Job Services provides instantaneous job information to O'Daniel. They also work with other employment agencies.

"A lot of the ex-offenders say, 'We're felons. We're American Indians. We're not going to get hired.' Most of the employers are willing to give these guys a chance," said Chambers. "The Rapid City area has been awful good to these folks. They have been willing to put guys to work."

But the cultural differences generated by poverty start emerging. "If you were born and raised on the reservation, then you know what it's like having nothing. But when you get that first or second or third pay check, you do what you always did before. You spend it foolishly. So they have to reestablish their way of behavior," said Jim Menard, a Counselor at the Detox Center with Pennington County Alcohol and Drug Programs.

Menard has worked at the Detox Center for twenty-two years, since the Center first began, and has seen hundreds of ex-offenders pass through his door. Growing up on the Rosebud Reservation, and a member of the Rosebud Sioux Tribe, he has firsthand knowledge of the frustrations and failures the parolees will be going through when they leave his program. Menard works helping inmates make the transition. His clients are either directly out of prison or off the streets. He also understands the difficulty in explaining the differences in lifestyles to people who have no knowledge of the reservation or poverty.

"It's hard for a lot of people to understand that when you come from nothing, and you have nothing, then why is all of this stuff so important? That's the frustrating part of it..." Menard said. "When they move here, I try to get them to take a view of themselves, to furthering their education, to going to a trade school or even finding a job. A lot of them, if they find a steady job, or have a steady paycheck coming in, they don't see the value of even staying in town instead of going back to the reservation. Once they get back to the reservation, they fall back into their old lifestyle. It hasn't changed since the time I graduated high school...back in '56."

The desire of ex-offenders to return home to the reservations is the biggest hurdle to the total success of the Fresh Start program.

"They're brought up here to go through this program off the reservations, and they may stay up here three to four months to complete these...we place them in jobs, and at the end of that period, they return to the reservations where there is no work, where the opportunities are not available. My biggest problem for this program is to have job retention for these clients because they decide to return to the reservations. Again, that's understandable. That's where they're from. That's where their family lives. Their loved ones are down there. But that is a major problem for this program and for our clients," said O'Daniel.

The problems of the reservations, primarily the depressed economic conditions and the lack of jobs lead inevitably back to alcohol and drug abuse, which in turn leads back to prison.

Menard tries to explain the motivation. "It's kind of hard for someone to see, if they've never had a drinking problem, or never had a drug problem. It's hard for them to see that maybe the individual may have the desire to have a better lifestyle and everything, but they don't know how to. That's primarily why, I think, the guys coming out of prison, they can go through all the programs in prison, but they have to look at the fact that the lifestyle that they came out of was only interrupted by their incarceration. So from the time that they're incarcerated to the time that they're released, nothing about them has changed. Their drinking was only interrupted because they couldn't drink," said Menard, "It was forced [sobriety]. Once they get out, they say, 'I don't have a drinking problem anymore because I've been sober for two years,' or six years, or ten years, or however long their sentence was."

"Everybody drinks for only one reason...it makes them feel good. That's why they keep drinking. That's the whole reason they drink. Everybody can say that they drink to hide their feelings, but they always take that drink because they know it makes them feel good," Menard said.

"The only time they're going to see a need to change that is whenever they can start asking themselves a question... 'If I take this drink, who's going to benefit from it?' If they say, 'I'm going to benefit from it,' then they're going to take that drink. If they say, 'I'm not going to benefit from it,' then they won't take it. Until then, they have to see a need for them not to drink. Until then, they're going to live their lifestyle drinking."

However, Menard has seen successes and says, "Before any program can work, it has to come from the individual that wants it to work. Any individual that wants to make the change, they can make it. But first, they have to reeducate themselves about finding out specifically who they are and what they really want. I think that probably any prison program could work if [the individual] knew how to make it work but they don't. Learning how to stay sober isn't something they teach on the reservation. They don't teach that any place. The individual themselves have to make a commitment to themselves to stay sober. In the end, they also have to make a commitment to ask for help. Because if they expect other people to read their minds, they're going to have an awful long wait. The help to stay sober, the help to further their education, the help to get school grants, whatever, it's all there. But the person has to teach themselves that it's okay to ask for help."

When ex-offenders leave the Detox Center, there is no tracking. They may spend four to six months on supervised release, or probation for a number of years. But when they start violating their conditions of probation and start drinking or using drugs, they will be returned to the Detox Center. Once there, if they violate the rules of the Center, then they will find themselves back in front of the judge. In many instances, Menard may act as a liaison between probation and prison.

The recidivism rate of all ex-offenders that come through the Rapid City office is approximately twenty-five percent, or about 50 individuals, according to Jeff Chambers. Of those numbers, more than half, or sixty-three percent, will be Native American. Yet the Native American population of the state is only ten percent.

IV

As the gap between the rich and the poor gets wider, to continue the current systems, (and I say systems because we are not just talking about prisons, we are talking about the economic system, the education system, the social services systems, the legislative system), will most definitely lead to the demise of these systems when the 'systems' can no longer provide for the needs of the millions and millions of people not in prisons who are falling below the poverty level. I'm not talking just about Indian reservations. I'm also talking about ghettos, slums, housing projects, poor farmers and ranchers, migrant workers, and many others who are increasing the numbers of the poor and impoverished in this country.

"The community as a whole has to look at it. If we want the crime rates to decrease, if we want recidivism to decrease, if we want prison building to drop and not have those multimillion dollar facilities...then we have to provide programs for offenders," said O'Daniel. "I think the judicial system, the correction system, and the communities have to work together. When you have 5.1 million people in the criminal justice system and it is growing daily, you've got to do something."

"With my population [of offenders], the majority being Native Americans, I have to ask and I have to wonder why we're not doing more on the reservations. There has to be community action. There has to be community belief that we want to keep our tribal members out of prison, out of incarceration, out of probation," O'Daniel said.

"[In] our economically disadvantaged areas, Shannon County being the poorest in the nation, and Pine Ridge being in Shannon County, job development and attracting new employers to that area is a must for the tribal members, if where they prefer to stay is on the reservation. Because the bottom line is that the recidivism rate on the reservation is astronomical. With no jobs down there and nothing to keep the people busy, there is a tendency either to recommit crimes or not to follow your probation guidelines. I see a revolving door from reservations to prison systems."

Are the reservations the miner's canary for the rest of the nation? Are the conditions of living in an inner city ghetto much different than living on a reservation? Has the circle come back, as Native Americans say, on the non-Indian world?

Are there any solutions, or is the problem so big and apathy so rampant that there will be no changes?

Our prisons are already overflowing. Yes, some programs can work...for a while. The problems of abject poverty and total dependence on the federal government are being felt more and more in larger and larger populations. The rich will not be, and are not now, exempt. Consider the amount of taxes that each working person pays. How much goes to pay the expenses of prisons? The problems of crime and punishment belong to everyone. The country as a whole needs to look at what it really values. When all human beings in this country are valued more than money, power, and things then maybe the way of living with each other and the world around us, a way of life that was destroyed, can begin anew.

Charmaine White Face is a member of the Oglala Lakota Nation and has a Bachelor of Science Degree in Education. She has written a book entitled Testimony for the Innocent which documents the current situation for the Oglala Lakota people on the Pine Ridge Reservation. She is a writer, a mom, and a grandma and resides in Rapid City, SD, with her husband, Varick Cutler.

JAY SHORT
"Legalizing Drugs"

I do not support the use of drugs. Yet I believe most attempts to stop drug use have been futile and expensive. Therefore, I have come to believe that drugs should be legalized.

I am not alone in this seemingly un-American proclamation. Conservatives like columnist William F. Buckley and economist Milton Friedman, as well as liberals like Dr. Benjamin Spock, support the legalization of drugs. Yet the most surprising support comes from law enforcement in our large cities.

Excessive alcohol and drug use is detrimental to youth and adults alike. The use of both can cause death. Both can harm and sometimes destroy relationships with the user's families and friends. And both can hurt individuals not associated with them—the innocent bystander. For example, an innocent person can be injured or killed by a drunk driver or a store clerk fatally wounded during a robbery by a person addicted to drugs. Therefore, based on this, shouldn't alcohol and drugs be illegal? For that matter, why not make anything potentially harmful illegal? Many people die every year by drowning—should we criminalize swimming?

How well did prohibition work? I think those who wanted to drink alcohol during that time did. Those people found a way to get the illegal alcohol and drank it. Were some people hurt? Yes. Many people died during the production and sale of the product rather than the consumption of it. Did the fact that it was illegal stop people from producing, selling or drinking alcohol? No. In some instances, the fact that it was illegal made people want to do it; it was the glamour of living on the edge. Many productive people spent a lot of time planning, wheeling and dealing to buy and sell alcohol. Just think of the benefit to society they would have been if this time and energy had been directed to more constructive pursuits.

How well does making drugs illegal work? It doesn't. Under our current laws, do drug addicts still use? Yes. In order to support their habits, do drug addicts hurt or kill other people? Yes. Therefore, the fact that it is illegal to use drugs, like prohibition, does not stop the production, sale or use of drugs and making it illegal does not stop tragedies from happening.

Many people think if drugs were legal, more people would use them. How many of you would start using drugs if they were legal?

I am not convinced the United States is a better place because drugs are illegal. The United States may even be a worse place. Think about the energy it takes to keep illegal drugs going. The addicts want and need it to the point that they lie, cheat, steal, abandon their children and sometimes kill for it. The dealers and pushers titillated by the money, sell and push to anyone, even a six-year-old. Some pushers also use their profits to support their own habits which increases the need to sell. However most large drug dealers run their businesses like any other corporation and do not indulge. They just want to make money. Police, lawyers, judges, jailers, and probation and parole officers get up each morning and fight this problem all day. Yet dealers, pushers and drug use endure.

How many new government programs and Drug Czars are needed? How many programs work? We spend billions on the fight against drugs and the problem continues and worsens because there is too much money to be made by the dealers. Young and old alike are enticed into dealing drugs by their huge untaxed profits. Education and hard work are not prerequisites for rising to the top in this business. Some can also offset meager welfare income by selling drugs. We cannot deny that it beats working at McDonalds for a minimum wage. In the end, the tax payers pay for more than the welfare checks. We also end up paying for the drugs because of the high cost of crime.

If drugs were legal, the incentive to deal is gone. Those involved in the business would have to find real work. Will all of them become good citizens? No. Will some continue to menace our communities? Yes.

Let me fantasize for a bit. Let's say that I could snap my fingers and all the drug lords and pushers were in prison or even dead. Is our problem solved? I don't think so. There is too much money to be made in selling illegal drugs for the problem to go away. There are new drug lords waiting in the wings to take over the business and drugs have been pushed from jails and prisons, even by some of the employees, because of money. Our jails and prisons are bursting at the seams because of drug users and small time pushers, not the kingpins and drug lords who are rarely caught. Most who are incarcerated, whether user or small time pusher, will not be there forever, and unless they receive intensive treatment and are employed after they are released, they will return to the job they know best—selling drugs—and they will seek out what gives the most comfort in their lives—using drugs. To these people, the huge profits made far outweigh the risks.

A professor studying gangs in Detroit took a few boys to the funeral of a gang leader killed over a drug territory dispute. The dead gang leader was twenty-one years old. In an attempt to persuade these boys away from using drugs and dealing, the professor pointed out to them how young the gang leader was and the reason he was killed. Unmoved by the professor's remarks, one young boy said, "Yeah, but look at all the money and stuff he had until he was blown away."

The point the professor made is more poignant than it appears on the surface. The dead gang leader did not die from ingesting drugs. He died, as do many, as a result of a drug war.

The authors of the book, The Mythology Of Crime And Criminal Justice, point out that "About 3600 people die each year from the consumption of all illegal drugs put together." Compare this figure to those who die from alcohol related deaths (about 200,000 a year) and tobacco related deaths (about 320,000 a year). Both alcohol and tobacco are legal drugs.

Most of the drug related deaths are due to adulterated drugs, not from abuse or misuse. Our current laws force drug users to buy unregulated products like heroin which are mixed with other dangerous substances, making them more potent than the user expects or needs. Our laws also prevent heroin users from engaging in good hygiene practices, giving rise to the potential of contracting infections from hepatitis B and AIDS. In the case of cocaine, drug laws force users to seek the cheapest more intense form that is smoked rather than snorted. Snorting is relatively safe, while 92 percent of cocaine deaths are caused from smoking. The authors of <u>The Mythology Of Crime And Criminal Justice</u> also site research that states the most widely used illegal drug in the United States, marijuana, has never been proven to be addictive, nor does tolerance develop to it. Marijuana is also the drug for which the most people are incarcerated.

So if our laws are actually encouraging the profitable production, sale and use of illegal drugs, and we cannot lock up or even do away with the pushers, dealers, kingpins, and the gangs cannot kill them off, how is the problem resolved? It is a well-known fact among researchers that if properly used and monitored, illegal drugs can be used safely and the user can lead a normal productive life, similar to those of us who are social drinkers. For example, heroin is a relatively benign drug if used under supervision, and has little direct or permanent psychological damage. Again, it is the adulterated drug on the streets now and bad hygiene practices that are the problems. Cocaine, if snorted and not smoked, as mentioned earlier, can be safe and cheaper.

It appears clear to me, if we take the "big business" and profits out of drug use, these drugs would become safe to use, far fewer deaths and illnesses would occur, drug related crimes would dramatically decline, and the users could function productively in our communities. We should legalize drugs so we can regulate them, tax the sale of them and monitor their use. We should use the money saved from legalizing drugs for better drug and alcohol education programs and counseling. These practices will make our communities healthier and our streets safer.

Jay Short contributes to this volume as a concerned citizen. He is a longtime Colorado resident where he owns and operates an insurance agency.

SPECIAL NEEDS

Death Row, Louisiana

December 15, 1995

"Being imprisoned isn't the problem, I've been in prison most of my life — not bars and concrete, but mentally wise. I'm wanting to and desperately needing help to deal with my mental problems, but there is no help given — even though it was promised. I suffer with delusions, pedophilia and numerous smaller things. These are the things that was a cause of me being here. These are the things that keep me troubled, confused and wishing death, so I can be free of the misery and torments that are brought by the above.

"All my life I've sought help the best I could and it is the one thing (it seems) that nobody wants to work with. Until these things are dealt with, my life will always be screwed up and pose a danger to myself and others. That is one reason I don't want to be sent back on the streets, but yet I don't want to waste away for years in prison. Prison doesn't meet the needs nor even try to. The general view is 'Lock them up for x amount of time — that will teach them to do better.' Only if that was true.

"I'm a Christian by faith. My days is spent reading and studying the Bible, doing correspondence courses and sharing with others that has a open mind. So many others don't realize what they are saying when they say, 'All you need to do is lay your problems at Jesus cross and that be that.' I know they mean good but they don't understand about brain damage and mental disabilities. Some tries to convince me that 'there is nothing wrong with me, that it is only Satan, and if I rebuke him he will flee from me.'

"Like I've said, I believe in the Lord deeply, have experienced his healing hand and know what He can do, but I also know the difference between being afflicted by Satan and having medical problems.

"Julie, I'm like any other person. I don't want to die, but will take that step if there's no other choice. All I want is professional help for my ills. As long as they go untreated, I will never be able to live a 'normal life' or have peace."

"ORGANIZED PSYCHOSIS" ©S.K. AINSWORTH DEATH ROW S.Q. 1993 (INK) 35/55

Steven King Ainsworth, "Organized Psychosis"

FRANKLYN GIAMPA
"The Self Mutilating Prisoner"

State Departments of Corrections have a primary mission and responsibility to accept prisoners at all security levels into a humane, safe and secure environment. A prisoner's right to health care within this setting is constitutionally mandated by the Eighth Amendment which prohibits cruel and unusual punishment and deliberate indifferences to a prisoner's health care needs. Health care is all encompassing and includes medical, nursing, dental and mental health services which are supposed to meet the community standard of care. These quality standards of care are set by various organizations that include the American Correctional Association, Center for Disease Control, US Public Health Service, Joint Commission on Accreditation of Health Care Organizations and the National Commission on Correctional Health Care.

Prisoners entering the correctional system, for the most part, have had limited access to quality health care in their home communities and tend to have had more exposure to health risk behaviors such as illegal drug use, poor nutrition and diet, violence and other stress related situations. Given the demands placed on the ever expanding prisoner system, it has become increasingly more difficult to provide adequate health care to a prison population that has a high need for services.

To further threaten access to limited health care resources, one finds that there is an increasing demand to provide targeted treatment programs to special needs populations within the prison setting. This further burdens an already stressed correctional system, which does not have a health care focus as its primary mission. One of the special populations in need of extensive medical and mental health services is the prisoners who mutilate their own bodies. Once an act of mutilation occurs, receiving the emergency medical care and then stabilization is the first priority. At this point the task of understanding why one commits this act must be addressed. This must occur for three very practical reasons:

A. Health care is constitutionally mandated; whether the correctional system cares about the prisoners well being or not, it is legally obligated to provide such services. Mental health service is usually the first intervention of choice.

B. If the behavior is not contained, the health care costs will continue to skyrocket out of control. Prisoners continuing to exhibit this behavior will require health care resources at a disproportionate rate.

C. A disruption to the correctional facility operation occurs, with custody officers treating the prisoner like a "hot potato" in an effort to transfer the prisoner to some other program or security status within the correctional delivery system.

This special prisoner, the Self Mutilator, is only one of many (e.g. substance abusers, developmentally disabled, mentally ill, dually diagnosed prisoners etc.) that is competing for the prison facility's limited resources. Although most of the special populations identified usually require the expertise of the mental health professional, the mutilator is one of the most costly and disruptive. The question as to whether their care can be delivered in a prison's general population is always raised, and a mental health evaluation is often, if not always, required. The qualified mental health professional will usually evaluate the prisoner's level of risk for suicide and/or self injury and make the appropriate referral for a comprehensive psychiatric examination.

For most correctional systems it is difficult to identify the appropriate housing unit necessary when dealing with the inmate exhibiting mutilative behavior. There are also various expert opinions as to the treatment offerings for an inmate. The options considered usually include a mental health or restricted custody unit. This decision is usually contingent on defining what was the motivation for the mutilative behavior. After the act, the medical emergency is handled, then a decision must be made as to whether this was a suicide attempt, behavior symptomatic of a serious mental illness, or an act to manipulate the correctional system to benefit the prisoner for some secondary gain.

Given the fact that the correctional system has an obligation to provide adequate health care that meets the individual need of this special population, a continuum of health services is necessary. Once the prisoner has completed an evaluation and his behavior has been assessed by a qualified mental health professional as either suicidal or suffering from a serious mental illness, the treatments of choice are clear. He will be admitted to the portion of the health care continuum that offers mental health services to the correctional facility. The mental health portion of the continuum, at a minimum, includes:

1. Out Patient Services: A team of mental health professionals provides services to the suicidal or mentally ill prisoner in general population who is stabilized and can function in the prison setting if follow up and support are provided.

2. Residential Programs: Mental health services are provided on specialized, protective housing units for prisoners coming from the acute care hospital setting. After a period of time they will be placed in general population with out patient team follow-up. The housing unit is supervised by a mental health professional in conjunction with custody direct care staff. Some prisoners will never transfer from a residential program and may need continuous mental health intervention.

3. Inpatient Care: Acute or chronic (long term) care is for prisoners in need of

voluntary or involuntary hospitalization for serious mental illness that is life threatening.

Although each state system is unique and may have different program labels, most would include the above essential mental health services. Prisoners with mental illness must receive adequate treatment. This was established by a US Supreme Court decision in *Estelle vs. Gamble* and *Bauring vs. Godwin*. Correctional systems may directly provide these services or contract for them. There appears to be little consequence as to the most appropriate arrangement for delivering services to the mentally disordered prisoner (Steadman et al 1982). Steadman's survey revealed that 16 states transferred most of their mentally disturbed inmates (75%) to facilities operated by State Departments of Corrections; 28 states transferred the majority to hospitals and units run by State Departments of Mental Health; and 6 states utilized a combination of both. Whatever the setting, transferring prisoners in need of mental health services to units other than the prison general population is a reasonable decision for Prison Administration. The prisoner now becomes a health care responsibility and the prisoner/patient is not mainstreamed back into the prison general population without behavior stabilization and out patient mental health team follow-up. If the prisoner decompensates, he is again transferred to a more restrictive health care setting. Prisoners that get transferred back and forth from mental health units to prison general population are commonly diagnosed with personality disorder, bipolar disorder, major depression, anxiety disorders, or psychoses such as schizophrenia. Although the mutilator is difficult to manage, if clinicians agree that the prisoner is suffering from a severe mental illness, the responsibility for care is clearly theirs. Whatever self injurious behaviors (cutting, ocular gouging, genital trauma, biting, pica, etc.) are exhibited, whatever the diagnosis, whatever the treatment required, the prisoner is mentally ill and stays within the health care setting.

But what if the qualified mental health professional (usually a psychiatrist) determines that the self mutilation is not caused by a serious mental illness and the prisoner is not suicidal; who is then responsible? Is the prisoner considered a discipline/management concern? Should they be placed on segregation status with limiting privileges or top of bed restraints or punished for inappropriate behavior or ticketed by an officer for not following a direct order? All these questions must be addressed in the absence of a diagnosis of serious mental illness. And this is where the "hot potato" game begins. The first question the layman asks is, "Why would anyone put their life at risk by mutilating their own body, if they weren't crazy?" Custody personnel find it difficult to fathom that a clinical professional would not think that this behavior is not caused by some type of mental illness. Who would enuculate an eyeball, cut at his genital area, slash open an arm or leg, etc.? This can't be normal and the clinician is accused of "dumping" a sick prisoner back to custody. Once the explanation is made as to why the prisoner is not appropriate for the health care units, custody must reluctantly take responsibility for the inmate.

When the correction facility and the correctional staff are responsible for this type of prisoner, the health care staff should work to develop a program that addresses the prisoner's needs as a self mutilator. Special units are usually placed in a high security segregation area for the management of prisoners who have been determined not to be suicidal and not seriously mentally ill, but who have deliberately and repetitively engaged in self mutilation. The mutilation is viewed as a maladaptive coping response with the intent to be manipulative, and can be characterized as a method for solving or escaping from life problems. Their acts may risk death, however mutilators cognitively distinguish their acts from suicide attempts. The mutilation is completed as a conscience effort to coerce prison staff into meeting the mutilator's demands. Baenman calls this "emotional blackmail." Inmates in Soviet prisons have cut their veins, sewn up their mouths, sewn buttons on their bodies and disemboweled themselves to get into the better conditions of a hospital setting. Motivation to commit such acts may also be related to avoiding gambling debts, securing favors or securing single cell placements.

Three major pieces of information must be identified prior to developing treatment program interventions for this type of mutilator. First, one must determine what the prisoner wants. Second, one must develop a realistic, achievable goal for the prisoner. Success is defined as reducing the frequency and intensity of the mutilative behavior. The prisoner should be able to participate in habilitative services and improve coping skills when dealing with life situations. Third, a number of scientifically acceptable treatment strategies must be available for use by the management team that will intervene with the prisoner. These interventions may include medical, psychodynamic and behavioral approaches. The management team coordinating services should include, at a minimum, upper level custody staff, a prison psychologist, and a medical doctor/psychiatrist. Additional staff may include custody officers working on the unit, a nurse from health care services, and other program staff (e.g. from education and housing.)

This team must develop a program that will provide the prisoner with an opportunity and a means for new and more appropriate coping and problem solving behavior. A plan dealing with psychological and program goals and interventions should be a product of the management team. This plan should be part of the health care and custody record. Also, a major contribution of the psychiatric staff is the verification that the prisoner is <u>not</u> suffering from a major mental illness nor is at high risk for serious injury due to manipulation. Assessing the prisoner's need for chemotherapy is invaluable as a part of the management team plan.

These types of mutilators are extremely dangerous to themselves and can have a contagious effect on other prisoners on their living units. The greatest concentration of affected males are found in prisons where the syndrome is usually endemic. Staff that participate in the management of the manipulative self mutilator must include both health care and correctional professionals. To address the needs of this special population is both challenging and rewarding.

Franklyn Giampa, Ph.D., Senior Program Administrator, is responsible for the implementation of United Correctional Managed Care contractual obligations with the Department of Corrections in the state of Michigan. His responsibilities include insuring that all sub-contractors, including hospitals, adhere to their respective contractual obligations. Dr. Giampa has 10 years of experience as the Director, Mental Health Services Division for the Bureau of Health Care Services, Michigan Department of Corrections. Dr. Giampa has numerous professional publications and he holds a position as Adjunct Professor at the University of Michigan School of Nursing.

JANE NELSON HALL
"Correctional Services for Inmates with Mental Retardation: The Right Thing to Do"

During the decade of the 1980s, interest was focused on persons with mental retardation within correctional facilities. In 1980 DeSilva found so few services for this population that he called it a problem without a program. In 1989 Brown observed that persons with mental retardation were over-represented in correctional facilities and under-represented in program services. Over the decade, however, the National Institute of Corrections (NIC) received so many requests for technical assistance in this area that it conducted national seminars to train staff in program development and designated certain grant funds for improving programs for offenders with retardation. Coffee, Procopiow, and Miller (1989) were able to locate sufficient resources to generate a guide for correctional administrators. The close of the decade, then, saw significant progress in this area.

Unfortunately these fledgling programs have been drastically affected by changes in social policy in the 1990s. National emphasis on cost cutting and punishment have resulted in extensive alterations to program services. Basic education has come to be regarded as a "luxury" rather than the crime-fighting tool research has shown it to be (Death Sentence 1996).

Established prison mental health programs have been depreciated to the extent that a federal magistrate has demanded a plan to remedy "unconstitutional treatment of mentally ill inmates." Federal judges have seen the emasculation of meaningful programs created in response to their rulings in precedent setting cases such as *Guthrie v. Evans.*

In a national survey, Englander (1996) found that only 14 states reported a system-wide program for inmates with mental retardation. Although these agencies reported having custody of over 350,000 inmates, they acknowledged providing services to fewer than 2,500 inmates with retardation.

Given the current state of affairs, it seems important to describe a viable program for inmates with mental retardation that has stood the test of time and escaped major budgetary dissection. The program will be described in terms of history and evolvement, component aspects and staffing needs, and qualitative evaluation.

History and Evolvement

The Program for Inmates with Mental Retardation at Georgia State Prison (GSP) was developed as part of the Georgia Department of Corrections (GDC) response to a class action suit, *Guthrie v. Evans.* While the issues of litigation in this suit were desegregation and overcrowding, the orders resulting from it extended into most aspects of prison operation. Judge Anthony Alaimo was specifically concerned about the "obvious ramifications of mental retardation in a maximum security prison setting" (*Guthrie v. Evans* Order of February 13, 1981), and required the state to provide meaningful intervention.

Dr. Albert Duncan, Director of Mental Health Services for GDC, established the theoretical base for services in the Georgia State Prison Mental Health/ Mental Retardation (MH/MR) Plan (1981). He said, *Whereas the use of psychotropic medications and other psycho-therapeutic techniques are the major methods for treating mental illness, the major emphasis with the mentally retarded is addressing his developmental needs through special education and other habilitation programs which emphasize the development of skills in vocational, personal and social spheres of functioning (p. 27).*

Simply stated, mental retardation is not seen as a disorder but rather a delay in human development. The MR program evolved from no services in 1976 (persons with presumed retardation were locked down in administrative segregation) to a comprehensive service system. Today there are six specialized housing units with counseling, special education, vocational and recreational programs. Staffing includes a Mental Retardation Specialist to administer and coordinate services, two mental retardation counselors to work primarily with inmates with retardation, two special education teachers, and shared access to psychological and psychiatric consultants, psychiatric nurses and an activity therapist.

<u>Program Components</u>

<u>In-service Education</u>. If a program is to be effective it must have broad-based institutional support. The heart of any correctional intervention is security staff (Hall 1992). If they understand why the program was developed, what its goals are and what their role in achieving these goals is they are more likely to invest in its implementation. In-service education is the first and most critical link in establishing this investment. Correctional officers were involved in the development of the GSP program; they reviewed proposed activities from a security standpoint and taught MH/MR professionals the realities of the correctional culture.

In-service modules were written and classes provided to all facility staff. The goal of these modules was to effect a change in the behavior of correctional officers and other staff. Desired behavioral changes included the following:

1. Increased ability to recognize and respond to problems related to mental retardation.
2. Improved written documentation.
3. Improved communication between inmates with mental retardation and treatment staff as evidenced by more appropriate inmate requests of staff and less frustration by service providers.
4. Increased participation by inmates with mental retardation in educational,

religious and recreational activities.

Instruction was underlaid with a respect for staff and the roles they played in the operation of the facility. The ability to communicate with persons of many educational and experiential backgrounds was emphasized. Pursuant to the MH/MR Plan, all existing staff received training in working with inmates with retardation. The modules have been integrated into all subsequent training developed by GDC and are now part of all basic security and program training.

Special Education. At GSP, special education was considered the essence of intervention for persons with mental retardation. All inmates who have been identified as having retardation are offered services. Since they are adults they have a right to refuse. If they do so, services are re-offered periodically. Methods of instruction vary as a function of the inmate's security status. Those who are able to participate in classes do so; those who are in lock-down by virtue of disciplinary sanctions, protective custody, or Hi-Max security status are taught in the cells.

The curriculum has two primary components, alternative academic instruction and social/vocational adaptation. Alternative academic instruction consists of literacy components and regards all academic teaching as a means to the end of social problem solving. Social/vocational adaptation is aimed at increasing the inmate's ability to recognize and respond appropriately to social problems.

Several factors can be identified as critical to the success of the special education program. They are as follows:

1. Consistency. For the first time in many of the inmates' lives they have a program which is stable and upon which they can count.
2. Positive Role Models. As inmates are able to see a variety of persons (officers, counselors, teachers) interact without anger or rage, they can obtain a new image of the manner in which a person can behave even when he is angry and/or has been mistreated.
3. Provision of an external significant other. The existence of administrators, counselors, teachers and officers who can observe and respond to positive behavior is a potent reinforcer.

Vocational Services. This component of the MR Program is primarily On-the-Job Training (OJT). This type of vocational education was considered particularly appropriate for developmentally delayed inmates because it allows them to learn by doing.

The OJT program has varied in accordance with institutional needs and has included groundskeeping, custodial maintenance, furniture assembly and horticulture. The programs have been supervised by specially trained correctional officers. A critical consideration in program operation was the fact that most of the inmates involved in the OJT program had never worked; the goal was, therefore, habilitation.

Recreation. Positive use of leisure time is essential to a fulfilling life. Many of the inmates with whom we dealt have never been taught to play in a cooperative manner. Goals of the recreation aspect of the MR program were as follows:

1. To increase socialization skills.
2. To decrease maladaptive use of leisure time.
3. To increase the individual's ability to make personal decisions and to adapt to structured and non-structured individual and group activities.

An activity therapist worked in concert with special education, work and counseling to coordinate the inmates' involvement in pro-social activities.

Counseling. The counseling aspect of the MR program unifies and reinforces all other treatment components. The counselor also serves as the inmate's consistent advocate. In this capacity the counselor functions as a liaison between the inmate and significant others both within and outside the facility. This would include medical staff, legal aid personnel, parole board members and family, friends and support groups.

Pre- and Post-Release Services. Pre-release planning and post-release follow-up are particularly important for inmates being released. Skills required for adjustment in a correctional setting may be diametrically opposite from those needed in the free world. Mental retardation staff work with various agencies such as the Department of Human Resources, Vocational Rehabilitation, and nonprofit support groups serving ex-offenders.

Over its 15 years of operation, the GSP MR program has served approximately 500 inmates. A definite weakness of the program was a failure to keep careful actuarial records. From its inception staff realized the importance of empirical quantitative evaluation. Demands of daily service delivery in combination with insufficient staff resulted in inconsistent recording of numbers. A quantitative component would be less demanding today with operational computer technology.

With respect to a qualitative assessment of the program, several conclusions can be drawn regarding its effectiveness. Perhaps the most significant is that the components of the program have become integral parts of institutional operations. Correctional staff routinely consider the impact of mental retardation in housing and work assignments, disciplinary action and program participation. Actions that were once performed to ensure procedural compliance with a court order have become substantive aspects of policy and daily operations.

Correctional officers who work in the supportive housing units have not only completed specialized training, they have also come to identify themselves with the MH/MR program. They are proud to work with special-needs inmates; as a consequence they are excellent role models.

Since GSP is a maximum security facility, most inmates have long sentences. Data on inmate transition to free-world society are so minimal as to be meaningless.

Transition emphasis, therefore, has been placed on movement from extremely expensive staff-intensive units to less structured environments. Although numbers are not exact, a conservative estimate is that 60 percent of all inmates with retardation assigned to a supportive living unit were able to achieve sufficient socialization skills to move into general population at GSP and/or be transferred to other less secure and less expensive GDC facilities. GDC realized significant tangible financial savings as a result of these changes in inmate behavior. In addition, there were countless intangible benefits in terms of institutional stress and resultant costs of illness and injury, property destruction and litigation.

From an ethical perspective, the paramount importance of the program is the difference it has made in the lives of individuals. The norms of the correctional culture can be starkly intimidating for any inmate; for those persons with mental retardation, these realities can be horribly overwhelming. The dangers of prisons are very real. Through the MR Program, inmates learned how to interact with authority figures and peers and as a result were better able to cope with the demands of incarceration. They received fewer disciplinary reports with less serious charges, i. e. insubordination rather than assault. Such changes resulted in dramatic improvement in their quality of life. These improvements translated into a calmer and more rational facility operation. In such an environment, real habilitation that can result in successful re-entry to society is possible.

Conclusion

The MR program has not totally escaped the budgetary scalpel. Within the last year GDC has instituted several policy changes that portend disaster. Special education, the heart of the intervention, was significantly affected by GDC's decision to replace all professional correctional educators with contract teachers. Experienced staff left the agency. Both continuity and consistency were damaged. Teachers have been replaced, for the most part, by retired public schoolteachers interested in part-time work. The difficulties and dangers of correctional work have affected recruitment. Some students still have no services.

The recreation component has also been affected. At one time there was an activity therapist who coordinated recreational activities in concert with MH/MR special education and vocational staff. As part of a "get tough policy," weights, game tables, musical instruments, and reinforcements such as movies were eliminated from all facilities. In addition, the number of recreational staff was dramatically reduced. As a consequence, this portion of the MR Program no longer exists. This seems particularly disturbing given the current emphasis on more stringent sentencing.

No rational person advocates a correctional system that is so pleasant and easy as to diminish the gravity of circumstances that lead one there; at the same time no responsible person supports policy so regressive as to raise issues of unconstitutional treatment.

I wish to extend special thanks to Johnny Skies, Warden Georgia State Prison, Glenn Rich, Director Wrightsville Youth Development Campus and to the Honorable Anthony A. Alaimo, Jr. Their goodness has enriched and empowered many people.

Jane Nelson Hall has a B.A. from Auburn University, an M.A. from the University of Alabama and an Ed.D. from Peabody College, Vanderbilt University. She went to Georgia State Prison in 1982 as Mental Retardation Specialist, and established the program for inmates with mental retardation there. In 1994, she became a special education teacher at GSP and worked at this job until all teachers in the Georgia Department of Corrections were terminated in January 1997. Since that time she has been teaching special education at the Wrightsville Youth Development Campus in the Department of Juvenile Justice.

References

Americans with Disabilities Act of 1990, 42 U.S.C.A. §12101-12213.

Bailey, S. (1996 March 6). "Magistrate urges plan to aid inmates." Birmingham New-Post Herald, March 6, 1966, pp. 1-8A.

Brown, R. (1989). Introduction. Programming for Mentally Retarded and Learning Disabled inmates: A Guide for Correctional Administrators (p.IX), U.S. Department of Justice, National Institute of Corrections,Washington, DC, 1989.

Coffee, O.D., Procopiow, N. & Miller, N. (1989). Programming for Mentally Retarded and Learning Disabled Inmates: A Guide for Correctional Administrators, U. S. Department of Justice National Institute of Corrections, Washington, DC, 1989.

"Death of Rehabilitation," The Atlanta Journal-Constitution, December 19, 1996, p. A10.

DeSilva, B. (1980). "The Mentally Retarded Offender: A Problem Without a Program," Corrections Magazine, 6 pp. 24-33.

Duncan, A.S. (1981). Mental Health/Mental Retardation Plan for Georgia State Prison, Atlanta: Georgia Department of Corrections, 1987, p. 27.

Education for All Handicapped Children's Act of 1975. 20 U.S.C.A. §1400-1461.

Englander, M. (1996). Habilitation Center: Manual and Final Report. Oklahoma Department of Corrections, Joseph Harp Correctional Center.

Guthrie v. Evans, 93 F.D.R. 390 (S.D. GA, 1981).

Hall, J.N. Model Program for Mentally Retarded and Severely Learning Disabled Inmates, Paper presented at American Correctional Association Seminars on Program Development for Mentally Retarded and Severely Learning Disabled Inmates, St. Louis, MO, November, 1987.

Hall, J.N. (1992). in R.W. Conley, R. Luckasson & Bouthilet (eds.) The Criminal Justice System and Mental Retardation, Baltimore: Brooks, 1992, pp. 167-190.

Individuals With Disabilities Education Act. 42 U.S.C.A. §12101-12213.

Mercer, J. (1970). "Sociological Perspectives on Mild Mental Retardation," in H.C. Haywood (Ed.) Socio-cultural aspects of mental retardation, New York: Appleton-Century-Crofts, 1997, pp. 378-391.

National Institute of Corrections, NIC Annual Program Plan for Fiscal Year 1983. Washington DC: U. S. Department of Justice 15, July, 1982.

SANITY IN SIGHT

From out of clearly defined territories
where men gnash their teeth
as ordinary mode of communication created by
manpredators and fear,

I hear different melodies near...
laughter it is...
clear appreciation of the human situation of blunder,
awe, wonder, and caring.

Healthier music it is,
akin to a hot bath at a hectic day's end:
people seeing in people veins of creativity,
the painters,
sculpturers,
leather and wood workers,
and poets,
hands guided by minds fashioning alike thoughts
into things of beauty, and practical use.

The air is fresher now.
I read verse and poetry written by quiet men,
and to them.
All is a simple request to find
definite horizons, direction...
and I'm willing to know exhaustion
and stuggle to arrive how I might.

Sanity in sight.

Don Callies
Lansing Correctional Facility, Kansas

"Sanity in Sight" is excerpted from Caged Freedom,
Edited by Louis Osei Cotton, Audenreed Press (1997)

MICHAEL B. ROSS
"Reflections from Death Row"

My name is Michael Ross. I am a condemned man on Connecticut's death row. When most people think of death row inmates, I'm the one they think of. I'm the worst of the worst, a serial killer who is responsible for the rape and murder of eight women in three different states. I have assaulted several other women, and stalked and frightened many more. I have never denied what I did and have fully confessed to my crimes. The only issue in my case was, and still is, my mental condition. For years I have been trying to prove that I am suffering from a mental illness that drove me to rape and kill, and that this mental illness made me physically unable to control my actions. I have met with little success.

So here I sit on death row, waiting for the judicial system to complete the tedious process which will in all likelihood result in my execution. And when I am finally executed, many people will celebrate my death. Sometimes, when I close my eyes, I can envision the hundreds of people who will likely gather outside the prison gates on the night of my execution. I can see them waving placards, drinking and rejoicing, and I can hear their cheers as my death is officially announced.

Who is Michael Ross? And what could possibly motivate a clearly intelligent individual, a Cornell University graduate, to commit such horrendous crimes? As you might expect, I have been examined by a multitude of psychiatric experts in the years since my arrest in June of 1984. All of them, including the state's own expert psychiatric witness, diagnosed me as suffering from a paraphiliac mental disorder called "sexual sadism"—a mental illness that, in the experts' words, resulted in my compulsion "to perpetrate violent sexual activity in a repetitive way." These experts also agreed that my criminal conduct was the direct result of uncontrollable sexual impulses that were caused by my mental illness. The state's only hope of obtaining a conviction and death sentence was to muddy the waters and to inflame the jury's passions and emotions so that they would ignore any evidence of psychological impairment. In my particular case that was quite easy to do, and the state succeeded in obtaining convictions and multiple death sentences.

What exactly is a paraphiliac mental disorder? It is something that is very difficult to explain, and even more difficult to fully understand—especially for the layperson [which unfortunately for me includes most jury members]. I'm not even sure that I fully understand this disease, and I have been trying to understand what has been going on in my head for a very long time now. Basically, I was plagued by repetitive thoughts, urges, and fantasies of the degradation, rape and murder of women. I couldn't get these out of my mind. These unwanted thoughts and urges filled my mind when I was awake. They were in my dreams when I slept. And the urges were insatiable. Imagine trying to control such urges, day by day, hour by hour. And try to imagine the self-hatred, loathing and abhorrence that I developed towards myself when I ultimately failed.

The best way for someone who is not plagued with this problem to understand the obsessive and repetitive nature of these thoughts, urges, and fantasies is to remember a time when you had a song or some catchy tune stuck in your mind, playing over and over and over again, driving you crazy. Even if you like the melody, its constant repetition, over and over and over again, becomes more than merely annoying. When this happens, the harder you try to push that melody out of your mind, the louder and more persistent it becomes. Now replace that sweet, little melody with noxious thoughts of physically and mentally degrading a woman, of raping her, and of strangling her, and you can begin to understand what I had running wild in my head. And I think you can begin to understand me when I say that it is not something that I wanted in my head.

The urge to hurt women could come over me at anytime, and at any place, powerful, and sometimes irresistible, urges that welled up for no apparent reason and with no warning. Even after my arrest—while facing capital charges—the urges continued. I remember one day being transported back to the county jail from a court appearance just prior to my trial. I was in the back of the Sheriff's van in full restraints—handcuffs, leg-irons, and a belly-chain—when we passed a young woman walking along a wooded stretch of road. I cannot begin to describe adequately the intensity of the urges that enveloped me that day. I wanted ... no, I had to get out of that van and go after her. The situation was ludicrous. There I was, in the back of the Sheriff's van on my way back to jail, and all I could think about was how badly I wanted to get hold of her.

Even after I was sentenced to death and living on death row the urges persisted. One day I was being escorted from the mental health unit back to my cell after seeing my psychiatrist. There is a small secluded stairwell that leads from the unit back to the main corridor. I was being escorted, without restraints, by a young, petite, female correctional officer. When I got to the stairwell, I suddenly felt this overwhelming desire to hurt her. I knew I had to get out of that stairwell, and I ran up the stairs and out into the hallway. I'll never forget how she shouted at me and threatened to write me a disciplinary report—she didn't have a clue as to what was going on. She never knew how badly I wanted to hurt her that day. She never knew how close I came to attacking her, and possibly even killing her.

You would think that being sentenced to death and living in a maximum security prison would curb such thoughts and urges. But this illness defies rationality. However, I am fortunate to have eventually found some relief. Almost three years after I came to death row, I started to receive weekly injections of an anti-androgen medication called Depo-Provera. Three years later, after some trouble with elevated liver function levels, my treatment was switched to monthly Depo-Lupron injections, which I receive to this day. What these drugs did was significantly reduce my body's natural production of the male sex hormone—testosterone. For some reason, be it because of some abnormal biological hook-up in my brain, or some sort of chemical imbalance, testosterone affects my mind differently than it affects the average male. A few months after I started to receive treatment, my blood serum testosterone levels dropped below pre-pubescent levels. And as this happened, nothing less than a miracle occurred. My obsessive thoughts, urges, and fantasies began to diminish.

Having those thoughts, urges, and fantasies is a lot like living with an obnoxious roommate. You can't get away from him because he is always there. What the Depo-Lupron does for me is to move that roommate down the hall to his own apartment. The problem is still there, but is easier to deal with because it isn't always in the foreground intruding on my everyday life. The "monster within" is still present, but the medication has rendered him impotent and has banished him to the back of my mind. And while he can still mock me—he kicks me in the side of the head from time to time so that I don't forget him—he no longer controls me. I control him. I am human once again.

You cannot begin to imagine what a milestone this was in my life. A whole new world opened up to me. I had my mind back—a clear mind free of the malevolent thoughts and urges. It was an unbelievable, incredible sense of freedom. It sounds strange for a condemned man to speak of being free on death row, but that is the only word that I can think of that adequately describes the transformation that I have undergone. And there are no words to express the gratitude that I feel towards the man who made this all possible—Dr. Fred Berlin, founder of the Johns Hopkins Sexual Disorder Clinic, and present Director of the National Institute for the Study, Prevention and Treatment of Sexual Trauma, both of which are located in Baltimore, Maryland. He testified on my behalf at my capital trial, but, more importantly, <u>after</u> the trial was over and I was sentenced to death, he continued to help me and was essential in my fight to get the Department of Corrections to acknowledge and treat my paraphiliac disorder. Without his letters and phone calls, I never would have received treatment for my disorder and to this day would still be captive to the monster that resides in my mind.

That's not to say all is well now. One of the results of all this was that I was forced to look at myself. I'm not talking about the cursory, superficial manner in which many people look at themselves, but rather a quite painful, unrelenting search into the depths of my very soul.

Many inmates in prison are able to lie convincingly to themselves, to see themselves as basically good people who are the innocent victims of a corrupt judicial system or of an unfair and uncaring society in general. Sometimes it is very difficult to see ourselves as we truly are, and much easier to blame others as justification for our actions. I know that to be true because for years this is exactly what I did. During this period I was angry—so very angry—at everyone and everything except for the one person that I should have been angry with—myself. It took a very long time, years in fact, for that anger to subside and for me to begin to accept who I was and what I had become, and even longer before I was ready and willing to accept responsibility for my actions.

Now I had a whole new set of problems, for not only did the Depo-Lupron free my mind, it allowed my moral judgment to awaken, which gave me back something that I thought I had lost forever—my humanity. For the first time in years, I began to see—really see. It was like a spotlight shining down on me, burning away the fog, exposing every shadow of my being. I began to be aware of things as they really were, as opposed to seeing things through the colored glasses of my mental illness. I began to be aware of things that I didn't like about myself. And many of the things that I now understood brought me great anguish.

I realized how weak and afraid I really was; I had always thought that I was strong and confident. I now understood how I had allowed the monster in my mind to take control of me. I saw what I had become. And worst of all, for the first time, I became truly aware of the pain that I had brought so many—such great and unceasing pain.

I began to feel the terrible agony and distress that I had brought to so many––my victims, the families and friends of my victims, my own family. And I also began to feel the awesome weight of my responsibility for my actions and of my responsibility to the people that I have harmed. And finally, I felt a profound sense of guilt. An intense, overwhelming and pervasive guilt that surrounds my very soul with dark, tormented clouds filled with a mixture of self-hatred, remorse, regrets, and sorrow. All of this leaves me with a deep desire to make amends and achieve reconciliation, something which under the present circumstances seems all but impossible.

Yet it is this sense of reconciliation that I yearn for the most. Reconciliation with the spirit of my victims. Reconciliation with the families and friends of my victims. And finally, reconciliation with myself and my God. If this happens it will be the final part of my transformation, and undoubtedly the most difficult part. If only science could create a drug to help me with this problem.

So what can be learned from this sad story? I'm not really sure because it seems pretty tragic all the way around. However, one thing that is surely true is that there are other "Michael Rosses" out there in various stages of development. They need places where they can go for help. One of the most difficult and painful things for me to deal with today is knowing that had I begun receiving just one little 1 cc injection of Depo-Lupron once a month fifteen years ago, eight women would be alive today. That ignorance, and its resulting guilt, are very heavy burdens on my mind, and burdens that I will carry with me for what remains of my life.

Society needs to learn from this tragic affair and needs to act now to make the necessary changes to prevent a failure of diagnosis and lack of early treatment, such as mine, from recurring in the future. Learn from my case and others like mine. It's easy for society to point its finger at me, to call me "evil," and to condemn me to death. But if that is all that happens, it will be a terrible waste. For in a sense society will be condemning itself—to future "Michael Rosses." Future tragic murders such as I committed can be avoided, but only if society stops turning its back, stops condemning, and begins to squarely acknowledge and treat the problem. Only then will something constructive come out of the events that took the lives of eight women, destroyed the quality of life of their families and friends, resulted in my incarceration and probable execution, and caused untold shame and anguish to my own family. The past has already happened; it's up to you to change the future.

Michael Ross, born and raised in Connecticut, graduated from the Cornell University College of Agriculture with a major in Agricultural Economics and Farm Business Management. He was arrested in 1984 and convicted of six counts of captial felony murder. In 1987, Michael was sentenced to death. Since 1994 when his death sentence was overturned, he has been fighting to be allowed to accept the death penalty in order to spare his victims' families the ordeal of another trial. As this book goes to press, the case is still unresolved.

FRED S. BERLIN, MD, PhD
"How Many People Need to be Eaten in Milwaukee?"

Serial killer Jeffrey Dahmer took the lives of 17 young men. For years prior to his apprehension and subsequent brutal murder in prison, he had been preoccupied with obsessive thoughts about meeting a man while he was still alive, and of then transforming him into a zombie-like individual who could continue to exist in a transitory state between life and death. He then wanted to continue relating to him in an intimate sexual fashion even after he had passed away. To fight the urge to enact such fantasies in a way that would cause harm to others, he had stolen a male mannequin from a department store, attempting to use it as a substitute for an actual human being. He had gone to a cemetery with the intent of digging up a dead body, with the same purpose in mind. He had frequented a number of gay bath houses, where he had slipped drugs into the drinks of unsuspecting strangers, hoping to then relate to them intimately, once again as "zombie-like" surrogates who would, in his mind at least, not be permanently harmed.

Later on, after ultimately succumbing to the urge to kill repeatedly and feeling out of control, Mr. Dahmer began wearing yellow contact lenses, wondering whether his destiny in life was to serve some evil force. He attempted to drill holes in the heads of several young men, pouring in caustic liquids while they were still alive, in an attempt to create zombies that would keep him company in an intimate sexual way. He came to believe that perhaps he could create a temple from the sacred skeletal remains of his victims, a temple that might give him special powers. While on work release from prison, he had taken with him, to keep him company, the skull of a young man whom he had killed. While working in a medical laboratory, he had intentionally tasted human blood. He had ingested various organ and tissue parts of some of his victims, feeling that, as a consequence, they would continue to live on through him.

At his insanity trial in Milwaukee, Wisconsin, in 1992, a jury of Mr. Dahmer's peers concluded that he did not have a mental disorder. After I had returned from Milwaukee to my east-coast home, subsequent to having testified at his trial, a good friend of mine, a very capable federal prosecutor, asked me only partially in jest, "How many people need to be eaten in Milwaukee before one can be considered to have a mental disorder?"

As reflected by the jury's decision, public cynicism about mental illness, particularly when one is facing criminal prosecution, and particularly when innocent victims have been harmed, is considerable. Such cynicism often becomes even more pronounced when the crimes in question have been sexual in nature. A frequent assumption is that the individual being prosecuted is simply feigning illness in an 11th-hour attempt "to beat the rap." Moral pronouncements tend to be made with certainty and conviction. If he was not prepared to do the time, he should not have done the crime.

Subsequent to his apprehension for questioning, Michael Ross, a serial sex offender and killer currently facing likely execution in Connecticut, voluntarily waived his constitutional rights and confessed, helping police to locate the bodies of a number of his young victims. Unlike Ted Bundy, with whom I also had a professional involvement, Mr. Ross has consistently been quite open. Mr. Ross' crimes, which included both the rape and murder of a number of young girls, were horrible, almost beyond belief. The sustained deep grief, suffering and understandable rage of his victims' families endures even now, years after his arrest, as an ongoing testimonial to the hopelessly sad aftermath of his tragic actions.

How could Michael Ross have become who he is? How could any human being, let alone this intelligent graduate of Cornell University, have done what he did? Why would someone arguably so evil, while still only a suspect, waive his rights and confess for the sake of his victims' families? A common public fear is that psychiatrists, in trying to understand these apparent paradoxes and mysteries, may try to argue that Mr. Ross, and not those whom he has harmed, is the real victim. Surely such doctors of the mind must not be allowed to excuse such obvious sin and moral depravity by relabeling it psychopathology.

All of the doctors who examined Mr. Ross after his arrest, including those who had done so at the request of the local prosecutor, agreed that he does suffer from a mental disorder. His diagnosis is Sexual Sadism. According to *The Diagnostic and Statistical Manual of Mental Disorders*, persons afflicted with Sexual Sadism experience recurrent, intense sexually-arousing fantasies and urges in which the psychological or physical suffering of a victim is sexually exciting. So what? That sounds so simplistic. How could such a condition, if it even exists at all, possibly have accounted for Mr. Ross' horrible crimes?

Almost all of us have been taught from the days of our earliest childhood that "all men are created equal." That is not true. Certainly we are all born equal in moral worth. Certainly we all have every right to expect equality of opportunity. However, we are not all equal to the extent that equal means the same. One important way in which we differ from one another is in our sexual makeups.

We differ from one another regarding (1) the types of partners towards whom we are, or are not, sexually attracted, (2) the types of behaviors that we either do, or do not, crave sexually, and (3) the intensity of our sexual desires. Remarkably, some persons are attracted sexually, as was the case with Jeffrey Dahmer, to corpses; others, as in the case of Pedophilia, to children. Some men sexually crave cross-dressing in female clothing, exposing themselves in a public setting, or coercive, as opposed to consenting, sexual acts. The spectrum of human sexual differences, though rarely discussed openly and maturely, is remarkably broad.

How have we come to differ from one another in such ways? There is still much to be learned. However, we do know that in some cases, when a young boy has been sexually abused, his ongoing erotic maturation can become warped, contributing to the subsequent development of abnormal sexual cravings. It is now believed that in some instances at least, biological factors, such as chromosomal, hormonal or brain abnormalities, may contribute to the development of unconventional or even pathological sexual makeups. What is certainly true about our sexual makeups is that we do not as children choose how they will develop. As a youngster I did not weigh my options deciding whether to grow up as a man who would be attracted to boys, girls, men or women.

No one in their right mind would decide as a child to grow up afflicted with recurrent intense sexually-arousing urges and fantasies about engaging in sex with corpses, or with children. Nor would they decide to be afflicted with recurrent intense sexually-arousing urges and fantasies about cross-dressing in female clothing, or about torturing and killing young girls. Persons such as Jeffrey Dahmer or Michael Ross, who have been plagued with abnormal sexual cravings, did not somehow simply decide to have them. Instead, they discovered themselves to be so afflicted. In my professional and personal opinion, no human being has ever deserved that.

Perhaps it is not Michael Ross' fault that he has been plagued by such disturbing cravings. Clinicians and researchers who contributed to the development of *The Diagnostic and Statistical Manual of Mental Disorders* had documented the existence of such aberrations of sexual makeup long before Mr. Ross was born. Clearly this is not a disorder whose existence was created to absolve him of his sins. However, even if it was not his fault that he had developed such an affliction, surely it had been his responsibility to do something about it. That something needed to be far more than fighting his urges by simply sitting at home, as he had so often done, hoping somehow that if he delayed going out this would help to overcome them. By failing to resist acting on his temptations, no matter how overpowering, had he not sinned? Surely such bad acts are not to be excused, explained or understood. Did he not have free will, and did he not choose to act irresponsibly? An eye for an eye and a tooth for a tooth.

I have trained for many years to become a physician. In the course of my work with patients, I have come to appreciate the power that biological drives can sometimes exert over human behaviors. Hundreds of thousands of Americans are currently spending literally millions of dollars in an attempt to diet. At this point in time, I can guarantee each and every one of them absolute success. Simply eat less. It is no more complicated than that. Weight loss is guaranteed. However, in spite of absolute sincerity and conviction, it is the presence of appetite, so invisible and unobservable to others, and even vague to one's self, that can in time so often be expected to overcome the would-be dieter's resolve. Gluttony is no longer thought of as a sin. Obesity is considered to be a potentially dangerous medical disorder. For some, biological cravings can sometimes compromise free will.

Obesity, however, relates to overeating. That is not sex. That certainly has nothing to do with sex involving sadism and murder. Overeaters, by sustaining their obesity, may victimize themselves. They do not directly victimize others. They certainly do not victimize innocent young females. Why should we believe Michael

Ross, who in seeking treatment in prison, insisted that he too had become weakened in his resolve in response to the repeated invisible incessant cravings of his pathological sexual appetite. In making such a claim, was he not just trying to absolve himself of responsibility?

God and/or nature has instilled within each one of us a number of powerful biological drives. Absent eating, the hungry man would die. Absent sexual behavior, the human race would die. It is important to eat, and it is important to have sex. When sexual drive becomes "aimed" in the wrong direction, for example towards children as in Pedophilia, or into sadistic cravings as in the case of Michael Ross, it still recurrently craves satiation.

As a moral person, could not Michael Ross have relieved himself of sexual tensions by masturbating, instead of acting upon his sadistic cravings? It is true that masturbation can often temporarily decrease sexual desire. On the other hand, for some it may also whet subsequent sexual appetite. In either case, recurrent masturbation does not necessarily facilitate celibacy. If a primary purpose of sex is to assure survival of the human species, then nature would not ordinarily want masturbation to prevent subsequent sexual acts with others. In some instances, frequency of masturbation may serve as a marker regarding intensity of sexual drive. For Michael Ross, going home and masturbating would not have amounted to successful self-treatment.

Even if one were to accept the argument that Michael Ross was so driven by his cravings that he could not control himself through willpower alone, surely he still had a moral obligation to seek help. The alcoholic may not be able to treat his own alcoholism. However, he should at least be expected to seek assistance before getting into a car and victimizing an innocent party. One of Mr. Ross' greatest regrets today, as he too finally grieves for the souls of his victims and for their families, is that he had not sought out such help. Instead he had repeatedly rationalized to himself that he would be able to stop on his own. On the other hand, where could he have gone for help without running the risk of being injured? Be that as it may, tragically, he did not muster up the necessary moral courage to come forward. Today, having finally received treatment in prison, his perceptions are no longer distorted by incessant sadistic cravings. As can be seen in his companion piece to this article, he currently lives on death row with a pervasive sense of ever present guilt and profound remorse.

Jeffrey Dahmer, too, had yearned for help for many years. He also had been afraid to openly discuss his situation with a mental health professional. Having accepted antidepressant medication treatment while still free, he had nevertheless been unable to bring himself to the point of discussing openly the nightmare of his necrophilic preoccupations. In his case, eight years had elapsed between his first killing and the other 16. During that period of time, he had tried prayer, sleeping with a mannequin, digging up a dead body, and sometimes pretending in his mind that drugged young men in gay bath houses were actually dead. He had desperately needed help, but had been afraid to speak up.

How is it that persons such as Jeffrey Dahmer and Michael Ross seem capable of denying, even to themselves, the enormity of their actions? As Jeffrey Dahmer related to me, "If a soldier feels that he has no choice but to take a human life, he cannot live with himself by thinking of those whom he has been trained to kill as a human beings with emotions and families." To accept in one's mind such a reality can cause unbearable pain. Thus, to preserve one's sanity, if one feels somehow compelled to take a life, the mind simply tries to blot out and deny the horror of such a truth. Presumably we as a society will also try to blot out the reality of Michael Ross as a suffering human being, undeserving of mercy or understanding, on the day that we lead him to his execution. Michael Ross has his explanations about why he felt compelled to kill. We, too, as a society will have our own explanations about why we feel compelled to kill him.

Were both Jeffrey Dahmer and Michael Ross lying when they claimed to be overpowered by their pathological sexual cravings? Perhaps they were. However, suppose just for the moment, that they were not. Making the moral argument that they should have been able to control themselves, doesn't prove that they were actually able to do so. Tragically at this very moment, there are many others in society afflicted with recurrent abnormal sexual cravings. Some may still be in their adolescence, or even younger. If in our zeal for moral certainty, we choose to deny the reality of such mental afflictions, thereby further retarding additional scientific/medical study and scrutiny, what a sad and unnecessary legacy this may leave for future potential victims.

Jeffrey Dahmer and Michael Ross are simply the extremes. Sex is a powerful force that touches the lives of each and every one of us. Too often we deal with it either through off-color jokes or by sweeping it under the carpet. As a society, we rarely reflect about it maturely. Instead we are quick to be judgmental and to point a finger. The sexually-active woman is "loose," and the sexually-active man a womanizer, no matter how solid in character they might otherwise be. Persons who experience unusual or unconventional sexual desires are labeled and stigmatized as "perverts." Is it not time for all of us to move beyond simply moralizing (while at the same time preserving our moral values), and to begin to approach such matters with a sense of open mindedness, thoughtfulness and scientific inquiry?

We need to learn how to preserve and demand from one another moral accountability and responsibility. At the same time, we must come to appreciate that at least in some instances we may not be dealing with evil that needs to be punished, but with a broken mind in desperate need of repair. How many people need to be eaten in Milwaukee to convince us that this might be so?

The minds, as well as the souls, of individuals such as Jeffrey Dahmer and Michael Ross can be disordered and tortured. They were not simply having fun. They were afflicted, and not of sound mind. This needs to be understood. To do so in no way whatsoever diminishes our compassion or concerns about victims and their families. To the contrary, it simply reflects our resolve to try to prevent future similar afflictions, and future similar victimizations.

Fred S. Berlin

Fred S. Berlin, MD, Ph.D., has received his training and been educated at a variety of centers including McGill University in Montreal, Canada, and The Maudsley Institute in London, England. He is currently an Associate Professor and attending physician in the Department of Psychiatry and Behavioral Sciences at The Johns Hopkins University School of Medicine, where he founded The Johns Hopkins Sexual Disorders Clinic. He is also the Director of the National Institute for the Study, Prevention and Treatment of Sexual Trauma.

ROBERT E. FREEMAN-LONGO
"A Public Health Model for Sexual Abuse"

Legislators and the public repeatedly turn to the criminal justice system to solve the violence in America. However, the series of tougher laws passed each year do not address the underlying causes of violence or sexual abuse, while the continued rise in sexual abuse suggests that a criminal justice model is not preventing sex offenses.

During the past few years, we have seen legislation that (1) mandates public notification of sexual offender release, (2) mandates use of Depo-Provera (chemical castration), and (3) imposes indefinite commitment of "predatory" sexual offenders. We cannot effectively apply these laws, based on extreme cases that are not representative of the majority of sexual abusers, to all sexual abusers. Recently, reports suggest that these laws have resulted in a decrease of sexual abuse reporting by victims. These mandated laws are examples of "feel good" legislation which may cause more harm than good as they drive the sexual abuser further into secrecy.

We must also come to grips with the unfortunate reality that sexual abuse commonly has its onset in childhood and adolescence. For example, 45% of child sexual abuse cases in Vermont are perpetrated by children and teens. Early identification and intervention by adults with these children would reduce, almost by half, the number of children sexually abused in Vermont! That is prevention.

People often ask us if there is a "cure" for sexual abusers. Generally, by cure they mean a treatment that renders the person safe and no longer at risk to engage in sexually abusive behavior. What we can say today is that hundreds of thousands of individuals have participated in specialized treatment programs and have gone on to lead productive lives and have not been rearrested.

During the past ten years, a number of studies regarding sex offender treatment and recidivism have been conducted and published. They are very encouraging and some show comprehensive treatment of pedophilia and other types of sexual abuse has a 90% or better success rate.[1,2,3,4] Rapists are a more difficult clientele and the success rates vary between 75-85% success, according to one expert,[5] and over 90% by others.[6] Research studies in the past few years have demonstrated strong enough evidence to convince even skeptics that treatment works better than no treatment.[7,8] Johns Hopkins University has reviewed treatment programs from around the world and discovered that even some of the most worrisome sexual predators, pedophiles and adult rapists, respond very well to rehabilitative efforts.[9]

So what works? Based on my experience as a clinician and trainer, the primary key to success is the ability of therapists to make a vital personal connection with each and every sex abuser being treated—even the most diabolical, brutal, and uncooperative of them.

All the science, technology, medicines and techniques are of limited value unless applied within a solid and respectful therapeutic relationship. Treatment providers have learned to put aside personal and political prejudices that have stymied success in times past. It is now clear that therapists who approach sex abusers with hateful, punitive and vindictive attitudes perpetuate abusive attitudes in their clients, rather than modeling how the client can learn to relate on a mutually respectful basis. Hate breeds more hate. Respectful firmness, however, is usually received well by abusers.[10]

If treatment is to be effective, relationships must be built between therapists and abusers that foster openness, disclosure, honesty and change. As with all human beings, sex abusers need to believe they will be treated with dignity and professionalism before they will let down their guard and risk being vulnerable.

Unfortunately, at times abusers have been shamed, brow-beaten, threatened with punishments for minor mistakes, and treated condescendingly by therapists who carry society's attitude of vengeance into the counseling session. Rather than punitive therapists and hard-line corrections personnel, sex abusers need a therapeutic community that is brave enough to challenge today's political climate of hate, look beyond the emotionalism, and strive to connect with each abuser who comes their way. In doing so, society can be better protected.

Now that research supports comprehensive treatment as effective, we should begin formulating rational public policy based on the findings. As responsible citizens and members of the media seeking to combat a serious public health problem, we must use this information to secure treatment for both sexual abusers and victims, knowing that not all sex abusers should be, or will be, behind bars until their deaths.

It is time for all of us to begin changing the way we think about sexual abuse. First, the most important action we can take to prevent the sexual abuse of our children is to educate ourselves. Because of the media's focus on high-profile sex crimes, and sex murders, these sensationalized news stories give the American public a biased, distorted and unrealistic view of sexual abuse. In addition, they foster an angry public who wants to castrate, use public notification, or imprison sexual abusers for life, regardless of what type, the frequency of their crimes, or the risk they pose to the community. Not all sexual abusers are alike, nor should they all be handled in a similar fashion.

Second, we must focus on early intervention and prevention of sexual abuse. For every individual we lock up in prison, there are at least one or more children at risk for acting out sexually. The same amount of money we spend to incarcerate one person for one year could fund state-of-the-art identification, intervention and treatment for at-risk youth.

Third, I believe that sexual abuse prevention requires a national campaign to acknowledge sexual abuse as a public health problem. If society expects people who are prone to act out sexually and abuse others to get help for their problem and stop their behavior, then society must offer the opportunity for sexual abusers, and persons prone to sexually act out, to step forward and get help. To prevent sexual abuse from becoming a more widespread epidemic, we must provide the potential abuser, and active abusers, the opportunity for hope and recovery.

It does not make sense to punish people afflicted with mental, emotional, or health problems that we can treat. We need to encourage, not discourage, these individuals to seek professional help. We need to develop and fund treatment, not close down programs. Using a public health model holds tremendous promise today for reducing sexual abuse in America tomorrow.

This essay is adapted from the book Sexual Abuse in America: Epidemic of the 21st Century by Robert E. Freeman-Longo & Gerald Blanchard, Safer Society Press, 1998.

Robert E. Freeman-Longo, MRC; LPC; CCJS, is the Director of the Safer Society Press, a nonprofit press and project of the Safer Society Foundation, Inc. He is an international consultant in the field of sexual abuser assessment, treatment and program development, and is founder and first President of the Association for the Treatment of Sexual Abusers. Mr. Freeman-Longo has trained professionals in law enforcement, mental health, protective service agencies, victim advocate programs and the judicial system internationally. He has written extensively in the area of sexual abuse treatment.

Footnotes

1. Olsen, S.S.(1997) Cognitive-Behavioral Treatment for Sex Offenders: A Look at Recidivism. Oregon Adolescent Sex Offender Network Newsletter, p. 1. EugeneOR
2. Lotke, E. Sex Offenders: Does Treatment Work? 1996, May 21(5) pp.1-3. Corrections Compendium: Lincoln, NE: CEGA Publishing.
3. Marshall, W.L. & Pithers, W.D. (1994) A Reconsideration of Treatment Outcome with Sex Offenders. Criminal Justice and Behavior, 21(1)pp. 10-27. American Assoc. for Correctional Psychology.
4. Nagayama-Hall, G.C. (1995) Sexual Recidivism Revisited: A Meta-Analysis of Recent Treatment Studies. Journal of Counseling & Clinical Psychology. 63(5) pp. 802-9. American Psychology Assoc. Inc.
5. McGrath, R.J., Hoke, S.E., & Vojtisek, J.E.(1997) Cognitive-Behavioral Treatment of Sex Offenders: A Treatment Comparison & Long-Term Follow-Up Study. Unpublished manuscript.
6. Berlin, F., Hunt, W., Malin, H., Dyer, A., Lehne, G., & Dean, S. (1991). A Five Year Plus Follow-Up Survey of Criminal Recidivism within a Treated Cohort of 406 Pedophiles, 111 Exhibitionists & 109 Sexual Agressives: Issues & Outcomes. American J. of Forensic Psychiatry, 12(3). Baltimore MD, pp. 5-28.
7. McGrath, R.J.(Winter, 1995) Sex Offender Treatment: Does It Work? Perspectives 9(1) pp. 24-26. American Probation & Parole Assoc.
8. Sex offender treatment program: initial recidivism study - executive summary. 1996, August 15. Alaska Dept. of Corrections Defender Programs & AK Justice Statistical Analysis Unit Justice Center: Univ. of AK. Justice Center Home Page: Microsoft Internet Explorer 12/7/96.
9. Berlin et. al. 12(3), pp. 5-28
10. Blanchard, G. (1995). The difficult connection. Brandon VT: Safer Society Press

HARRY NIGH & HUGH KIRKEGAARD
"Circle of Support"

June 1994 - The First Circle

When this all started, we never conceived of it as a ***program.*** We just wanted to do something to help one guy - Eddie.

I got a call from Bill Palmer, Psychologist at Warkworth Institution, a penitentiary 100 miles northeast of Toronto. "Do you think we could find a home on a Mennonite farm for Eddie?" he asked.

I had known Eddie for15 years through my work with M2/W2 Ontario, a ministry of friendship that linked prisoners who had no visits with Christian sponsors. We had matched him with two men, Adrian and John, who had faithfully befriended him for over 10 years. Eddie had lived in institutions from the age of 4. He had never learned to read or write.

At age 41, he was approaching release after serving a 7 year sentence for sexual assault against an adolescent boy. It was his 4th conviction over a 20 year period. This time he was coming out on "warrant expiry," which meant that he would serve every single day of his sentence without any community supervision following release. With the rising hostility among Canadians towards sex offenders, parole officials had become increasingly reluctant to grant conditional releases for which they might later be held to account.

Les Horne had known Eddie even longer than I had. Les had been Child Advocate for the province of Ontario. He was retired now, but still very committed to Eddie, who regarded him with the affection and respect of a son to a father. We knew that if <u>we</u> didn't come to Eddie's aid, he had no one else. How do you turn your back on a friend?

But if we had known what was going to happen on Eddie's release, I'm sure I would have found an excuse, any excuse, to side-step Bill's plea.

So Les and I drove to Warkworth, met with the case manager, and with Bill and Eddie. We explained that the Mennonite farm idea would not fly, but we would try to create a "circle of support" for Eddie when he hit the street. We agreed to help him find accommodation, help him re-establish his disability pension, and try to build a circle of friendship and support in his new city.

We also agreed to make contact with the local police. The institution was required to inform the police 60 days prior to Eddie's release.

When I walked into Detective Bob's office, he had Eddie's file on his desk. He candidly told me, " We don't want him here." Based on institutional reports, the police felt Eddie was sure to re-offend, and soon. A few months before, our police force had taken a pounding when another offender escaped from the Psychiatric

Hospital and re-offended against a young boy. The public had not been warned of his escape.

Released to the Community

This time, within two days of Eddie's release to the community, the Police made his picture available to the media and warned the community of his presence among us. He was front page news. One headline read, *"Streets of Fear."* The school boards photocopied the press release and gave one to every school kid in our region of 300,000 citizens. Within hours, his picture was posted throughout the neighborhood.

Someone in the system leaked that "a Mennonite Pastor" was part of the group helping this guy. In no time the media descended upon our church. We had a quick prayer meeting with our staff and I went out to face the cameras. I feared pickets in front of our home (they never materialized). I bought a telephone answering machine!

The police mounted a 24 hour surveillance on Eddie. They felt sure he would re-offend within a short period. They also wanted to ensure Eddie's safety. We heard that the cost of the 6 week surveillance amounted to more than $300,000.

Eddie, however, looked on the police as his neighbors. One day he brewed a pot of coffee and took it out to the officers on surveillance behind his house. They shooed him away: "You're not even supposed to know we're here," they said.

All of this community uproar was unnerving for our little church. How would they react to this mess that I had got them involved in? How would they receive Eddie's presence among us?

We had two congregational meetings at which everyone was invited to speak. Fears for our kids were expressed. What resources did we have as a little group to cope with this complex, polarizing issue?

In the midst of the discussion, dear Eleanor, who had lived on social assistance all of her life, spoke up, "If Jesus hadn't welcomed me, where would I be today?" The group decided unanimously to welcome Eddie, recognizing that we would all need to work together to help him avoid problem situations.

At the height of the community turmoil, the church threw an apartment-warming party for Eddie to let him know that he was welcome among us. Eddie invited his police "friends" to the party too!

Police Support Made the Difference

At Police headquarters meetings were called involving all levels of the justice system, mental health people, community representatives and ourselves. It was clear to me that if a legal and expeditious avenue could have been found to remove Eddie from the community, it would have been taken.

Yet out of those meetings some bridges were built. One of the most vocal and angry of the community leaders agreed to meet Eddie face to face. They talked for over an hour in a donut shop. The community leader saw Eddie as a person, and recognized the mental and emotional disabilities that he coped with. They exchanged phone numbers. With police approval, we planned a face to face meeting between Eddie and other neighbors, but at the last minute the neighbors declined.

Throughout this time, Eddie's circle of support met regularly with him. Individually we contacted him every day (and still do after almost 4 years). We would take him to do his laundry, shop for groceries and find furniture for his apartment. For the first 6 weeks, because of police surveillance, every time we took Eddie out of his apartment 2 police cars followed us everywhere.

Gradually the police became supportive of what we were trying to do, and without their participation this effort might never have worked. Detective Bob proved to be a wonderfully patient, humorous contact. He would come to our Circle meetings and would check in with us frequently. He served as a buffer with the community, correcting rumours and diffusing problems.

Bob established a good-natured rapport with Eddie. The first night Bob gave Eddie his pager number and told him to call any time if there were problems. At 11:30 that night, Bob was awakened by a call through the pager. Alarmed, he returned the call quickly.

"Eddie, what's the matter?"

"Bob, I can't sleep....," Eddie said.

"Well, Eddie, that makes two of us!" Bob responded sleepily.

A Public Testing

The hospitality of our congregation was tested dramatically one Sunday morning when an intoxicated neighbor began screaming at Eddie and the group of us visiting outside after service.

"You're not welcome here...," he shouted, pointing at Eddie,

"We don't want you here...do you know what he's done... if you come back, I'm going to shoot you..."

I sent a frightened Eddie home and went over to talk to the neighbor, but he was beyond rational talk.

Our little church was shaken by this verbal attack and what it could portend in relations with our community. Eddie himself called Bob, and an officer went to talk to the neighbor.

The next morning, our neighbor, whose name was John, called me over to apologize. I listened to his story. He told me of his own victimization as a kid in one of our provincial training schools. I sensed his loneliness in raising two young kids as a single parent and I invited him and his kids to come to our church.

To the amazement of all of us, the next Sunday John and his kids came to church. We watched John and Eddie shake hands and reassure each other that there was no reason for fear.

Almost 4 Years Later

This was not the last crisis. There have been others. As a result of the media's attention, he occasionally faces rejection and unfair treatment. But Eddie's life has settled into a comfortable pattern. He maintains a clean, comfortable apartment. He occasionally volunteers to help seniors who need accompaniment. He's slowly developing a small network of friends, although trust takes a long time.

The circle of support has filled a number of roles: *advocating* with the system to secure the benefits that were rightfully his; *confronting* Eddie about his attitudes and behavior; *walking* with him through emergencies; *providing* financial backing when his kitten needed emergency surgery; *mediating* landlord-tenant conflicts; and *celebrating* anniversaries and milestones, all the small victories in Eddie's journey of reintegration.

The circle has felt keenly a dual responsibility: to be a ***caring*** community for Eddie in the midst of the hostility of the larger community, but also to be a ***responsible*** community, concerned that community safety not be compromised. We have always hoped that our presence might avert a situation developing in which someone else becomes a victim. No one can ever guarantee that Eddie will not re-offend, but we do not find this dual responsibility to be incompatible.

Nor do we find it a burden. Eddie has goals and a positive outlook on his life. He is a generous, caring friend.

Harry Nigh

The Story Continues

During the first weeks of this journey I became involved to support Harry, encouraging him, sharing mid-night phone calls to discuss the next move and generally affirming that he and the the small group around Eddie were doing something courageous and necessary. Little did I suspect that our turn would come mere months later when another ex-offender, released under the same circumstances, arrived on our doorstep in Toronto. His history was similar to Eddie's. Sam was lower functioning, had an alcohol problem and long history of trouble with the law. He too had been released at the end of his sentence. In addition to the personal challenges he faced, by the time he had come to Toronto he had been chased from a distant community as the result of an aggressive media campaign. He feared for his life. For months after, Sam had a high profile in the media and his name became synonymous with danger to children in the community. He became a leper.

Following the example of Harry and his congregation in Hamilton, we created a circle of friends around Sam. Within twenty-four hours of his surfacing in Toronto, the police determined to place him under a peace bond,[1] and we had a group of four people in the courtroom with Sam to indicate our willingness to work with him in the community. The police were not sure what to make of us, a group of Christians involved with such a case, they thought we were 'religious fanatics.' For our part, we had become involved with Sam's predicament, not necessarily because we knew what we were doing, but because we felt that it was right! If we, as people of faith, were not prepared to deal with the difficult issues which people like Sam represented in our communities, then who would?

Our convictions were put to the test in the ensuing days and weeks as we attempted to assist him in finding housing, getting settled in the community, and finding appropriate work. It seemed that we were stymied at every turn. For four weeks Sam stayed in a cheap motel room on the outskirts of the city as we tried to find a religious community, or some other form of safe accomodation, even temporarily. When they heard of the situation, many church members said, "We can't help you with housing, but we'll make a contribution to help with his expenses." So we paid for the motel room and food for Sam with their support. Every day for a month, one of us would make the trip to meet with Sam and take him out for lunch or dinner. He had been so traumatized by his initial experience that he would not leave the room alone for fear that he would be recognized.

Finally, an Alcoholics Anonymous (AA) connection paid off as a member was found who was willing to have Sam share his apartment and the rent. This was helpful in two ways—Sam had a place to live and a roommate who could keep an eye on him. As we had gotten to know him better we had recognized that his history as an alcoholic and his involvement in paedophilia were bound together.

The Challenges of Community

We continued to meet with Sam on a daily basis as he got established in the city and began to look for work. In addition, the group working with him began to meet together with Sam in the church where one of our number was the parish priest. These meetings became places where we could support and encourage him as well as help him problem solve and hold him accountable for his actions in the community. Sam had worked as a waiter in restaurants in the past and was interested in finding similar work again. He thought that work in a family restaurant where no alcohol was served would be a good place for him to seek employment. The circle was very clear with him that this was not an option as there may be children there and he would both be 'at risk' of re-offending and in contravention of his bond. These and many other issues would be dealt with in our meetings together as Sam both pushed the limits of our support of him and came to trust our care for him. For all of us it was an exercise in discovering the boundaries that should exist in healthy community.

The most difficult test of the circle came late one Friday evening when I received a call from Sam's roommate. He had arrived home to discover a collection of empty liquor bottles in the kitchen and Sam in his bed, dead drunk. I agreed to come to the apartment. When I arrived, I found Sam incoherent and his roommate didn't know what to do with him. I called a couple of the others who were involved with the support circle and we had a midnight meeting at the apartment. Even after several doses of strong coffee, we couldn't converse with Sam, so we felt that we had to make a decision on the right course of action. We had had suspicions about the possibility of his drinking previously, but he had always denied it. This was the first time that he had been caught. We had been clear with him that if he were drinking, we would have no recourse but to turn him in. So at 12:30 a.m. we called our contact with the Police, a detective who had been involved with the circle around Sam, and explained the situation. She and her partner came to the apartment, arrested him and put him in jail to dry out for the weekend.

Our decision that night was not an easy one but we felt that for Sam's sake and that of the community we had no other option. Similarly, we agreed that we would meet in court on Monday morning to support his release back into the community if he would be willing to take an alcohol rehabilitation program. The Police, who now recognized that we were indeed concerned with the safety of the community, as well as with Sam being supported in the community, backed us in the decision to have him released into a residential treatment program.

Circles of Support

We began to explore how we could help others who were released under the same circumstances as Eddie and Sam. Harry had the idea that what we were doing for them could be used for others in their situation. The vision took shape as we thought about the capacity of the faith community to welcome refugees, offering sanctuary; the experience of the L'Arche Community with the developmentally delayed, creating community; and our own commitments to a biblical vision of Restorative Justice, seeking healing. Out of our conversations together and our contact with the Mennonite Central Committee, the idea of developing intentional "Circles of Support and Accountability" was birthed.

Our research revealed a dramatic increase in the numbers of sex offenders in our prisons over a twenty year period. This appeared to be the result of decreased tolerance in the community for sexual and physical abuse and the increased reporting that has resulted from this shift in public opinion. The problem has become that even after many sex offenders have 'done their time,' taken treatment programs, and sought conditional release on parole, the community has remained intolerant of them. Widespread use of the "warrant expiry," detention legislation noted above, has been the result. We realized that the Circle model addressed both the need of the released offender for support and the concerns of the community for some structure and accountability for the offender.

As we began to formalize our work into the "Community Re-integration Program," we experienced support from the Mennonite and other faith communities, case management personnel in the prisons and the community, from mental health professionals and from the police. The 'turf wars' that often create problems working with these diverse groups and agencies were not an issue for us. The support we received both encouraged and enabled us to begin to tackle more difficult cases.

Over the past two years as the program has grown, we have welcomed ten more men into Circles in the community. The criteria for involvement of a core member are that they are considered to be high risk, with high needs, have little or no community support, are potentially high profile and are willing to be involved with us. Several of the men have connected with us a few months prior to their release, others have sought us out after release to the community when they realized that they could use the support we offer. Even the Police have referred men to our program.

Each Circle has four to six volunteers who have been recruited largely from churches in the areas where the offender or 'core member' has settled. The individual needs of each core member are addressed by the Circle volunteers, from practical concerns to legal issues related to the peace bonds, social needs to birthday celebrations. For many of the core members this has been their first experience of a supportive community. Similarly, the accountability that the Circle demands has been a new experience for many. Fortunately, there have been no re-offenses to this point.

The Victim's Voice

The foundation of the Circles approach in the principles of restorative justice requires that the needs of the victims of sex offences be taken seriously. For this reason we have attempted to recruit a person to each Circle that can represent "the victim's voice." In one of our early Circles a woman minister concerned about the offense history of the core member reminded him regularly that "the children in our community are not safe until you are and you're not safe until they are." Other volunteers have been interested in working with us in order to understand the victimization of family or friends and to prevent further victims.

We recognize that the real challenge in taking the needs of victims seriously is offering to them the same kind of support that the Circle extends to the offender. This remains a need that the existing community and criminal justice structures do not address well, if at all. Perhaps one day we will be able to form Circles of Support and Healing around victims early in the justice process.

Big Things

As the Circles have expanded in southern Ontario and interest in what we are doing has spread to other parts of Canada and the United States, we have recognized that we are into something much bigger than we ever anticipated. Our initial concerns for Eddie and Sam and their safe re-integration into the community have led us to the possibility of what we have come to see as 're-creating community' for those who have 'fallen out of community.' This is a far greater task than just working with ex-offenders. It involves the re-empowering of people to care for all those who have fallen out of the life of the community by virtue of their own actions or of circumstances beyond their control. This includes the elderly, the unemployed, the poor, and the sick, among others. John McKnight's observations of the increasing professionalization of human services and the subsequent dis-empowerment of the traditional capacity of the community for compassion and care, has provided a helpful framework for understanding this greater challenge. In The Careless Society, he affirms that...

"Our essential problem is weak communities. While we have reached the limits of institutional problem-solving, we are only at the beginning of exploring the possibility of a new vision for community. It is a vision of regeneration. It is a vision of reassociating the exiled. It is a vision of freeing ourselves from service and advocacy. It is a vision of centering our lives in community."[2]

The emergence and use of the Warrant Expiry Detention legislation has in effect signalled the limits of the Criminal Justice system to solve 'the problem of sex offenders.' The parole system that historically has provided a safety net in the community has in effect, failed. Circles of Support are about re-kindling the capacity of the community to respond to these difficult situations creatively, re-weaving the most despised of people back into the fabric of the community in a responsible and compassionate way. This is crucial, not only for Eddie, Sam and the others with whom we work, but for a healthy and vital community life. For as Judge Barry Stuart has suggested:

"The health of a community improves when its members participate in conflict resolution. When they leave the task to others, the quality of community life declines. Gone is a collective sense of caring, of respect for diverse values, and ultimately a sense of belonging. Gone as well is the community's natural capacity to prevent crime, redress the underlying causes of crime, and rebuild the broken lives and relationships caused by crime."[3]

Stuart's views are based on his experience with the use of 'Sentencing Circles' in largely Aboriginal communities. He is concerned with the tendency of 'criminal justice professionals' to steal the 'conflict' from the community which is where it happens and where it must ultimately be addressed.[4] The work of Circles of Support, like that of Sentencing Circles, is about returning 'criminal conflict' to its rightful place in the community.

Circles of Support have captured the imagination of many both inside and outside the formal Criminal Justice systems. This seems to support the potential of the Circles to harness the resources of the community to deal with the hard issues of crime and the re-integration of offenders. The field of 'community corrections' involves professionals but it is ultimately a challenge for the community; the choice is one of living in fear and reacting out of that fear or welcoming people back into the community, creating the means to both support them and hold them accountable.

The strength of Circles of Support is that they are composed of community volunteers doing what the professionals alone cannot, creating safer and healthier communities.

Hugh Kirkegaard

Harry Nigh has served for the past 8 years as Pastor / Executive Director of Welcome Inn Community Centre and Church, a Mennonite-sponsored ministry in north end Hamilton. This small congregation became the base for the first "Circle of Support" when a warrant expiry offender came to the community in a highly-publicized release. In 1973, Harry helped form the Ontario program of M2/W2, which matched community volunteers one-to-one with prisoners. He served as Director of M2/W2 for 14 years, leaving in 1987 to take a position as Personnel Manager of a printing firm in Niagara. In 1989, he was invited to enter a position of ministry with the Mennonite Church.

Hugh Kirkegaard is the National Chaplaincy Co-Ordinator for Circles of Support with the Chaplaincy Dept. of the Correctional Service of Canada. He previously worked as a Community Chaplain with Offenders, ex-offenders and their families in Toronto, Ont. Hugh is an ordained Baptist minister and has been involved in prison ministry for 19 years.

Footnotes

1. The peace bond, or section 810.1 of the Canadian Criminal Code, is known as the "Paedophile Peace Bond". It restricts the movement of such offenders in the community, and until recently was the only legal mechanism which the police could use to deal with the perceived risk which people like Sam posed to the community.

2. John McKnight, The Careless Society: Community and Its Counterfeits, New York: Basic Books, 1995, p. 172.

3. The Church Council on Justice and Corrections, Satisfying Justice: Safe Community Options that attempt to repair harm from Crime and reduce the use or length of imprisonment,
Ottawa: The Church Council on Justice and Corrections, 1996, p. XII.

4. Judge Stuart is a Territorial Court Judge in the Yukon Territory of Canada. He has been instrumental in the creation and use of "Sentencing Circles" or "Peace-Making Circles" as they have come to be called in the Aboriginal Community, as a community-based means of resolving criminal conflict. He has published a document about this work: Building Community Justice Partnerships: Community Peacemaking Circles, Aboriginal Justice Directorate, Department of Justice, Canada:1997

Jesse Roberts, "Careful Going Over the Fence"

A BRIDGE TO THE COMMUNITY

Michigan

February 12, 1995

"I'm not on death row, but I have 17 years in prison! I'm a young black man, 35 years, 5'7", 172 lbs., 100% vegetarian. I only look to be 23 or 24 yrs. of age. I lose my Mom and Dad. I'll be release in 14 months. I have a positive heart and a lot of goals. But I know I can't do it all alone. The State of Michigan don't have no program set up for prisoners that's being release, other than $50 bucks and you know that really aren't going to go far. I'm scare as hell. But I'm ready to go."

February 2, 1998

"I hope and pray that this letter finds you in great spirit and health. Okay - some very nice news. I'm being released Feb. 25, 1998. I'm paroling to St. Paul Minnesota. I'm not returning home. I'm going to start a whole new life there. I have church aid and A JOB and a place to live. God bless your heart and keep up the good work and wish me luck."

STEPHEN FRALEY
"Community Preparation Workbook"

Introduction

In late 1992, the former Pre-Release programs were designated Community Preparation programs. This chapter was written in the form of a booklet to provide a general structure for all Community Preparation programs. Each program will naturally have an individual character, but a general framework should be applied throughout the state of New York. It describes how we have designed the Community Preparation program at Attica Correctional Facility. It also provides details on each group and our method of facilitating it.

In addition to the monthly Community Preparation cycle of twelve sessions, we have self-help therapy groups that address issues in the following problem areas: drug abuse, anger and violence, maladaptive personality, and HIV/AIDS. We always have long waiting lists for these workshops, and we give preference to those closest to the parole board. Through these efforts we hope to prepare inmates in such a way that the Hub Pre-Release facility will function more to reinforce positive changes than to attempt a two-week transformation of inmates facing the parole board.

Here at the Attica Community Preparation Center we use diverse and flexible methods of counseling. Briefly, they include: 1) Rational-Emotive Therapy techniques, challenging the irrational thoughts and beliefs of group members and offering more reasonable self-statements which are more adaptive in our society; 2) Lecture and Discussion sessions, supplemented by handouts, in which the peer counselor gives a very brief talk on a subject, and then opens the group for rational discussion, which he will facilitate; and 3) Video and Discussion sessions, which involve showing a topical video, discussing the reactions of the group members, and challenging irrational or self-destructive responses.

We hope that our efforts will help provide the atmosphere and opportunity for all inmates to actively seek rehabilitation.

I. Orientation

Orientation is the first session of the Community Preparation (CP) cycle. During this time we will present an overview of the program. The overriding purpose of CP is to help you prepare for a successful transition back to your community.

Resident Director

1. Introduce staff.
2. Articulate the following information:

A. CP is strictly voluntary.
B. The major purpose of CP is to:
(1) Assist you in preparing to re-enter society.
(2) Point out some of the obstacles you may face upon release.
(3) Provide you with ID and other resources or services.
C. Summarize the CP cycle
3. The rules are: no smoking, no hanging out, and mutual respect.
4. (Introduce the Assistant Resident Director.)

Assistant Resident Director
1. There are tables set up for services, including birth certificates, social security cards, addresses for drug and alcohol counseling, housing, education, social services, and employment.
2. Guidelines for birth certificates and social security cards:
A. If you were born in New York state, you can obtain a copy of your birth certificate free; otherwise the cost will vary.
B. We can only replace your old social security card. No charge.
3. (Introduce the Senior Counselor.)

Senior Counselor
1. To earn a CP certificate you must attend 8 of 12 sessions; the Guidance Unit issues the certificates and Parole gets a copy.
2. (Invite the junior CP staff to comment briefly.)
3. Supervise the services operation, and take attendance.

II. Family Concerns

Intense emotions related to family are often unconscious. Many of you believe that your families and friends abandoned you. You are hurt, but may find it more acceptable to express this through anger than to honestly address the pain. Family issues are delicate; therefore we approach them with gentleness and understanding. We discourage bitterness toward family members, focusing instead on how to build strong family ties. The core issues include:
1. Rejoining your family
2. Communication
3. Bitterness about abandonment
4. Family adjusting to you
5. Adjustment to your family
6. Realistic expectations
7. Avoiding negative family influence
8. Parenting skills
9. Strengthening family relations

III. Interpersonal Relations

Placing special emphasis on positive relationships and current attitude, the major themes that we will address include:

1. Relations with peers, family, and support personnel (e.g. P.O.)
2. Domestic violence
3. Forming strong support networks

Cultural Diversity

As part of interpersonal relations, it is important to discuss diverse cultural values in a multicultural society. This naturally includes discrimination, self-esteem, and social influences.

We hope to enhance your self-esteem and sense of identity by broadening your cultural awareness. We have encountered large numbers of men who not only have serious difficulties relating to people of other cultures but who also lack knowledge of their own heritage. If this is the case with you, it can severely compound your life-adjustment challenges. Evidence indicates that low self esteem contributes to these interpersonal and intrapersonal problems. Low self-esteem is the cornerstone of drug abuse, violence, and other patterns of criminal behavior. Although no one comes to prison charged with a lack of self-knowledge and pride or with not understanding and accepting people of other racial and ethnic groups, it appears that these kinds of issues contribute to the negative outlook which makes criminal activity more appealing. In essence, we can reduce the recidivism rate by raising awareness and self-esteem. The topics we wish to focus on include:
1. Ethnic and racial diversity
2. Religious Diversity
3. Age and sexual diversity
4. Stereotypes
5. Cultural pluralism in America
6. Prejudice and discrimination

IV Career Counseling

What types of programs are you now involved in? There are many institutional and community-based career development options, such as vocational training and college.

You cannot teach an old dog new tricks, right? Wrong! Life is one long learning process. More adults today than ever are taking classes or job training. They realize that education is essential.

Furthering your education or training can provide you with many benefits, such as a good job. If you plan to stay out of prison, you must prepare yourself for the job market. The type of job you get depends largely on how well you prepare. Virtually all employers demand a basic education. Experience is not enough.

Education can also boost your self-esteem. Being nervous about going back to school is natural. Here are some areas of concern:

1. The school's reputation
2. Financial aid (grants and loans)
3. Scholarships; company-financing
4. Placement services
5. Learning a trade
6. Apprenticeships

V. Decision-Making

The decision-making process involves weighing the advantages and disadvantages, and taking responsibility for your choices, rather than putting blame elsewhere. Good decision-makers are good problem solvers, and effective communication is crucial to both. Examples of decision-making considerations include:

1. How to approach a tense situation?
    A. Why is the situation tense?
    B. How will I feel in the situation?
    C. How do the other people in this situation feel?
    D. Can I do anything to relieve the tension?
    E. What strategies can I use to calm myself and others?
    F. What are the pros and cons of each strategy?
    G. Among all the potential strategies, which one is the best?
2. How to respond to an angry person?
    A. Why is he angry?
    B. Do I understand what led to his anger?
    C. Do I need to ask him to clarify the cause of his anger?
    D. Did I cause his anger? If so, what can I do to alleviate it?
    E. What optional responses do I have available to me?
    F. Which option is the most positive at this time?
3. Should I move back into my old neighborhood upon release?
    A. Do I want to return to my old neighborhood?
    B. What are my positive motives? Negative motives?
    C. Can I change those negative motives?
    D. Would I be able to avoid negative influences and patterns?
    E. What are my options?
    F. Can I arrange other living arrangements in a new environment?
    G. What is really best for me at this point in my life?

VI. Health

There are direct links between mental and physical health. Maintaining good health means eating and sleeping properly, exercising, and having a positive attitude. Your body is the only one you will ever have. Here is some information that will help you to take good care of it.

1. What is AIDS and how is it spread?
   - A. AIDS is a fatal virus, for which there is no known cure.
   - B. It is spread in the following manners:
     - 1) Blood to blood-IV drug use.
     - 2) Semen to blood-intercourse with either sex.
   - C. AIDS infection is greatest among IV drug users.
   - D. You cannot catch AIDS through casual contact.
   - E. It takes 3 to 10 years for a person to develop symptoms.
2. What are sexually transmitted diseases and how are they spread?
   - A. The most common STDs are gonorrhea, herpes, and syphilis.
   - B. STDs are transmitted through unsafe sexual practices.
   - C. STDs are not usually fatal (like AIDS).
   - D. If you do contract an STD, seek medical help immediately.
3. What is stress and what is stressful for you?
   - A. A certain amount of stress is normal and adaptive.
   - B. We have negative distress and positive eustress.
   - C. Distress results from unwelcomed pressures and hassles.
   - D. Eustress follows major achievements (e.g. making parole).
   - E. Stress affects both our physical and mental well-being.
   - F. Positive adaptations to stress include:
     - 1) Diversions and exercise
     - 2) Conflict resolution
     - 3) Talking it out
     - 4) Time management
   - G. Negative adaptations to stress include:
     - 1) Drug and alcohol abuse
     - 2) Denial
     - 3) Excessive worry
   - H. How can alcohol and drugs affect your health?
     - 1) Alcohol kills more people than all other drugs combined.
     - 2) All illegal drugs are harmful and should be avoided.

VII. Drug Abuse

There is a definite connection between drugs and crime. The major underlying cause of drug abuse is low self-esteem, which we address, along with the following issues:

1. Ways drugs have hurt you and others
2. Alternatives to drug use (i.e. positive coping strategies)
3. Your feelings about current attitudes toward drug abuse

4. Whether marijuana is safe
5. Dealing with drug testing by your parole officer or employer
6. Triggers or indicators that you want to use drugs
7. Your positive role models and sources of support
8. How to avoid a drug relapse:
    A. Remain alert
    B. Prepare for risky situations
    C. Use positive self-statements
    D. Deal with drug-free people
    E. Be open and honest
    F. Don't test yourself
    G. If you relapse, don't give up
9. Enjoying a drug-free lifestyle
    A. Engaging in new activities
    B. Patience in new situations
10. Drug abuse and mature intimacy
    A. Meet new people
    B. Include mate in recovery
    C. Seek outside help
    D. Communicate and compromise

VIII. Budgeting

It's easy to go from financial problems to criminal justice problems. Here are a few budgeting concerns:

1. Individual design
2. Income limitations
3. Realistic expenses

<u>Sample Budget</u>

<u>Income</u>

Your monthly net income	$ 800
Your spouse's monthly net income	+800
Total monthly net income	1600

<u>Fixed Expenses</u>

Rent or mortgage	500
Car note	300
Telephone	50
Insurance	50
Savings	+50
Total monthly fixed expenses	950

Total net income	1600
Total fixed expenses	-950
Income to be budgeted for flexible expenses	650

Flexible Expenses

Food	$200
Clothing	100
Transportation	50
Household items	25
Medical and dental care	75
Entertainment	100
Pocket money	50
Savings	+50
Total flexible expenses	$ 650

IX. Employment I

The New York State Department of Labor (Bureau of Labor Statistics, Bldg. 12, State Office Campus, Albany, NY 12240) can provide you with counseling, consultation, and information about the New York State Job Service. Programs available specifically for ex-offenders include Work Opportunity Tax Credit (WOTC), On-The-Job Training (O.J.T.), Office of Vocational Rehabilitation (O.V.R.), Federal Bonding, and Dislocated Worker. These can be quite helpful to you, at least in the beginning. This session will focus on:

1. Job search strategies
2. Resumes
3. Applications
4. Interviews

X. Employment II

This is your opportunity to role-play the job interview and evaluate your performance and that of others. Proceed as follows:

1. Set up video equipment
2. Record mock interviews
3. Play them back
4. Invite comments

If for any reason it is not feasible to videotape the role-plays, you can do the interviews without taping. Another option is to discuss interview scenarios, posing such questions as, "Why is there such a gap in your work history for the last several years?"

XI. Parole

An institutional parole officer will explain the rules and regulations for parolees, individual parole concerns, pre-parole interviews, and preparing for the parole board. Address Earned Eligibility and Temporary Release questions with your counselor.

The main parole issues include:

1. Parole experience
2. Problems
3. Successful strategies

The Certificate of Relief from Disabilities is available upon release if you have only one felony conviction. With two or more felonies there is a Certificate of Good Conduct. When the most serious conviction is an A or B felony you must wait five years before applying; otherwise three years.

XII. Recidivism

Issues you should address before returning to society include:

1. Fear of responsibility
2. Deceiving loved ones
3. Inability to trust
4. Confronting a new environment
5. Distorted judgments
6. Weak or false confidence
7. Refusal to seek help
8. Relapse

Ready To Go Checklist

	Ready	Need to Work on
Place to live (housing, shelter, etc.)	____	____
Job	____	____
Job leads	____	____
Plans for formal education	____	____
Addresses for therapeutic programs (drugs/alcohol, anger, ex-offenders)	____	____
Realistic goals and action-plan	____	____
Personal funds and/or sources of income for immediate living expenses	____	____

Last Words

We hope this booklet has been beneficial in preparing you to re-enter society. Almost everyone eventually gets out of prison. Your adjustment in society depends in large part on how prepared you are to face the challenges of freedom.

This is not an attempt to be exhaustive about inmate counseling. Nor do we expect this booklet to teach you everything about survival on the street. In fact, we are not teaching you at all. What we hope to do is open your mind and inspire you to make a long-term commitment to change. And so, if the contents herein touch your core humanity and give you reason to hope for a better life, then our goal has been achieved. The real work now begins.

The complete 40 page, spiral bound Community Preparation Workbook by Stephen Fraley is available for purchase; see page 370.

Stephen Fraley, a prisoner-counselor, earned his B.S. in psychology at the Consortium of the Niagara Frontier (Canisius College) while in prison. He is also senior counselor of the Relapse Prevention program at Collins Correctional Facility. He has spent 17 years in prison counseling, teaching, and writing. Fraley is doing 20 years to life for murder and will be eligible for parole in 2001.

JUDITH B. FOX, JD and ROBERTA RICHMAN

"The Evolution of the Rhode Island Women's Prison Mentoring Program 1990-1997"

Every year, approximately 200 women in Rhode Island are released from prison. Over 75% of these women are mothers, and the majority of these are the primary caretakers of their children. For the most part, these women are in early recovery from substance abuse problems, with limited life skills, and little or no work experience. They are often homeless, and may be ineligible to access shelters or other housing programs because of their criminal records.

These women are critically unprepared to provide for themselves or their children. Without help, even those with the best intentions may find it difficult to remain drug and alcohol free and refrain from criminal activity. Circumstances often force them to return to the same unsafe and unsupportive environments they frequented before being incarcerated. Moreover, help is becoming increasingly unavailable as the stigma of criminal and/or drug involvement is being used more to disqualify women for supportive services.

The estimated cost of incarcerating a woman in Rhode Island is $40,000 a year. This does not include the cost of providing foster care for her child while she is incarcerated, at a cost of about $20,000 per year. Programs which keep women out of prison and help them adopt a healthy lifestyle can reduce this economic burden while simultaneously reclaiming the women and their children as current and future contributing members of our community.

I

The Rhode Island Women's Prison Mentoring Program is designed to assist female inmates with the ongoing challenge of transitioning from incarceration to an independent lifestyle. The Mentoring Program, which began in 1991, fosters a personal relationship between volunteers and inmates, geared toward providing the inmate with a positive role model.

Through May 1997, the Mentoring Program has provided services to approximately 200 female offenders. Based on a study of 96 women one year after release, the recidivism rate for women who participated in the Mentoring Program was 25% compared to 40% for those who did not participate.

The core element of the Program is the Mentor/Mentee match. The Mentoring Program recruits volunteers from the community who agree to act as Mentors to motivated inmates. Mentors are expected to make a one-year commitment to the Mentee, and provide the Mentee with support and guidance in the transition from incarceration to the community. The Mentors receive extensive training to provide them with the necessary skills and background needed to undertake this Mentoring responsibility.

Mentors are matched with the inmate several months before release. During this pre-release period, the Mentor meets regularly with the Mentee and, with the help of the Case Manager, assists her in developing and implementing a Discharge Plan. The Plan includes goals for successful independent living and concrete actions necessary to reach these goals. The Case Manager assists the Mentee in locating affordable housing. The Mentee also meets with the vocational staff, who conduct a vocational/educational assessment, provide small-group pre-vocational classes and then assist the Mentee in obtaining employment. Following release, a Mentor continues to meet weekly with the Mentee to provide ongoing support and assistance in implementing the Discharge Plan. The Mentors attend monthly support meetings throughout the Mentoring process. There are also monthly workshops, attended by both Mentors and released and incarcerated Mentees, which offer information about a specific topic as well as an opportunity for socialization and mutual support.

In 1991 the Mentoring Program began operations out of an office in the Women's Prison. It was initially met with suspicion among some correctional staff. Some staff felt it was a waste of time to provide support for the women inmates. They believed that these women were entrenched in a negative lifestyle and would continue on a negative path regardless of interventions. Other staff felt threatened by the Mentoring Program and the influx of volunteers into the prison. In fact, shortly after the Program started, the office was relocated outside of the inmate living area due to complaints about volunteers walking in secured areas. In addition, correctional staff confiscated Mentoring Program training materials, which were being copied by an inmate, because they felt it was improper for inmates to have a copy of the Code of Ethics.

When the Mentoring Program began, very few mentoring programs for women leaving prison existed in the country. Therefore, there were many fundamental questions which had to be explored and resolved, including: the criteria to use for selecting inmates to participate; whether men should mentor women; how long to monitor and maintain the relationship; how to recruit, screen and train volunteers; how best to limit liability and secure safety for volunteers. Information was gathered from similar programs as well as inmates and correctional staff to determine the initial program design.

A critical element was the selection of inmates to participate in the Mentoring Program. The goal in inmate selection was to identify women who could most benefit from the support of a community volunteer.

It was decided to have an initial group of 20-25 matches during the first year, out of a prison population of about 200. In light of the limited number of opportunities to participate, the Mentoring Program was not advertised to all of the women in the facility. Instead, custodial and non-custodial staff members were consulted for recommendations. Selected inmates were interviewed and asked to fill out a written application if interested in participating.

The development of guidelines for the selection of Mentors was equally fundamental. Since many women in prison historically have had problematic relationships with men, only women were selected as Mentors. Maturity, stability and open-mindedness were quickly recognized as important characteristics for the volunteers. Mentors were asked to give a one-year commitment to meet with their Mentee. The relationship was allowed to continue after the year, but was regularly monitored. If the Mentee lost contact with the Mentoring Program or did not continue to work on issues she identified as critical to her reintegration into the community, she received a written termination notice.

In order to support the volunteer Mentors, a comprehensive training manual and guidelines were developed. Volunteers were given strict rules to follow to protect their safety and foster healthy boundaries.

Matches were made based on the oral interviews of Mentors and Mentees, their written applications and observing them in group settings. Since both Mentor and Mentee entered into the relationship voluntarily, and great emphasis was placed on matching based on interests, need, geography, and background, matches seldom failed.

Mentees see their Mentors as an important source of support in their lives. For many women, the Mentor is the first link to a new culture they must integrate into if they are serious about changing their lives. As the program has evolved, motivated women in prison in RI have developed an attitude that they need a Mentor to make a successful transition into the community.

Based on comments from Mentors and Mentees as well as from other programs, two regular monthly gatherings were initiated early on and continue to date. The first is a meeting for both Mentors and Mentees, held in a non-prison building on corrections grounds. Because this facility is a non-prison building, released women participating in the Program, who ordinarily are prohibited from entering prison buildings, were allowed to return to the non-prison building for the monthly meeting. However, since the building is located on corrections grounds, minimum security/work release women are also permitted to attend. These women are transported by a correctional staff person who remains at the building for security purposes.

This regular interchange between current and recently released inmates is unusual for a prison, and has benefited both groups of women. For the recently released inmates, this provides an opportunity to visit with friends and have a night out with their Mentors. More importantly, it allows them to feel connected to a group and feel proud about their progress. They often have been very helpful in giving advice and feedback to incarcerated women. For the women still in prison, these monthly meetings are eagerly anticipated. At these meetings, they can socialize, in a positive way, with people from the community.

The content of these meetings has been varied. Examples of activities have included cookouts, Thanksgiving dinner, athletics, life-skills workshops on topics ranging from nutrition to anger management to non-traditional careers, craft projects, creative writing and discussions about the difficulties of transitioning out of prison. Refreshments are always served.

The second monthly meeting is a support meeting for Mentors only. The idea started from the volunteers themselves, who felt a need to talk about their experiences on an on-going basis. These meetings have served several purposes. They provided a forum for learning about the issues that arose in the relationships and their impact on the volunteers. They also provided both peer and supervisory support for participants.

II

It soon became apparent that Mentoring was only one important component of a woman's successful transition into the community. The Program Manager/Coordinator and Mentors realized that without other critical elements, such as mental health treatment, employment and appropriate housing, the effectiveness of the Mentor and the likelihood of the women successfully making the transition into the community dramatically diminished.

In order to address these needs, the Program Manager/Coordinator, together with the Advisory Committee and other community volunteers, decided to seek out funding to begin to address the areas of identified unmet need. The Program, in collaboration with a community based non-profit organization, successfully submitted a $29,500 United Way grant proposal for part-time staff in the areas of case management, housing and mental health. The new staff was housed at the prison and provided direct services to women in the Mentoring Program.

The addition of these new positions allowed for a team approach to the provision of services. The Case Manager helped the women plan for release by identifying critical needs and appropriate community services to meet those needs. Appointments were set and essential documents obtained before release. When necessary, the Case Manager arranged to accompany the Mentee to an appointment. The Housing Specialist assisted women with difficult housing issues, developed written materials for the program on housing options and created liaisons with community housing resources. The mental health counselor, who has an MSW degree, met individually with each woman before release and offered to continue to counsel her post-release, at no cost.

This funding was in place from the spring of 1993 through November 1994. During this period, the Mentoring Program worked with 20-30 women a year. This grant enabled the Program to provide comprehensive services for each woman. Each woman not only was matched with a Mentor, but also received specialized help in three critical areas. The services began while the woman was in prison and continued post-release as long as the woman continued to work on issues identified in the discharge plan developed with the guidance of the Case Manager.

Staff met weekly to discuss each woman's progress and to ensure comprehensiveness of services. The monthly Mentor meetings were now facilitated by the MSW mental health counselor. This counselor used the group meetings as an opportunity to supervise and educate the Mentors and ensure that they maintained appropriate boundaries with their Mentees. This served a critical need since, despite explicit training to the contrary, Mentors sometimes placed themselves in potentially dangerous situations to help their Mentees.

Program policies were developed and refined regarding qualifications for Mentors and Mentees, how to handle emergencies, reincarcerations and noncompliance with discharge plans, as well as tracking and monitoring Mentees and Mentors.

III

In 1994, the Mentoring Program applied for and received a research grant to assist the women in obtaining and maintaining employment. Women are chosen based on demonstrated motivation through involvement with other prison programs, interest and ability to work, participation in education and prison drug treatment programs, recommendations from other prison treatment staff, level of education and past work history. Women selected to participate are required to complete a Gainful Employment Training course while in prison and work on the development and implementation of a comprehensive discharge plan for release with a case manger and Mentor. Each woman also meets with a Job Developer before and after release to review her employment status and plan for training and work for the future.

As before, the therapists meet each woman one to two months before release and offer ongoing services, post-release, on a voluntary basis. If necessary, money is now available through the grant to pay for transportation and child care so that the women can get to work or access support services. Funds are also available for follow-up treatment with a psychiatrist, if necessary, and to pay for other necessities.

The Mentoring Program developed an educational video for the Mentees to explain the purpose of mental health treatment. This was done because many women had never been introduced to the concept before and associated "social workers" with welfare and child protection organizations, both of which evoked strong negative associations for many of the women. The video helped to break down some of those barriers.

Since housing had repeatedly been identified as a critical need, the Program took advantage of an offer by one of the collaborating grant partners to experiment with jointly running two transitional two bedroom apartments for Mentees. Policies regarding resident selection for the units were jointly developed. Two single women were placed in one unit and a family in the other. All of the women came directly from prison.

This experiment was short-lived. Despite intensive off-site case management, none of the women placed in the apartments was able to follow the rules established and did not remain in the apartments. Staff decided to end the arrangement unless more intensive structured supervision could be provided. Unfortunately, the unavailability of structured, supervised living opportunities in the community (whether imposed or voluntary) has been a missing critical ingredient for many women's successful transition. While women can be taught basic life skills in prison, they need an opportunity to practice what they have learned so that it can be internalized. This can only be done in a supervised, structured setting outside of prison.

The wealth, breadth and duration of service provided by the Mentoring Program through this research grant made it a very desirable program for inmates hoping to change their lives. The Mentoring Program's attractiveness was further bolstered by the introduction of a new residential drug treatment program at the Women's Prison beginning in March, 1994, and the addition of other group educational programs at the Women's Facility focusing on parenting skills, sexual abuse and domestic violence.

The addition of these programs, coupled with word of mouth testimonials from released women who had worked with Mentors, encouraged inmates who wanted to change their lives to articulate a need for a Mentor. The prison programs were giving them a sense of hope that their lives could be different if they worked on it. They began seeing a relationship with a Mentor as a critical ingredient in their process of change. The relationships provided an opportunity for the women to learn fundamentals about friendship and trust which most women in prison have not experienced. They also provided a safe place to learn about a world that was foreign to them.

IV

The Mentoring Program at the RI Women's Prison is still evolving. What is interesting to observe is the development pattern of the Program, particularly those critical elements of its evolution that allow it to continue.

Before any innovative programs such as this one can begin to germinate, there must be supportive, progressive leadership at the prison. The structure and culture of most prisons do not provide an environment conducive to new social service programs. Support from top management is critical. At the RI Women's Prison, the Warden embraced community involvement in the prison, which allowed this program to start up.

The impetus for the Program came from some members of an educational leadership group from the community. Moved by their observations during a tour of the prison, they voluntarily wrote a successful grant proposal. Their ongoing involvement in the Program as an Advisory Committee combined with the vision and support of the Warden of the Women's Prison and the Program Manager/ Coordinator provided the momentum for two important events.

The first was the creation of the position of the Women's Prison Mentoring Program Manager/Coordinator as a permanent position within the Rhode Island Department of Corrections. Advocacy and community pressure from both the Advisory Committee and Mentors played a significant role in institutionalizing a new program at a time when basic services to inmates were being cut back. No similar program exists for men incarcerated in Rhode Island.

The second was the decision by the Advisory Committee to establish a separate non profit organization, Women in Transition, Inc. The decision to create this organization came after many debates about whether the complex needs of this population could be met by existing organizations. The more the Committee learned about these women, their families and the barriers they faced, the more it became apparent that this population needed its own voice in the community. While Mentoring is one important ingredient, a woman's chances of successfully transitioning out of prison are dramatically diminished unless other critical needs are also being addressed. The purpose of Women in Transition is to coordinate, enhance, advocate for and, when necessary, develop opportunities for these women and their families.

The creation of Women in Transition is also an important first step to bring the dilemma of how a society addresses a complex social issue into the community. Collaborations with community agencies during the course of the grants this program received as well as the increased sensitivity of funders and the trained volunteer Mentors have begun to impact on the public perception of the female offender.

Rhode Island Women's Prison has a state funded position for a Mentoring Program Manager/Coordinator. Without ongoing grant funds, the Program will be reduced or have to find other funding sources. Initial data on recidivism for this program indicate a 15% reduction in recidivism for those who participate in the Program. Assuming an annual cost of incarceration of $40,000 per inmate, a 15% reduction in recidivism results in total savings of approximately $600,000 per year for every 100 women inmates.

Although our success has not yet translated into additional staffing for the program, we expect to develop creative ways to compensate and continue to build an effective and meaningful support network for women in conflict with the law.

An expanded article on this program is available; see page 370.

Judith Fox has been the Program Manager of the Mentoring Program since its inception in 1992. She has successfully developed the program as well as a series of significant grants designed to offer support services such as mental health counseling, job training and job development to inmate mentees and to women after release. Ms. Fox has also played an important role in assisting a group of community volunteers who initiated the program to form a non-profit organization called "Women In Transition," which is intended to work in partnership with the Mentoring Program. Ms. Fox is dedicated to facilitating the transition from prison to community for female inmates by providing counseling and support groups for as long a period of time as the woman chooses to remain involved.

Roberta Richman has worked in corrections since 1979 serving in succession as Administrator of Educational Services, Deputy Assistant Director of Prison Industries and, since 1991, as Warden of the Women's Facilities for the State. In this capacity, Ms. Richman has introduced several program and treatment interventions for female offenders including the Mentoring Program, Intensive Residential Substance Abuse Treatment, and counseling for a variety of gender specific issues such as domestic violence and childhood sexual abuse. Ms. Richman is committed to working in partnership with community agencies who offer services both inside the prison and follow inmates as they transition back into the community after release.

THE FORTUNE SOCIETY

"The Birth of the Fortune Society" DAVID ROTHENBERG

Once upon a time I worked in a theater...back in the '60s. It was a period of time in America when it was all right to care about people. I was working in the theater, and in 1966 I produced a play about the Vietnam war.

In 1967 I had read a play called *Fortune And Men's Eyes.* I didn't know anything about prisons. I grew up in a small town in New Jersey in a middle class environment. And when I read *Fortune And Men's Eyes,* I realized that even if I didn't know much about prisons I did know an honest play when I read one, and I knew this had to have been written by a guy who had been in prison. It was a play about what happens to young people in jail and how the system destroys them. And I was determined to see that the play got on. We got a group of actors together and we went to Rikers Island. It was my first visit to a jail. I was devastated by what I saw. There was a newspaperman there and he said, "What is your opinion of this?" I said, "The only thing I can say is that anybody who has gone there because he has done something wrong...how would he be better as a result of that experience?" I went into jails and prisons all over the world, and I never went into an institution where I didn't come out thinking, "What kind of society takes people who they think have done something wrong and puts them in a cage for a period of time and thinks they are going to be anything but enraged when they come out? It doesn't make sense."

So we did the play. About a month into the play's run, a group of students came from their school to the theater and they asked if they could stay afterwards to discuss the play. We thought it was a great idea because we were very interested in what the play had to say. We invited the entire audience to stay and talk with me, one of the actors, and the stage manager who then revealed to us that he had done time in Iowa. We stayed on the stage and invited the audience to ask us questions about the play's message. And some guy in the audience said, after about 10 minutes, "This play is exaggerated. The characters are exaggerated. This couldn't happen in a jail." And from the back of the room a man named Pat stood up and said, "If my 20 years in the joint around this country account for anything, this play tells the truth and not even all of it. You couldn't watch what they did to us." So we said, "Come on up on the stage." And Pat came and joined us on the stage and that was really how the Fortune Society began. Pat spoke for about an hour, knocking us all out with stories about jails and prisons, and we said to him afterwards, "Could you come back next week. We'll do it all over again; we'll invite the audience to stay." Pat said, "I would, but I think I ought to bring somebody else. I did White time, in the '50's and '60's. In jail, there's White time and there's Black time. I think I ought to bring Clarence." And Clarence joined us the following week and he talked to us about his time as a Black man in prison and how the system would divide inmates and pit them against each other, just as it does on the outside. We did this every week for about 8 or 10 weeks until we realized that people were coming back regularly. And we started meeting wives of inmates and a lot of ex-cons. Most of the ex-cons who were coming were people who had found some stability, who had dealt with alcohol problems. We realized that while they were dealing with their sobriety, with AA, there were still a lot of pent up feelings about their time in prison that wasn't getting dealt with.

So we decided to call ourselves Fortune Society since the play was called *Fortune And Man's Eyes* and *Fortune And Man's Eyes* is from a Shakespearean sonnet, recited in the play, that begins, "When in disgrace with fortune........" So you can tell people that the Fortune Society is rooted in Shakespeare. It has also rooted the lives of thousands of men and women who have committed themselves to reaching out to other people and making a difference. Because, from those early days at my one room office, four of the guys from Fortune Society went on the David Susskind show. In 1968 four ex-cons went on TV. Ex-cons were never on television before, because of shame and because society didn't want to hear their stories. But in the '60's, when major institutions were being challenged and new voices were being heard, these guys went on TV and then gave the name of the Fortune Society if anyone wanted to get in touch with us, and they wrote my name and the Fortune Society address across the screen. The next morning about 200 people—all ex-cons—were at my office. We were inundated with men—no women—all of whom were sick and tired of jail, sick and tired of bouncing back and forth like a ping pong ball on the streets of NY, and they didn't have a clue how to begin. There was a man named Kenny Jackson and Kenny said to me, "You don't have any idea what you are doing," and he started counseling right there, and Mel Rivers too, and Mel and Kenny stayed around and became the nucleus for the next five or six years. And an army of men and women who had done their time, were tired of the system, wanted to tell their experiences to the public, and wanted to reach out to other men and women became involved in that period.

I find that rarely a week goes by when I'm not walking down the street or going somewhere and somebody stops me, and he tells me his name and says, "I came to Fortune and it made a difference." There is no reward so great as having someone come up to you and remind you who they are, that your being there made a difference, and that they are walking the streets and having a productive life with a family and loved ones. And our being here had made the difference. That is the excitement and the challenge that Fortune Society has always provided in a city, in a state, in a country, that sometimes seems so divided that coming back here is an oasis and a reminder that people can make a difference in the lives of other people, that we can reach out to one another. And that's why we celebrate together, why we come together from time to time to remind each other that there are options to the death penalty, options to locking people up. That reaching out and caring about each other is the heart and soul of the whole thing.

"What Fortune is Doing to Help" BIENNIAL REPORT

The Fortune Society has been working with ex-offenders since 1967, helping them change their lives and stay out of prison. At Fortune we know what it's like for people coming home from prison and what makes the difference between staying straight and returning to crime. There are so many voices shouting for ever-harsher punishment of criminals, including many politicians who know they can win elections by pandering to voters' fear and frustration. The public needs to hear more from the other side of the debate, from the growing movement of people who see that current policies have done more damage than good and that fighting crime requires more innovative responses than perpetual prison-building. Here is what Fortune is doing to help:

Fortune helps ex-offenders make the difficult transition to crime-free living by supplying...

Role models. All of our counselors and most of our staff are either ex-offenders or recovering substance abusers. They share key life experiences with their clients and, by their example, prove that there are better ways to live.

Peer support. People meet others who are trying to rebuild their lives. Fortune clients and staff are a community, sharing a common struggle.

A safe place and a new social network. For people trying to learn a new way of life, it's important to get away from environments that pull them back to crime and drugs. At Fortune they find new friends, new things to do and a safe harbor from destructive influences.

Counseling. Fortune counselors help their clients set and achieve goals, and give support that many don't get from their families. They help clients work through difficult changes, and remind those who want to give up that the consequence of crime is most likely a return to prison.

Education. Fortune offers one-on-one tutoring, from basic literacy to GED preparation, making students more employable, improving their self-esteem, and broadening their vision of life's possibilities.

Training. Clients get help in how to look for a job (including how to prepare a resume and talk about a criminal record in an interview), job placement and how to keep a job.

Substance abuse treatment. Fortune's relapse prevention services are licensed by the NY State Division of Substance Abuse Services. Participants attend discussion groups that teach them to recognize and evade "relapse triggers."

Referrals. Fortune refers clients to agencies for such services as housing, medical care, residential drug treatment, HIV/AIDS treatment, and others.

In addition to services for ex-offenders, Fortune speakers address churches, schools and community groups, to make the public more aware of the brutal conditions and inhumanity with our criminal justice system, and to offer better solutions, such as alternatives to incarceration. Audiences are encouraged to get involved in local community improvement efforts and to elect representatives who care about these issues. As was true when The Fortune Society was founded, ex-offenders, who had seen the truth from the inside, serve as the voices of those still incarcerated. Clients, staff and volunteers continue to advocate vigorously for a more humane, educated approach to criminal justice.

"The Health Link Program" RICARDO MARTINEZ

The Health Link Program, administered by The Fortune Society, builds bridges between low income communities and ex-offenders returning to the community. The program works to reduce recidivism, drug use, and the spread of infectious diseases through a continuum of care services for incarcerated women and adolescents. Many inmates return to communities that lack supports, such as substance abuse treatment, jobs and housing. During this vulnerable period after release when assistance is needed the most, Health Link connects these individuals with much needed services.

Health Link's nine case managers conduct health education sessions in the jails. Eligible clients who request assistance are then assigned a case manager who, in one-to-one sessions, helps them set short and long range goals during the transitional period.

After their return to the community, the program continues to provide clients with support services such as career counseling, skill development, substance abuse treatment and adequate housing. Services are furnished by sub-contracted community-based organizations in Harlem and the South Bronx. Health Link believes that low income neighborhoods have tremendous problems, but also a wealth of services available to them. Health Link leads a coalition of approximately 30 community organizations which meet monthly through its Community Coordinating Council which assists organizations in supporting the needs of ex-offenders returning to the community.

By connecting individuals to services, Health Link anchors individuals in an attempt to prevent them from returning to drugs and crime.

The Fortune Society
Photo credit: Toshi Kazama

"Being a Volunteer" SHEILA MAROONEY

The first time I actually came to Fortune was on a chilly October day in 1989. The elevator doors opened on 7 and I stepped into a wood paneled area that was called Reception. I said to myself, "I've been here before!"

The reception area reminded me of so many storefront churches in Mississippi where I'd done voter registration when I worked with the NAACP during the '60's. It was slightly dingy, poorly lighted, and random posters were tacked up on the walls. There at the front desk was a harassed but polite young man who had me sign in, while he answered the phones and greeted people coming in and out.

I waited to be interviewed in a large auditorium-like area. Around the walls were open cubicles where tutors and students were working together. People were hiking back and forth across the room, some had books and papers, some had radios. I couldn't tell who was staff and who was not, but it didn't matter to me. I glanced at some heavy plastic cartons with books spilling over the edges, a coat rack wobbling under jackets and coats. I saw people stop to make quick sandwiches from the open jars of peanut butter and grape jelly, and a couple of opened loaves of whole wheat bread. I saw people dozing on battered couches.

Watching over this with me was Martin Luther King Jr. in the brooding photograph where he's resting his chin on his right fist.

The atmosphere was mellow and informal, and I thought, "I wonder whether this place has room for me?" Inside me lives a person who wants to be wanted, and one way to be wanted, I thought, is to do things for others. Now I was here at Fortune, feeling as though my puppy-dog nose was pressed against the window, wanting to work to help people who'd spent time in jail.

The head of the education unit accepted me as a tutor. One of my first students, Claudine, asked, "Why do you tutor? How much do you get paid?" When I told her I came because it made me happy, and that I didn't get paid at all, she said, "Ain't nobody can be that dumb." When she earned her GED, she said, "You are the whole nine!" That many years ago neither of us could have known how rich I was going to become as a Fortune volunteer.

I am proud to be in charge of <u>The Fortune Society Home News</u>, our in-house news publication. Six years ago, when we only had 23 staff members on one floor, the Executive Director, JoAnne Page, decided we needed such a publication. Now that there are almost 80 staff members on three floors, <u>Home</u> is both a news source and reference for background information.

Now, as I work at Fortune each day, I am part of an agency where, indeed, we fight against crime, one life at a time, and where everyone has the chance and opportunity to change and grow. The riches I am earning are unexpected, personal and incomparable.

"Fortune's Mission and Voice" JOANNE PAGE

The Fortune Society began as a self-help and education organization that drew its strength from the desire of ex-offenders to rebuild their lives, and from the shock and horror of good people in the community who found it unacceptable that prison conditions were so dehumanizing. The strength of ex-offenders' commitment to change their lives and the vulnerable hope that drives that commitment are as strong today as they were in 1967, when the agency was founded.

What has changed dramatically is the number of people in prison, which has more than quadrupled. The culture in which we are working has changed dramatically, as well, and the general public's response to descriptions of dehumanizing prison conditions is more one of celebration than dismay. We have taken many steps backward in our humanity since 1967, as evidenced by the reinstitution of the death penalty and by the choice to build steel cages instead of schools.

Fortune is still here, still strong, still feisty. We hold onto our dream of change, the dream that change is possible, not just on an individual level, but on the level of systems and the soul of a nation. Day to day at Fortune, we work within a community that is inspiring. Adults come to us, just released from prison, seeking to fight the barriers they face and succeed in returning to their neighborhoods and families as positive forces. Young people come to us with the hope that they can use our services to keep from being locked up and to build a future that offers more options than being killed or being caged. Volunteers come to us seeing a way to make a difference in the world instead of simply giving up or being angry. They receive incredible gifts of being able to touch other persons' lives and help to build hope.

I feel privileged to have the opportunity to be Fortune's Executive Director.

David Rothenberg grew up in New Jersey and worked as a theatrical agent in New York City. His production of a play about brutality in prisons, Fortune and Men's Eyes, eventually led to the founding of The Fortune Society, which Mr. Rothenberg headed for 18 years. He was a member of the Attica Observation Committee during the Attica Prison riots; this group came to the prison for arbitration at the request of the inmates. He now hosts a radio show on WBAI every Saturday morning in which he covers such topics as theater, politics and "whatever I feel like talking about."

Ricardo Martinez, born in Detroit of Mexican parents, graduated from high school, earned a BA in Political Science at the University of Michigan. In 1988 he came to New York, worked for the Legal Aid Society, then as a legal assistant at a law firm, and at another non-profit. In 1993 he started working with Health Link as a Project Administrator when it was headquartered at Hunter College. He is currently enrolled at the School of Public Affairs, Baruch College graduate school, working towards a Masters in Public Administration.

Sheila Maroney was a UPI press photographer during World War II working out of the Chicago and Kansas City offices. She worked in the Public Relations departments of both The National Urban League and the National Association for the Advancement of Colored People in New York during the Civil Rights era. She went to Cuba during the first year of the Cuban revolution, met Fidel Castro and danced in the streets with Che Guevara en las navidades of 1960. She and her pet, g, have been volunteers at The Fortune Society for almost nine years.

JoAnne Page joined The Fortune Society in March of 1989 as Executive Director. She graduated from Yale Law School with a Juris Doctor degree in 1980, and worked through 1983 in Brooklyn as an attorney with Legal Aid Society. During 1983, she began working with the Court Employment Project as Director of Court Programs, developing and implementing the alternative to incarceration and detention programs. Her experience in criminal justice dates back to 1972, when she first began teaching and couseling in New York State prisons.

THOMAS H. ZOET
"180 Degrees"

Listening to the media, it would be easy to get the idea that halfway houses just popped up recently in our communities, probably because of some fuzzy-headed liberal scheme to keep criminals from going to prison where they really belong. The truth is, the idea of halfway houses and other community-based facilities for offenders has been around for a long time. New York City's Isaac P. Hopper House, a halfway house for female offenders, was founded in the 1840's. The Salvation Army and Volunteers of America were among many other organizations who started programs during the latter part of the 1800's.

The first half of the 1900's, however, saw a swing away from these community based approaches towards the building of large institutions to deal "efficiently" with social problems. It wasn't until the 1960's that halfway houses and group homes again began to emerge as serious correctional resources. Today, estimates place the number of halfway houses and other release facilities for offenders at around 800. 180 Degrees, Inc. is one of them.

Robbie Robinson, the program's founder, was not a man likely to be described by the words "polished professional." At six-feet-four and 240 pounds with a loud, gravelly voice that could cut through the noisiest confrontation, "imposing" was a better fit. Robbie spent 20 years in and out of prison before coming to the conclusion that he had something better to do with his life. He often described himself as having been "a very bad burglar, who was a very good drunk." Alcoholics Anonymous led Robbie to take a look at the lessons his own life had taught him and direct his prodigious energy towards improving the odds for other ex-offenders. He wanted to help them make the same 180 degree turn that his own life had. With the help of his parole officer and other "experts" like himself, he wrote up a proposal laying out his dream. In 1971, 180 Degrees was incorporated. About half of its first board were other "drunks" and ex-offenders from Robbie's AA support system. What they may have lacked in sophistication, they made up for in the passion they shared for Robbie's vision. In 1973, 180 opened its doors as a halfway house for men coming out of prison. Its stately, red-brick building, once the home of the founders of General Mills, had room for 37 ex-offenders. Today, 2,000 residents later, it's still going strong.

From a 1990's perspective, the idea of a bunch of alcoholics and habitual criminals starting a halfway house seems unlikely, at best. The fact that many of the early staff members fell into the same category sounds more like a topic for "20/20" than a formula for success. Of course, those were different times, before mandatory minimum sentences, routine background checks, offender registration and the many other measures we now take for granted as public policy. They were times when the belief that ex-offenders could become productive citizens extended even to allowing them to work in corrections. They were times before public and political reaction precluded any chance of starting halfway houses in neighborhoods, or anywhere else for that matter. It wasn't that Robbie had an easy time realizing his dream; he had many hurdles to surmount. Even then, the idea of returning offenders to the community was not a popular one. Robbie simply had the right combination of bull-headedness and vision at the right time. Lucky thing for the thousands of men, women and juveniles who have gone through 180's programs since its humble beginnings.

Like most halfway house directors, Robbie always had one eye on the offender and the other on the community. For him, 180's mission was first and foremost to offer a safety net for the community. He firmly believed that his program could make a difference for the men who were sent there. Sometimes that belief meant taking risks in deciding who could enter the program. This, in itself, wasn't an unusual attitude for a director to have. New facilities often established themselves by taking the clients that no one else was willing to deal with. Usually, once a stable referral base was established, acceptance criteria would get tighter; someone else could take the tough ones. Robbie refused to do that. He felt that 180 should always be willing to take the offenders no one else wanted, that community-based programs were obligated to take the bad risks with the good. Over the years, his confidence in the strength of 180's program has only rarely been undermined by residents committing new offenses. Of those few, none committed crimes within the facility's immediate neighborhood. That fact touches on the importance of a condition critical to 180's continued existence. All successful community-based programs come to understand that *both* the needs of clients and the concerns of the community must always be balanced against each other. Without the hard-earned confidence of its community, no halfway house can expect to survive. When Robbie died in 1982, he left a philosophical legacy which has driven 180's program development ever since. Its mission to "build a safer society by assisting offenders as they re-build successful lives in the community," owes much to this unlikely correctional leader.

Who goes to 180 Degrees? Each year roughly 10% of the men released from Minnesota's state prisons come live at its facility in Minneapolis, Minnesota. They are individuals whom the Department of Corrections has decided should be closely monitored as they begin their transition back into the community. In many respects, these men reflect Minnesota's general inmate population. Their average age is 33. The majority are single or divorced. Most of them come from the Minneapolis/St. Paul metropolitan area. There are some significant differences, as well. Where 36% of Minnesota's inmate population is African American, they comprise 56% of 180's residents. Of Minnesota's prisoners 64% have committed person offenses (sex offenses, homicide, assault, robbery), but more than 70% of 180's residents fall into that category.

With any discussion of halfway houses eventually come the questions, "Why are these guys being let out of prison to go to halfway houses, anyway? Why not just keep them locked up?" Looking at the description of 180's average resident, it's easy to see what prompts that concern. In Minnesota, however, the question doesn't reflect the reality of how most men are referred to a halfway house. Under Minnesota's sentencing guidelines system, offenders are given a set supervised release date soon after they enter prison. The significance of that release date is that once it arrives, he leaves wherever he's doing time and begins his supervised release time in the community. This is the point where halfway houses usually come into the picture, when the question is not halfway house vs. prison, its halfway house vs. the street. In other words, rather than providing an excuse to release people early, halfway houses provide a means of extending close supervision into the community, just without the bars.

The importance of including halfway houses as resources for any strategy to reduce recidivism among offenders has been well documented. A 1990 research report by the Massachusetts Department of Corrections looked at the effect of community reintegration on recidivism rates. Surveying data from 1971 through 1987, they noted the following findings:

• Individuals who received a furlough prior to release from prison had significantly lower rates of recidivism than did individuals who had not. This trend was observed throughout the fifteen years for which data was available.

• Participation in pre-release programs was correlated with reduced rates of recidivism.

When follow-up periods were extended from one to five years, the findings above remained constant; so much for the idea that nothing in corrections works.

These findings stress the importance of easing the transition between prison and freedom in the community. They argue for a step between these two conditions, where the process of re-connection with the community can begin in a closely supervised setting. Halfway houses fit this need very well. Looking at 180's graduates, for example, after two years, 92% show no new felonies. In a 1997 study by Minnesota's Legislative Auditor's Office, three years after release from prison, sex-offenders who did *not* complete 180 were found to be *three times* more likely to be reconvicted for a new gross misdemeanor or felony than those who did.

Other studies point to the fact that there are critical points where offenders make decisions about the future direction their lives will take. In its recidivism studies, Massachusetts found that of those people placed on probation who commit new crimes, one-third do so within the first month after being placed on probation. Almost 90% of those new offenses happen within six months of sentencing. Minnesota studies found that half of those offenders convicted of three felonies will get a fourth within three years. Seventy-five percent of that group will get a new conviction within the first year of their return to the community!

The first months after release from prison seem to be a critical point for many offenders. Considering how many men fail during that time, it is prudent to involve halfway houses in the offender re-entry process. They are in a position to help determine which men are serious about making the changes necessary to keep from returning to prison. Talking with 180's residents, many express how tired they are of wasting their lives, of how they want to stay out for the sake of their families, that they are trying to make a fresh start. In spite of this motivation, close to half of the men coming to halfway houses do *not* complete the program. They may run away and eventually be picked up and returned to prison or they may be terminated and returned as supervised release violators. If 180 decides to terminate a resident, it's usually because he has been found to be using drugs or alcohol rather than because of a new offense. Statistically, a very high percentage of offenders were under the influence at the time of their offenses, so any potential use is monitored closely and taken very seriously when discovered. On an individual basis, however, 180 often considers taking ex-residents back into the program after they've done some new prison time. Roughly 10% of its residents in a given year have left the program and returned during that time period.

From a strictly financial point of view, halfway houses also serve to protect the huge investment made whenever an individual is locked up. In Minnesota, for example, it costs $109,000 to lock an adult up for the state's average sentence of 3.6 years. When that man leaves prison, the daunting task of finding a place to live and generating the income necessary to pay for it is often a challenge he meets alone. It's not unusual to find that family and friends are no longer available to an offender for support and $100 gate money is all he has in his pocket. In a halfway house, less than $3,000 buys that man the time he needs to start again. In the two months most graduates stay at 180, over ninety per cent are able to establish steady employment and find an acceptable place to live. After years of being totally supported by the state, these men are able to re-enter society as tax paying citizens. Even while they're still residents, they start paying $10.00 per day towards their room and board, once they secure a steady job.

In 1996, 180 Degrees was among fifty-four programs honored by the American Correctional Association as "programs that work." The formula for 180's success goes back to Robbie Robinson: clear, consistent expectations, personal accountability and individualized program planning. There's nothing unusual about this focus. Most successful community-based programs would probably come up with a similar list. Translated into practical terms, 180's day to day programming is directed towards helping its clients make a personal shift in how they approach the world, moving them from an outlook of violence, dependency and victimization to one of self-responsibility and independence. Toward this end, the program couples an expectation for change with the tools necessary to accomplish that transformation.

House rules are explained to every new resident. Zero tolerance for violence or threatening behavior towards staff or other residents is given special emphasis.

Other rules weave a web of accountability through procedures for house jobs (daily chores), checking in and out of the facility, completing goal sheets, writing down schedules with verification phone numbers, curfew times, etc. This helps protect the community while reinforcing habits necessary for success. Through the structure of consistent program rules and expectations, clients learn the routines most people take for granted as necessities for being able to find and maintain employment, housing and relationships. A class on critical thinking skills is required of all residents. Its message is "stop and think *before* you act," an elementary idea to most people, but a powerful tool for success for 180's residents.

For residents with more specialized needs, case managers coordinate 180's internal resources and those available in the community to match up the best possible fit. This touches on another trait that it shares with other successful programs, the realization that the halfway house is part of a larger team. 180 sees itself with a very clear role to play in the corrections/criminal justice system, but it's not working in a vacuum. A major component of that role is maintaining lines of communication with a multitude of professionals (prison caseworkers, corrections agents, social workers, police, etc.) who share its mission to build a safer society.

Where is 180 unusual? Probably in the program's emphasis on continual self assessment. It is fanatical about the need to evaluate past success, building on it to ensure a successful future. In other spheres, this would be called marketing. At 180, it's called survival.

Each time a resident leaves the halfway house, regardless of the reason, a service evaluation goes to his supervising agent. This form is complete enough to cover the major areas of program concern (appropriateness of referral, staff cooperation, communications, etc.), yet easy to complete in a reasonable amount of time. There's about a 45% return rate on these forms.

When the form comes back to the program, it's routed to the case manager who worked with that client, the Supervisor, the Program Director and finally the Executive Director. This accomplishes several things. If there's a high rating or special comments from a "customer," all of the critical people are informed of a job well done. If there are low ratings or comments, all of the critical people are involved in determining why and improving the program where necessary. This process keeps the program in touch with how it's doing on the individual client level.

Another important tool is the service evaluation completed by all graduates of the program. It is an unsigned document given directly to the Executive Director. It includes questions that cover all aspects of the halfway house experience, from quality of food to personal growth. This gives the program a glimpse of how it's doing from the client's point of view. Interestingly, these evaluations cover the full range of responses, from genuine appreciation and thoughtful suggestions, to recommendations that the whole program be shut down.

Probably the most important source of program information for 180 is in the database maintained on each of its clients. An ongoing process of data collection allows the program managers to easily monitor how 180 is meeting the needs of its clients and the community. It also provides identifying information from which outside agencies can do independent assessments. Since 1990, components of 180 have been included in research and evaluation projects done through the National Institute of Justice, Minnesota Department of Corrections, Minnesota Legislative Auditor's Office, et al. Its openness to examination has helped 180 keep focused on what works best in accomplishing its mission to build a safer society.

When it comes to working with people, success can be an elusive quantity to measure. How clients do while they're involved in a program is only part of the picture, the beginning of a new way of living. How the lessons learned stand up under the test of time, in day to day interactions with others, that's the real measure. As one man wrote upon leaving 180, "I thank all the 180 staff for helping me out, for being there as a friend. Most people have different viewpoints about this place. I try not to let those views dictate what I think. 180 is what a person makes of it. I have gained a lot being here, most of all another chance and a start at being a good human being."

Thomas Zoet began his correctional career in 1970, working at the Hennepin County Home School and its Juvenile Detention Center. From 1971 to 1983, he worked with Washington County Court Services. While there, he was a juvenile probation officer, an adult probation officer and eventually supervised in both its adult and juvenile divisions. Also during that time, he supervised a private juvenile group home and a juvenile emergency placement/ detention facility. In 1983, he became the Executive Director of 180 Degrees, Inc. Under his leadership, 180 has grown from a correctional halfway house working with 125 clients per year to a correctional services agency providing residential and non-residential services to over 1,800 clients per year. Mr. Zoet received his Master of Social Work from the University of Minnesota in 1978. He has written numerous national journal articles on corrections and electronic home monitoring topics.

DORIS LUTHER
"Victim-Offender Mediation: A Return to Community and Accountabililty"

Hasn't every kid experienced (or known someone who experienced) stealing candy from the local "Mom & Pop" store? Remember the thrill and the terror of that first gum-snatching? You got away with something. It gave you power, while at the same time, your conscience was beating time with your heart. Remember the agony and mortification of getting caught and your parents making you apologize to "Mom & Pop?" The act of apologizing was a statement of recognition that, "Yes, I did it, and I'm here to be held responsible and accountable."

We thought we were being tough—screwing up the courage to steal that pack of gum or candy bar. Little did we know or anticipate the courage it would take to return to the scene of the crime, admit guilt, and take responsibility for our actions. So difficult, in fact, it was enough to discourage most kids from ever stealing again!

Here lies the underlying premise of Victim-Offender Mediation (VOM) also known as Victim-Offender Dialogue and the Victim-Offender Reconciliation Program (VORP). VOM is a face-to-face meeting between an offender and his or her victim, mediated by a trained community volunteer. The "heart" of it is that "an offender meets with the person he or she has wronged, the victim, in order to discuss what has happened, its effects, and what [if anything] can be done to make things right."[1]

The Victim-Offender Reconciliation Program in Kitchener, Ontario is recognized as the forerunner of this process in North America when, in 1974, a judge ordered two young men to meet with twenty-two victims whose property they had vandalized. Within three months, the youths had met with all but one of their victims (who had moved away) and reimbursed them for their losses.[2]

According to Dr. Mark Umbreit,[3] results of VOM are:

1. Mediation in juvenile proceedings results in very high levels of client satisfaction (victims, 79%; offenders, 87%) and perceptions of fairness (victims, 83%; offenders, 89%).
2. The process has a strong effect for both victims and juvenile offenders in humanizing the justice system response to crime.
3. Mediation reduces fear and anxiety among victims. Prior to mediation, nearly 25% of victims were afraid of being victimized.
4. Mediation has a significant impact on the likelihood that offenders will complete their restitution obligation (81%) to the victim, when compared with similar offenders in court administered programs without mediation (58%).

5. Juvenile offenders do not perceive mediation as a significantly less demanding response to their criminal behavior than other options available to the court. Mediation is consistent with efforts to hold young offenders accountable for their crimes.
6. Mediation has strong support from court officials, including both judges and probation staff, and is increasingly becoming institutionalized in juvenile courts.
7. Mediation is perceived to be voluntary by the vast majority (81%) of juvenile offenders who participated.
8. Mediation is perceived to be voluntary by the vast majority (93%) of victims who participated.
9. Victims in mediation were far more likely to experience the justice system as fair, when compared with similar victims who went through the normal court process.
10. Considerably fewer and less serious additional crimes were committed within a one-year follow-up period by juvenile participants in mediation programs, when compared with similar offenders who did not participate. Although consistent with two recent English studies, this important finding was not statistically significant because of the size of program samples.

The process of VOM is similar to other mediation: it is voluntary; the parties are trying to come up with their own solutions; the mediator is a neutral facilitator, not a judge or lawyer; it is designed to provide a "safe" setting that allows communication to take place without threat. VOM does, however, differ in many crucial ways. VOM requires that mediators have specialized training in victim sensitivity, offender sensitivity, mediation, conflict management skills, and self awareness. The sensitive nature of the process demands that victims not be re-victimized. It is critical that cases be screened for appropriateness (i.e. both victim and offender can participate willingly and in a manner that is not threatening or damaging). Mediators must spend the time up front to meet with both parties, get their stories (the facts and the feelings), clarify expectations, screen the parties, and have a thorough understanding of what each party wants to say in the mediation. I feel it is important that, as much as is possible, there be no surprises when victim and offender come together.

Mediator self-awareness is essential because they are placing themselves in what may be a highly charged situation. Mediators need to be able to keep themselves from being drawn into or personalizing people's stories, and they need to avoid making judgments about either victim or offender. In almost all VOM cases, the mediators are volunteers. Charging fees for VOM is very tricky. Often the offender has no money, and that burden should not fall on the victim. Even if a victim is willing to pay, that may have an effect on mediator neutrality, either because the victim perceives that the mediator is working for him/her or the mediator feels obligated.

The concepts of offender accountability and community involvement are not new. Ancient societies used to conduct their own justice, without the benefit of courts, through community involvement that included accountability and restitution from offenders.[4] As societies grew and laws were enacted, the sheer complexity of it all moved the judicial process out of the hands of the community into the court system.[5] One unfortunate aspect of our judicial system today is that a criminal offense is treated as a crime against the state, rather than against the victim. Howard Zehr describes it as "Retributive Justice" in that "Crime is a violation of the state, defined by law-breaking and guilt. Justice determines blame and administers pain in a contest between the offender and the state directed by systematic rules."[6] Zehr suggests that it is time for us to look at justice "through a new lens" called "Restorative Justice:" "Crime is a violation of people and relationships. It creates obligations to make things right. Justice involves the victim, the offender, and the community in a search for solutions which promote repair, reconciliation, and reassurance."[7] Victim-Offender Mediation is one of many processes that fosters these concepts.

I first became aware of Victim-Offender Mediation at a workshop led by Mark Umbreit in 1992. I was deeply touched by the concept. Remember the kids I referred to who had to apologize for stealing candy? I hung out with those kids, but I was not caught and never had to apologize. I saw what they went through and was misguidedly grateful that I didn't have to endure accountability and learn the impact of my actions on others.

As an adolescent, I was totally unsupervised. With my friends, my extracurricular activities were comprised of letting air out of peoples' tires, throwing eggs at houses and cars, writing 'dirty' words on lawns with salt water, and other obnoxious and illegal behaviors. At the time, I viewed them as harmless pranks. The truth is, I had NO IDEA—no concept of the trouble I was causing for my victims. Today I know the impact of finding four flat tires—the hassle and the expense. I would be devastated if someone did it to me!

I felt that VOM would be a great process for helping offenders (particularly juveniles) to be accountable and learn the impact of their actions. I began to pursue the idea of starting a VOM program in Maine. With the help of Cushman Anthony, attorney and mediator; Bob Philbrook, Quaker and activist; Evelyn Hanneman of the Maine Council of Churches; New England Yearly Meeting; Anita Jones of the Community Dispute Resolution Center and others too numerous to list, the plan began to take form. We all felt that the criminal justice system wasn't as effective as it could be. We all knew of too many kids who got caught and were incarcerated, only to be released into society, with no rehabilitation, to continue a life of crime. Or they got caught, were put on probation, and promptly fell through the cracks. Juvenile probation and parole officers don't have the time to keep up with all of these kids. The pieces that were missing, we thought, were community involvement, victim involvement, and accountability of offenders. The human elements that were missing were the exchange of feelings, the offender having a chance to learn the impact of his or her actions, and the opportunity to "make things right."

Our purpose became: "To undertake face-to-face meetings between victims and offenders in a controlled setting in selected and carefully screened cases, as an alternative means or as a procedure supplementary to prosecution. In this process, facts surrounding the events can be determined, feelings of victims can be aired, and offenders can be made personally accountable for their actions."

In 1994 I mediated our first case. A juvenile had assaulted another juvenile in front of the high school. After meeting with each side, we brought them together. An apology was made, the uninsured medical bills were paid, and most importantly, the victim's mother was able to relay to the offender the distress and fear she had experienced when she saw her son's bloodied face. The victim was able to relate his embarrassment at being beaten up in front of everyone at school. It was also important for the victim and his mother to hear the offender say he knew he was wrong and would not do it again. While restitution may have been ordered by a court in this case, the expression of feelings would probably not have been allowed, which far and away had the most impact on the offender. All participants related that they were glad they went through the process.

At this time, efforts were underway to form the Community Dispute Resolution Center (CDRC) in Portland. The Center's mission became "to strengthen the capacity of the people of Greater Portland to resolve conflicts through the provision of dispute resolution services, including mediation, negotiation, and facilitation, using trained volunteers." We felt their mission dove-tailed with that of the VOM project and the two groups merged in 1995. Since then, we have received 32 VOM referrals, 16 of which have gone to mediation, the others being inappropriate because of unwillingness on the part of either the victim or the offender.

Our reputation is growing. We have received referrals from defense attorneys, police departments, judges, juvenile case workers, and the community policing program. Funding for our program has been difficult. Our first grant came from New England Yearly Meeting. We have received an anonymous grant, some funding through grants for CDRC, and we will be paid by the Department of Corrections for approved cases. Ideally, VOM and restorative justice programs should be part of our Corrections system and have legislated funding. Some states, such as Texas and Minnesota, do receive state funding for VOM. For us, it is a constant struggle. While our volunteer mediators donate their time, we have administrative costs to cover: scheduling mediations, finding mediators, taking referrals, and following up on cases.

As a mediator, I find VOM to be very challenging and very satisfying. As a white middle class woman, I often have to cross class barriers and gain people's trust, not showing my shock at what they tell me or the words they use. I have to clear my mind of any preconceived notions about class, gender, and people who commit crimes. I have to be more careful (than in Court and family mediation) about remaining neutral and not let my own personal experiences influence how I react to participants. I must always be prepared to hear how other people view life and how they respond to their own experiences. I have to listen to people's horrendous life situations and have empathy for them without becoming depressed about their misfortunes.

In my seven years of mediating, the power of the process never fails to impress me. In VOM cases, that power is magical. I have seen a church group meet with their offenders and embrace them into their community. I have seen connections made between victim and offender. I have witnessed true forgiveness and the positive impact this process has for offenders. If something like this had been available to me as a teenager, maybe I wouldn't have hurt so many people...but then again, maybe I wouldn't have been drawn to this work.

Doris Luther has a Master's Degree in Conflict Resolution. She is a mediator for Maine's Court Alternative Dispute Resolution Service and a partner in "Mediation First," a partnership of consultants, trainers, and mediators. Much of her work takes place in schools teaching peer mediation and conflict resolution to students and teachers. She is a volunteer for the Youth Alternatives Family Mediation Program and the Community Dispute Resolution Center in Portland.

Footnotes

1 Pact Institute of Justice, The VORP Book. Michigan City, IN, no date.

2 Peachey, Dean. "The Kitchener Experiment." In M. Wright and B. Galaway (Ed.), Mediation and Criminal Justice. London, Sage Publications, 1989, p. 14-16.

3 Umbreit, Mark S. and Coates, Robert. Victim Offender Mediation: An Analysis of Programs in Four States of the U.S. Minneapolis, MN: Minnesota Citizens Council on Crime and Justice, 1992.

4 Wright, Martin. Introduction. In Wright & Galaway (Ed.) Mediation and Criminal Justice. London: Sage Publications, 1989.

5 Donegan, Susan L. "ADR in Colonial America: A Covenant for Survival." Arbitration Journal. No. 48, vol. 1, June 1993, p.14-22.

6 Zehr, Howard. Changing Lenses. Scottdale, PA: Herald Press, 1990, p. 181.

7 Ibid.

TIMOTHY TOWNSEND
"Things Are Better Now"

My twin brother and I got busted two years ago for doing crimes. We were accused of arson, burglary, and attempted murder. Every night we would go out and break into people's cars and take cigarettes, light them and smoke them. Then we started going into people's houses and we took things. We did this for a couple of months, always together, and at the last house we broke into, we got caught. The people woke up because they heard us and they stood behind the door and caught me. My brother got away, but they called the police on me and asked me where I lived. They took me to the Youth Center and called my home and my father brought my brother over there. We were thirteen years old at the time. After a week, I was transferred to the Jackson Brook Institute for psychological evaluation and I stayed there for seven or eight weeks. They thought I was crazy or something. My brother stayed at the Youth Center, which was a lot worse than being at Jackson Brook. After this we went to court and we were able to settle things without our having to do time, because we were put in our grandfather's custody and we agreed to do community service. We met with the victim and did 120 hours of community service, half of that with the victim. We pulled weeds, painted, and did other odd jobs. Then we were put on probation for two years. We both got the same sentence, and we used to have to meet with our probation officer every week, then every other week, but we haven't gone lately because they keep changing people. I've had about seven different probation officers in less than two years. That will be over pretty soon. It's working pretty good for both of us, and we haven't been in trouble again.

At the time all this happened I was really angry. There were a lot of problems in our family. My mom died when I was 10. It was after that that we started getting in trouble. I feel differently now. We are not doing community service anymore. We go to school and we work when we are not in school. We get one day off when we go up to camp with our grandfather, but the rest of the time we are either in school or we work for our grandfather. I am a year behind in school, but I was able to get back into things without many problems. My friends accepted things, although they did ask questions. In general, people were OK about our having made mistakes. Actually, I don't think most people around here even knew about it. Now I am just trying to get through high school so I can get into pro wrestling. I want to make a career of wrestling.

It was our family situation that caused our problems. I was definitely depressed, both because I tend to get depressed and because of things in the family. Sometimes I can talk to someone about it, but not so much lately. But I'm not as angry anymore. I also get a little more freedom now. Once I can prove to my grandparents that I can do something right, they trust me more and they allow me this freedom. I also think I can handle things better now because I am older. But if my grandparents hadn't come forward, I would have got a sentence and I would have had to be at the Youth Center, which would have been terrible. It was a lot better for me at Jackson Brook than it was for my brother at the Youth Center for those two months before we were released into our grandparents' custody. I have friends there and they are still messed up.

My message to kids that are getting in trouble is: Don't do bad stuff. Talk to a friend. I talk to my cousin. Even though he is younger, he understands. He has been in trouble too, but he is a good talker. Talking releases the stuff inside, but talking to grown ups doesn't really help. They just don't understand. A kid talking to another kid is what works. Now that I am better, I sometimes even try talking to other kids to keep them out of trouble, but I don't know if I've really helped very much. Anger is the main thing that gets kids in trouble. Booze and drugs don't help either.

When I got caught I was scared. I had thought of the consequences of what I was doing, but I didn't really care. In fact, in some ways I wanted to get caught, and it was a good thing that I did get caught because I felt bad then and I feel a lot better now. What really helped me was that some people started listening to what I had to say. That really makes a difference. And I've learned to listen to others. But I've learned the hard way. I still can't talk about things with my dad, but I do see him. We don't discuss the stuff that made me angry, and at school, there is no time for talking about things. But I can talk with my grandparents and I have a real home with them. Without them, my brother and I never would have made it. Around them we can be ourselves, and we stay out of trouble. Things are pretty good for us.

Timothy Townsend is a high school student in Maine. He and his brother were juvenile offenders who participated in victim-offender mediation, each performing 120 hours of community service. They have been released to the custody of their grandparents.

STEVE NOTIS
"Healing our Community"

I am the pastor of a United Methodist church. As I walked across the parking lot to enter the church building early Sunday morning, I wondered what I might find. It had been a difficult two weeks. The church had been broken into twice.

On Wednesday evening the organist entered the building and heard the water running in the kitchen. On investigating, she found that a softball-sized rock had been thrown through a window, slid across the counter and hit the faucet, turning the water on. As she looked around the deserted building she found that the choir's book shelf had been pushed over and all their hymnals and books lay in a mess on the floor.

The following Sunday morning at 6:30 a.m., as I was getting ready for the service, I noticed a strange smell coming from the kitchen. Given the last break-in, I warily approached the kitchen; all over the floor was a disgusting combination of sugar, ketchup, vinegar, milk, coffee, and juice. From the looks of it, much of what had been in the refrigerator was now on the floor. I immediately phoned several of the more faithful workers of the church and asked them if they could clean up this mess so we could have something like a normal Sunday. We then called the police, who were concerned that, in our cleaning up the mess, we had destroyed evidence. Our first concern was to have our church ready for the many people who would soon be there.

After the services, we tried to decide what might be going on. Because a space that we consider sacred had been violated twice, it felt personal. We wondered if we had been victims of an anti-church hate crime. Some considered that perhaps one of our members had "gone off the deep end." We really didn't know what to think. Feelings of anger, mistrust and suspicion hung over the church community.

So as I walked across the parking lot to the church, after not the best night's sleep, I wondered what would greet me this Sunday morning. As I walked in the door, I noticed several large kitchen knives lying in the lobby. All over everything was a fine white powder—every fire extinguisher in the building had been discharged. Our potted plants had been slashed to stubs. The kitchen was even worse than last time. Even the walls and ceiling were covered. Butter had been smeared over everything in the restrooms. The Sunday school class rooms were trashed, the sofa and wing chairs in the library had been slashed. Someone had defecated in a storage room. In the sanctuary of the church, the cross had been thrown off the altar and our new organ had been urinated on. This time I called the police immediately.

Soon after the police arrived, I learned from them that the town's middle school had been broken into and vandalized in much the same way. I hate to say it, but I immediately felt relief. That meant that it wasn't a hate-crime nor was it a member who had had some sort of mental breakdown. It was probably, the police said, adolescents.

After the police had collected all the evidence they wanted, we cleaned up enough to have our Sunday services. As the pastor, I decided that we needed to worship, especially now. It was obvious to everyone that something was going on and for part of the service we talked about it, but we also gathered to pray, sing and praise God, as we do every week. The regular routine of worship had a calming effect on all of us.

Later that week I was told by the police that three young boys, two aged twelve and one thirteen, had confessed to the crimes. Two of the boys were brothers. The juvenile district attorney called it the worst case of juvenile vandalism and aggravated criminal mischief he had ever seen.

Over the next few weeks, the vandalism made us the center of attention. The media called, letters and donations flowed in, and we all wondered "why?" Why would three boys do that sort of thing? All the while I was feeling more and more angry with the boys and their parents; no one had even dropped us so much as a note of apology. We later found out legal counsel had advised them to have no contact. We read in the papers that they had pled "not guilty" to a crime they had confessed to just a few weeks before. This was not the first time that we experienced the legal system as counter to the deeper needs of the victim and the offender. As victims we felt like it was all a game.

My anger at "the system" prompted me to feel that there must be a better way. I imagined that a face to face meeting with the boys might do us and them a world of good. Even though the local police had been great throughout the whole process, we felt ignored and forgotten.

A few weeks after the crime, I happened to be at a meeting with many of my clergy colleagues. A room full of clergy is a room full of advice! One thing stuck, however. There was a group in the community that was doing dispute mediation and I wondered if we might be candidates for this sort of process. I hoped that it might enable us to make something good come out of a horrible situation. I made a few phone calls and found out that the people who do mediations had been thinking about us and felt that our case would be ideal.

Eventually, it got back to us that two of the boys, the brothers, had been advised by counsel to try victim offender mediation. The other boy, it was felt, had psychological issues that kept him from such a process. For us, just the idea that we would eventually meet the boys came as a relief. Our need to understand, move on and perhaps even help these boys seemed, at last, to find some hope in victim offender mediation. It was explained to us that the process was only done in situations when it was felt it would benefit both parties.

As a church we began working on who would represent the church and what our agenda might be. This proved to be a much more complicated process that I had imagined. There was a great deal of diversity regarding our perceived role. What we eventually agreed to was that the church was not of one voice and that the many different voices were indeed valid and should be allowed to contribute. While it was not easy, this diversity proved to be a great strength. It was a strength because it took just such a variety of perspectives and voices to finally break through the defenses of the boys.

As the day of mediation approached, many of us were filled with a mix of anxiety and hope. Facing those who had trashed our church was not easy. We were angry and wondered what kind of people they would be. We also hoped that they might see how much pain they had caused us and truly feel sorry for what they had done. We also hoped we might feel better knowing that we had done all that we could do to resolve the situation. We felt the prayers of many and knew that if we could allow good to come from evil, we would be living out the best of our religious tradition.

Our prayers and hopes were answered. The mediation experience went as well as we hoped it might. The people of the church had a chance to share what happened and how they felt about it. The boys were able to tell us why they did what they did. Even more importantly, the boys were able to feel the shame of what they had done. We were able to hear it and work out ways for them to earn back the trust of the community. It was a transforming experience for all involved. We agreed on a system of work service to the church, which the boys carried out. Best of all they became people to us. No longer were they faceless little demons who trashed our church; they were two troubled boys who had admitted their mistakes and were working to make amends. It took a great deal of courage for them and their parents and I will always respect them for it.

Out of the mediation, a relationship with the boys and their family began. It was a healing, forgiving experience. I can remember telling members of the church that we had to stop calling them "the boys who vandalized the church" and call them by name.

A few weeks after the mediation the boys and their parents were in the congregation on Sunday morning. When they came forward for Communion, many of us were moved to tears. It was a moment I will never forget. Communion speaks of many things but most essentially it speaks to our connection with God and one another. To have the boys and their parents participate in this ritual was powerfully moving.

The family has continued in their relationship with the church. Most Sundays finds them in the pews and the boys are involved in our youth programs. Real healing and reconciliation occurred. Victim-Offender Mediation had given us a way to live out the best of our beliefs.

Steve Notis grew up in the state of Maine and graduated from the Boston University School of Theology. He served as pastor for a central Maine church for six years, and is currently pastor of a United Methodist Church in Southern Maine. It was under his leadership that the congregation participated in Victim-Offender Mediation after the church was damaged during several episodes of severe vandalism.

NEW ENGLAND YEARLY MEETING STATEMENT ON RESTORATIVE JUSTICE

As a Quaker I believe there is that of God in all people, though it's sometimes hard to find. Punishment ought to be a way of helping people to realize the hurt they are doing to this sense of worth in themselves and others. Harvey Gillman

We, members of the Religious Society of Friends, believe that God is leading us to adopt, and live in accordance with, a testimony of Reformative Justice which calls for justice without retribution and without vengeance. It also calls for healing of all parties in any conflict, whether familial, civil, criminal, racial, or international. It is based on unconditional love and forgiveness, love of victims and offenders equally.

In our peace testimony we affirm that Jesus taught us to love our enemies. As Friends we believe there is that of God in every person and the power of God can transform violence to peaceful goodwill.

When crime occurs, producing harm and injury, Restorative Justice must focus on meeting the needs of every one involved. Victims have the right to be secure, to receive support from others, to experience justice, to seek restitution, and to grant forgiveness. Offenders need to be brought to justice, to accept responsibility, to repent and apologize, to make restitution, and to seek forgiveness. Communities need to create the conditions in which both victims and offenders can reach agreement, be healed, and be restored to wholeness.

Restorative Justice recognizes that we must all be held accountable for our actions and the consequences of our actions. Society has a legitimate right to public safety and protection from violence. Restraint and other disciplinary measures must be applied humanely and only to the extent necessary. Where offenders are restrained in institutions, the restorative and healing process should be extended into the institutions.

Restorative Justice is not the justice system which prevails today. The present system relies far too heavily on the concepts of punishment and retribution and not enough on restitution and healing relationships. We Friends in New England believe that God is calling us to renew our traditional concern for those in prison, to challenge our justice systems to act in radically different ways, and to implement restorative justice systems in our communities.

We ask God's spirit to lead us in our efforts.

James Lee, "Snowy Owl"

EPILOGUE

Death Row, Louisiana

July 26, 1996

"Well, I started the process of legal penalties against three workers. Last Thursday, after putting me in full shackles, hands cuffed to the waist, and leg irons, they escorted me into the visiting room, out of sight of others, and whip up on me. All the blows given was done to my head. I went to the hospital with a busted head. Today the doctor referred me back to the hospital for head xrays and xrays on my eyes. The workers now realize that their claim, 'I felled against the bars," isn't standing up — too much damage was done. All three has asked me not to pursue charges because they have families to support. I guess I'm mean, because I told them they should have thought of that before hitting me.

"They whip up on me because, in their own words, 'We don't like baby killers and you need to be taught a lesson.' Like a death sentence isn't enough! I'll close, my ole head is still aching. Be glad when Monday comes so the xrays can be done."

August 17, 1996

"The doctor isn't letting me know much — said they can't read the xrays!?! But this past Tuesday, I was called out and informed about an appointment with a neurologist. After I kept pressing the doctor 'why,' he finally told me that there is a 'red mass' that has shown up. After he didn't give anymore information, I pressed him some more. The only other thing he said was that the red mass could be a result of a ruptured blood vessel. I know one thing, I'll be glad to find out what is causing my head to ache steadily, hazy sight and the numbing on my right side of body."

August 28, 1996

"Yes, my symptoms still persist and it is aggravating. I'm still waiting on the appointment with the neurologist. The medical in these places are less than second rate and they do not get in any rush, especially if something is wrong that was a result of one of the employees."

BO LOZOFF

"Let's Not Settle For Too Little"

The prison system in modern-day America is a terrible mess. Because so many things about it are terrible, there is obviously no limit to the improvements which could be made, many of which are described in this book. An innovative program here or there, a productive rather than destructive modality here or there, can be a tremendous lift for the people involved. But it would be a grave mistake to assume this is the best we can do. A criminal justice system predicated on fear, anger and retribution is beneath us. It cannot be fixed by a few compassionate people bringing in a little fresh air around the edges.

I am one of those people who has been working around the edges for over twenty-five years, so I mean no disrespect to myself or the other contributors in this volume. We all must continue to do our work so long as it is necessary. Like Mother Teresa said, it may be a drop in the ocean, but the ocean would be one drop less without it. We should applaud and support every program which makes things better for the people who are locked up right now.

But we must also bear in mind that billions are being spent on new prison construction while only hundreds of thousands are being spent on programs such as the ones in this book. Make no mistake about it: we are in extremely bad shape and we are moving into worse shape. It would be serious denial to pretend that these few programs and ideas are heralding in a new, compassionate era of corrections. They are not.

The simple fact is, the most fundamental assumptions we make about imprisonment need to be changed, and they need to be changed soon. We don't need a single one of the hundreds of new prisons currently being planned. Not one. But if we allow them all to be built, and new ones continually added each year, then they will always be filled, every single one of them. There will be too many political and economic forces at stake for us to change our minds and say that we were wrong to build them.

Our model of retributive justice, of harsh and angry punishment, is making things worse rather than better. This is clear; it is not debatable. It is an urgent priority for our civilization to explore models of justice which are restorative rather than retributive, which heal rather than harm. We need to set aside our infantile tough-on-crime political rhetoric, take a deep breath, step back and notice how terrible a failure such a system has been. We are not soft on crime, we have not *been* soft on crime. We are extremely tough on crime; we routinely *ruin* people's lives rather than help them to change.

We must also abandon our notion of a "war on drugs" and acknowledge drug abuse to be the serious public health problem which it is. Millions of our people, millions of our children, are turning to drugs because American life has become too shallow, manic, competitive, and confusing. We have found it easier to build more prisons than to look honestly at what is lacking in the spiritual and psychological makeup of our culture. People don't rush into drug addiction when they are happy or when they feel a sense of connection to the world around them. Using punitive rather than therapeutic responses to their addiction is totally counterproductive. It truly demeans us all. We need more depth; we need a chance to breathe calmly and slow down; we need a sense of meaning beyond the unfulfilling consumerism of our day.

Even the architecture of modern prisons is shameful to the human spirit. Let's see the architects and judges spend six weeks of their lives in a supermax institution like Pelican Bay, and then ask them their philosophical views about imprisonment. Many of them would be seriously traumatized, even mentally ill, in that short a time. Yet those are the institutions we continue to build and to fill. We are in serious trouble. Those buildings will be with us for a long time. They will house our own grandchildren.

Most of the people we send to prison shouldn't be sent out of their communities in the first place. Incarceration must be a last resort for violent and dangerous people, not a first response to selfish, confused, dysfunctional behavior. Nationwide, nearly **seventy percent** of our prisoners are serving time for nonviolent offenses. In other words, they were not necessarily violent or dangerous when they entered prison. But they certainly are likely to be by the time they leave.

Most new prison inmates are scared to death and just want to get out of prison alive. Their increasing capacity for violence during their incarceration is a direct response to factors which are very much under our control: the profoundly negative tone of our prisons, the dominant note of scorn expressed toward inmates throughout the day by staff and other inmates, the lack of opportunities to learn responsibility, decency, altruism, the lack of safety from predators in the prison population.

In short, we place people who are mostly confused, dysfunctional and selfish into a hellacious environment which turns their confusion into hopelessness, their dysfunctions into sociopathy, and their selfishness into a ceaseless struggle for sheer survival. We cannot be surprised at the occasional Attica or Lucasville or Santa Fe. To the contrary, I am always surprised there are not many more such riots. Between the sinister new architecture and the increasing harshness of prison sentences, such as the many three strikes laws which strip inmates of all incentive to reform or behave well, we're definitely pressing our luck.

Worse yet, from the way we speak about criminals, the way we cheer over executions, the way we celebrate the return of chain gangs, our children are picking up the message of the times that it is acceptable to humiliate or brutalize or even execute bad guys. The problem is, we cannot control our children's perceptions of who the bad guys are. On any given day, it may be their teachers or friends at school or even us, their parents.

The name Lizzie Borden is at least vaguely familiar to most of us because over a hundred years ago, she was arrested for something so rare, so unthinkable, it became legendary—murdering her parents. Last week alone, I came across four teenagers who had killed at least one parent. Nationwide, such a story is in the news now about once a week. The governmental response to this astonishing devolution has been merely to pass legislation sentencing juveniles to adult institutions if they commit such violence. Wouldn't it make more sense to figure out why it's happening, instead of building more prisons for the children who are now five and six years old, who may be sentenced to life imprisonment by the time they're fourteen? We are not thinking clearly.

We now imprison millions instead of thousands. The vast majority of those millions will one day be released and walk among us. It is mere sanity to want them to be happier, more compassionate and more capable human beings instead of damaged time bombs waiting to go off. To accomplish this, we need a more mature view and the courage to fly in the face of contemporary political sloganeering. We need the foresight to *trash* our current prison model rather than improve upon it.

When our children do wrong, we don't hate them for the rest of their lives. We don't place them in situations where they may be raped and battered. We do whatever we can to get them to see what they did was wrong and deepen their values so they become the decent human beings we know they are capable of becoming. We must have similar faith in other people's children who do wrong, too.

A justice system must have at its core a solid belief in human goodness and redemption. Otherwise there will (literally) continue to be hell to pay. We can blame anyone we want, but we all suffer for this reckless disregard of the basic tenets of a humane society. We must cherish our citizens, even after they have committed crimes. We must strive mightily to get them back into the fold instead of abandoning and exiling them forever.

We could reduce the prison population by about 70% and not see even a 1% increase in violent crime. In fact, it is incredibly naive to think we could treat offenders the way we do and expect to derive a safer society from it. What are we thinking? With a fraction of the money we are currently using to build new prisons, we could create community programs which empower rather than incapacitate people on the margins of society. This is not naive idealism, it is patriotism of the highest, most urgent order.

Bo Lozoff is an American spiritual teacher and the director of Human Kindness Foundation. He and his wife, Sita, are founders of Kindness House, a small spiritual community in rural North Carolina which runs the foundation. Human Kindness Foundation is best known for its Prison-Ashram Project, which helps prisoners and prison staff throughout the world turn inward and use their harsh environments to develop deep kindness and compassion. Bo's first book, We're All Doing Time, is now in its tenth printing.

STILL A HUMAN BEING

I may be a prisoner
But I'm somebody's child
I'm somebody's brother
I'm somebody's uncle
I'm somebody's nephew
I'm somebody's cousin
I'm somebody's friend
And even though I'm somebody's pay check
I'm still a human being.

Vincent Johnson
Iowa State Penitentiary, Iowa

"Political Prisoner" is excerpted from Iowa on the Inside,
by Vincent Johnson, Audenreed Press (1997)

The following chapters from Frontiers of Justice, Volume 2: Coddling or Common Sense? were written for a professional audience and were shortened for use in this anthology. They can be ordered in their entirety for the cost of photocopying and shipping.

"Brain-Building Basics, Parenting & Literacy Skills,"
Mary-Garrett Bodel - $1.50
"Resocialization: Teaching Accountability, Social Skills and Victim Empathy," Judy Briscoe - $1.50
"The Evolution of the RI Women's Prison Mentoring Program,"
Judith Fox & Roberta Richman - $1.50
"Reducing Recidivism: Amity and the CA DOC Demonstrate How to Do It," Mullen, Schuettiger, Arbiter & Conn - $3.75
"Resource Center for High Risk Youth Sex Offenders,"
James Smith & PhilipTedeschi - $3.00
"Why Cognitive Restructuring?" Pamela K.Withrow - $1.50

"The Community Preparation Workbook" by Stephen Fraley was written in both outline form, as presented in this anthology, and as a full length, 40 page booklet. This booklet can be ordered for the cost of photocopying, spiral binding and shipping. $6.00

Frontiers of Justice is a series with the goal of promoting humane and effective criminal justice policy. The authors of Frontiers of Justice, Volume 1: The Death Penalty have been touched by capital punishment personally (the inmates, their families and their victims' families) or professionally (in the areas of law, criminal justice, government, religion, journalism and advocacy). This powerful anthology represents men and women of reason and conscience, both the incarcerated and the free, who deplore the use of legalized killing to solve America's criminal justice problems. Edited by Claudia Whitman and Julie Zimmerman

TO THE EXECUTIONER

Inject my veins with poison-
Hang me by the neck-
Fill my cell with cynaide gas-
Put me on the rack.

Blind-fold and shoot me-
Chop off my head-
Make me walk the plank-
Kill me till I'm dead.

There's nothing you can do-
That's not been done before-
I'm the John that has to pay-
And you're the system's whore.

John Yarbrough
Federal Bureau of Prisons, Texas

INDEX

Georgia

March 5, 1998

Dear Julie,

I received your letter a few weeks ago. It's taken me this long to gather up enough strength to write you back, not only because of Ms. Karla Tucker's demise, but because of my own. I don't mean to sound selfish. Honestly, I don't want to be, but during the same time period, I received some very disturbing and devastating news of my own. I won't be going home! I was really hurt, actually everyone was. Especially since I've done everything humanly possible to correct problems within myself, but I guess that'll never be good enough for Georgia's Politicians. It's an election year and everyone is out to prove how hard they (the candidates) can be on convicts. As a result I've been set off until 2006. That means I will have done 15 years for a simple armed robbery (no injuries). While the norm has been 5 to 6 years for the same crime I committed, yet I'm being denied.

Right now I'm feeling hurt, disappointed and alone. My future is uncertain and I'm very confused. In a sense I've gone back to court and received a new sentence for the same offense. The Parole Board cited their reason for turning me down was "the circumstances of my crime." The fact that I robbed the store won't ever change. What about the positives that have resulted from the negative?

I read a case in the Atlanta Journal-Constitution where this guy was in prison for 20 armed robberies and he also had a life sentence. But because he had a friend who was politically connected, he was sent to a transitional center where he would be eligible for parole in about 9 months. It's unfair how the system overlooks the poor. I came into this system young and naive, but I've learned very fast about the racism, bias, discrimination and powers of the privileged.

I didn't want to have to cry on your shoulder, but—what are friends for? I'll be writing you again very soon, but for now take good care of yourself.

Yours Truly,
Willie

Death Row, California

March 10, 1998

About 2:30 p.m. this date, I got a message from the Legal Affairs Coordinator to call my attorney. I did....and it was bad news! The 9th Circuit reversed the District Court's ruling reversing my capital crime conviction and they denied by cross appeal....umph! Big loss for me!! Not lethal, but a major step toward death's door. I still got some moves and will fill you in later on what I'm expecting after I get a chance to think about it. (It's 4:01 p.m.) I just found out about 1 1/4 hr. ago....so my mind is kinda bouncin' around right now.

I assume that AJ's execution gave you a bit of a callous and you realize that it can and does happen, and that you are to remain strong and keep up the fight for us and humankind.